Cost Management in Supply Chains

Stefan Seuring
Maria Goldbach
Editors

Cost Management in Supply Chains

With 109 Figures
and 26 Tables

Physica-Verlag
A Springer-Verlag Company

Dr. Stefan Seuring
Maria Goldbach

University of Oldenburg
Institute of Business Administration
Faculty for Business, Economics and Law
Uhlhornsweg
26129 Oldenburg, Germany

ISBN 3-7908-1500-4 Physica-Verlag Heidelberg New York

Library of Congress Cataloging-in-Publication Data applied for
Die Deutsche Bibliothek – CIP-Einheitsaufnahme
Cost Management in Supply Chains: S. Seuring; M. Goldbach (Eds.). –
Heidelberg; New York: Physica-Verl., 2002
   ISBN 3-7908-1500-4

This work is subject to copyright. All rights are reserved, whether the whole or part of the material is concerned, specifically the rights of translation, reprinting, reuse of illustrations, recitation, broadcasting, reproduction on microfilm or in any other way, and storage in data banks. Duplication of this publication or parts thereof is permitted only under the provisions of the German Copyright Law of September 9, 1965, in its current version, and permission for use must always be obtained from Physica-Verlag. Violations are liable for prosecution under the German Copyright Law.

Physica-Verlag Heidelberg New York
a member of BertelsmannSpringer Science + Business Media GmbH

http://www.springer.de

© Physica-Verlag Heidelberg 2002
Printed in Italy

The use of general descriptive names, registered names, trademarks, etc. in this publication does not imply, even in the absence of a specific statement, that such names are exempt from the relevant protective laws and regulations and therefore free for general use.

Cover design: Erich Kirchner, Heidelberg

SPIN 10879566   88/2202-5 4 3 2 1 0 – Printed on acid-free papaer

Foreword

Supply chain management has gained considerable attention in recent years, both from practitioners and academics. It enables companies to achieve competitiveness beyond the factory gates to serve customers. Still, specific issues have not been discussed so far. One prominent example is cost management. While cost management has seen a broad development of concepts and instruments, few transfers to supply chain management have been made so far.

This volume brings together papers which address this intersection between cost management and supply chain management. Such innovative research approaches are needed to further our understanding on how companies interact along the supply chain.

In 2001, the Supply Chain Management Center (SCMC) was established at the University of Oldenburg to advance our research in supply chain management. This volume is our first major contribution to the internationalization of our activities, which is fostered through our cooperation with many of the researchers that contributed to this volume.

Within the Supply Chain Management Center, research on cost and performance management in supply chains is carried out which shows how target costing and activity-based costing or the balanced scorecard can be applied in supply chains.

Furthermore, concepts from strategic management and organization theory are taken up, as they build the link to comprehend how supply chains are formed, restructured, gain competitive or build chain-wide core competencies.

Stefan Seuring, the research director of Supply Chain Management Center (www.uni-oldenburg.de/scmc), and Maria Goldbach, the coordinator of the EcoMTex research project (www.uni-oldenburg.de/ecomtex), who edited this book, did a great job and I am looking forward to jointly advancing our research on supply chain management.

Prof. Dr. Uwe Schneidewind

Preface

Cost Management in Supply Chains seems to be a rather specific issue. Yet, if a single performance measure is used in a supply chain, costs usually are applied. Therefore, costs and their reduction are a frequently stated objective in supply chain management. Yet, only few works seem to have been conducted regarding the issue. This is why we decided to organize a research workshop and document it in a book.

When we set out to plan the research workshop, we hoped to bring researchers together conducting work in a similar field as ourselves. We would like to thank all people contributing to the workshop and this book for sharing their work and ideas with us, as we learned a great deal from them. We are happy to have brought together authors from Austria, Denmark, England, France, Germany, Italy, Russia, Spain, Switzerland, and the United States of America.

A special thanks we would like to give to our support team in Oldenburg. Before, during and after the workshop, Lars Rauprich, Sven Stührenberg, Benjamin Walter, Mathias Guderle, Tim-Hagen Hardt and Magnus Westhaus did a great job to support our efforts, by maintaining the website, preparing the conference documentation, picking up and returning participants to the airport, filling the cookie plates and all the other little things needed.

Concerning the book, Lars Rauprich and Sven Stührenberg supported the editorial work. Dave Kloss did a major review of the text and helped improve the English for the non-native speakers. By now most of them have gained their degree and left the University of Oldenburg. We wish them all the best for their career.

This book and the research work it helps form part of, would not have been possible without the constant support of Prof. Dr. Uwe Schneidewind. We would like to express our deep gratitude to him and look forward to continuing our work at the University of Oldenburg.

Oldenburg, Germany, January 2002

Stefan Seuring and Maria Goldbach

Acknowledgement

This book forms part of our work in the research project EcoMTex (Ecological Mass Textiles, Reference No. 07OWI14/0), which is funded by the German Federal Ministry for Education and Research (BMBF) and administrated by the National Research Center for Environment and Health (GSF). We would like to express our gratitude to both the BMBF and the GSF for their financial and administrative support, specially to Alexander Grablowitz (BMBF) and Dr. Jens Hemmelskamp (GSF).

For further information on the research project see:
www.uni-oldenburg.de/ecomtex

Contents

Foreword V

Preface VII

Acknowledgement VIII

Contents IX

Cost Management in Supply Chains – Different Research Approaches.   1
Stefan Seuring

Part 1 - Developing Concepts for Cost Management in Supply Chains

Supply Chain Costing – A Conceptual Framework 15
Stefan Seuring

Proactive Cost Management in Supply Chains 31
Peter Kajüter

A Framework for Extending Lean Accounting into a Supply Chain 53
Peter Hines, Riccardo Silvi, Monica Bartolini, Andrea Raschi

Managing Costs Across the Supply Chain 75
Regine Slagmulder

Organizational Settings in Supply Chain Costing 89
Maria Goldbach

Part 2 - Applying Cost Management Instruments

Supply Chain Target Costing – An Apparel Industry Case Study....... 111
Stefan Seuring

Integrating Life Cycle Costing and Life Cycle Assessment for
Managing Costs and Environmental Impacts in Supply Chains........... 127
Gerald Rebitzer

Transfer Pricing in Supply Chains: An Exercise in
Internal Marketing and Cost Management.. 147
Messaoud Mehafdi

The Role of Finance in Supply Chain Management............................ 165
Lars Stemmler

Non-Hierarchical Production Networks
– Order Fulfillment and Costing 177
Tobias Teich, Marco Fischer, Joachim Käschel

Efficient Consumer Response
– Increasing Efficiency through Cooperation 195
Khurrum S. Bhutta, Faizul Huq, Francine Maubourguet

Improving Supply Chain Productivity Through Horizontal
Cooperation – the Case of Consumer Goods Manufacturers................ 213
Kourosh Bahrami

Cost Efficiency in Supply Chains – A Conceptual Discrepancy?
Logistics Cost Management between Desire and Reality..................... 233
Herbert Kotzab, Christoph Teller

Part 3 - Building Cost Management Models

Interdependencies between Supply Contracts and Transaction Costs.. 253
Stefan Voß, Gabriele Schneidereit

Decision Support by Model Based Analysis of Supply Chains............ 273
Michael Kaczmarek, Frank Stüllenberg

A New Customer-Oriented Methodology to Evaluate Supply Chain
Lost Sales Costs Due to Stockout in Consumer Goods Sectors............ 289
Marco Perona

Global Supply Chain Management: Extending Logistics'
Total Cost Perspective to Configure Global Supply Chains................. 309
Rolf Krüger

Managing Stocks in Supply Chains: Modeling and Issues................... 325
Layek Abdel-Malek, Giovanni Valentini, Lucio Zavanella

Some Optimization Tools to Improve Manufacturing and
Supply Chain Performance 337
Riurik Skomorokhov

An Options Approach to Enhance Economic Efficiency in a
Dyadic Supply Chain 349
Stefan Spinler, Arnd Huchzermeier, Paul R. Kleindorfer

Part 4 - Extending the Scope Beyond Cost

Using Internet-based Purchasing Tools in Supply Chains
– Insights from a Retail Industry Analysis... 363
Mirko Warschun, Uwe Schneidewind

Complexity Management in the Supply Chain: Theoretical Model and
Empirical Investigation in the Italian Household Appliance Industry.. 381
G. Miragliotta, M. Perona, A. Portioli-Staudacher

Using the Balanced Scorecard for Interorganizational Performance
Management of Supply Chains – A Case Study 399
Klaus Zimmermann

Editors 417
Authors...418
Index 433

Cost Management in Supply Chains – Different Research Approaches

Stefan Seuring

1 Defining Basic Terms 2
2 Developing Concepts for Cost Management in Supply Chain Management .. 5
3 Applying Cost Management Instruments 6
4 Building Cost Management Models 8
5 Extending the Scope Beyond Cost 9
6 Suggestions for Future Research 10
7 References 10

Summary:
Supply Chain Management and Cost Management are among the top issues on the agenda of business practitioners and academic researchers. Yet, while this proves the importance of these issues, it does not necessarily point towards their integration. Still, the links between the two approaches exist. Cost reduction is among the most cited objectives in supply chain management. Additionally, if costs are to be reduced, companies increasingly turn their attention to their supply chain partners, so both suppliers and customers reach out for new frontiers of competitiveness and profitability. Yet, few approaches exist so far, addressing, how cost management in a supply chain can be carried out. This book charts the journey as it puts together different approaches capturing the extend of existing research and business practice.

Keywords:
Supply Chain Management, Cost Management, Supply Chain Costing

1 Defining Basic Terms

Among the objectives most frequently stated in supply chain management is the reduction of cost along the supply chain.[1] Active partnering with suppliers and customers enables companies to achieve optimization potential beyond the factory gate. Often, these cost reductions are achieved rather as a side effect to other measures implemented in supply chain management. Yet, the developments in cost management thought in recent years have proven the importance of the issue.[2]

Therefore, the establishment of a stream of research addressing the management of costs in supply chains forms an important development[3] influencing both the future development of cost and supply chain management.

1.1 Supply Chain Management

Various defintions of Supply Chain Management have been given. Among the most widely used is the one provided by Handfield and Nichols: "The supply chain encompasses all activities associated with the flow and transformation of goods from raw materials stage (extraction), through to the end user, as well as the associated information flows. Material and information flow both up and down the supply chain. Supply chain management (SCM) is the integration of these activities through improved supply chain relationships, to achieve a sustainable competitive advantage."[4]

It is emphazised that this definition brings together the two major issues of supply chain management; the management of material and information flows is combined with the management of relationships. Only the combination of both aspects addresses the full content of supply chain management. Looking at the material and information flows only addresses logistics issues, while covering the relationships only has already been done in other bodies of literature, such as organization, network management or industrial relationships.

Still, the term Supply Chain Management is in its infacy and a general lack of concepts is aknowledged. Few concepts such as the product-relationship-matrix[5] exist, that specially aim to address both dimensions. Future research will have to improve such concepts and prove their validity. In total, Supply Chain Management is not an issue limited to a certain theory or practice, but a rapidly developing field.

---

[1] See e.g. Stevens (1989), p. 3; LaLonde, Pohlen (1996), p. 1; Christoper (1998), p. 25.
[2] See e.g. Franz, Kajüter (1997a); Fischer (2000); Brinker (2000).
[3] See Cooper, Slagmulder (1999); Kajüter (2000); Seuring (2001).
[4] Handfield, Nichols (1999), p. 2.
[5] See Seuring (2001), p. 17.

1.2 Cost Management

What has just been established for Supply Chain Management is also true for Cost Management. In earlier years, both students at universities and practitioners in their companies had a set of instruments that evolved from management accounting. Data was put together and figures were calculated. As the competitive environment of companies changed, it was not sufficient any more, to arrange past data. Instead, accomplished cost information is needed to manage the future. This has led to the introduction of the term cost management, which can be defined in this way: "Cost management encompasses all (control) measures, that aim to influence cost structures and cost behavior precociously. Among these tasks the costs within the value chain have to be assessed, planned, controlled, and evaluated."[6] The proactive management of costs[7] extends much further than management accounting and has lead to the establishment of a full set of new concepts, such as target costing, activity-based costing, life cycle costing and many more.[8]

1.3 Cost Management in Supply Chains

As both cost management and supply chain management are rather platforms for a wide variety of methods, concepts and instruments, it cannot be expected, that looking at the intersection will lead to a single, clear concept.

This volume brings together many of the exiting approaches to cost management in supply chains. As given by Seuring, the issue addressed can be defined as methods or concepts allowing analysis and control of all costs within a supply chain.[9] While this is a wide definition, originally used for Supply Chain Costing, it covers all approaches taken and does not limit practices used to a certain set. In a particular context, it might be necessary to limit the assessment to a certain set of parameters, i.e. costs, resulting in a meaningful analysis of the model.

Taking into account the SCM definition given above, it becomes evident, that costs are not only created by material and information flows along the supply chain, but also by the relationships with the supply chain itself. The papers that are put together in this book aim to illustrate this.

The remainder of this chapter will provide an overview of the papers presented in the book. They are arranged according to four tracks, explained subsequently:

---

[6] Dellmann, Franz (1994), p. 17.
[7] See Kajüter (2000).
[8] See e.g. Brinker (2000); Fisher (2000), which cover many of the existing approaches.
[9] Seuring (2001), p. 126.

1. Developing Concepts for Cost Management in Supply Chains,
2. Applying Cost Management Instruments,
3. Building Cost Management Models,
4. Extending the Scope Beyond Cost.

Each section contains a set of papers that offer an insightful discussion of recent research. Concerning the practical content of the papers, here too four different approaches can be found in the papers.

1. Descriptive Examples show how the research findings presented have drawn from or can influence business practice.
2. Calculated Examples present data either from real world examples or use model data to exemplify the issues addressed.
3. Case Studies are used to illustrate the concepts or instruments introduced.
4. Survey Data shed light on the issues presented drawing from a wider analysis.

Table 1 puts together the two dimensions used to systemize the papers and places each paper in the resulting field. As the table emphasizes, a wide range of different approaches is taken.

Theoretical Basis	Empirical Data			
	Descriptive Example	Calculated Example	Case Study	Survey Data
Developing Concepts	Seuring I Slagmulder Goldbach		Kajüter Hines*	
Applying Instruments	Mehafdi Teich*	Stemmler	Seuring II Baharami Rebitzer Bhutta*	Kotzab*
Building Models	Voß* Kaczmarek* Skoromokhov	Krüger Abdel-Malek* Spinler*		Perona
Extending Beyond Cost	Warschun*		Zimmermann	Miragliotta*

* Indicates that more than one author contributed to the paper. Only the first name is given.

Each paper is allocated to one field only, but several cover more than one issue in each dimension.

Table 1: Overview to the Papers on Cost Management in Supply Chains

The following sections will use the four theoretical bases to discuss some general issues of the papers. This aims to provide some general insights and point at some links between the papers.

2 Developing Concepts for Cost Management in Supply Chain Management

The first section of the book provides insights on how cost management in supply chains can be conceptualized. Common to all papers is the aim to go beyond the limitations of exiting cost management concepts, as they are not capable of considering a supply chain perspective. The papers emphasize that both cost management and supply chain management integrate contributions from other theories such as transaction costs, principal agent theory, or lean management.

Author	Concept	Characteristics
Seuring	Supply Chain Costing	Three cost levels need to be analyzed: direct, activity-based, and transactions cost to account for all costs in a supply chain and find the right partner to control them.
Kajüter	Proactive Cost Management	Proactive cost management is a market-oriented, anticipatory system. Specific techniques are used to coordinate activities, as a case study from the car industry shows.
Hines, Silvi, Bartolini, Raschi	Lean Management Accounting	Linking strategic and operational levels to understand customers and processes, and thus enhance customer value. A case study from car sales offers details.
Slagmulder	Interorganizational Cost Management	Managing supplier and customer costs in coordinated cost reduction programs are carried out during product design and manufacturing.
Goldbach	Organizational Settings	Cost Management has a functional and an institutional dimension. Principal-agent-relationships are important in the application of cost management in a supply chain.

Table 2: The Conceptual Papers

Each paper has a specific perspective (see Table 2), and contributes different ideas. Seuring (Chapter 2) shows that traditional cost management is not prepared to take into account the supply chain perspective. Integrating transaction costs would be able to introduce an analytical level to the cost management system. Kajüter (Chapter 3) presents a framework that allows capturing how cost management systems can be structured to fulfill specific tasks and coordinate activities. Hines, Silvi, Bartolini, and Raschi (Chapter 4) integrate lean management and strategic cost management to provide a case study how his can be put into action. Slagmulder (Chapter 5) looks at the buyer-supplier-interface and shows how interorganizational cost management is carried out. While the previous papers touch on the issue, Goldbach (Chapter 6) addresses how organization of and cooperation in the supply chains influences costs.

Two prevailing perspectives form an important part of all papers. The first is addressed in target costing, as this looks at how targets are set and can be achieved. A process perspective as in activity-based costing accompanies this. Looking at cost management objectives can systemize this. Starting with customer needs, products are brought to the market to fulfill these, while various processes (productive and administrative) are carried out using resources. Hence, reference to target costing and activity-based costing is the unifying topic of the conceptual papers. Furthermore, these two cost management instruments play a major role in the next section.

3 Applying Cost Management Instruments

This section contains papers that provide insights on, how specific cost management instruments or other techniques can be used in a supply chain to reduce costs.

As Table 3 summarizes, most papers are based on existing cost management or accounting techniques, e.g. target costing, life-cycle costing, activity-based costing, transfer pricing or finance instruments. Still, other approaches, such as electronic data interchange (EDI) or virtual enterprises help restructure or control costs. A wide range of issues is addressed showing that no one single approach will be able to solve all arising problems.

Target Costing is one of the most discussed cost management techniques. Seuring (Chapter 7) builds on target costing methodology and integrates the three cost levels of supply chain costing. A case study from the apparel industry gives evidence how this methodology can help to analyze and reduce costs. Rebitzer (Chapter 8) builds on life-cycle assessment and integrated cost data into this framework to calculate life-cycle costs in two case studies from the automotive and aerospace industry. Transfer pricing plays an important role in internal supply chains. Mehafdi (Chapter 9) shows how this can be used and extended towards the development of a balanced scorecard. Financial issues play an important role in these. Stemmler (Chapter 10) provides evidence, how financial instruments can help improve supply chain performance.

Regional production networks can be organized efficiently building on virtual enterprise thought. Information technology assists in fulfilling orders and manage costs, as Teich, Fischer and Käschel (Chapter 11) present. Bhutta, Huq and Maubourguet (Chapter 12) look at the same objectives with the use of electronic data interchange (EDI), which facilitates customer centric approach. Distribution performance and costs play a major role satisfying customers' needs. Bahrami (Chapter 13) shows how horizontal cooperation can help reduce such costs in a consumer goods case study. The last paper of the section stays with the topic of distribution, as Kotzab and Teller (Chapter 14) conducted a survey on how logistics costs are managed in small and medium sized Austrian retail companies.

Author	Basic Instrument	Link to Supply Chain Management
Seuring	Target Costing	The paper shows how target costing in a supply chain helps to analyze direct, activity-based and transaction costs. Case study from apparel industry.
Rebitzer	Life-Cycle Costing	Life-Cycle Assessment methodology and data are used for costing issues as case studies from car and aerospace Industry portray.
Mehafdi	Transfer Pricing	The importance of internal supply chains in multinational companies is emphasized and linked to the external chain. A balanced scorecard is integrated.
Stemmler	Finance	Finance intermediates are used to improve supply chain performance, specially in reducing stock levels. Sample calculation provides evidence.
Teich, Fischer, Käschel	Virtual Enterprise	A competence based approach helps non-hierarchical production networks join forces between SMEs for improved order fulfillment and costing.
Bhutta, Huy, Maubourguet	Electronic Data Interchange	Changing to a customer centric approach, where activity-based costing assists in reducing costs and improve service levels.
Bahrami	Distribution Costs	Horizontal cooperation in a distribution network allows reducing costs by restructuring the distribution network, as sample data emphasizes.
Kotzab, Teller	Logistics Costs	A survey on Logistic Cost Data Usage in small and medium sized Austrian retail companies reveals that cost management is a neglected function, still.

Table 3: The Intrumental Papers

While these papers usually report on current practice that is brought together with theoretical or conceptual developments, the next section of the book looks at how models are built, as they often portray an ideal supply chain.

4 Building Cost Management Models

Models play an important role in the management of both costs and supply chains. Consequently, this section brings together a total of seven papers that take a modeling approach. Still, the papers do not contain only formula, but emphasize how models can help improve supply chain solutions.

The papers show how models can help to generalize problems observed. Reference Models play an important part in such solutions, as Voß and Schneidereit (Chapter 15) as well as Kaczmarek and Stüllenberg (Chapter 16) present. While the first paper mentioned integrates this with game theory, the second does with simulation, respectively.

While the customer is meant to be the focus of all supply chain activities, it is usually hard to evaluate what effect lost sales have in the supply chain. Perona (Chapter 17) presents a model to do so in a three stage supply chain and compares the results of his model to survey data.

Author	Issue Modeled	Characteristics
Voß, Schneidereit	Supply Contracts and Transaction Costs	Classifying supply contracts and building a reference model for supply chain planning, where decentralized decisions are modeled with game theory.
Kaczmarek, Stüllenberg	Process Chain and Cost Model	Using simulation to model costs of inventory oder policies to evaluate and improve supply chain performance.
Perona	Calculating Lost Sales	Using a three-stage supply chain to model the effects of lost customer sales on all stages. Comparison to survey data from Italian Apparel Industry.
Krüger	Logistics Total Costs	Using weight, volume and freight rate to illustrate the influence of transportation costs on global supply chains. Logistic Cost and Reach as evaluation criteria.
Abdel-Malek, Valentini, Zavanella	Inventory Modeling	Modeling inventory in a supply chain under uncertainty to reduce stock levels Comparison of two models.
Skoromokhov	Job Shop Scheduling	The logic of job shop scheduling is applied. In an analogy this allows to balance capacities along the supply chain.
Spinler, Huchzermeier, Kleindorfer	Options Trading	Using game theory to model options for logistics services and assessing cost influences. Sample calculation provided.

Table 4: The Modeling Papers

Krüger (Chapter 18) calculates the logistics reach as an example of a measure, that can be used to reduce logistics costs and enhance performance in a global supply chain. Abdel-Malek, Valentini and Zavanella (Chapter 19) reduce the scope further and look at specific stock keeping models among uncertainty. As a lot of capital still sits in stocks, this will improve supply chain efficiency. Within operations planning, various approaches have been developed. Looking at small and medium sized companies which operate in job shops, it arises that job scheduling and sequencing is an important issue. Skoromokhov (Chapter 20) argues, that the job shop scheduling problem to balance capacities can be used as a model for supply chain optimization, where supply chain partners are treated as the single jobs conducted in a job shop. The last paper of the section by Spinler, Huchzermeier and Kleindorfer (Chapter 21) also uses game theory. Trade options are modeled to help to improve the buyer-supplier interaction in dealing with non-storable goods such as transport capacities.

While the modeling techniques presented help to solve specific problems, the last section of the book contains three papers that even go beyond the scope of cost management.

5 Extending the Scope Beyond Cost

The final section of the book extends the scope of supply chain management beyond cost. The challenges arising from the developments in information technology form an important part of supply chain management. Warschun and Schneidewind (Chapter 22) address the question, how Internet based purchasing tools can be applied in the retail industry. Therefore, the purchasing process is structured, so to assess in which phase the single tools can be applied.

Author	Extension	Characteristics
Warschun, Schneidewind	Internet Technology in Purchasing	Internet technology helps to reduce purchasing costs for retailers. The purchasing process is structured.
Miragliotta, Perona, Portioli-Staudacher	Complexity Management	A conceptual model for complexity management in supply chains is developed and tested in a survey in the Italian household appliance industry.
Zimmermann	Balanced Scorecard	A balanced scorecard for a supply chain is developed allowing developing performance measures. A case from the chemical industry portrays first results.

Table 5: The Papers beyond a Cost Focus

Still, information technology is often only partially able to reduce complexity, so this has to be management in its own regard, as Miragliotta, Perona and Portioli-

Staudacher (Chapter 23) show. Their conceptual framework and model is evaluated in a survey carried out in the Italian household appliance industry. The link to the management of complexity costs will have to be addressed.

Supply chain performance cannot only be measured in terms of cost, so future research must continue and integrating cost issues with other performance measures. The paper by Zimmermann (Chapter 24) looks at how the balanced scorecard can be applied in a supply chain. This addresses the wider issues of performance management in a supply chain, which already forms an important part of supply chain management literature. A case study from the chemical industry portrays the application.

The three papers offer some insights into how supply chain management will be developed further. They complement the previous sections of the book and chart the course towards future research.

6 Suggestions for Future Research

This book brings together a set of different research approaches that address how costs are managed in supply chains. By integrating conceptual work, cost management instruments and models, a great variety of research work is presented. Future work will have to build on the papers presented. Supply chain management is a rapidly developing field, drawing on a multitude of theories, concepts and instruments. This is also the case for cost management in supply chains. Hence, it is of crucial importance to go into further detail of the organizational implications of cost management in supply chains. The need to meet customers' needs and create value while reducing costs through supply chain management will provide challenges and opportunities for companies and researches, so issues discussed in this book will remain on the agenda.

7 References

Brinker, B. J. (ed.) (2000): Guide to Cost Management, Wiley, New York.

Christopher, M. (1998): Logistics and Supply Chain Management – Strategies for Reducing Cost and Improving Service, 2nd Edition, Financial Times, London.

Cooper, R., Slagmulder, R. (1999): Supply Chain Development for the Lean Enterprise – Interorganisational Cost Management, Productivity Press, Portland.

Dellmann, K., Franz, K.-P. (1994b): Von der Kostenrechnung zum Kostenmanagement (From Accounting to Cost Management), in: Dellmann, K., Franz, K.-P. (ed.): Neuere

Entwicklungen im Kostenmanagement (New Developments in Cost Management), Stuttgart, S. 15-30.

Fischer, T. M. (ed.) (2000a): Kosten-Controlling – Neue Methoden und Inhalte (Controlling Costs – New Methods and Contents), Verlag Schäffer-Poeschel, Stuttgart.

Franz, K.-P., Kajüter, P. (eds.) (1997): Kostenmanagement – Wettbewerbsvorteile durch systematische Kostensteuerung (Cost Management – Competitive Advantages through Systematic Cost Controlling), Verlag Schäffer-Poeschel, Stuttgart.

Handfield, R. B., Nichols E. L. (1999): Introduction to Supply Chain Management, Prentice Hall, New Jersey.

Kajüter, P. (2000): Proaktives Kostenmanagement. Konzeption und Realprofile (Proactive Cost Management. Theoretical Concept and Empirical Evidence), Verlag Gabler/DUV, Wiesbaden.

LaLonde, B. J., Pohlen, T. L. (1996): Issues in Supply Chain Costing, in: The International Journal of Logistics Management, Vol. 7, No. 1 (1996), p. 1-12.

Stevens, G. C. (1989): Integrating the Supply Chain, in: International Journal of Physical Distribution & Logistics Management, Vol. 19, No. 8 (1989), p. 3-8.

Part 1
Developing Concepts for Cost Management in Supply Chains

Supply Chain Costing –
A Conceptual Framework

Stefan Seuring

1	Introduction	16
2	Supply Chain Management with the Product-Relationship-Matrix	17
3	Cost Management Issues in Supply Chains	21
4	Supply Chain Costing	24
5	Conclusion	27
6	References	28

Summary:
Within Supply Chain Management, the reduction of costs is a frequently cited objective. Yet, no concepts have been presented so far, that allow assessing the total costs in a supply chain. This paper provides a framework for supply chain costing in three steps. First, the product-relationship-matrix offers a systematic approach to decision in supply chain management. Next, three cost levels are distinguished to allow a separation of costs that can be influenced within a single company – single and activity-based costs – and within the supply chain – transaction costs. Taken together, the three dimensions product, relationships and costs form the conceptual framework for supply chain costing.

Keywords:
Supply Chain Management, Cost Management, Product-Relationship-Matrix, Cost Levels, Single Costs, Activity-Based Costs, Transaction Costs

1 Introduction

The reduction of total costs is a frequently stated objective in supply chain management.[1] In contrast to these statements, no conceptual framework for a systematic assessment of cost in supply chains has been presented. Mostly, other objectives, specially the reduction cycle times and inventories along the supply chain prevail.[2] As these goals are reached, costs will decrease.

This simplified assumption does not take into account the full range of decision that influences costs within a supply chain. This paper provides a conceptual framework for supply chain costing. Definitions of supply chain management include two aspects, the management of products with their material and information flows and the management of relationships along the supply chain.[3] These two dimensions of supply chain management form the basis of the product-relationship-matrix.

Cost management techniques center on companies as the unit of assessment. Yet, direct and indirect costs are distinguished. This separation does not allow analyzing how the decision of one company in the supply chain influences the costs of suppliers and customers. Hence, transaction costs have to be integrated with activity-based costs and direct costs.

The three dimensions, product, relationships and costs together form the conceptual framework of supply chain costing. Four decision fields will be explained to show, which cost level can be optimized at what stage of the supply chain.

---

[1] See e.g. Jones, Riley (1985), p. 21; Houlihan (1985), p. 26; Lee, Billington (1992), p. 68; Christopher (1998), p. 25.
[2] See Towill (1996), p. 41-53; Rich, Hines (1997), p. 210-225.
[3] See Handfield, Nichols (1999), p. 2.

2 Supply Chain Management with the Product-Relationship-Matrix

2.1 Material and Information Flows and Relationships

Various other terms are used as synonyms for supply chain management, which is still the most used one. Some examples in a non-exhaustive list are: value chain management, value stream management, demand network management, and value net management.

Beside these different wordings, it is evident that two issues form the constituents of supply chain management, as the definition of Handfield and Nichols expresses: "The supply chain encompasses all activities associated with the flow and transformation of goods from raw materials stage (extraction), through to the end user, as well as the associated information flows. Material and information flow both up and down the supply chain. Supply chain management (SCM) is the integration of these activities through improved supply chain relationships, to achieve a sustainable competitive advantage".[4]

The management of material and information flows links supply chain management to its conceptual basis in logistics. While logistics tries to optimize material and information flows between single facilities, supply chain management looks much further, as the second part of the definition states.

The interconnected links of material and information flows along the supply chain can only be achieved by managing relationships among partners. Therefore, the needs and abilities of all companies must be taken into account, as the competitiveness of the chain will only be as strong as the weakest part of it.[5] Hence, the decisions that frame the supply chain have to be integrated into a conceptual framework for supply chain management.

2.2 The Decision Fields of the Product-Relationship-Matrix

Cooper and Slagmulder propose a two dimensional framework for supply chain management, that builds directly on the definition mentioned. They distinguish a product and a relationship dimension, which are each subdivided into a constitutional and an operational phase.[6]

---

[4] Handfield, Nichols (1999), p. 2.
[5] See Croom, Romano, Giannakis, (2000), p. 67.
[6] See Cooper, Slagmulder (1999), p. 10.

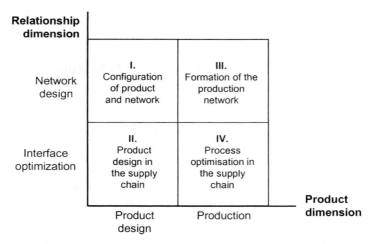

Figure 1: The Product-Relationship-Matrix of Supply Chain Management[7]

This separation of two phases builds on life-cycle thinking. Therefore, within the product dimension, the two phases product design and production are separated, while the relationship dimension is split into network design and interface optimization. Still, Cooper and Slagmulder do not integrate the two dimensions with each other. Taking the two dimensions and their interrelations together, the product-relationship-matrix is formed (Figure 1).

Within the matrix four fields result that can be used as a decision framework for supply chain management. These decisions will be described subsequently.

2.2.1 Configuration of Product and Network

The configuration of product and network covers the basic decisions in which products and services are offered in cooperation with other companies.[8] This includes the question, which kind of coordination among supply chain partners[9] is most efficient, as this can range from market to hierarchy.[10] In this context, hierarchial companies fully integrate all activities along a supply chain. There is a clear governing structure, guaranteeing that all decisions made by top management are executed accordingly. But on the other hand, there is the disadvantage of high sunk costs throught the investment in structures and

---

[7] Seuring (2001), p. 17.
[8] See Fine (2000), p. 213.
[9] See Corsten, Gössinger (2001), p. 51f.
[10] See the arguments of transaction cost theory, e.g. Williamson (1998).

equipment that cannot be used for other purposes. Markets in contrast represent the traditional form of how products are exchanged between companies. Within these arms-length relationships, the exchange of material and information flows happen on a case-by-case basis.

Within supply chain management, it is assumed, often without any reference or reason given, that intermediate forms of coordination that have neither the disadvantages of hierarchies nor those of free, unlimited markets are superior to both extremes of the continuum.[11] These decisions depend on the distribution of competencies, power and trust among the supply chain partners.[12] The following three fields of the matrix specify the framework set.

2.2.2 Product Design in the Supply Chain

Product design in the supply chain aims at utilizing the research and development know-how of suppliers. This leads to strategic sourcing or outsourcing decisions, where a company has to determine, which parts of the product development process belong to its core competencies, which can be outsourced in strategic partnerships or can be purchased on commodity markets. In some case, it might even be suitable to develop suppliers that can supply product design as part of their support.[13]

In recent years, companies have introduced supplier pyramids to reduce the number of suppliers dealt with. The company at the end of the supply chain orders pre-build components from their suppliers (first-tier suppliers), which must in turn organize their sub-suppliers (second-tier suppliers). Within the car industry, this has led to the transfer of parts of the product development to the supplier network. Traditionally, parts were fully specified and ordered to be built to these specifications. These days, companies define the parts and their technical requirements, while suppliers have to conduct all activities necessary to be able to deliver the parts, including the design and development needed.[14] This leads to the development of design for supply chain management.[15]

2.2.3 Formation of the Production Network

As a single company is not able to provide all pre-products necessary, a network of suppliers has to be organized. Again, the aim is to minimize the costs created by fulfilling the customer service demanded at the end of the chain. The decisions to be made within the formation of the production network cover the choice of

---

[11] See Stadtler (2000), p. 9.
[12] See Maloni, Benton (2000), p. 49-73; Blois (1999), p. 197-215.
[13] See Quinn, Hilmer (1994), p. 43-55.
[14] See Dyer, Cho, Chu (1996), p. 42-56; Scannel, Vickery, Dröge (2000), p. 23-48.
[15] Lee, Billington (1992), p. 71.

production partners and the definition of their specific role. The processes carried out at the single production facilities, stock holding points and cycle times have to be specified.

The postponement principle can be used to illustrate this. Within production systems, two controlling mechanisms prevail. Traditionally, production systems are driven by a forecasted demand. Products are pushed through the production lines and kept in stock so as to satisfy upcoming demand. This allows a rather easy production, but leads to high stock levels and low production flexibility, so that products cannot be modified according to customer requests. Pull driven production responds directly to customer demand, as an incoming order triggers the production of a specific product. Problems found in these systems arise from capacity costs, as highly flexible machines have to be used, and opportunity costs, if customer orders cannot be fulfilled.

Applying postponement, companies try to avoid the problems associated with both systems. Within production, postponement products are manufactured up to a level where they easily can be customized. Furthermore, logistical postponement aims at an optimized stock keeping.[16] Hewlett Packard combined these two ideas within the design and delivery structure of their printers. Taking the power supply unit out of the printer body allows a preproduction of printers and delivery to a central stock keeping point in Europe. Depending on the demand in single countries, the printers are customized by adding the country-specific power supply unit and distributing the printer to the point of sale.[17]

2.2.4 Process Optimization in the Supply Chain

Most of the supply chain management literature falls into the last field of the product-relationship-matrix. Process optimization in the supply chain accepts the structures given, but looks at optimization potentials within these structures. As previously mentioned, the guiding objectives are the reduction of cycle times and inventories along the supply chain. Regularly, information technology is employed to enable a better transfer of information between supply chain partners, such as in efficient consumer response (ECR) solutions that use electronic data interchange (EDI).[18]

For the management of processes, reference models are applied to systemize and depict them. The Supply Chain Operations Reference Model (SCOR)[19] builds on the input, throughput, and output scheme used in operations management and defines four basic processes, as Figure 2 shows.

---

[16] See Pagh, Cooper (1998), p. 15.
[17] See Davis (1993), p. 35-46.
[18] See Lummus, Vokurka (1999), p. 13.
[19] See Stewart (1997), p. 62-67.

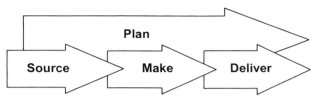

Figure 2: The Basic Processes of the SCOR-Model[20]

Any process receives material and information via the source process from its predecessors. Within the make process, these materials and information are transformed to then be carried on to the next stage of the process or supply chain within the delivery process. To coordinate these operational processes a plan process is introduced. The SCOR Model can be used to depict processes on various levels and detail them step by step.

So far, the product-relationship-matrix has been introduced and explained as a framework for supply chain management. If costs are to be analyzed and managed within a supply chain, they have to be integrated into this framework.

3 Cost Management Issues in Supply Chains

3.1 Some Remarks on Cost Management

Traditionally, management and cost accounting techniques have focused on the reverse allocation of costs. The information provided has lost its relevance to managers on all levels for cost analysis and controlling,[21] a result of the changing cost structure of companies, specially the dramatic rise of indirect costs.[22] This has led to the development of cost management techniques that are used to support specific decisions and the overall management of organizations.

"Cost management encompasses all (control) measures that aim to influence cost structures and cost behavior precociously. Among these tasks the costs within the value chain have to be assessed, planned, controlled, and evaluated."[23] This has led to a wide range of new cost management techniques. Target costing and

---

[20] Supply Chain Council (1997), slide 42.
[21] See Kaplan, Cooper (1997), p. 2.
[22] See Miller, Vollmann (1985), p. 143.
[23] Dellmann, Franz (1994), p. 17.

activity-based costing are among the most prominent, emphasizing the managerial application of cost data, leading to a proactive cost management.[24]

The recent development of the total cost of ownership concept by Ellram[25] and the work on interorganizational cost management by Cooper and Slagmulder[26] provide examples on, how supply chain related issues are integrated into cost management thoughts. Total cost of ownership helps to analyze the interface to suppliers. It centers on selecting suppliers and optimizing the interfaces towards them, as it is part of field four of the product-relationship matrix.[27]

The approach offered by interorganizational cost management builds on lean management. Various management techniques are taken up to improve the lean design and operation within a supplier network. As previously mentioned, both the product and the relationship dimension are taken into account, but the step of linking them together is missing. Hence, the single cost management techniques addressed are presented rather separately. An integrative framework for supply chain costing is missing so far.

3.2 Distinguishing Three Cost Levels

Most cost management techniques look at the internal cost of companies. Direct and indirect costs are distinguished to manage cost according to the decisions create these costs. In a supply chain, various decisions can only be made considering the needs and abilities of suppliers and customers. Therefore, managerial instruments are needed to allow for the classification of costs within the supply chain that provide the opportunity to analyze and control costs in a supply chain setting.

Such a supply chain costing has to take into account both production and transaction costs. This terminology is taken from the concept of transaction costs that plays an important part within the new institutional economics.[28] Without referring to this concept in detail, the term transaction costs within the concept of supply chain costing is applied in a simplistic way that disregards the variables and explanations given by Williamson's theoretical concept. Building on the traditional separation of direct costs and indirect or activity-based costs, this leads to a differentiation of three cost levels, direct costs, activity-based costs and transaction costs (Figure 3). The three terms are defined as follows:

---

[24] On proactive cost management, see Kajüter (2000).
[25] See Ellram (1994), p. 171-192; Ellram (1995), p. 22-30.
[26] See Cooper, Slagmulder (1999).
[27] See Seuring (2001), p. 55.
[28] See Williamson (1998).

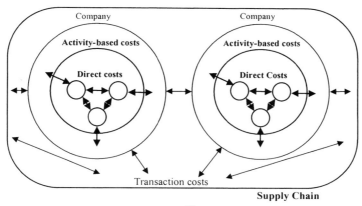

Figure 3: Cost Levels in Supply Chain Costing[29]

1. Direct costs

Direct costs are caused by the production of each single entity of a product and include such costs as materials, labor and machine costs. Mainly, these costs are controlled by prices for material and labor.

2. Activity-based costs

Activity-based costs are caused by activities that cannot be directly related to products, but are caused by administrative activities that have to be performed in order to be able to manufacture and deliver products to customers. These costs arise from the organizational framework of the company.

3. Transaction costs

Transaction costs encompass all activities dealing with the information of and the communication with suppliers and customers. Therefore, these costs arise from interactions with other companies in the supply chain.

The three cost levels provide a basis for the analysis and optimization of costs in the supply chain, yet must be integrated with the two dimensions of the product-relationship-matrix.

---

[29] Seuring (1999), p 22.

4 Supply Chain Costing

4.1 Integrating Product, Relationship and Cost Dimension

In the previous section, the product-relationship-matrix as a concept of supply chain management and the three cost levels were introduced. Taking these ideas from supply chain management and cost management together, a conceptual framework for supply chain costing results (Figure 4). Within supply chain costing, all costs within a supply chain must be analyzed and controlled. The concept assesses cost directly, but does not refer to surrogate measures, such as cycle time and inventory. However, it also integrates the perspective taken by total cost of ownership, which looks at all three cost levels but only at the production stage and interface optimization.[30] The concept of interorganizational cost management describes the product and the relationship dimension, but does neither integrates them nor takes a cost dimension into account.

Again, the four fields of the product-relationship-matrix are used to structure the discussion.

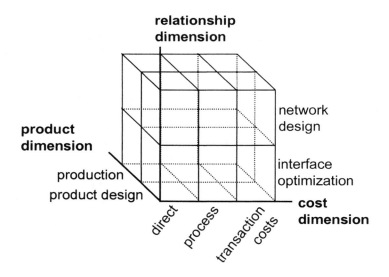

Figure 4: A Conceptual Framework for Supply Chain Costing

---

[30] See Seuring (2001), p. 126.

4.2 Cost Analysis in the Four Decision Fields

4.2.1 Configuration of Product and Network

The first field, configuration of product and network, deals with the basic decisions that determine the products and services offered and the partners involved. These decisions often are seen as separate ones, so the costs challenges are not taken. Purchasing tends to look at the price, so only the direct costs are into consideration. Strategic sourcing decisions must look further and consider the activities carried out and the transactions necessary between suppliers and customers. This might lead to strategic investments in supplier and customer relationships that create rising transaction costs. As these transaction costs are often one time investments, they pay off by reducing the activity-based costs of the long term cooperation, as the processes between the companies along the supply chain are integrated and optimized. The resulting effects are explained subsequently. Within this decision field, usually only limited direct costs occur.

4.2.2 Product Design in the Supply Chain

Depending on the products or services offered to customers, an intensive cooperation between companies is needed in the design phase. Advanced suppliers offer sophisticated parts at the specification of the customer. The cooperation is highly dependant on the products and their characteristics, so transaction costs for first-time settlement of the relationship still constitute an important part of the total costs. The lower the competence of the supplier, the higher these transaction costs will be, as an intensive, almost continual contact to the supplier will be needed.

Yet, the center of the costs is within the activity-based costs. Research and development activities can only be attributed to the product in total and depend on the internal structures. Know-how transfer to the supplier might lead to shorter development times. Again, this raises transaction costs, but lowers activity-based costs. For the materials needed during the design and development process, some minor direct costs may appear, but most direct costs would have already been determined by these decisions.

4.2.3 Formation of the Production Network

Product and supply chain must be compatible with each other, so the cost implications of these decision have to be obeyed. The investment into information technology might significantly reduce the operating costs of data exchange between companies, so transaction and activity-based costs are effected. Yet, the limits of this approach have to be obeyed. For products with a steady, predictable demand, e.g. canned soups, efficient supply has to be ensured.[31]

Fashion products, such as apparel, need a regular review of the amount delivered and stocked along the supply chain. Unsold products will have to be marked down at the end of the season, while lost sales opportunities cannot be compensated.[32] Hence, for the optimal design of the supply chain, the constant occurrence of transaction costs and activity-based costs for internal and supply chain-wide processes are typical.

4.2.4 Process Optimization in the Supply Chain

The process optimisation in the supply chain looks at single measures for cost reductions, which are usually achieved on the direct cost and activity-based cost level. The supply chain wide analysis of production processes and stock-keeping points allow identification of weak spots. These can range from the use of wrong materials that lead to higher scrap to the redesign of a production process or an optimized order fulfillment between a company and its supplier. The introduction of electronic data interchange, a decision made within the former field, will lower the direct and activity-based costs of information exchange significantly.

4.3 Integrating the Four Fields in Supply Chain Costing

The discussion within the four decision field is now taken as a whole. As can be seen in Figure 5, a step by step shift from transaction costs to activity-based and direct costs is evident as the supply chain becomes operational.

The relative importance of the three costs levels is highly dependent on the product or service offered. Products with long life cycles will need much lower transaction costs for supplier selection, relationship building, and product and process design between companies.

Products within short fashion or technological cycles will lead to increased costs in early decision phases. As the time on the market of these products is often shorter than the product development time, there is a high risk that investments will not pay off. This emphasizes the importance of transaction and activity-based costs and calls for their active management.

---

[31] See Fisher (1997), p. 108.
[32] See Fisher (1997), p. 109.

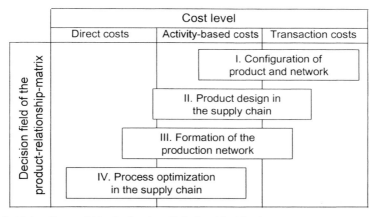

Figure 5: Major Costs within the Product-Relationship-Matrix

5 Conclusion

The explanations given show that the borders between single fields are weak. Still, the conceptual framework for supply chain costing has proven to be suitable for the analysis and controlling of cost in supply chains. The product, relationship and cost dimension comprise all major decisions within the supply chain and allow their cost influences to be addressed.

The paper illustrates, how increased costs on one level, especially the transaction cost level, help to reduce costs at other levels. So far, transaction costs and activity-based costs created at supplier and customer facilities are often not taken into account, as companies tend to focus on their own production lines. Within the increasingly competitive global environment, supply chains have to consider the competitiveness of the whole supply chain. Cost management will have to form an integrative part of supply chain management on all stages of the supply chain.

Beyond that, the further development of trust and confidence within the supply chain will be necessary, so that the supply chain is seen as a single entity by all partners involved, where the competitiveness of the chain and the customer satisfaction created can only be improved jointly and for mutual benefit.

6 References

Blois, K. J. (1999): Trust in Business to Business Relationships: An Evaluation of its Status, in: Journal of Management Studies, Vol. 36, No. 2 (1999), p. 197-215.

Christopher, M. (1998): Logistics and Supply Chain Management – Strategies for Reducing Cost and Improving Service, 2nd Edition, Financial Times, London.

Cooper, R., Slagmulder, R. (1999): Supply Chain Development for the Lean Enterprise – Interorganizational Cost Management, Productivity Press, Portland.

Corsten, H., Gössinger, R. (2001): Einführung in das Supply Chain Management (Introduction to Supply Chain Management), Oldenbourg Verlag, München.

Croom, S., Romano, P., Giannakis, M. (2000): Supply Chain Management: An Analytical Framework for Critical Literature Review, in: European Journal of Purchasing and Supply Management, Vol. 6 (2000), p. 67-83.

Davis, T. (1993): Effective Supply Chain Management, in: Sloan Management Review, Vol. 34, No. 2 (1993), S. 35-46.

Dellmann, K., Franz, K.-P. (1994): Von der Kostenrechnung zum Kostenmanagement (From Cost Accounting to Cost Management), in: Dellmann, K., Franz, K.-P. (ed.): Neuere Entwicklungen im Kostenmanagement (New Developments in Cost Management), Verlag Paul Haupt, Stuttgart 1994, p.15-30.

Dyer, J. H., Cho, D. S., Chu, W. (1998): Strategic Supplier Segmentation: The next "best practice" in supply chain management, in: California Management Review, Vol. 40, No. 2 (1998), p. 57-77.

Ellram, L. M. (1994): A Taxonomy of Total Cost of Ownership Models, in: Journal of Business Logistics, Vol. 15, No. 1 (1994), S. 171-192.

Ellram, L. M. (1995): Activity-Based Costing and Total Cost of Ownership: A critical linkage, in: Journal of Cost Management, Vol. 8, No. 4 (1995), S. 22-30.

Fine, C. H. (2000): Clockspeed-Based Strategies for Supply Chain Design, in: Production and Operations Management, Vol. 9, No. 3 (2000), p. 213-221.

Handfield, R. B., Nichols E. L. (1999): Introduction to Supply Chain Management, Prentice Hall, Upper Saddle River, NJ.

Hines, P., Rich, N., Bicheno, J., Brunt, D., Taylor, D., Butterworth, C., Sullivan, J. (1998): Value Stream Management, in: The International Journal of Logistics Management, Vol. 9, No. 1 (1998), p. 25-42.

Houlihan, J. B. (1985): International Supply Chain Management, in: International Journal of Physical Distribution & Logistics Management, Vol. 15, No. 1 (1985), S. 22-38.

Jones, T. C., Riley, D. W. (1985): Using Inventory for Competitive Advantage through Supply Chain Management, in: International Journal of Physical Distribution & Logistics Management, Vol. 15, No. 5 (1985), S. 16-26.

Kajüter, P. (2000): Proaktives Kostenmanagement. Konzeption und Realprofile (Proactive Cost Management. Theoretical Concept and Empirical Evidence), Verlag Gabler/DUV, Wiesbaden.

Kaplan, R. S., Cooper, R. (1997): Cost and Effect – Using Integrated Cost Systems to Drive Profitability and Performance, Harvard Business School Press, Boston.

LaLonde, B. J., Pohlen, T. L. (1996): Issues in Supply Chain Costing, in: The International Journal of Logistics Management, Vol. 7, No. 1 (1996), p. 1-12.

Lee, H. L., Billington, C. (1992): Managing Supply Chain Inventory: Pitfalls and Opportunities, in: Sloan Management Review, Vol. 33, No. 1 (1992), p. 65-73.

Lummus, R. R., Vokurka, R. J. (1999): Defining Supply Chain Management: A Historical Perspective and Practical Guidelines, in: Industrial Management & Data Systems, Vol. 99, No. 1/2 (1999), p. 11-17.

Maloni, M., Benton, W. C. (2000): Power Influences in the Supply Chain, in: Journal of Business Logistics, Vol. 21, No. 1 (2000), p. 49-73.

Miller, J. G., Vollmann, T. E. (1985): The Hidden Factory, in: Harvard Business Review, Vol. 63, No. 9/10 (1985), p. 142-150.

Pagh, J. D., Cooper, M. C. (1998): Supply Chain Postponement and Speculation Strategies: How to choose the Right Strategy, in: Journal of Business Logistics, Vol. 19, No. 2 (1998), p. 13-34.

Quinn, J. B., Hilmer, F. G. (1994): Strategic Outsourcing, in: Sloan Management Review, Vol. 34, No. 3 (1994), p. 43-55.

Rich, N., Hines, P. (1997): Supply-Chain Management and Time Based Competition: The Role of the Supplier Association, in: International Journal of Physical Distribution & Logistics Management, Vol. 27, No. 3/4 (1997), p. 210-225.

Scannell, T., Vickery, S. K., Dröge, C. L. (2000): Upstream Supply Chain Management and Competitive Performance in the Automobile Supply Industry, in: Journal of Business Logistics, Vol. 21, No. 1 (2000), p. 23-48.

Seuring, S., (1999): Gestaltungsoptionen durch Kostenmanagement – Das Beispiel der Wertschöpfungskette von Öko-Textilien (Opportunities through Cost Management – The example of the supply chain for eco-products in the apparel industry), in: Umweltwirtschaftsforum. Vol. 7, No. 4 (1999), p. 18-23.

Seuring, S. (2001): Supply Chain Costing – Kostenmanagement in der Wertschöpfungskette mit Target Costing und Prozesskostenrechnung (Supply Chain Costing with Target Costing and Activity Based Costing), Verlag Franz Vahlen, München.

Seuring, S., Schneidewind, U. (2000): Kostenmanagement in der Wertschöpfungskette (Cost Management in Supply Chains), in: Wildemann, H. (ed.): Supply Chain Management, TCW Verlag, München, p. 227-250.

Stadtler, H. (2000): Supply Chain Management - An Overview, in: Stadtler, H., Kliger, C. (ed.): Supply Chain Management and Advanced Planning - Concepts, Models, Software and Case Studies, Springer Verlag, Berlin, p. 7-28.

Stewart, G. (1997): Supply Chain Operations Reference Model (SCOR): The First Cross-Industry Framework for Integrated Supply-Chain Management, in: Logistics Information Management, Vol. 10, No. 2/3 (1997), p. 62-67.

Supply Chain Council (ed.) (1997): Introduction to the Supply Chain Operations Reference-model (SCOR), Release 2.0, Pennsylvania (see: www.supply-chain.org).

Towill, D. R. (1996): Time Compression and Supply Chain Management - a Guided Tour, in: Logistics information management, Vol. 9, No. 6 (1996), p. 41-53.

Williamson, O. E. (1998): The Economic Institutions of Capitalism - Firms, Markets, Relational Contracting, Simon and Schuster Trade Division, New York.

Proactive Cost Management in Supply Chains

Peter Kajüter

1	Introduction	32
2	Review of Previous Research	33
3	Framework for Proactive Cost Management	39
4	Empirical Evidence from the Automotive Industry	42
5	Summary and Outlook	48
6	References	48

Summary:
With increasing competition many companies have extended the scope of their cost management activities across organizational boundaries. Yet, the theoretical foundation of this trend is still limited. A literature review reveals several deficiencies, above all the lack of a comprehensive conceptual framework for proactive cost management in supply chains. The paper seeks to close this gap by presenting such a framework which has been used in an exploratory case study in the automotive industry. The empirical evidence of this case study is described and directions for further research are suggested.

Keywords:
Cost Management, Supply Chain, Conceptual Framework, Automotive Industry

1 Introduction

In recent years, many companies have extended the scope of their cost management efforts as a result of increasing competition. At first, the focus has been shifted from production to product development. Although the emphasis on cost management in the product design stage offers significant opportunities for improving the cost position, cost management activities are still restricted mainly to the company's boundaries. Hence, interorganizational synergies are frequently neglected. Taking advantage of these synergies, however, is vital in today's world and requires a broad focus encompassing the entire supply chain.

A supply chain, though different definitions exist[1], comprises all firms from raw material extraction to the ultimate consumer. Within such a group of entities the flow and transformation of goods, the associated information flows as well as the relationships between the entities are subject to analysis and improvement.[2]

Cost management covers all activities aiming to improve the efficiency of a company or supply chain. In practice, cost management efforts are often a temporary reaction to declining profits. Since short-term improvements are necessary in such cases, cost problems are rarely analysed in depth. Instead, cost cutting programs dominate. There are multiple reasons for this but the lack of a comprehensive framework for a systematic and continuous approach to cost management seems to be a major reason. Such an approach meeting the requirements for effective cost management in a highly competitive environment and integrating various single research findings is called *proactive cost management*.[3]

It is the purpose of this paper to present a conceptual framework for proactive cost management in supply chains. The next section therefore briefly reviews previous research to analyse the theoretical foundation of managing costs in supply chains. Based on this analysis, a conceptual framework is introduced in section three. The results of an exploratory case study on cost management activities in the supply chain of an international automotive manufacturer, derived by using the framework, are discussed in section four. The final section provides some concluding remarks and suggests directions for further research.

---

[1] See Harland (1996), p. S64; Berry et al. (1997), p. 74. As in this article, the term "supply chain" is generally used synonymously with "value chain".

[2] See Handfield, Nichols (1999), p. 2; also Macht, Hartlieb (1997), p. 416.

[3] See Kajüter (2000), (2001).

2 Review of Previous Research

A review of previous research in the area of cost management faces the problem that within management science several disciplines address single aspects of cost management and analyse them in the discipline's specific context. The literature of strategic management, organizational theory, management accounting, and supply chain management has contributed several insights to managing costs in supply chains. In addition to these individual contributions, there are a few attempts to integrate these research findings into a more comprehensive framework. The following sections 2.1 and 2.2 provide an overview of empirical and theoretical research in both fields leading to a conclusion in section 2.3.

2.1 Previous Research by Management Disciplines

2.1.1 Strategic Management

Strategic management deals with the design and implementation of strategies that aim to create a competitive advantage. As lower costs are a source of competitive advantage, cost issues are frequently subject to research in strategic management. A major influence on strategic thinking about cost advantages stems from the value chain concept developed by Porter.[4] The value chain is a generic tool to analyse the strategically relevant activities of a company. These activities are potential sources of competitive advantage in terms of cost or differentiation. A cost advantage can be gained by the control of cost drivers or the reconfiguration of the value chain.

Figure 1: Industry Value Chain

A company's internal value chain is not an isolated system. It interacts with the value chains of suppliers and distributors (channels) and is therefore part of the industry value chain (Figure 1). This broad view of the value chain concept allows expanding the focus on the linkages existing between independent companies. The procurement and inbound logistics of a firm, for instance, interact with the order entry system of its supplier, and similarly outbound logistics interrelate with channel activities. Such linkages are a major cost driver. Improving the coordination

---

[4] See Porter (1985), p. 33.

and jointly optimizing the interfaces between value chains frequently offers opportunities to reduce costs at both partners.

The value chain concept stimulated the discussion for a strategic approach to cost management. It distinguishes two perspectives – the internal value chain of a firm and the industry value chain. The practical application of the former is limited though: Assigning costs to the value chain activities is rather difficult because cost accounting systems are not designed to provide data for value chain analysis.[5] Moreover, the concept provides little help for the identification of cost drivers. It only lists ten strategic factors (economies of scale, learning, linkages etc.), but does not discuss how they relate to each other. However, by emphasizing the need for a broad view encompassing the entire industry value chain the concept forms a basis for inter-firm cost management efforts.

2.1.2 Organizational Theory

The transaction cost approach[6] constitutes an important contribution of organizational theory to cost management in supply chains. Originally developed to explain the existence of organizations, it provides a theoretical foundation to decide which activities of the overall industry value chain a company should perform itself. For this purpose, the transaction cost approach focuses on costs caused by the information of and communication with supply chain partners. Transaction costs are thus defined as costs arising from the design, agreement and control of contractual relationships. In general, these costs are not under control of a single company; they are rather influenced by all supply chain partners. In doing so, supply chain partners should consider the amount of transaction-specific investments, the degree of uncertainty and the frequency of transactions as major drivers of transaction costs.

Although the transaction cost approach addresses some important issues of cost management in supply chains from a theoretical perspective, its practical application causes problems due to the difficulty of separating transaction costs from other indirect costs.[7] This limitation restricts transaction cost theory to deliver primarily qualitative aspects (e.g. reducing transaction costs by definition of standards). Furthermore, it also explains the lack of empirical studies which measure the level of transaction costs in companies.

Apart from the transaction cost approach, other contributions of organizational theory to cost management can be found in the area of business process design and redesign. The latter gained much attention in the early 1990s in the form of reengi-

---

[5] See Hergert, Morris (1989); Partridge, Perren (1994), p. 22.
[6] See Coase (1937); Williamson (1979), (1981).
[7] This is, however, primarily a deficit of management accounting, not of transaction cost theory.

neering concepts developed by consulting firms.[8] Although reengineering concepts generally did not meet their expectations and consequently received a lot of criticism[9], they contributed a few new aspects to organizational theory and cost management. First, they state that process improvement is not restricted to the company itself, but rather has to take cross-company processes into account as well. This is combined with an emphasis of the need for an increased customer focus in designing business processes. Reengineering concepts confirmed the findings of earlier research identifying human factors (e.g. resistance against organizational change) as the major reason for the failure of corporate restructuring.

2.1.3 Management Accounting

The implications of extending cost management efforts across the supply chain have also received increasing attention in management accounting research. The literature discusses various aspects, e.g. the issue of disclosing and sharing cost data between supply chain partners[10], the technical problem of collecting cost data across the supply chain when accounting systems are not compatible with each other[11], the impact of supply chain accounting on the traditional firm-specific accounting systems (which was found to be rather small)[12], and above all, the application of available cost management techniques within supply chains[13].

Target costing gained particular interest in this context.[14] It proved to be well-suited for inter-firm cost management because it allows transmitting the cost reduction pressure throughout the supply chain by linking the target costing systems of buyers and suppliers (chained target costing). In addition, the applicability of life cycle costing[15], activity-based costing[16], kaizen costing[17], benchmarking[18] and the balanced scorecard[19] has been analysed as well. The conceptual design of an accounting system for transaction costs, however, is still a largely unsolved question.[20] Despite the increasing amount of literature published in recent years, the discussion remains on a fairly general level in most cases. Empirical research is, if at all, undertaken in the form of single case studies. While these case studies usu-

---

[8] See e.g. Hammer, Champy (1993).
[9] See e.g. Earl, Khan (1994).
[10] See Munday (1992); Berry et al. (1997), p. 75; Ellram, Feitzinger (1997), p. 15.
[11] See Dekker, van Goor (2000), p. 47.
[12] See Cullen et al. (1999), p. 32.
[13] See LaLonde, Pohlen (1996); Cullen et al. (1999), p. 32.
[14] See Cooper, Slagmulder (1999a), p. 181; also Dyer (1996), p. 52; Ellram (2000).
[15] See Taylor (1981).
[16] See Dekker, van Goor (2000).
[17] See Lingscheid (1998); Cooper, Slagmulder (1999a), p. 271.
[18] See Donelan, Kaplan (1998), p. 12.
[19] See Cullen et al. (1999), p. 31; Brewer, Speh (2000); Kummer (2001).
[20] For a transaction cost accounting system in purchasing see Matje (1996), p. 210.

ally describe joint cost management efforts in bilateral buyer-supplier relationships, supply chains of more than two partners (supply networks) are seldom analysed.

2.1.4 Supply Chain Management

Supply chain management emerged as a field of research during the 1990s integrating recent developments in logistics, procurement, marketing and information technology. As a major objective of supply chain management is to increase efficiency, the literature contains several aspects refering to cost management.

Estimates indicate that about 30 billion USD are wasted annually in the US food industry due to poor coordination among supply chain partners.[21] Thus, improving the interfaces between buyers and suppliers is a key source for cost savings. The standardization of material and information flows frequently offers significant opportunities in this respect. It allows eliminating non-value added activities and streamlines business processes. As a consequence, cycle times and inventory can be reduced. In the past few years, new and more efficient ways to organize the flow of material and information across companies evolved by the increasing use of the internet.[22] Still, research in this area does not provide any comprehensive approach to effective cost management in supply chains. Nevertheless, it emphasizes the need for inter-firm process optimization.

Other studies in the area of supply chain management supplement this issue. In particular, the results of empirical research reveal that positive effects on profitability can be achieved by long-term relationships between suppliers and buyers due to lower overhead costs compared to those firms employing a transactional approach to servicing customers.[23] Finally, literature suggests that different types of products (innovative vs. functional products) require different supply chains.[24] This fact raises the question whether and how product strategy influences the way costs are managed effectively in supply chains.

2.2 Conceptual Approaches to Cost Management

In addition to the investigation of single aspects, some conceptual work has been conducted as well. Conceptual approaches to cost management in general are rare, and only very few of them specifically address the management of costs in supply chains. These are briefly discussed below.

---

[21] See Fisher (1997), p. 106.
[22] See e.g. Cross (2000).
[23] See Kalwani, Narayandas (1995), p. 2.
[24] See Fisher (1997), p. 107.

2.2.1 Strategic Cost Management

A notable approach that gained much attention internationally is *Strategic Cost Management*.[25] Based on Porter's work, the concept comprises three key ideas:

- *Value chain*: The focus of cost management efforts is extended beyond the organizational boundaries to include the value chain partners.

- *Strategic Positioning*: The competitive strategy – cost leadership or differentiation – influences the relevance of cost management activities (e.g. competitor cost analysis) and thus the design and application of cost management techniques.

- *Cost Drivers*: Not volume, but a number of strategic cost drivers are crucial for creating and sustaining a cost advantage. Two kinds of cost drivers can be distinguished: structural cost drivers (e.g. scale) and operational cost drivers (e.g. linkages with suppliers and distributors).

The Strategic Cost Management approach emphasizes some important aspects of managing costs in supply chains. It introduces the idea of strategic positioning and provides another set of strategic cost drivers. However, a few weaknesses must be mentioned. First, the three key ideas remain rather separate pillars of the concept. No specific reasons are given for their selection except a hint to strategy literature. Hence, the concept has been supplemented with cost management tools like target costing or activity-based costing.[26] Finally, a study providing empirical evidence for the approach as a whole is missing.

2.2.2 Interorganizational Cost Management

Interorganizational Cost Management (IOCM) is a structured approach to cost management in supply chains.[27] It demands close cooperation of buyers and suppliers to reduce costs in the total supply network. IOCM comprises two dimensions – relationship and product. The relationship dimension establishes the environment for joint cost management efforts. It aims, at the network level, to build stable, cooperative and mutually beneficial relations allowing extensive information sharing to fully identify cost reduction opportunities. Such opportunities exist within the relationship dimension at the *buyer-supplier interface*. As to the product dimension, inter-firm cost improvements can be realized during the entire product life cycle. At *product development*, target costing and chained target costing are disciplining mechanisms that indicate the need for cost reduction. Enabling mechanisms such as value engineering, functionality-price-quality trade-offs (FPQ), interorganizational cost investigations, and concurrent cost management

---

[25] See Shank (1989); Shank, Govindarajan (1992), (1993).
[26] See e.g. Horváth, Brokemper (1998), p. 590.
[27] See Cooper, Yoshikawa (1994); Cooper, Slagmulder (1999a), (1999b).

help the companies in the supply chain find ways for cost improvements. Similarly, kaizen costing and value analysis are the primary techniques disciplining and enabling inter-firm cost management during *manufacturing*.

The IOCM approach has been developed after extensive exploratory field research in Japanese firms. Compared to most other empirical studies, the research has not only focused on the interaction of two companies, but also includes supply networks of three independent entities. Although it is difficult to generalize the research findings, they represent a major contribution to a better understanding of cost management in supply chains. From a theoretical viewpoint, the identification of factors influencing its effectiveness, e.g. the buyer-supplier environment or the nature of thebuyer-supplier relationship, provide a valuable basis for theory development.

2.2.3 Supply Chain Costing

The concept of *Supply Chain Costing* offers a framework for the analysis and management of costs within and across companies.[28] It builds on the relationship and product dimension of IOCM and the differentiation of three cost categories: direct costs, activity-based costs, and transaction costs. The latter refer – in a broad sense – to transaction cost theory and include costs arising from interactions with suppliers and customers. Applying this differentiation to the methodology of target costing allows distinguishing between product-level, process-level, and transaction-level target costing. Necessary cost reductions, derived from a market-driven target setting, can be realized on all three levels. For this purpose, trade-offs between the three cost categories can be taken into account. As illustrated by examples from the textile industry, it might be favorable to improve the coordination between supply chain partners despite an increase in transaction costs due to an even higher decrease of direct and activity-based costs.

By integrating the transaction cost approach, the concept of Supply Chain Costing includes the relationships between supply chain partners in the search for cost reduction opportunities. Thus, it shows a way to extend the focus of cost management across organizational boundaries. Because of the problems in measuring transaction costs, however the analysis stays on a qualitative level.

2.3 Conclusion

The above review of previous research reveals a considerable gap between the practical relevance of cost management in supply chains and its theoretical foundation. The deficiencies of current research can be summarized as follows:

---

[28] See Seuring, Schneidewind (2000); Seuring (2001a), (2001b).

- Most studies focus on a narrowly defined problem which is analysed from the perspective of a particular management discipline. Research in management accounting, for example, is centered to a large extent on the application of single cost management techniques. Organizational aspects of cost management are neglected in most cases.

- Empirical research is limited to case studies. The vast majority of them are single case studies describing specific cost management efforts in a bilateral buyer-supplier relationship. Only very few empirical studies investigate supply chains that encompass more than two partners. Cross-case analysis[29] to identify general patterns of cost management in supply chains is seldom used. Research findings are thus hard to compare and difficult to generalize.

- There is a lack of a comprehensive conceptual framework integrating existing theoretical and empirical research. Existing conceptual approaches only consider certain individual contributions and therefore focus on specific aspects of cost management in supply chains.

All in all, it can be concluded that "cost management is in its infancy"[30]. Research is still in an early exploratory stage and has not yet developed a consistent theory for managing costs across organizational boundaries. In view of this, the following section presents a conceptual framework for proactive cost management in supply chains.

3 Framework for Proactive Cost Management

In addition to the lack of a comprehensive conceptual framework for effectively managing costs across organizational boundaries, the characteristics of effective cost management have not been defined in detail. It is therefore necessary to briefly outline these attributes before the conceptual framework is presented.

To be effective in a highly competitive environment cost management must be:[31]

- *Market-oriented*: Cost management considers customer needs and competitive behavior.

- *Holistic*: Cost management takes a broad focus including the entire supply chain and product life cycle.

- *Anticipatory*: Cost management starts in the product design stage and aims to influence the future cost position.

---

[29] See Eisenhardt (1989), p. 540; Yin (1994).
[30] Brinker (1992), p. 3.
[31] See Kajüter (2000), p. 14.

- *Continuous*: Cost management is a permanent task. It ensures continuous improvements.
- *Participatory*: Cost management requires involvement of virtually every employee.
- *Cross-functional*: Cost management integrates business functions.

A cost management approach characterized by these attributes is called hereafter *proactive cost management*. The attributes apply to cost management in general, but also specifically to cost management in supply chains. They are specified by various parameters which are part of the conceptual framework to be developed.

In designing the framework a few formal requirements must be met. Since the framework shall provide a comprehensive description of proactive cost management from a theoretical perspective, it has to be able to integrate all relevant aspects. Further, it shall be used for empirical research. Hence, it must be possible to operationalize the framework. Finally, the framework should be flexible so that new developments can be considered.

Given these requirements, systems theory seems to be a suitable theoretical approach to describe and analyse cost management. It allows concentration on specific aspects (dimensions) of the system while at the same time taking a broad perspective. Thus, a *cost management system* can be defined as the sum of subsystems and elements of cost management serving to enhance the efficiency of a company or supply chain by influencing costs.

To become more concrete, the subsystems and elements of the cost management system must be specified. For this purpose, reference is made to the definition of cost management as well as to the above literature review which provides a valuable pool of research findings. Since cost management is considered to be a task, it comprises several *activities* which form the first dimension or subsystem of cost management. Such activities are discussed extensively in the various fields of literature, for instance cost analysis in strategic management or issues of implementation in organizational science. All in all, cost planning, action planning (based on the analysis of the cost position and cost drivers), action implementation and cost monitoring are major activities of cost management.

Costs are influenced by certain actions (e.g. reduction of product complexity) which relate to specific objects within the value added process. These *objects* constitute the second dimension of the cost management system. Three objects must be distinguished: *resources*, like material or personnel which are the input of any value added process, the *process* itself, and the *product* which is the output. Accordingly, a resource-oriented, a process-oriented, and a product-oriented cost management can be differentiated.

Finally, cost management activities are supported by several tools and techniques. Examples are target costing, value engineering, activity-based costing, and benchmarking. These tools serve to structure the activities and support decisions by generating cost data. Thus, cost management *techniques* are the third dimension of the cost management system.

Still, the issue of cost management is not yet completely captured. By implementing the cost management system, decisions about its organizational design must be made. This includes the definition of responsibilities (who shall execute the cost management activities?), and the choice of coordinating mechanisms. As a result, the *cost management structure* is defined encompassing two dimensions – specialization and coordination.[32]

The cost management system and cost management structure are the two basic parts of the conceptual framework. So far, this framework is rather general and does not consider the specific characteristics of proactive cost management described above. Hence, these attributes specifying the cost management system and cost management structure must be added (Figure 2).

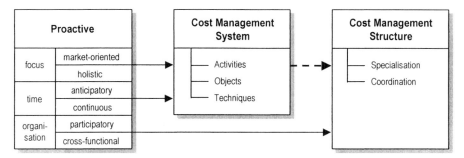

Figure 2: Conceptual Framework for Proactive Cost Management

This yields a comprehensive conceptual framework enabling the integration of the numerous cost management parameters and puts them into a broader context. In this way, the framework offers a guideline for a structured approach to proactive cost management in practice. In addition, it can be operationalized and thus used in empirical research to gain further insights into cost management. The results of such an exploratory case study are presented in the next section.

---

[32] For a similar approach see Pugh et al. (1968).

4 Empirical Evidence from the Automotive Industry

4.1 The Eurocar Supply Chain

Eurocar[33] is an international automobile manufacturer. Due to intense competition in the industry, the company introduced new ways of managing costs in the 1990s. In particular, it extended its cost management efforts and developed a structured approach to analysing and managing costs within the supply chain. At Eurocar, this approach is called Total Cost Management:

> "How we manage cost is fundamentally changing as we expand our focus from looking strictly at material costs to identifying cost reduction opportunities throughout the entire Value Chain. Total Cost Management (TCM) is a tangible sign of this commitment and continues to define our relationship with our Value Chain partners." (Eurocar)

Although TCM centers on the upstream part of Eurocar's value chain and thus excludes dealers and ultimate customers, other cost management programs exist to exploit cost reduction opportunities in the downstream part of the value chain. To make TCM work, Eurocar has established cooperative and stable relationships with its key suppliers:

> "Partnership is the basic foundation upon which our Total Cost Management strategy is built. TCM requires the joint commitment of our company and our supply base to successfully identify and implement opportunities to reduce costs. In addition, TCM allows us to develop plans that are preventative in nature. Our suppliers are our partners and contributors in the development of these plans." (Eurocar)

For a normal passenger car, Eurocar usually works together with about 50 key suppliers which are called "Full Service Suppliers". They get involved in the early stages of product development and coordinate in turn sub-suppliers. Full Service Suppliers dispose of significant opportunities to influence cost as they develop and produce complex modules, components and systems.

4.2 Cost Management System

4.2.1 Cost Management Activities

Eurocar applies a market-driven approach to *cost planning*. Product cost targets are derived during product development by subtracting an adequate profit margin

---

[33] The name of the company is disguised for reasons of confidentiality.

from the potential selling price of the proposed product. Hence, cost targets consider competitive pressure from the market. A cost breakdown leads to detailed cost objectives on the component level, too. Comparing these market-driven cost targets with current or estimated costs usually indicates the need for cost reduction. This cost reduction pressure is transmitted to the suppliers if a component is not developed and manufactured by Eurocar itself. In this case, the component-level cost targets are the price limit for the sourcing agreements with the supplier.

In order to achieve the cost targets and ensure continuous improvements, Eurocar closely cooperates with its suppliers according to the TCM approach during the entire life cycle of a product. This includes a comprehensive analysis of the cost structure and cost drivers in the value chain, joint action planning and implementation as well as regular monitoring of target achievement.

The *cost analysis* encompasses all major stages of the value chain up to the final assembly of a particular module, component or system at Eurocar. For this purpose, the Tier 1 Supplier prepares a Value Chain Flow Chart (Figure 3) which contains the names and locations of the Tier 2 and Tier 3 suppliers, the flow of material (distances and means of transportation), and the value added cost ("on-cost") of each stage. The total cost of the system can be determined by adding up the value added cost of the entire supply chain.

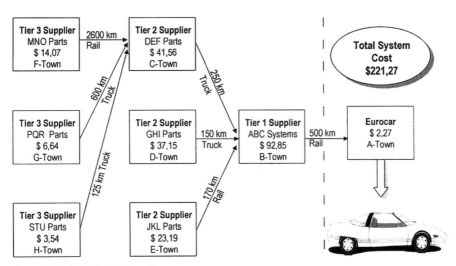

Figure 3: Value Chain Flow Chart

The Tier 1 Supplier further provides a detailed breakdown of the cost structure for the system it supplies (Figure 4). Similar cost element structures are set up by the Tier 1 Supplier in cooperation with the sub-suppliers for the parts produced on earlier stages of the value chain. This requires an open-book accounting policy throughout the supply chain. It allows identifying important cost elements and helps discover cost reduction opportunities.

Cost Element	On-Cost ($)	% of On-Cost
Raw Materials	N/A	N/A
Direct & Indirect Labour	27.00	29%
Manufacturing Overhead	37.00	40%
Corporate Overhead	15.20	16%
Packaging	1.00	1%
Transportation	N/A	N/A
Warranty	3.85	4%
Research & Development	5.00	6%
Profit	3.80	4%
Total	$92.85	100%

Figure 4: Tier 1 Supplier Cost Element Structure

The cost structure analysis is followed by an investigation of the *cost drivers* in the value chain. Cost drivers are defined at Eurocar as anything driving up cost without adding value to the customer. Examples are over-specification of materials, prototype policy, and product complexity. The identification of such factors can generate ideas for improving the cost structure. These ideas may refer to any partner within the value chain or to the interfaces between them.

	Target Achievement Plan (TAP)				
	Year 1	Year 2	Year 3	Year 4	Totals
Commercial	1.8	2.5	2.5	1.5	8.3
Process Improvement	2.5	2.5	1.9	1.6	8.5
Policy	0.7	1.3	0.6	1.5	4.1
Design	2.5	5.2	0.5	0.3	8.5
Other/To Be Identified	0.0	0.0	0.0	0.6	0.6
Total TAP	7.5%	11.5%	5.5%	5.5%	30%
Less: LTA/PA*	-2.5	-2.5	-2.5	-2.5	-10
Net Incremental to LTA/PA	5.0%	9.0%	3.0%	3.0%	20%

* only where a Long Term Agreement or Productivity Agreement exist

Figure 5: Target Achievement Plan (TAP)

The cost reduction opportunities that have been identified and selected for implementation are incorporated into the Target Achievement Plan. This *action plan* is jointly developed by Eurocar and the Tier 1 Supplier and distinguishes four categories (Figure 5): *Commercial* captures cost reductions at the Tier 1 Supplier and the sub-suppliers; *Process Improvement* includes the elimination of inefficiencies in business processes; *Policy* contains cost savings to be realized by optimizing business practices like quality control; *Design* comprises actions requiring changes in the design or material specifications by Eurocar. The overall objective is to define cost reduction opportunities within the total value chain over a four-year period that will result, on average, in a 20% cost decline of the component based on the purchase order price to Eurocar. This target can be achieved, however, without reducing the purchase price a full 20% because cost savings at Eurocar count towards achievement of the target as well.

After a three month planning process, the Target Achievement Plan is presented to the management of both Eurocar and the Tier 1 Supplier to enhance the commitment and discuss potential roadblocks for *implementation* and ways to overcome them. The Target Achievement Plan finally serves for *cost monitoring*, too. It shows to what extent the planned cost savings are actually realized and eventually demonstrates the need for additional actions.

4.2.2 Cost Management Objects

The four categories in the Target Achievement Plan indicate that a variety of cost improving actions are defined by both Eurocar and the Tier 1 Supplier. These actions relate to products, processes, and resources. In the field of *product*-related cost management, considerable efforts are made to manage complexity caused by the number of parts and product variants. Priority is given to ways that prevent or reduce complexity rather than transfer it from one value chain partner to another. For instance such a transfer of complexity from Eurocar to the supply base could be realized by modular sourcing. This might lead to lower costs at Eurocar, but will in general not reduce costs in the total supply chain. Thus, a broad view on managing product complexity offers mutual benefits that can contribute to improving the cost position of all supply chain partners.

In addition, particular emphasis is given to continuous *process* improvements in the supply chain. All primary and support processes impacting the component studied are subject to collaborative optimization. To identify process improvement opportunities, representatives of both Eurocar and the Tier 1 Supplier jointly walk through the manufacturing sites of the two firms. These "Process Walks" enable a better understanding of how the processes in the supply chain are linked with each other and thereby allow optimization of buyer-supplier interfaces. Process improvements can take various forms, however, the elimination of non-value added activities is fundamental. Non-value added activities are a waste. They consume resources but do not contribute to satisfying customer needs. As they are often hard to identify, Eurocar differentiates eight types of waste that cause such non-value added activities: overproduction, time delays, unnecessary motion, holding of excessive inventory, unnecessary transportation, overprocessing, correction, and not utilizing human resources by ignoring people's suggestions and ideas for improvement. If not yet applied, Eurocar helps introduce Kaizen principles at the Tier 1 Supplier to ensure continuous elimination of non-value added activities.

Resource-related cost management efforts address primarily material. Eurocar usually makes long-term contracts for components and agrees with the supplier on regular reductions of the purchase price. In exchange for this, the suppliers profit from stable demand and joint cost reduction programs. In case of a single sourcing relationship, the suppliers frequently benefit from economies of scale due to higher volumes, too. The use of carry-over and commonality parts further enhances this advantage.

4.2.3 Cost Management Techniques

As part of TCM, a number of cost management techniques are applied. The most important tool is (chained) target costing. At Eurocar, it is called Affordable Business Structure (ABS) and serves as an umbrella for other methods helping to generate more concrete cost reduction ideas. Among them are common techniques such as benchmarking, reverse engineering, and value analysis/value engineering. In addition, Eurocar has developed specific tools used not only within the company but also across its boundaries to manage supply chain costs. An example for such tools is the Cost Reduction Ideas Database (CRID). This database contains previously developed cost improvement ideas and is accessible by design engineers worldwide.

4.3 Cost Management Structure

4.3.1 Specialization

TCM activities are conducted by a *cross-functional team* that includes representatives of Eurocar and the Tier 1 Supplier (Figure 6). The TCM team must not exceed 16 members, eight from each company.

TCM Team	
Eurocar	Tier 1 Supplier
Purchasing Manager, Commodity Buyer, Cost Estimator, Design & Releasing Engineer, Manufacturing Process Engineer, Supplier Technical Assistance Engineer, Customer Services Division Representative	Sales Executive, Commercial Manager, Design Engineer, Finance Representative, Manufacturing Process Engineer, Quality Engineer, Buyer

Figure 6: TCM Team Members

A facilitator and other experts as appropriate may support it. Individual data gathering responsibilities are assigned to each team member according to his/her functional expertise.

TCM team membership is an additional task to the "normal" job. Attendance at the team meetings is mandatory, however, in some cases it is at the discretion of the team. The presence of the Customer Services Division Representative, who shall provide an end-customer focus to the team, is usually not always necessary for instance. The TCM team is finally broken up after the Target Achievement Plan has been completed and agreed upon. Implementation and regular monitoring of target achievement is the responsibility of each company.

4.3.2 Coordination

As cost management activities are performed by several individuals, there is a need for coordinating mechanisms. This need is considered in two ways. First, structural mechanisms are used. A central TCM Office has been established at Eurocar to coordinate all TCM activities. This department further develops the TCM approach and transfers experience from one project to the other. Moreover, the team structure itself serves as a coordinating mechanism as it integrates representatives of two companies and allows a direct and efficient exchange of information between them. Specific forms and well defined rules and procedures are a second type of coordinating mechanism employed. They are documented in a TCM Handbook and facilitate TCM activities in the supply chain.

4.4 Implications

The inter-firm cost management activities described above are mainly driven by Eurocar. Close and cooperative relationships with the Tier 1 Suppliers are necessary to fully identify and exploit existing cost reduction opportunities. However, only direct and indirect costs are considered whereas there are no attempts to take transaction costs into account as well. The main reason for this is the difficulty in measuring these costs.

Although TCM activities are an integral and permanent part of cost management at Eurocar, each activity itself has the character of a project. Thus, there seems to still be scope for an even closer integration between the supply chain partners, for example in the area of harmonizing performance measures and accounting systems.

5 Summary and Outlook

Despite the increasing relevance of extending cost management efforts across the entire supply chain, a consistent theory has not been developed so far. Theoretical and empirical research is still in an exploratory stage and focuses to a large extent on specific, narrowly defined aspects. In view of missing conceptual approaches that integrate previous research findings, this paper presents a comprehensive theoretical framework for proactive cost management in supply chains that explicitly considering organizational issues. The case study of the Eurocar supply chain demonstrates that this framework allows collecting empirical data in a structured way and thereby ensures a systematic description of cost management practice. Furthermore, it may also provide a guideline for systematically managing costs in supply chains as it considers all relevant parameters.

However, further research is needed to enhance our understanding of cost management in supply chains. Future research should not only explore issues like the impact of e-business, the application of common performance measures across organizational boundaries or the design of transaction cost accounting systems, but should also seek to further develop and refine the conceptual framework presented above. This could then allow more empirical research to be conducted. As previous studies have mainly examined bilateral relationships, future field research should also include supply chains of more than two partners. In addition, more cross-case analysis might indicate general patterns of inter-firm cost management and help to identify factors influencing its effectiveness. Continuous research efforts will contribute to further theory building and will finally allow definition and test hypotheses based on a larger sample of supply chains.

6 References

Berry, T., Ahmed, A., Cullen, J., Dunlop, A., Seal, W., Jonston, S., Holmes, M. (1997): The Consequences of Inter-Firm sSupply Chains for Management Accounting, in: Management Accounting (UK), November (1997), p. 74-75.

Brewer, P. C., Speh, T. W. (2000): Using the Balanced Scorecard to Measure Supply Chain Performance, in: Journal of Business Logistics, Vol. 21, No. 1 (2000), p. 75-94.

Brinker, B. (1992): The State of Cost Management, in: Journal of Cost Management, Vol. 5, No. 4 (1992), p. 3-4.

Coase, R. H. (1937): The Nature of the Firm, in: economica, Vol. 4 (1937), p. 386-405.

Cooper, R., Slagmulder, R. (1999a): Supply Chain Development for the Lean Enterprise – Interorganizational Cost Management, Productivity Press, Portland.

Cooper, R., Slagmulder, R. (1999b): How to Undertake Effective Interorganizational Cost Management in Product Development, in: Controlling, Vol. 11, No. 6 (1999), p. 245-252.

Cooper, R., Yoshikawa, T. (1994): Inter-Organizational Cost Management Systems: The Case of the Tokyo-Yokohama-Kamakura Supplier Chain, in: International Journal of Production Economics, Vol. 37 (1994), p. 51-62.

Cross, G. J. (2000): How E-Business is Transforming Supply Chain Management, in: Journal of Business Strategy, Vol. 21, No. 2 (2000), p. 36-39.

Cullen, J., Berry, A. J., Seal, W., Dunlop, A., Ahmed, M., Marson, J. (1999): Interfirm Supply Chains – The Contribution of Management Accounting, in: Management Accounting (UK), June (1999), p. 30-32.

Dekker, H. C., van Goor, A. R. (2000): Supply Chain Management and Management Accounting: A Case Study of Activity-Based Costing, in: International Journal of Logistics: Research and Applications, Vol. 3, No. 1 (2000), p. 41-52.

Donelan, J. G., Kaplan, E. A. (1998): Value Chain Analysis: A Strategic Approach to Cost Management, in: Journal of Cost Management, Vol. 12, No. 2 (1998), p. 7-15.

Dyer, J. H. (1996): How Chrysler Created an American Keiretsu, in: Harvard Business Review, Vol. 74, No. 4 (1996), p. 42-56.

Earl, M., Khan, B. (1994): How New is Business Process Redesign?, in: European Management Journal, Vol. 12, No. 1 (1994), p. 20-30.

Eisenhardt, K. M. (1989): Building Theories from Case Study Research, in: Academy of Management Review, Vol. 14, No. 4 (1989), p. 532-550.

Ellram, L. M. (2000): Purchasing and Supply Management's Participation in the Target Costing Process, in: The Journal of Supply Chain Management, Spring (2000), p. 39-51.

Ellram, L. M., Feitzinger, E. (1997): Using Total Profit Analysis to Model Supply Chain Decisions, in: Journal of Cost Management, Vol. 11, No. 4 (1997), p. 12-21.

Fisher, M. L. (1997): What is the Right Supply Chain for Your Product?, in: Harvard Business Review, Vol. 75, No. 2 (1997), p. 105-116.

Handfield, R. B., Nichols, E. L. (1999): Introduction to Supply Chain Management, Prentice Hall, New Jersey.

Hammer, M., Champy, J. (1993): Reengineering the Corporation, Harper Collins, New York.

Harland, C. M. (1996): Supply Chain Management: Relationships, Chains, Networks, in: British Journal of Management, Vol. 7, Special Issue (1996), p. S63-S80.

Hergert, M., Morris, D. (1989): Accounting Data for Value Chain Analysis, in: Strategic Management Journal, Vol. 10, No. 2 (1989), p. 175-188.

Horváth, P., Brokemper, A. (1998): Strategieorientiertes Kostenmanagement (Strategic Cost Management), in: Zeitschrift für Betriebswirtschaft, Vol. 68, No. 6 (1998), p. 581-604.

Kajüter, P. (2000): Proaktives Kostenmanagement. Konzeption und Realprofile (Proactive Cost Management. Theoretical Concept and Empirical Evidence), Verlag Gabler/DUV, Wiesbaden.

Kajüter, P. (2001): Kostenmanagement in der Automobilindustrie (Cost Management in the Automotive Industry), in: Zeitschrift für Automobilwirtschaft, No. 3 (2001), p. 36-43.

Kalwani, M. U., Narayandas, N. (1995): Long-Term Manufacturer-Supplier Relationships: Do They Pay Off for Supplier Firms?, in: Journal of Marketing, Vol. 59, No. 1 (1995), p. 1-16.

Kummer, S. (2001): Supply Chain Controlling, in: Kostenrechnungspraxis, Vol. 45, No. 2 (2001), p. 81-87.

LaLonde, B. J., Pohlen, T. L. (1996): Issues in Supply Chain Costing, in: International Journal of Logistics Management, Vol. 7, No. 1 (1996), p. 1-12.

Lingscheid, A. (1998): Unternehmensübergreifendes Kaizen Costing (Kaizen Costing Across Organisational Boundaries), Verlag Franz Vahlen, München.

Macht, M., Hartlieb, C. (1997): Kostenmanagement in der Automobilindustrie (Cost Management in the Automotive Industry), in: Franz, K.-P., Kajüter, P. (ed.): Kostenmanagement, Schäffer-Poeschel Verlag, Stuttgart, p. 405-419.

Matje, A. (1996): Kostenorientiertes Transaktionscontrolling (Transaction Cost Controlling), Gabler Verlag, Wiesbaden.

Munday, M. (1992): Accounting Cost Data Disclosure and Buyer-Supplier Partnerships: A Research Note, in: Journal of Management Accounting Research, Vol. 3 (1992), p. 245-250.

Partridge, M., Perren, L. (1994): Cost Analysis of the Value Chain: Another Role for Strategic Management Accounting, in: Management Accounting (UK), July/August (1994), p. 22-26.

Porter, M. E. (1985): Competitive Advantage, The Free Press, New York.

Pugh, D. S., Hickson, D. J., Hinings, C. R., Turner, C. (1968): Dimensions of Organization Structure, in: Administrative Science Quarterly, Vol. 13 (1968), p. 65-105.

Seuring, S., Schneidewind, U. (2000): Kostenmanagement in der Wertschöpfungskette (Value Chain Cost Management), in: Wildemann, H. (ed.): Supply Chain Management, TCW-Verlag, München, p. 227-250.

Seuring, S. (2001a): Supply Chain Costing – Kostenmanagement in der Wertschöpfungskette mit Target Costing und Prozesskostenrechnung (Supply Chain Costing with Target Costing and Activity Based Costing), Verlag Franz Vahlen, München.

Seuring, S. (2001b): A Framework for Green Supply Chain Costing. A Fashion Industry Example, in: Sarkis, J. (ed.): Greener Manufacturing and Operations: From Design to Delivery and Back, Greenleaf Publishing, Sheffield, p. 215-226.

Shank, J. K. (1989): Strategic Cost Management: New Wine, or Just New Bottles?, in: Journal of Management Accounting Research, Vol. 1, Fall (1989), p. 47-65.

Shank, J. K., Govindarajan, V. (1992): Strategic Cost Management: The Value Chain Perspective, in: Journal of Management Accounting Research, Vol. 4, Fall (1992), p. 179-197.

Shank, J. K., Govindarajan, V. (1993): Strategic Cost Management, The Free Press, New York.

Taylor, W. (1981): The Use of Life Cycle Costing in Acquiring Physical Assets, in: Long Range Planning, Vol. 14, No. 6 (1981), p. 32-43.

Williamson, O. E. (1979): Transaction-Cost Economics: The Governance of Contractual Relations, in: Journal of Law and Economics, Vol. 22 (1979), p. 233-261.

Williamson, O. E. (1981): The Economics of Organization: The Transaction Cost Approach, in: American Journal of Sociology, Vol. 87 (1981), p. 548-577.

Yin, R. K. (1994): Case Study Research, Design and Methods, 2nd edition, Sage Publications, Beverly Hills.

A Framework for Extending Lean Accounting into a Supply Chain

Peter Hines, Riccardo Silvi, Monica Bartolini, Andrea Raschi

1	Introduction	54
2	An Integrative Approach	55
3	Methodology	59
4	Results	65
5	Conclusions	70

Summary:
The Lean Transformation of the Supply Chain represents a major challenge in Lean Management studies and involves both the reduction of waste (both within and between companies) and supply chain alignment to the actual needs of the final customer. At the same time, Lean Management is looking for an information system able to support a Lean Transformation by incorporating all the drivers of company performance in the development of a cost system. In order to explore the possibility of an integration between the Cost Management practices, the Lean Management principles, and the Value Analysis studies, this paper presents a new integrated methodology, as well as the results of an international and interdisciplinary research project: the Le.M.A. (Lean Management Accounting) Program. The case study approach adopted reviews an internal supply chain with a view to extending the work at a later point to an external supply chain.

Keywords:
Lean Management, Lean Accounting, Customer Value, Integrated Approach

1 Introduction

Ever since the pioneering work of Jay Forrester in the 1950s academics, consultants and practitioners have been searching for the 'holy grail' theory, method or solution that will cure all of their supply chain ills. Theories or approaches have come from systems dynamics, time compression, lean thinking, business process re-engineering, agility, mass customization and virtual organization.[1]

Such research has provided many insights into the improvement of both the internal operations of companies and the wider network of customers and suppliers. However, almost invariably it has been attempted from a functional rather than process basis[2] and in most cases has concentrated on finding the most efficient or effective way to sell the products or services produced.[3] Attempts to integrate the real demand or customer perspective into supply chain thinking, although not unknown, are far too rare.[4]

In addition, in many previous approaches researchers have attempted to develop an appropriate solution to the improvement of the real case supply chain based on a specific methodological approach, which often leads to predictable solutions.[5] What is called for is an integrative approach that seeks to gain a more holistic and contingent decision-making method.

Moreover, the Cost Accounting System's ability to support the planning and control processes strongly depends on its coherence with the competitive environment. This also means that changes in the competitive philosophy necessarily impact the measurement system's effectiveness, involving a need for continuous adaptation.

In terms of applying any new integrative approach to the supply chain the authors were faced with a choice of defining the most appropriate supply chain scale. A spectrum of increasing complexity has been discussed in the literature ranging from internal supply chains, dyadic relationships, linear supply chains and networks.[6] Analysis of past logistics research shows that about 38% of papers address internal supply chains, 40% dyadic or linear supply chains and 22%

---

[1] See respectively: Forrester (1961); Stalk, Hout (1990); Womack, Jones (1996); Hammer (1990); Kidd (1994); The Economist (2001); Davidow, Malone (1992).
[2] See Schonberger (1986); Ostrenga, Probst (1992).
[3] See Porter (1985); Towill (1996).
[4] See Christopher (1992); Womack, Jones (1996).
[5] See Towill (1996); Wilding (1998).
[6] See Harland (1998).

address a supply chain network.⁷ In this pilot research, due to the complexity of the approach attempted, a simple internal supply chain approach has been chosen. In later research the Le.M.A. method will be applied to the more complex supply chain environments.

2 An Integrative Approach

In order to develop an integrative approach the authors have attempted to draw from four complimentary management areas, namely: Process Based Lean Management, Strategic Cost Management, Marketing and Policy Deployment.

Presently none of these approaches with their respective existing tool kits on their own are capable of a truly holistic approach. Each has its own strengths and weaknesses (see Table 1).

The Lean Management approach relies on five key principles: 'Understanding Customer Value', 'Identifying the Value Stream that Adds This Value', 'Creating Flow of Product and Information', 'Using Customer Pull' and in so 'Doing Seeking a Wasteless Perfection State'.⁸ In order to implement such a Lean System, a series of tools and approaches have been developed which primarily fall into two categories: diagnostic/analytical and implementation.⁹ Within the diagnostic/analytical area are the Value Stream Mapping Tools.¹⁰ The implementation tool kit includes a wide variety of tools drawn from the Just In Time and Total Quality / Six Sigma schools.¹¹ Central to this logic is a detailed understanding of the waste or inefficiencies that lie in existing systems. Such an understanding is required for radical or incremental improvements.

However, optimizing each piece of the supply chain in isolation does not lead to the lowest cost solution. In fact, it is necessary to look at the whole sequence of events, from the customer order back to the order given to the raw materials producer and forward through all successive firms making and delivering the product to the customer. Focusing on the whole chain is the first step; focusing on the product is the second and focusing on the flow of value creation, and not on the more traditional performance measurement of departments and firms, is the third step. This allows the mapping of a *Value Stream* - a new and more useful unit of analysis than the supply chain or the individual firm.

---

7 See Hines (1998).
8 See Womack, Jones (1996).
9 See Bicheno (2000).
10 See Hines, Rich (1997); Rother, Shook (1999); Hines, Taylor (2000).
11 See Shingo (1989); Ishiwata (1991).

Although the Lean Paradigm is widely accepted in manufacturing industry[12], it has yet to make a major impact away from the shop floor and particularly outside manufacturing firms. In addition, it does not presently have a widely accepted, rigorous customer focus approach, although research is ongoing in this area.[13]

	Process Based Lean Management	*Strategic Cost Management*	*Marketing*	*Policy Deployment*
Strengths	Effective Non-Financial Measures	Able to Develop Effective Financial Measures	Effective Tools to Understand Customers	Holistic Business Approach
	Analytical Fact-Based Approach	Not Overly Bureaucratic	Effective at Integrating with Business Strategy	Links Financial & Non Financial Measures
	Practical Approach	Can Be Linked to Tangible Benefits		Deploys Strategy to Operational Areas
	Addresses Processes not Functions	Addresses Processes and/or Functions		
Weaknesses	Lack of Financial Measures	Lack of Non-Financial Measures	Lack of Integration with Internal Processes	Lack of Detailed Operational Tools
	Lack of Rigorous Tools to Understand Customers	Lack of Rigorous Tools to Understand Customers	Lack of Integration with Financial Performance	
	Often Only Employed in Manufacturing Shop Floor Environment	Lack of Rigorous Tools at the Shop Floor Level		

Table 1: An Integrative Approach

---

[12] See Ohno (1988).
[13] See Hines et al (1998); Brunt et al (1998).

Moreover, this approach fails in offering a global picture of a process performance, as it does not provide any financial and cost information. This is also the consequence of a traditional lack of participation and involvement of accounting in improvement management teams, so that they can develop methods and measures coherent with the key business priorities and actually support and drive efforts to achieve continuous improvement.

Strategic Cost Management[14] can address most of these shortcomings, as it has the stated objective of using cost information, often gathered from several heterogeneous sources, to define and create a competitive advantage.[15] «In the Strategic Cost Management environment, managers look for ways to leverage the industry value chain in unique ways that reduce the cost and complexity of completing transactions. The key contribution of Strategic Cost Management is that it takes an external view of cost and raises the understanding of how company activities can be better leveraged and aligned with the market to improve performance».[16] In particular, Strategic Cost Management provides an innovative perspective on the way that choices of task environment can affect costs structure. It focuses its attention on the distribution of activities within the whole system, in order to reconstruct the value generated overall by the industry, and to grasp how value is distributed between the different companies.[17] Cost information should play a fundamental role in the placement of the boundaries of the firm. Indeed, cost estimation for the resources employed and for the related benefits should shape how managers make decisions about the rational level of vertical integration for their firms. But management accounting and strategic management studies to date have not provided much explicit financial analysis regarding this trade-off. Typically, make or buy decisions are framed in managerial accounting from a short-run, differential cost perspective. This approach ignores long-run costs related to the management activities involved and also ignores linkages with customers and suppliers.

A recent development of Strategic Cost Management tools[18] provides an innovative framework to describe a company cost structure in a form compatible with the engineering business process analysis, typical of a Lean Management approach. In sum, it makes capturing the potential relationship possible between customer/market requirements, defined as an array of value attributes with unique weightings by customers, and the firm's economic and activity structure. This model assumes that the resources available to provide products and support internal operations are channeled into a number of processes, or activity streams, that result in any number of outcomes. As these outcomes are depicted as value-

---

[14] See Shank, Govindarajan (1993a,b).
[15] See Porter (1985); Shank, Govindarajan (1993a,b).
[16] See McNair et al (2001b).
[17] See Shank, Govindarajan (1989, 1993a,b).
[18] See McNair et al (2001a,b).

added (in the eyes of customer), business value-added (required for the business, but not directly perceived by the customer), and waste, the model adopts the same typical language of a Process Value Analysis (PVA). So, compared with a basic Activity-Based Costing (ABC) approach, the Strategic Cost Management perspective also provides a useful distinction between the activities based on their respective value[19], according to a process-based orientation, and allows a better understanding of customer needs.

The possibility to match this cost approach with the Lean Management view is mostly related to the common object of analysis: the process. In fact, the Strategic Cost Management perspective differs from the traditional cost accounting and also from a basic Activity-based Accounting thanks to its focus on processes, instead of on simply products and services or disconnected activities. It assumes that in order to analyze the cost behavior you need to explore the causal relationship between the use of resources and the root causes of their consumption. Following the Strategic Cost Management approach, resource consumption is driven at a process level.[20]

As a result, the application of Strategic Cost Management can help firms and wider Supply Chains enable change rather than inhibiting or misdirecting it, as often occurs with many more traditional accounting approaches. However, many applications of Process Cost Analysis (PCA) tend to preserve a departmental logic, as they map the process configuration starting from the activities performed in each company function, instead of from the customer requirements and the related information and physical flows. The effect is that the current accounting systems often undermine improvement activities and can, in the worst case, drive firms in the wrong direction.[21]

However, neither Lean Management nor Strategic Cost Management can on their own resolve concerns about how to understand the customer value proposition. Nevertheless, to create a bridge between the firm and its customer is the first step in transforming cost from financial function to a strategic tool and in starting a lean transformation. As a consequence, moving to a "total firm perspective", a third role should be played by some marketing tools, through the identification of the key attributes in the eyes of the customers and the assessment of their respective weighting[22] in order to drive companies' efforts better in designing and improving processes.

It is our contention here that an integrated or holistic process-based approach is the most effective way to drive companies towards a competitive advantage. As a result, the research team faced the challenge of developing marketing, cost, and

---

[19] See Ostrenga, Probst (1992).
[20] See Ostrenga, Probst (1992).
[21] See Johnson, Kaplan (1987).
[22] See Lancaster (1971); Green, Srinivasan (1990); Wayland, Cole (1997).

operations approaches, tools and languages in order to be able to speak to one another. As the market environment facing many companies and their production processes have changed radically, both internal and external changes have important implications for management accountants. The tendency towards «continuous improvement required new philosophy for manufacturing, engineering, and marketing. Manufacturing philosophy emphasized new approaches such as people involvement [...] and visual control [...]. Engineering philosophy emphasized design for cost, quality, flexibility, and overall customer value rather than for mere improvement of the product's engineering features. Marketing philosophy focused on matching the needs of the customer with *the* ability to deliver value, instead of on expanding the number of product variations as a means of increasing market share».[23]

In carrying out the research it was necessary to integrate these different approaches in order to guide the direction of the company or wider Supply Chain. The approach chosen to do this was *Policy Deployment*. Policy Deployment may be described simply as an approach to focus the operations of a whole company according to a set of expected results by the use of a rigorous set of guidelines for the achievement of these targets. Policy Deployment is generally regarded as a Westernized, and often simplified, version of the Japanese Hoshin Kanri approach to strategic alignment.[24] In its simplest form[25], it involves a firm codifying its strategic direction, aligning a set of Key Performance Indicators to this and then checking that all its improvement activities are designed to produce optimum results by being directly aligned with the achievement of these results.

3 Methodology

The research method is based on the use of case studies, due to the need for a very flexible and holistic research design[26] involving a combination of different methods in order to deal with the complexity and variety of data.[27] The complexity is mostly related to the kind of analysis, which involves a global approach to a company (including its market) and the combination of several techniques and methods, such as combining secondary data, observational techniques, interviews and surveys. In particular, the present work uses the case study as an "instrumental case"[28], where the case itself is of secondary interest, as it simply facilitates the

---

[23] See Turney, Anderson (1989), p. 97-98.
[24] See Akao (1991).
[25] See Hines, Taylor (2000).
[26] See Hakim (1987).
[27] See Yin (1989); Hartley (1994).
[28] See Stake (1998).

understanding of more general issues. In addition, several previous studies can support most of the critical findings of this research, even though they involved only elements of the approach taken here. In particular, empirical evidence could be found in studies taking place under the Strategic Cost Management umbrella[29] and the Lean Thinking Paradigm.[30] These previous works could also be considered as significant pilot studies, as they highlighted the main implementation issues of the different techniques and suggested how the specific weaknesses of each approach could be avoided.

A framework has been conceptualized within a joint UK/Italian research program involving various methods drawn from a marketing, engineering, accounting, and strategy background. The diverse backgrounds of the team members reflect this need for synergy between disciplines.

As it is necessary to have the full (and time consuming) involvement of management, the selection of cases has been based most of all on the company's willingness to take part in the study and their expectation of gain from an Action Research approach.[31] In fact, this propensity guarantees full access. At the same time, companies were also selected as characterized by traditional accounting systems and the contemporary awareness of their insufficiency. Moreover, they had to be interested in potential operations improvements emerging from the lean tools implementation.

A limitation of this research is how the detailed findings relate to the particular case company and what they should do. Although the findings may have a wider applicability in industry, this cannot be inferred from this single case.

3.1 The Research Approach

According to the research model presented in Figure 1, the research first attempted to understand the firm's existing business strategy and general policy. The approach sought to establish the Critical Success Factors for the firm, a review or definition of appropriate Key Performance Indicators, the key business processes, and an understanding of which processes need detailed analysis. After this had been established, the research followed arrows 1 in Figure 1 to the operational level.

In order to understand the customer view, the marketing approach adopted in the Le.M.A. and in other previous research programs[32] considers as basic assumptions

---

[29] See Lorenzoni et al (1999); McNair et al (2001a,b).
[30] See Hines et al (2000).
[31] See Wass, Wells (1994).
[32] See McNair et al (2001a,b).

that «[...] any object [...] can be described according to a state of levels on a set of attributes, variables, properties, characteristics, factors or criteria.

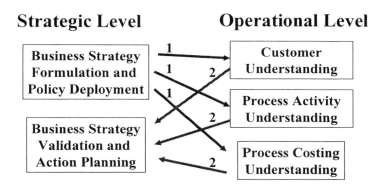

Figure 1: The Research Model

The attributes of an object are assumed to be evoked by the decision maker; that is, they are mental percepts and may or not may be related to objective characteristics».[33] A value attribute is then directly valued by the customer and considered as core criteria in making a purchase decision. Examples of value attributes could be: the quality of the product and service, the ability to customize, the post-purchase service, etc. The complete customer value profile is described by their relevant value attributes and relative importance. As a consequence of this basic assumption:

1. It is possible to split the total value proposition related to a product-service into a list of main relevant attributes in the eyes of the customer;

2. Customers could perceive a different level of importance for each of them;

3. Each product-service will have their own specific attributes list;

4. Even though managers think they know the customer value profile, it must be evaluated directly by the customers;

5. Understanding what is most important can help companies focus their efforts/investments and increase the value provided/perceived.

Different methods could be applied to reconstruct the customers' value profiles: a simple key manager brainstorming (where managers define a set of value attributes and give their perception of the relative importance to customer),

---

[33] See Green, Wind (1973), p. 13-14; Lancaster (1971).

customer focus groups (representative of the current mix and distribution of the companies and/or the total market customers), customer surveys (including analysis like cluster analysis and conjoint analysis[34]). The choice between these different approaches represents a key stage, as they involve vastly differing inputs of time, efforts, knowledge, as well as different degrees of academic rigor. However, the use of a variety of triangulated methods will add to the rigor of the research even if the most detailed method is not employed.

Acquiring customer understanding has been carried out through a number of different stages:

1. Managers brainstorming in order to identify relevant analysis processes (new and used car sales, service), and the list of relevant dimensions in the customer decision making process for each of the business areas selected;

2. Face-to-face customer structured interviews at the dealership (95 interviews), in order to test the list of relevant attributes, the list of variables that could affect the attribute profile, and the questionnaire structure, making it as rigorous and easy to complete as possible;[35]

3. Mail questionnaire survey (1,520 questionnaires sent with a 33% return rate), covering 100% of the new car customers and most of the used car and the service customers of the dealership;

4. Data processing and analysis (cluster analysis and correlations), concerning the key attributes importance and satisfaction for new and used cars and services.

In order to understand the internal processes, the New Cars Order Fulfillment, the Used Cars Order Fulfillment, and the Servicing process were mapped using diagnostic techniques (the Value Stream Mapping toolkit[36]): the Big Picture Map (BP Map), the Detailed Process Activity Map (PAM), with Value Adding Profile, the Supply Chain Response Matrix, the Production Variety Funnel, the Quality Filter Mapping and the Demand Amplification Mapping. This mapping work was facilitated by the researchers using a process facilitation approach. It involved three different internal expert groups, one for each process, together with one of the senior managers acting as a research champion.

With reference to the cost perspective, in this research program the Strategic Cost approach aims to translate into financial and non financial terms the outcomes of the processes analysis and related improvement plans. As a result, costs must be developed coherently with the structure and languages used by the Lean Tools.

---

[34] See Green, Srinivasan (1990).
[35] See Frankfort-Nachmias, Nachmias (1996).
[36] See Hines, Rich (1997); Rother, Shook (1999); Hines, Taylor (2000).

New dimensions (like time, delays and quality issues), neglected by most of the traditional performance measurement systems, assume key relevance.

As Lean Management approaches are generally process-oriented, a Process-Based Cost (PBC) analysis appears to be a natural consequence. It also meets the logic of a Process Value Analysis (that plays a significant role in LM, particularly in detailed Process Activity Maps). Thus, we assume that what the final customer receives is the result of a global process rather than one of single disconnected activities. A PBC[37] system can address most of the weaknesses of a basic ABC application, as in many implementations this tends to keep a functional view, exploring the activities performed inside each department. Thus, according to a process-based view, costs have been developed after the BP mapping work, as it provides the main activities to consider and investigate inside each department.

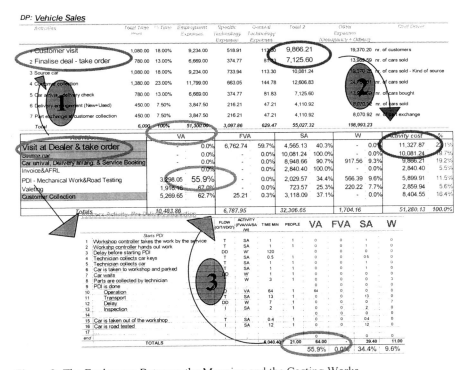

Figure 2: The Exchanges Between the Mapping and the Costing Works

As Figure 2 shows, those activities become part of the department job descriptions (exchange no. 1). These descriptions could then be completed thanks to structured

---

[37] See Lawson (1994).

interviews with the employees and through direct observations of the work of each department. This pattern of methods provides a global view of activities by department compatible with the traditional functional structure of cost centers. Therefore, it allowed us to use the data already supplied by traditional accounting systems to obtain activity costs. The information provided represented an input for completing the Process Activity Map (or PAM) and integrating the operations data with the financial ones (exchanges no. 2 and 3).

The cost information provided could then be used at different levels:

1. Global Process Level: in this case, the purpose is to offer a global picture of the consumption of resources by each main activity along the process in a certain period of time, solving the problem of department boundaries. This approach is affected by capacity issues because it takes into consideration the total costs paid in the same period, without paying attention to the level of capacity actually used.

2. Single Product Level: the activity costs can be also translated in unit terms. It is possible, for instance, to obtain the cost of a single minute or hour. These unit costs, if applied to the PAM information (in particular, to the unit lead time) enable the user to evaluate the resources consumed by a single car or service. This result is conceptually very different from a unit cost obtained dividing the global process cost for the number of units actually produced. In fact, while the former considers only the time directly spent for the single car-service, the capacity utilization level heavily affects the latter.

As a consequence, it is possible to obtain *the cost of the unused capacity*[38], through the difference between the Total Resources Consumption (Global Process Cost) and the Unit "Lead Time" Cost, multiplied for the Actual Volume. This logic provides data that can be used to simulate variations and hence estimate the effect on profitability.

Once this operational data have been recorded, the final stage was to validate the business strategy and develop an improvement plan. The result of these final sessions was a set of action plans appropriately correlated back to the earlier defined Key Performance Indicators.

---

[38] See Cooper, Kaplan (1992).

4 Results

4.1 Business Strategy Formulation & Policy

In order to codify the strategy the researchers facilitated a discussion using several traditional strategic development tools, including SWOT, Environmental Scanning and Growth Vectoring. Together with a related discussion it was thus possible to define a set of Critical Success Factors for the dealer. The factors are a mix of external or market-facing criteria and internal efficiency and effectiveness areas. As these had been established as important areas to address, the next facilitated workshop sought to see how well this existing (implicit) strategy was being deployed into the business by the existing measurement approach. The reason for this is that, in general, individuals and departments in a business tend to focus on how they are measured rather than business strategy when making strategic and operational decisions.[39] The existing set of measures had largely been influenced by the retailer's supplier of new cars. However, it was necessary to check whether this set of measures would help motivate the right behavior in the dealer.

4.2 Customer Understanding

This part of the study sought to understand what the customers really wanted from the retailer from the three key business processes responsible for delivering new and used car and after-sales service. As a result, it helps validate how sensible the existing business strategy is and whether it is related to true customer needs. In addition it can also help suggest how this strategy may be achieved.

From the data analysis, new and used car buyers seem to have a very similar relevant value attributes profile (see Figure 3), apart from the fact that used car buyers, compared to the new car buyers, evaluate the price, payment terms and dealer reputation more closely. On the contrary, the new car buyers pay more attention to the staff at the dealership, dealer facilities and after-sales service.

If we consider that dealer reputation, staff, facilities and service are directly managed by the retailer (at least, much more than product characteristics, price, payment terms and brand), these findings suggest that the analysis and development of the internal processes can provide good opportunities. Moreover, the entire service process could become the target area for continuous improvement programs with strong impacts on time, quality and costs. This is evidence of how the marketing analysis can facilitate priority identification, highlighting the strategic role of the service in the customer's choice of a dealership.

---

[39] See Dimancescu et al (1997).

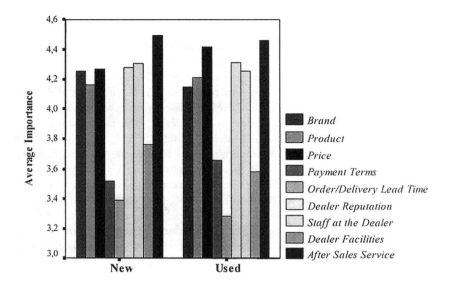

Figure 3: Key Customer Value Attribute Scores for New and Used Cars

The cluster analysis shows that it is not possible to split dealership customers into many significant clusters, as they already represent a specific target: customers of the same strong brand. Thus, in order to obtain a real understanding of the different car buyers segments it would have been necessary to extend the survey to the entire market. Therefore, it is possible to compare only two significant clusters. While the biggest one tends to give a higher importance to every attribute and, in particular, to the dealer reputation, staff and after-sales service (that is, exactly what the firm can control), the second cluster perceives only the product characteristics and price as very important (that the dealer can't greatly affect). This consideration again supports the idea that a better management of the internal processes can highly affect the value perceived by most of the customers.

If we compare the importance and satisfaction levels (see Figure 4), product characteristics, price, dealer reputation, and after-sale service are the criteria receiving the lower score. The process analysis then becomes strategic in order to explore how to align performance with expectations.[40]

---

[40] Actually, the collected data have been used for a number of other analyses (i.e. key attributes and satisfaction levels by purchase reason, car use, personal characteristics, type of service, etc); the same has been done for the mechanical & parts service business area. Moreover, the research team is carrying out the same customer survey

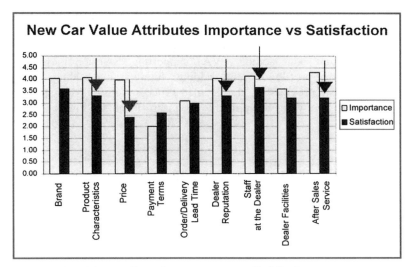

Figure 4: New Car Value Attributes Importance versus Satisfaction

In particular, the cluster analysis applied to the level of satisfaction shows the presence of two very differentiated groups. This means that there is a significant group of relationships that could be improved through a better understanding of the customers' needs or increasing their value perception.

4.3 The Lean & Strategic Cost Management Perspective

On the basis of the outcomes reported above, the mapping work allowed describing the main activities inside the new car sales, used car sales, and service processes, collecting data about production and set up times, stock accumulation, people involvement, information flows, etc. Figure 5 provides just an example of Big Picture map[41] concerning the service process.

The Big Pictures represented only the highest level of each process, whereas much more detailed mapping has been run producing a number of detailed PAMs (see

---

with another brand dealership, characterized by a different position on the market. This second work has two main purposes:
- to test the ability of the research techniques to describe the different customer profiles that should differentiate two distinctive brands;
- to enable the dealerships involved to understand better the reasons why groups of car buyers choose another company and/or another brand.

[41] See Rother, Shook (1999).

the third table in Figure 2).[42] These maps explain more in depth the micro-activities behind the main ones considered in the Big Picture map and, most of all, they provide a sufficient level of detail to classify the activities by their nature (operation -O-, inspection -I-, delay -D-, transport -T-) and in terms of value adding (VA), future value adding (FVA), supporting (SA) activities and waste (W). As such, the profile of value adding, future value adding, supporting activities and waste provided by the detailed Process Activity Mapping for each main activity can afterwards be applied to the macro-level (see Figure 2, exchange 3).

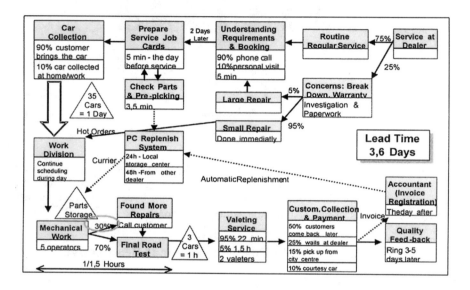

Figure 5: The Service Big Picture Map

Starting from the picture provided by every detailed PAM and the cost information already available from the firm's accounting system, it has been possible to obtain the cost of the activities inside every department. The first table in Figure 2 shows an example concerning the Vehicle Sales department.

Figure 6 presents the time and labor cost related to each macro-activity inside the service process and also shows that only 29.7% of that cost is due to value adding activities. This consideration suggests a deeper investigation of the nature of the micro-activities, paying attention to the efficiency improvement opportunities.

---

[42] See Bicheno (2000).

Activities	Labour Cost		VA	FVA	SA	W
U.R. & Booking	1.06	6.2%	0.59	0.02	0.21	0.25
Prepare Service Job Cards	1.71	10.0%	-	-	1.29	0.42
Check parts & Pre-picking	0.42	2.5%	-	-	0.30	0.12
Car Collection & Work Division	1.24	7.3%	-	-	0.72	0.52
Mechanical Work	5.10	29.9%	1.85	-	2.06	1.20
Road Testing	1.25	7.3%	1.03	-	0.23	-
Valeting Service	2.43	14.2%	1.60	-	0.83	-
Customer Collection & Payment	3.85	22.5%	-	-	3.51	0.34
Total Labour Cost	17.07	100.0%	5.06 29.7%	0.02 0.1%	9.15 53.6%	2.84 16.6%

Figure 6: The Labor Cost of a Typical Service

However, in the case of new cars, a considerable part of the delay is caused by the customers themselves (and thus could be excluded from consideration in a time compression program). Thus, the delay time can be subdivided as follows: 49% Customer Delay, 23% Dealer Delay, 27% Manufacturer Delay. Other Lean Management tools can then offer a deeper description of the reasons of the delays depending on the firm and on the supplier (the car manufacturer, in this case). The Delay Filter Map, for instance, shows the percentage of incoming cars presenting a delay due to the manufacturer (20%), the percentage (2%) of cases with an internal delay in transactions between different departments (PDI: Pre-delivery Inspection and Valeting) and the percentage of cars delivered late to the customer (15%). The Quality Filter Map shows that there is a serious issue concerning incoming quality of cars (mainly due to minor damage such as "undulations" or dents) and that around a sixth of cars are returned with warranty claims. In addition, one in twenty cars must be returned for further rework after repair or servicing.

Further detailed analysis allowed the description of other sub-processes, such as Cars Movements, T-Cards and Job-Cards Management, and Quality Inspections. This kind of approach aims to increase the operations efficiency, as it highlights «[...] when an activity involves hand-offs from one department to another, and when an activity is highly fragmented, involving people from several different departments performing various or even the same aspects of the activity».[43]

4.4 Business Strategy Validation and Action Planning

At the completion of the operational level data capture and analysis (Figure 1), the researchers, with a university industry expert, facilitated a strategic level discussion with the firm's senior managers. Various opportunities were identified in terms of Creating Value in the eyes of the customers (VC), Waste Reduction

---

[43] See Kaplan, Cooper (1998), p 141.

from the existing processes (WR), Developing the firm's Infrastructure (In), and External supply chain change (Ex).

Finally, in order to complete the planning phase, the researchers took this outline plan and estimated the Profit Potential of this activity using the earlier financial and simulation information. The term Profit Potential was borrowed from McNair (1994), where she used it to describe the amount of resources a firm can generate by reducing or eliminating supporting activities and waste. In this context, we take a broader definition of Profit Potential to include the results of any activity (either on the demand or supply side) that can change the propensity for profitability of the focal company whether it is under their direct control or not.

5 Conclusions

The primary aim of this research has been to develop, test and if possible validate an integrative approach seeking to gain a more holistic and contingent decision-making approach. In order to do this, a single case study was chosen, due to the expected complexity of the research and volume of research time required. The first area of discussion focuses on how effective this integration process was as a research method. It was judged that this pilot study was effective in terms of integrating the language used, the cultures of the research team and the functional specialties of the researchers. An example of the effectiveness of the approach was the evolution of some of the Lean, Strategic Cost Management and Marketing language and definitions into a common lexicon for this service industry case. The other major area for integration was that of the cultural and functional backgrounds of the research teams.

The integration of Lean Thinking, Strategic Cost Management, Marketing and Policy Deployment has proven effective at both the strategic and operational levels. However, this initial work has suffered from a number of limitations, particularly due to its time consuming nature. Further research is required in order to correct, or at least restrict, these limitations. This should include further integration of other elements of Strategic Cost Management such as cost driver analysis.[44] Also, of benefit would be longitudinal research on the case firm described here to observe whether they can fulfill the potential of their improvement plans. In addition, further testing of the approach in other automotive retailers, industrial sectors and outside the UK will help gauge whether the approach can overcome cultural and sectoral institutional barriers.[45] Once the approach can be further streamlined it can also be applied to a wider supply chain setting.

---

[44] See Shank, Govindarajan (1993a,b).
[45] See DiMaggio, Powell (1983); Hofstede, Bond (1988); Whitley (1992).

6 References

Akao, Y. (1991): Hoshin Kanri: Policy Deployment for Successful TQM, Productivity Press, Cambridge, Mass.

Bicheno, J. (2000): The Lean Toolbox, 2nd Edition, Picsie Books, Buckingham.

Brunt, D., Rich, N., Hines, P. (1998): Aligning Continuous Improvement Along the Value Chain, in: Proceedings of the 7th International Annual IPSERA Conference, 80-88, International Purchasing and Supply Education & Research Association, London.

Cooper, R., Kaplan, R. S. (1992): Activity-Based System: Measuring the Cost of Resources Usage, Working Paper Harvard Business School, Harvard.

Cooper, R., Slagmulder, R. (1998): Operational Improvement and Strategic Costing, in: Management Accounting, September (1998), p. 11-12.

Christopher, M. (1992): Logistics and Supply Chain Management: Strategies for Reducing Costs and Improving Services, Pitman Publishing, London.

Davidow, W., Malone, M. (1992): The Virtual Corporation: Structuring and Revitalizing the Corporation for the 21st Century, Harper Business, New York.

DiMaggio, P., Powell, W. (1983): The Iron Cage Revisited: Institutional Isomorphism and Collective Rationality in Organizational Fields, in: American Sociological Review, Vol. 48 (1983), p. 147-160.

Dimancescu, D., Hines, P., Rich, N. (1997): The Lean Enterprise: Designing and Managing Strategic Processes for Customer-Winning Performance, AMACOM, New York.

The Economist (2001): A Long March, Special Report Mass Customisation, in: The Economist, July 14th (2001), p. 79-81. (also at www.economist.com/business).

Forrester, J. W. (1961): Industrial Dynamics, MIT Press, Massachusetts.

Frankfort-Nachmias, C., Nachmias, D. (1996): Research Methods in the Social Sciences, 5th Edition, St. Martin's Press, New York.

Green, P. E., Srinivasan, V. (1990): Conjoint Analysis in Marketing: New Developments with Implications for Research and Practice, in: Journal of Marketing, Vol. 54 (1990), p. 3-19.

Green, P. E., Wind, Y. (1973): Multiattribute Decisions in Marketing: A Measurement Approach, The Dryden Press, Illinois.

Hakim, C. (1987): Research Design, Allen Unwin, London.

Hammer, M. (1990): Re-engineering Work: Don't Automate, Obliterate, in: Harvard Business Review, July-August (1990), p. 104-112.

Harland, C. (1998): Supply Network Strategy: Observations on Structure, Infrastructure and Operations Performance, in: Proceedings of the 2nd Worldwide Symposium on Purchasing and Supply Chain Management, IPSERA, London, p. 248-267.

Hartley, J. (1994): Case Studies in Organisational Research, in: Cassell, C., Symon, G. (ed.): Qualitative Methods in Organisational Research, Sage, London.

Hines, P., Rich, N. (1997): The Seven Value Stream Mapping Tools, in: International Journal of Production & Operations Management, Vol. 17, No. 1 (1997), p. 44-62.

Hines, P. (1998): Supply Chain Management: From Lorries to Macro-Economic Determiner, Key Note Speech, in: Proceedings of the Logistics Research Network Conference, Cranfield University, p. 1-23.

Hines, P., Rich, N., Hittmeyer, M. (1998): Competing Against Ignorance: Advantage Through Knowledge, in: International Journal of Physical Distribution & Logistics Management, Vol. 28, No. 1 (1998), p. 18-43.

Hines, P., Lamming, R., Jones, D., Cousins, P., Rich, N. (2000): Value Stream Management: Strategy and Excellence in the Supply Chain, Financial Times Prentice Hall, Harlow.

Hines, P., Taylor, D. (2000): Going Lean: A Guide to Implementation, LERC (Lean Enterprise Research Centre), Cardiff Business School, Cardiff.
(also at www.cf.ac.uk/carbs/lom/lerc/centre/goinglean.pdf).

Hofstede, G., Bond, M. (1988): The Confucius Connection: From Cultural Roots to Economic Growth, in: Organisational Dynamics, Vol. 16, No. 4 (1988), p. 5-21.

Ishiwata, J. (1991): Productivity Through Process Analysis, Productivity Press, Cambridge, MA.

Johnson, H. T., Kaplan, R. S. (1987): Relevance Lost. The Rise and Fall of Management Accounting, Harvard Business School Press, Boston.

Kaplan, R. S., Cooper, R. (1998): Cost & Effect. Using Integrated Cost Systems to Drive Profitability and Performance, Harvard Business School Press, Boston.

Kidd, P., (1994): Agile Manufacturing: Forging New Frontiers, Addison Wesley, Wokingham.

Lancaster, K. (1971): Consumer Demand: a New Approach, Columbia University Press, New York and London.

Lawson, R. A. (1994): Beyond ABC: Process Based Costing, in: The Journal of Cost Management for the Manufacturing Industry, Vol. 8, No. 3 (1994), p. 33-44.

Lorenzoni, G., Shank, J. K., Silvi, R. (1999): Networked Organizations: A Strategic Cost Management Perspective, Babson Working Paper Series No. 99 109 NB.

McNair, C. J. (1994): The Profit Potential: Taking High Performance to the Bottom Line, Oliver Wight Publications Inc, Essex Junction, VT.

McNair, C. J., Polutnik, L., Silvi, R. (2001a): Outside-In: Cost and the Creation of Customer Value, in: Advances in Management Accounting, Vol. 9 (2001), p. 1-41.

McNair, C. J., Polutnik, L., Silvi, R. (2001b): Cost and the Creation of Customer Value, in: Shank, J. (ed.): Handbook of Cost Management, Warren, Gorham, and Lamont Publishing Company, New York, Forthcoming.

Ohno, T. (1988): Toyota Production System: Beyond Large-Scale Production, Productivity Press, Portland, OR.

Ostrenga, M. R., Probst, F. R. (1992): Process Value Analysis: The Missing Link in Cost Management, in: Journal of Cost Management, Vol. 6, No. 3 (1992).

Porter, M. E. (1985): Competitive Advantage, The Free Press, New York.

Rother, M., Shook, J. (1999): Learning to See, The Lean Enterprise Institute, Brookline.

Schonberger, R. J. (1986): World Class Manufacturing: The Lessons of Simplicity Applied, The Free Press, New York.

Shank, J., Govindarajan, V. (1989): Strategic Cost Analysis. The Evolution from Managerial to Strategic Accounting, R. D., Irwin, Homewood, IL.

Shank, J., Govindarajan, V. (1993a): Strategic Cost Management, The Free Press, New York.

Shank, J., Govindarajan, V. (1993b): What "Drivers" Cost? A Strategic Cost Management Perspective, in: Advances in Management Accounting, Vol. 2 (1993), p. 27-45.

Shingo, S., (1989): A Study of the Toyota Production System from an Industrial Engineering Viewpoint, Productivity Press, Cambridge, MA.

Stake, R. (1998): Case Studies, in: Denzin, N., Lincoln, Y. (ed.): Strategies of Qualitative Inquiry, Sage, California.

Stalk, G. J., Hout, T. M. (1990): Competing Against Time, The Free Press, New York.

Towill, D., (1996): Industrial Dynamics Modelling of Supply Chains, in: International Journal of Physical Distribution & Logistics Management, Vol. 26, No. 2 (1996), p. 23-43.

Turney, P. B. B., Anderson, B. (1989): Accounting for Continuous Improvement, in: Sloan Management Review, Winter (1989), p. 95-105.

Wass, V., Wells, P. (1994): Principles and Practice in Business and Management Research, Dartmouth Publishing, London.

Wayland, R. E., Cole, P. M. (1997): Customer Connections. New Strategies for Growth, Harvard Business School Press, Boston.

Whitley, R. (1992): Business Systems in East Asia: Firms, Markets and Societies, Sage Publications, London.

Wilding, R. (1998): Chaos Theory: Implications for Supply Chain Management, in: International Journal of Logistics Management, Vol. 9, No. 1 (1998), p. 43-56.

Womack, J., Jones, D., Roos, D. (1990): The Machine that Changed the World, Rawson Associates, New York.

Womack, J., Jones, D. (1996): Lean Thinking: Banish Waste and Create Wealth in your Corporation, Simon & Schuster, New York.

Yin, R. (1989): Case Study Research: Design and Methods, Sage, California.

Managing Costs Across the Supply Chain

Regine Slagmulder

1	A New Perspective in Cost Management	76
2	Cost Management Beyond the Factory Walls	77
3	Cost Management Beyond the Boundaries of the Firm	79
4	The Relational Context of Interorganizational Cost Management	85
5	Summary	86
6	References	88

Summary:
Supplier and customer-focused cost information enables firms to identify opportunities for improving the cost efficiency of their transactions with supply chain partners. It is the first step towards interorganizational cost management, which is a structured approach to coordinating the activities of firms in a supply chain so that overall costs are reduced. Coordinating the cost-reduction programs of firms across the supply chain can help them identify ways to make their interfaces more efficient. In addition, it can help the firms and their buyers and suppliers find new ways to jointly reduce the manufacturing costs of their products, both during product design and manufacturing.

Keywords:
Interorganizational Cost Management, Supply Chain, Activity-Based Costing, Target Costing, Buyer-Supplier Relationship

1   A New Perspective in Cost Management

After decades of relatively little change, management accounting practice has been characterized by a stream of innovations in recent times, including such techniques as activity-based costing, target costing, and kaizen costing. Many of these innovations fit under the umbrella of strategic cost management, whose objective is to reduce costs while simultaneously strengthening the strategic position of the firm.[1] Given this objective, strategic cost management systems cannot limit themselves to either the four walls of the factory or the boundaries of the firm. A perspective that is gaining increased attention in the business world is the idea that cost and performance management should be applied across the entire supply chain.

Traditional costing systems, however, are limited to analyzing production costs and are used to determine the cost of products only. Other potential cost objects such as suppliers and customers are treated either as general overhead and arbitrarily allocated to products, or as period costs and assigned directly to the income statement. The problem with this approach is that these non-manufacturing costs cannot be managed effectively because the underlying reasons for their occurrence are blurred by the firm's costing system. The use of activity-based costing enables firms to assign costs in a more causal manner not only to products, but also to suppliers and customers. Armed with the insights provided by this extension of cost management, a firm can begin to manage supplier and customer related costs more effectively.

While supplier and customer focused costing enables firms to extend their cost management efforts beyond the production area, it does not necessarily require joint action by buyers and suppliers. In contrast, the objective of interorganizational cost management is to find ways to reduce costs through the cooperative actions of firms in a supply chain. This objective is achieved by encouraging all the firms involved to act in ways that increase the efficiency of the entire supply chain in which they operate, not just themselves. Interorganizational cost management can help reduce costs in three different areas. First, it can help identify ways to make the interface between the firms more efficient. Second, it can help the firm and its buyers and suppliers find new ways to design products so that they can be manufactured at a lower cost. Finally, it can help the firm and its suppliers find ways to further reduce the cost of products during manufacturing.

The remainder of this article is organized as follows: The next section discusses the shortcomings of traditional costing systems and the insights that can be gained

---

[1]   See Cooper, Slagmulder (1998).

from activity-based costing approaches for managing the costs of transactions with suppliers and customers. Section three extends the subject beyond the firm's boundaries and discusses various approaches for interorganizational cost management during product design and manufacture. Section four highlights the characteristics of buyer-supplier relations that enable the effective use of these cost management techniques. The final section concludes the paper with a summary.

2 Cost Management Beyond the Factory Walls - Supplier and Customer Costing

The implications of extending cost management beyond the factory walls means that costs can not only be assigned to products, but also to suppliers and customers (see Figure 1). One of the primary techniques for meaningfully assigning non-manufacturing costs is activity-based costing. The advantage of this technique over traditional costing methods lies in its ability to assign costs in a causal manner to a broad range of cost objects including products, suppliers, and customers.

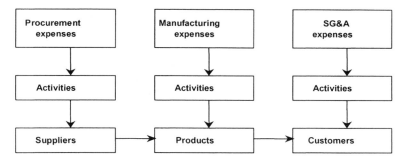

Figure 1: The Activity-Based Costing Approach to Supplier and Customer Costing

2.1 Managing Supplier Costs

Without proper assignment of procurement costs, purchasing managers typically select suppliers based on the purchase price of their products. Such decision making may lead to suboptimal buying behavior weakening the firm's strategic position, for example, by purchasing components from suppliers whose quality, reliability, and delivery performance are below acceptable levels. These purchasing decisions inevitably hinder the firm's ability to satisfy its customers and earn adequate profits because on-time delivery of high-quality products is affected. However, if purchasing managers are rewarded solely on the purchase prices they negotiate with suppliers, it will be almost impossible to change their approach to supplier selection.

Strategic cost management resolves the conflict in two ways – first, by taking a broader view of component costs and, second, by assigning procurement costs to products in a causal manner. Instead of just looking at the purchase price, strategic cost management includes the costs associated with low quality, reliability, and delivery performance. Purchasing managers now are expected to evaluate suppliers on total cost, not just purchase price. The resulting buying behavior leads to a strengthening of the firm's strategic position as suppliers are chosen based on their ability to help the firm produce high-quality products timed to customer demand.

In the next step of the process, supplier costs are assigned causally to products using activity-based costing principles. This way products are assigned their specific procurement costs, not the average for all products. For example, products containing large numbers of unique components that rely upon specialty suppliers will be seen as more expensive than products that contain only standard components that can be bought in the open market. Only if the specialty components add value to the end product and this value is reflected in its selling price will the use of such components be justified.

2.2 Managing Customer Service Costs

In traditional cost systems, selling, general, and administrative (SG&A) expenses are treated as period costs and are expensed to the income statement. Under this accounting treatment, they are often taken into account indirectly through rules of thumb about how profitable products should be. For example, "SG&A costs are 25%; therefore, we need to make a 35% profit margin to make an adequate return." Essentially this rule of thumb spreads the SG&A costs evenly over products based on their sales dollars. The outcome is a totally distorted view of the cost of serving customers because customers either appear to cost nothing to serve, or they all appear to cost the same percentage of their sales revenue. Without proper assignment of customer costs, sales representatives select customers based almost exclusively upon the way they are rewarded. Typically, this means either on the volume sold (if the representatives are evaluated on revenue generated) or on the relationship between the selling price of the products and reported product costs (if they are evaluated on product profitability). Such a treatment can lead to a strategic weakening of the firm because there is no way that individual customer profitability can be determined accurately. Therefore, the sales representatives are unable to manage the firm's customer mix effectively.

Strategic cost management provides a more accurate view of customer profitability by assigning customer-related costs to the customers causing them to use activity-based costing principles. For example, customers who order in small, unpredictable quantities and require considerable post-sales support will be seen as more costly than customers who order in high, predictable quantities and require little or no support. Using this enhanced knowledge of customer profitability, sales representatives can strengthen the strategic position of the firm by attracting and retaining high-profitability customers, even at the risk of losing low-profitability ones. For example, they can identify clusters of high-profitability customers and try to increase their satisfaction through higher service levels or lower prices. By contrast, for unprofitable customers they can try to deliver the services in a more efficient way or increase prices to reflect the cost of the resources consumed. Finally, they may reduce selling efforts to unprofitable customers.

Even though extending cost management beyond the walls of the factory can provide eye-opening insights into the economics of supplier and customer relationships, it may still not be sufficient. The next step in strategic cost management is extending the cost management process beyond the firm's organizational boundaries and identifying ways to reduce costs across the supply chain. By coordinating their cost management programs with those of their suppliers and customers, firms can take advantage of any cost management synergies that may exist between themselves and their supply chain partners.

3 Cost Management Beyond the Boundaries of the Firm

For the majority of the twentieth century, management accounting practice has limited its scope to the boundaries of the firm. This limitation makes it difficult for the firm to take advantage of any cost-reduction synergies that exist across the supply chain. Such synergies can only be achieved by coordinating the cost-reduction activities of multiple firms in the supply chain. Interorganizational cost management is a structured approach to coordinating the activities of firms in a supply chain so that total costs in the chain are reduced. The objective of interorganizational cost management programs is finding lower-cost solutions than would be possible if the firm and its buyers and suppliers attempted to reduce costs independently. Coordinating the cost-reduction programs at multiple firms in the supply chain can help reduce costs in various ways. It can help identify ways to make the interface between the firms more efficient. In addition, it can help the firm and its buyers and suppliers find additional ways to reduce the manufacturing cost of products, both during product design and during manufacturing.

3.1 Increasing the Efficiency of the Buyer-Supplier Interface

The first step in interorganizational cost management consists of the firm getting together with its buyers and suppliers to find ways to make their interfaces more efficient. An important element in making the interface more efficient is reducing uncertainty, for example by increasing information sharing and shortening cycle times. Reducing uncertainty in such a way may lead to significant savings as both the buyer and the supplier can keep lower levels of buffer inventory.

Suppliers can help increase the efficiency of the buyer-supplier interface by changing their behavior to reduce procurement costs at the firm. For example, if the firm is operating in just-in-time mode, late deliveries by suppliers are very expensive. Based upon its analysis of procurement costs, the firm can show the supplier the high costs associated with poor delivery performance. The supplier can then initiate a program to increase on-time deliveries. The firm can help in this process by transferring the expertise it has gained in its own journey towards lean thinking. Other potential improvements for the supplier include improved quality, smaller batch deliveries, and shorter lead times.

Alternatively, buyers can change their behavior in ways that reduce the firm's customer service costs. For example, the buyer may be placing a large number of small orders with the firm. If the firm has high sales order processing costs, then the firm's cost to serve that customer will be high. The firm can use the insights it gains into the economics of customer service to suggest new ways for the buyer to order products. For example, the buyer might agree to undertake data entry that feeds directly into the firm's sales order systems. Other potential improvements for the buyer include reducing its reliance on custom as opposed to standard products, ordering as many different products at a time as possible, increasing sales order lead-times, and reducing the number of changes to sales orders.

The interfaces between the firm and its buyers and suppliers will only become truly efficient when they in turn ask the firm to modify its behavior to reduce their costs. Many of the recommendations will lead to cost savings at both sides. For example, adopting Total Quality Management not only reduces costs at the buyer by removing the need to inspect incoming items or return defects, but also at the supplier by eliminating rework or scrap. Similarly, both sides can achieve savings by adopting electronic data interchange (EDI). The critical point is that there are win-win scenarios that can be identified by extending cost management beyond the walls of the factory and realized by extending it beyond the boundaries of the firm.

In addition to optimizing the buyer-supplier interfaces, the supply chain can also be made more efficient by having the firm and its buyers and suppliers jointly look for ways to reduce manufacturing costs. Some cost management techniques are applied to reduce costs during the product design stage, whereas others are used to reduce costs during the manufacturing stage.

3.2 Interorganizational Cost Management During Product Design

Interorganizational cost management during product development is of particular importance to lean enterprises because these firms often outsource as much as 70% of the value-added of their products. With such a high degree of outsourced value, coordinating product development throughout the supply chain is critical to the firms' success. As firms become lean and undergo vertical desegregation, they discover that it is no longer adequate for each firm in the supply chain to undertake cost management independently. Instead, they find that product development programs must become coordinated across buyer-supplier interfaces. Techniques enabling firms to jointly reduce costs during product design are target costing, functionality-price-quality trade-offs, interorganizational cost investigations, and concurrent cost management.

1. Target Costing

During the product design phase, interorganizational cost management involves close interactions between the design teams of the firm and its suppliers. The objective of these interactions is to find lower cost solutions than would be possible if the design teams acted in isolation. The primary cost management technique used to trigger these interactions is target costing. Target costing is a structured approach to determining the life-cycle cost at which a proposed product with specified functionality and quality must be produced to generate the desired level of profitability at its anticipated selling price.[2] Achieving this product-level target cost requires the application of value engineering (VE). VE is a multidisciplinary effort to analyze the functions of the product so a firm can find ways to achieve those functions while meeting its target cost. The objective of most target costing and VE programs is not to minimize the cost of products in general, but to achieve a specified level of cost reduction established by the firm's target costing system.

Once the target cost of a new product is established at the product level, multifunctional product design teams decompose it to determine component and subassembly target costs. The cost-reduction objective is not spread evenly across all the components and subassemblies. Historical trends, competitive designs, and other data are used to estimate how much cost can be removed from each component or subassembly. An iterative process is used to ensure that once the component and subassembly target costs are set, they add up to the product-level target cost. By establishing the cost-reduction objectives for the products and the components they contain, target costing becomes a disciplining mechanism for interorganizational cost management. By chaining target costing systems, that is, connecting the target costing system of the buyer to that of its suppliers, the

---

[2] See Cooper, Slagmulder (1997).

discipline of target costing can be extended from a single firm to multiple firms in a supply chain.

2. Functionality-Price-Quality Trade-Offs

One of the outcomes of target costing is that the firm establishes its suppliers' selling prices. Since these prices reflect the cost pressures that the firm faces in the marketplace, it communicates these pressures to the firm's suppliers. When a supplier finds that it cannot achieve the target costs set by the buyer's component-level target costing process, it can initiate additional interorganizational cost management activities (see Figure 2).

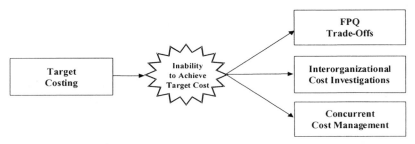

Figure 2: Triggering Interorganizational Cost Management During Product Design

The degree to which the design teams of the two firms interact under the various techniques varies significantly. At one end of the spectrum are functionality-price-quality (FPQ) trade-offs, which involve only minor reductions in the outsourced component's quality, functionality, and cost, and which have no impact on the specifications of the end product. Under an FPQ trade-off, the buyer and supplier negotiate to lower the level of quality and functionality required so the supplier can generate an adequate profit at the buyer's component-level target cost. For example, costs might be reduced if a casting is used instead of a more expensive forging. The firm's engineers know by how much surface tolerances can be relaxed before the quality and functionality of its product suffer, and the supplier's engineers know the tolerances that can be achieved using castings and forgings. Thus, only when the two design teams interact and coordinate their activities can an acceptable, low-cost castings solution be identified.

The feasibility of an FPQ trade-off depends upon the willingness of the buyer to relax the quality and functionality specifications established for the component. If the supplier can negotiate such relaxations, it will be easier to achieve the component's target cost. For example, if the component is allowed to have lower functionality, its design might be simplified so that the number of parts it contains can be reduced. Such a parts reduction can lead to lower cost. The willingness of the buyer to allow such relaxations is constrained by the need to maintain the specifications of the end product itself. The supplier must understand the role of the component in achieving the end product's functionality so that it can make appropriate recommendations.

3. Interorganizational Cost Investigations

The interaction between the design teams can be extended to several firms in the supply chain. For example, imagine a situation in which one firm produces a forging or casting, another one machines its surface, and a third one uses the final component in its end product. In this scenario, the knowledge required to find new low-cost solutions resides at three firms. Therefore, to find creative ways to reduce costs requires that design teams from the three firms get together. These interactions are called interorganizational cost investigations. The important point is that a new lower cost solution can only be identified through the coordinated effort of the three design teams. In an interorganizational cost investigation, the design teams of the firms get together to determine whether the specifications set by the buyer can be altered in ways that enable the component's costs to be reduced significantly. The changes to the component's specifications usually are greater than those considered under an FPQ trade-off.

The objective of interorganizational cost investigations is to find ways to redesign the products and the components they contain so that they can be manufactured at their target costs. Consequently, the first consideration is what changes can be made to the design of the end product and the components it contains. Since the design changes made to the components may affect the specifications of the end product, the supplier cannot initiate them unilaterally. Instead, the buyer and supplier design teams must get together to identify which design changes are acceptable to the buyer and reduce costs across the supply chain.

The second consideration deals with changes in the production process that require moving production activities across organizational boundaries. If certain activities can be performed more efficiently at another firm in the supply chain, then costs will be reduced if these activities are moved. Second, if collocating two activities allows costs to be reduced, then shifting one of the activities so it is performed in the same location as the other will allow costs to be reduced. Finally, if changing the production process can eliminate certain activities, then costs will also be reduced. For example, if there is a way to start with raw material that has a smooth surface as opposed to a rough one, then the production step preparing the surface of the rough component can be eliminated.

As the product design and production processes are modified, the costs incurred in each firm change. These changes often require the target costs of the components to be modified. For example, if costs are increased at one firm and decreased at another (but reduced overall), then the target cost of the component at the firm with increased costs may need be raised and at the firm with the lower costs, reduced. These changes redistribute the cost-reduction objectives and hence profit levels among the firms in the supply chain. Typically, the firm that is most upstream in the supply chain sets the new target costs.

4. Concurrent Cost Management

Under concurrent cost management, the most interactive of the interorganizational cost management techniques, the design of the entire major function is outsourced to the supplier. Consequently, this interorganizational cost management technique involves intensive interactions during the product design phase, where both sides make suggestions for cost reduction leading to significant changes in the design of the product and the components that it contains.

For concurrent cost management to be practiced, the suppliers need to develop the necessary expertise so that the buyer can relinquish design responsibility to them. If the two design teams can operate essentially in isolation, then parallel engineering is appropriate. The buyer's team provides the supplier's team with high-level specifications such as size, capacity, and effectiveness. The two teams are then free to operate independently as long as they do not make any design changes violating the high-level specifications of the product or the component. While the two design teams operate in isolation, they maintain contact with each other to ensure that they achieve their joint objectives.

However, if the buyer and supplier design teams cannot effectively operate in isolation, simultaneous engineering is used to design the product and component concurrently. In simultaneous engineering, the two design teams work closely together to identify ways to increase the quality and functionality of the end product and its major function, while at the same time reducing overall costs. The two design teams make suggestions to alter the design of both the end product and the major function, which could not be made if the two teams acted in isolation. For example, redesigning the component to reduce its costs may require some major changes in the design of the end product. Identifying the scope of such changes and whether they reduce overall costs without sacrificing quality and functionality requires frequent interactions between the design teams.

3.3 Interorganizational Cost Management During Manufacturing

Additional opportunities for joint cost reduction in the supply chain occur during the manufacturing phase. Interorganizational cost management during product manufacture is a structured approach to coordinating the production activities of firms in the supply chain so that the products and components those firms produce can be manufactured at their kaizen costs. The starting point for setting a kaizen cost-reduction objective is the price pressure that the firm is exposed to in the marketplace. This kaizen cost-reduction objective then has to be decomposed to the supplier level. In kaizen programs, suppliers usually are subjected to a flat cost-reduction rate, for example, 3% per year. This approach differs significantly from the one used for target costing, where specific targets are set at the individual product level. In kaizen costing, specific cost-reduction objectives are set only for very expensive components (for example, 6% for radiators and 3% for starter motors).

If some suppliers are unable to achieve the cost-reduction objective, additional cost-reduction efforts are required. The buyer and supplier can cooperate in three ways to further reduce costs. First, the buyer can use its engineering expertise to help the supplier find lower-cost ways to manufacture the components it sells to the buyer. Second, if such solutions cannot be identified, the buyer can change the design, but not functionality, of its product to enable the supplier to develop new, lower-cost components. For example, several integrated circuits might be combined into a single chip. This solution lowers the cost for the supplier, but requires that the buyer change its circuit design. Finally, the buyer can agree to change its production processes, but not product designs, to accommodate changes in the supplied component. For example, the buyer might agree to perform machining operation in house because it can be integrated with an existing one at a lower cost than the supplier can undertake. In that case, the supplier's kaizen cost might be adjusted downwards to allow for the additional cost borne by the buyer, but overall the supplier will be better off because the downward reduction is less than the avoided costs. Alternatively, the buyer can agree to shift some operations to the supplier and accordingly adjust the kaizen cost upward. Again, the supplier will be better off if the increase in the kaizen cost is greater than the costs incurred to perform the new operations. The firm can also help its suppliers reduce costs in other ways. For example, the firm can use the combined buying power of the supply chain to negotiate better discounts than its suppliers can achieve on their own.

4 The Relational Context of Interorganizational Cost Management

The objective of interorganizational cost management programs is for firms to find lower-cost solutions through coordinated actions with their buyers and suppliers than would be possible if the firms attempted to reduce costs independently. Given its heavy reliance on cooperation, interorganizational cost management can be undertaken only in supply chains where the buyer-supplier relations are characterized by high levels of trust and resource sharing.

For interorganizational cost management to be effective, it must start as a cultural process with the establishment of the appropriate buyer-supplier relationships. The relationships are shaped primarily by the degree of cooperation, stability, and mutual benefit. Cooperation is required for all three areas of interorganizational cost management – buyer-supplier interface, product development, and manufacturing – because they all require the firm and its buyers and suppliers to change their behavior. While unilateral behavior changes may be beneficial, it is only when several firms in the supply chain change their behavior that the real savings of interorganizational cost management are achieved. In addition, stability is required both to motivate and justify these behavioral changes.

The principle of mutual benefit ensures that all the firms involved share in the increased profitability resulting from the behavioral changes. Since lower overall costs mean higher profits for the entire supply chain, all the firms are potentially better off if they adopt interorganizational cost management. For interorganizational cost management to work, the additional profits from any improvements have to be shared among all the firms involved. This sharing creates an incentive for everyone to cooperate irrespective of how powerful they are. The weaker firms will not cooperate unless some of the benefits are shared with them and the powerful firms will only be willing to share additional profits if they believe that sustaining the supply chain's ability to undertake interorganizational cost management is to their benefit.

All three areas of interorganizational cost management also require intense information sharing. This is particularly true in the case of product development, where information sharing is needed to ensure coordination of the design process at all the firms involved. The degree of information sharing depends on the outsourced item. Some items need very little information sharing, and the buyer-supplier relationship can be relatively simple and at arm's length. In contrast, for items that are major functions, such as in concurrent cost management, almost total information sharing is required as the teams simultaneously design the end product and its major functions.

5 Summary

Interorganizational cost management is an approach to cost and profit management that takes advantages of synergies existing across multiple firms in a supply chain. Unlike traditional costing systems that have failed to provide an accurate analysis of costs beyond the production domain, activity-based costing systems help firms to more accurately assign the costs associated with supplier and customer relationships. This supplier and customer-oriented cost information enables firms to identify opportunities for increasing the cost efficiency of their trading relationships within the supply chain.

Cost synergies can also be realized by actively coordinating activities among firms in the supply chain, with the aim of reducing overall supply chain costs.

Interorganizational cost management involves three major areas of coordination. The first area focuses on increasing the efficiency of the interface between buyers and suppliers. As these interfaces become more efficient, the cost of transferring goods between the firms decreases.

The second area requires coordinating the product development processes of the firms in the supply chain. Experience has shown that it is easier to design costs out of products than to find ways to eliminate them after the products enter production. When a firm outsources a large percentage of the value-added of its products, it is not sufficient for just that firm to develop low-cost products. Rather, it is necessary for all the firms involved in the development process to develop low-cost designs. Often, the choices made by one firm about how to design its part of the product have cost implications for the other firms involved in the process. Consequently, only if all these firms cooperate will the end product be low cost.

Target costing acts as the disciplining technique that identifies where individual firms are having problems achieving sufficiently low-cost designs. By joining the target costing systems of several firms in the supply chain, the competitive cost pressures the end firm encounters in the market can be communicated throughout the supply chain. Failure to achieve a target cost indicates that interorganizational cooperation is required. Three interorganizational cost management mechanisms foster such cooperation: functionality-price-quality (FPQ) trade-offs, interorganizational cost investigations, and concurrent cost management programs. Each of these mechanisms causes the product design teams of two or more firms to interact, with the specific objective of reducing costs through improved design.

The third area of interorganizational cost management requires coordinating the manufacturing processes of the firms in the supply chain. The kaizen costing systems in the firms create pressure on their suppliers to continuously reduce the costs of the products they manufacture. When a supplier finds that it cannot achieve the required level of cost reduction, it can ask the buyer to help it lower its costs. The two firms can reduce costs together in various ways. They can either jointly find ways for the supplier to manufacture the component at a lower cost, or they can move activities between them so that these activities can be performed more efficiently at a lower cost. For all three forms of interorganizational cost management to operate effectively, the buyer-supplier relations in the supply chain must be characterized by high levels of trust, stability, and mutual benefit so that they create an incentive for all firms involved to cooperate and share the necessary resources.

6 References

Cooper, R., Slagmulder R. (1997): Target Costing and Value Engineering, Productivity Press, Portland, OR.

Cooper R., Slagmulder R. (1998): Strategic Cost Management – What is Strategic Cost Management?, in: Management Accounting, Vol. 76, No. 1 (1998), p. 14-16.

Cooper, R., Slagmulder R. (1999): Supply Chain Development for the Lean Enterprise. Interorganizational Cost Management, Productivity Press, Portland, OR.

Cooper, R., Yoshikawa T. (1994): Inter-Organizational Cost Management Systems: The Case of the Tokyo-Yokohama-Kamakura Supplier Chain, in: International Journal of Production Economics, Vol. 37 (1994), p. 51-62.

Dyer, J. H. (1996): Specialized Supplier Networks as a Source of Competitive Advantage: Evidence from the Auto Industry, in: Strategic Management Journal, Vol. 17 (1996), p. 271-291.

Dyer, J. H., Ouchi W. G. (1993): Japanese-Style Partnerships: Giving Companies a Competitive Edge, in: Sloan Management Review, Vol. 34, Fall (1993), p. 51-63.

Hines, P. (1994): Creating World Class Suppliers, Pitman Publishing, London.

Kamath, R. R., Liker J. K. (1994): A Second Look at Japanese Product Development, in: Harvard Business Review, Vol.16, Nov.-Dec. (1994), p. 154-170.

Kaplan, R. S., Cooper, R. (1997): Cost and Effect, Harvard Business School Press, Boston.

Lamming, R. (1993): Beyond Partnership. Strategies for Innovation and Lean Supply, Prentice Hall, New York.

Womack, J.P., Jones, D. T. (1996): Lean Thinking, Simon & Schuster, New York.

Organizational Settings in Supply Chain Costing

Maria Goldbach

1	Introduction	90
2	Conventional Cost Management	91
3	Supply Chain Costing	94
4	Organizational Settings in Supply Chain Costing	97
5	Summary and Perspectives	104
6	References	106

Summary:
Cost management in supply chains currently focuses on the functional level, i.e. the management of activities and transactions causing costs. The institutional level, i.e. the management of the decision makers, is equally crucial for the application of cost management in the supply chain, as its success depends upon the interactions between both the functional and institutional level. This paper presents two concepts for supply chain costing. Activity based supply chain costing provides a cooperative framework for cost management in supply chains. Supply chain target costing may serve either as a cooperative, i.e. trust-based, or a confrontative, i.e. power-based framework. The developed concepts are illustrated with an example from the textile industry.

Keywords:
Supply Chain Management, Cost Management, Supply Chain Relationships, Organizational Implications, Textile Industry

1 Introduction

Cost management in supply chains gains increasing importance for two major reasons

1. Competition between companies is more and more replaced by competition between supply chains.[1]
2. Additional cost optimization potentials can only be realized by managing the costs along the entire supply chain.[2]

Research for cost management in supply chains generally focuses on the costs related to activities and transactions. Even though relationships are considered to be one of the most important elements in supply chain management[3], the existing approaches merely focus on a functional level, discussing strategies and instruments. They do not take an integrated perspective, including reflections of cost management, from an institutional point of view. These are crucial for the application of cost management in the supply chain as its success depends upon the interactions between both the functional and institutional level. Cost management instruments and strategies have to be implemented by the involved actors which raises the question regarding the organizational implications of cost management concepts as well as the required organizational settings. This prompts a further question: Which different supply chain costing strategies and instruments organizational settings require and provoke?

This paper presents two supply chain costing concepts from an organizational perspective, supply chain target costing and activity based supply chain costing, with the objective to find out which organizational settings correspond to these instruments.[4]

In the first part, after some general remarks on cost management, the concepts of activity based costing and target costing are presented both from a conventional point of view as well as in the supply chain context. Following that, an analytic, organizational framework, agency theory is introduced.[5] The supply chain costing concepts are reflected in the background of agency theory. A combination of both concepts is discussed in this context. The theoretical reflections are illustrated with an example from the textile chain before the paper concludes with a summary and perspectives on further research.

---

[1] See Vollmann, Cordon, Raabe (1998); Christopher (1998), p. 28ff.
[2] See Cooper, Ellram (1993).
[3] See Handfield, Nichols (1999), p. 67-93.
[4] For a description of these concepts see Seuring (2001).
[5] For other approaches in new institutional economics see Pfaff, Weißenberger (2000).

2 Conventional Cost Management

2.1 The Scope of Cost Management

In order to manage costs, data required need to be collected by the involved actors. These data provide the necessary empirical basis for applying cost management instruments. Both cost data and cost management instruments as well as their combination need to be implemented and applied by the actors. Cost management instruments do not allow cost optimization due to their mere existence, just as a musical instrument does not make music by itself. They require actors or musicians which use or play the instruments in order to have the desired effect.

Figure 1: Organizational Setting in Cost Management.

The interaction of cost data, cost instruments and actors needs to be embedded in the organizational setting of the company and supply chain (see Figure 1).

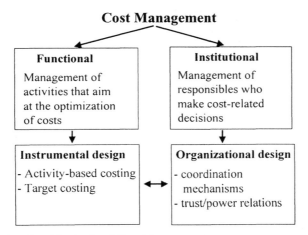

Figure 2: Functional and Institutional Cost Management.

Cost management can therefore be divided into a functional and an institutional dimension.[6] The functional dimension refers to the management of activities that aim at the optimization of costs. The institutional aspect alludes to the management responsiblefor cost-related decisions.

The functional dimension leads to the implementation of an instrumental design using cost management instruments such as activity based costing and target costing. The institutional aspect requires a suitable organizational design enabling cost management via co-ordination mechanisms as well as trust or power driven relations.

2.2 Activity-Based Costing

Activity-based costing (ABC)[7] is based on the idea that overhead costs are caused by different activities[8]. These activities are related to drivers which influence costs both in a positive and negative way. Glad and Becker define these cost drivers as *"the causal factors (such as business policy) that cause costs of an activity to change"*.[9] The objective of ABC is to attribute overhead costs more appropriately to total product costs by using cost drivers. Activities which do not contribute to final customer utility are identified and reduced or eliminated in order to optimize overhead costs. This permits better response to market demand and therefore increases competitiveness.

The concept of activity based costing is traditionally applied within a single company. If a firm purchases a good, e.g. yarn, the involved actors, i.e. the different departments (institutional dimension) identify the activities related to the purchasing of yarn (functional dimension). One of the main cost drivers in this example is the number of orders. This procedure permits differentiation between both value-adding and non value-adding activities. Purchasing yarn is value-adding.

Overhead: Activity-Based Costs

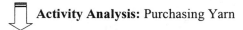
Activity Analysis: Purchasing Yarn

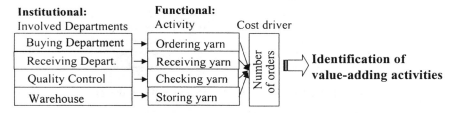

Figure 3: The Concept of Activity Based Costing.

---

[6] See Gräfe (1997), p. 168.
[7] See Cooper (1988); Franz (1992), p. 606.
[8] See Coenenberg, Fischer (1991), p. 25.
[9] See Glad, Becker (1997), p. 23.

From an organizational perspective, the activities and related critical cost drivers are jointly identified, discussed and classified by the departments involved in the process of purchasing yarn within the company.

2.3 Target Costing

Target costing takes up the idea of customer satisfaction, starting from the assumed market price of a product. This implies the analysis of value-cost relations in target costing:[10] *"An ideal resource input is therefore to put resources in, the way it corresponds to the desired product value relations of the customer"*.[11]

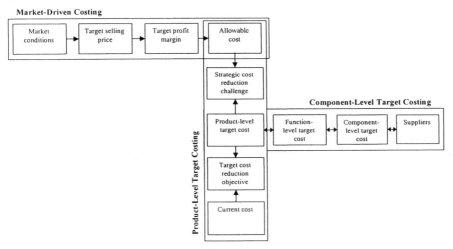

Figure 4: The Concept of Target Costing.[12]

This refers to the management of the cost-related activities (functional). Having set the market price, e.g. through marketing analyses, competitor analyses etc.[13], the company, more specifically the management responsible, fix the desired margin they would like to obtain (institutional). Subtracting the margin from the market price, it acquires the costs a product should cause, resulting in the so-called allowable costs. This procedure is called market-driven costing. In a second step, the costs a product is susceptible to cause, called standard or current costs, are calculated. These current product costs are then confronted with the allowable ones. If a difference occurs, which is rather probable in practice, the firm has to take measures to adjust costs. Generally, the standard costs will exceed the allowable

---

[10] See Horvath, Seidenschwarz (1992), p. 143.
[11] Horvath, Seidenschwarz (1992), p. 145, translation by the author.
[12] Cooper, Slagmulder (1999), p. 166.
[13] See Freidank (1993), p. 394.

ones, which means that the firm has to take actions to reduce the current costs. *"It's got to sell for x. Let's work backwards to make sure we can achieve it."*[14] The measures to be taken can be divided into procedures of product and component-level target costing (functional). These are carried out by the different departments within a company (institutional). Among the different possibilities of adjusting allowable and standard costs is ABC which will be discussed in section 4.4.[15]

From an organizational perspective, the actors in the departments of a company aim at adapting their internal costs to the market requirements.

3 Supply Chain Costing

3.1 The Scope of Supply Chain Costing

The scope of conventional cost management is a single firm. The basic idea of cost management in supply chains is to extend the cost management approach to the entire supply chain which implies an approach beyond organizational boundaries.

Three authors have largely contributed to the development of a concept for supply chain costing, Cooper/Slagmulder[16] and Seuring[17]. As in conventional cost management, they consider both the direct and indirect or activity-based costs of the product .Moreover, they take into account the costs of the network, especially the costs that occur from the management of supply chain relationships. In this context, Seuring introduces the so-called transaction costs as a third level of costs (direct – activity-based – transaction costs)[18]. They are defined as information and coordination costs which occur in the negotiation, control and adaptation of mutual transaction relations.[19] They are caused through the interaction of the different supply chain partners and may therefore only be influenced jointly.[20]

---

[14] Worthy (1991), p. 50.
[15] See Freidank (1993), p. 394 and Mayer (1993), p. 79.
[16] See Cooper, Slagmulder (1999).
[17] See Seuring (2001). Shank/Govindarajan have equally largely contributed to strategic cost management, even though they focus mainly on the cost driver perspective. Shank, Govindarajan (1993).
[18] See Seuring (2001), p. 168-216.
[19] Definition according to Seuring (2001), p. 116.
[20] A obstacle in management practice is that transaction costs are very difficult to quantify so that so far, their integration into supply chain costing merely stays on a conceptual level. See Seuring (2001).

Organisational Settings in Supply Chain Costing   95

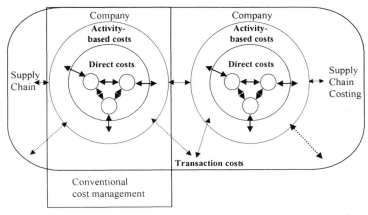

Figure 5: Scope of Conventional Cost Management and Supply Chain Costing.[21]

Supply chain costing aims at the identification of cost optimization activities and transactions along the entire chain by the involved actors both within the company and the supply chain.

3.2 Activity-Based Supply Chain Costing

ABC in supply chains aims at optimizing total product costs by analysing overhead costs based on both activities and transactions taking a chain-wide perspective. Therefore, in activity-based supply chain costing, both the overhead costs on firm level (activity costs) which have been presented in the conventional scope, as well as on supply chain level (transaction costs) need to be analysed. The transaction costs are analysed according to the transactions linked to them (meeting a customer/supplier, negotiating a contract etc.).

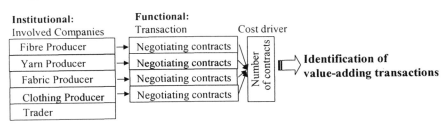

Figure 6: Transaction Based Costs in Activity Based Supply Chain Costing.[22]

---

[21] Based on Seuring (2001), p. 115.

The transactions and activities[23] as well as their related cost drivers are jointly identified, discussed and classified by the companies and departments involved in purchasing yarn within the chain member companies.

3.3 Supply Chain Target Costing

Target costing in supply chains equally extends the scope of cost management to the entire chain.[24] Taking the conventional procedure of target costing, the scope of action within one firm ends with component level target costing. On this level, the chain perspective comes into play. The costs identified on the component level serve as the market target costs for the upstream supplier. This effect goes down all the way through the chain up to the raw materials suppliers.[25]

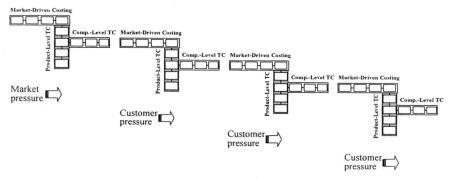

Figure 7: The Concept of Supply Chain Target Costing.[26]

Final customer requirements are identified and communicated back into the chain. The market pressure which serves as the basis of the market target price is translated into customer pressure from the second level in the supply chain.

The actors representing the companies of the supply chain as well as the responsible of departments within the company aim at adapting chain-wide costs to market requirements, equally taking into account internal costs.

---

22 Own.
23 See figure 3.
24 Target costing in supply chains has been described by a multitude of authors such as Ellram (2000); Lockamy, Smith (2000) and Cooper, Slagmulder (1999) and Seuring (2001).
25 See limits discussed in Cooper, Slagmulder (1999).
26 Based on Cooper, Slagmulder (1999).

4 Organizational Settings in Supply Chain Costing

4.1 An Organizational Perspective On Supply Chains

"Organizations are continually faced with the challenge of managing the 'people' part of the equation. [...] A number of supply chain initiatives fail however due to poor communication of expectations and resulting behaviors that occur. [...], the management of interpersonal relationships between the different people in the organizations is often the most difficult part." [27]

Agency theory[28] provides an analytical framework for the analysis of relationships in supply chain management.[29] It takes into consideration complexity and uncertainty of the environment as well as interest conflicts and information asymmetries between the supply chain partners involved in the transactions. Jensen/Meckling define *"an agency relationship as a contract under which one or more persons (the principal(s)) engage another person (the agent) to perform some service on their behalf which involves delegating some decision making authority to the agent."*[30] The agent disposes of a greater knowledge and specialization than the principal. Therefore, the principal uses the agent's lead of know-how to achieve better performance and increased utility for himself.[31] As a result of his services, the agent receives a payment in monetary form.[32] The objective in agency relations is to reduce uncertainty and complexity in transactions and by this reduce costs.

The actors in agency theory are utility maximisers who dispose of preferences and act in a rational way. But, in extension to the conventional *homo oeconomicus*, the actors only behave rationally within certain limits.[33]

Considering the basic assumptions concerning the characteristics of the actors (information asymmetries and interest conflicts), opportunistic behavior becomes likely. *"If both parties to the relationship are utility maximizers, there is a good reason to believe that the agent will not always act in the best interests of the principal".*[34] Due to this, two interacting problems called agency problems arise:

---

[27] Handfield, Nichols (1999), p. 67.
[28] For an introduction to agency theory see Ebers, Gotsch (1995); Jensen, Meckling (1976); Richter, Furubotn (1999).
[29] See Goldbach (2000), (2001).
[30] Jensen, Meckling (1976), p. 308.
[31] Another reason could be the limited temporal responsibility or the setting of priorities through the principal.
[32] See Pratt, Zeckhauser (1991), p. 2.
[33] Simon describes this phenomenon as bounded rationality. The bounded rational actor searches „*very selectively through large realms of possibilities in order to discover what alternatives of action are available, and what the consequences of each of these alternatives are. The search is incomplete, often inadequate, based on uncertain information and partial ignorance [...]*". Simon (1985), p. 294.
[34] Jensen, Meckling (1976), p. 308.

1. Interest conflicts describe the diverging interests of the involved actors and result from their different roles in the relationship and differing preferences.
2. Information asymmetries occur when both actors do not dispose of the same information. They result from great uncertainty and complexity in the actors' environment as well as their bounded rationality.

Only the simultaneous occurrence of information asymmetries and interest conflicts causes the so called agency problems. On the one hand, interest conflicts only become a problem when no possibility of entire action control, necessarily based on complete information, exists. On the other hand, information asymmetries only lead to opportunistic behaviour when interest conflicts between the actors occur.

There are three kinds of mechanisms capable of breaking the vicious circle of information asymmetries and interest conflicts to solve agency problems. Control is an explicit contractual measure which aims at reducing opportunistic behaviour by reducing information asymmetries between the involved partners. It reflects a confrontative attitude from the principal towards the agent in which the former plays on power. Incentives are equally explicit contractual measures which aim at reducing interest conflicts between the actors by inducing win-win solutions. This approach is characterized by a cooperative attitude of the principal towards the agent. Trust aims at reducing both information asymmetries and interest conflicts. It is defined as the voluntary production of performance, refraining from explicit coordination measures against opportunistic behaviour, expecting that the other will not behave opportunistically in spite of lacking protective measures.[35] This mechanism reflects a cooperative attitude between the partners.[36]

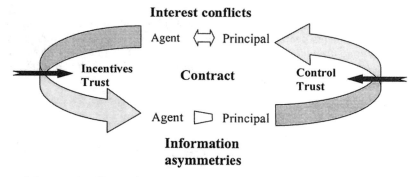

Figure 8: Interest Conflicts and Information Asymmetries in Agency Relationships.

---

[35] See Ripperger (1998), p. 45.
[36] The problems of information asymmetry and interest conflicts increase when taking into consideration the entire supply chain. In general, a trader will be better informed about the interests of his direct supplier than about the interests of the raw material supplier. See Goldbach (2001), p. 34.
This remark is not examined any further in this work, though.

The analysis criteria related to the agency relationship may be categorized as follows[37]:

- Cooperative ⇔ confrontative strategy
- Trust/incentives ⇔ control as coordination mechanisms
- Trust-based ⇔ power-based relationship
- Win-win solutions ⇔ win-lose solutions

These criteria will serve as a basis for the organizational analysis of the two supply chain costing instruments in the following.

4.2 Organizational Settings in Activity-Based Supply Chain Costing

In activity-based supply chain costing, the activity-based costs (functional) lie primarily in the responsibility of the departments of each single supply chain member (institutional), characterized by internal agency relationships which are not further investigated. The transaction-based costs (functional) though, are a common responsibility of all companies in the supply chain (institutional). It is difficult to specify who is the principal and who the agent in the relationship. Both partners seem to hold a double role of being principal and agent at the same time or alternatively changing roles. Both actors define their expected performance towards the other partner while at the same time fulfilling the requirements of the latter. This means that they identify, discuss and classify the cost drivers of their transactions within the supply chain jointly.[38] The relation between the two actors involved can be described as cooperative. The underlying coordination mechanisms are trust and incentives with the entire relationship being based on trust. The objective is to realise win-win solutions (see figure 9):

Hence, activity-based supply chain costing seems to be an ideal concept in supply chain costing from an organizational point of view.

---

[37] The presented criteria describe two extremes between which hybrid constellations are of course possible.

[38] The image of man underlying the activity-based supply chain costing is therefore that of an intelligent, motivated human being that requires some freedom to develop full productivity. See McGregor (1960), p. 33ff and 47f.

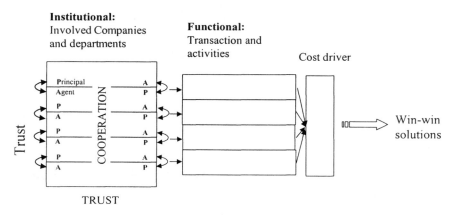

Figure 9: Organizational Activity-Based Supply Chain Costing

4.3 Organizational Settings in Supply Chain Target Costing

In supply chain target costing, the upstream members of the chain take the roles of agents and the downstream members act as principals. The objective of supply chain target costing consists in achieving a fixed market target price through adaptation of value-cost relations throughout the entire supply chain. With the allowable costs being set by subtracting the desired profit margin from the market price (functional), the involved partners throughout the entire supply chain then must try to achieve this cost target (institutional). The supply chain partner closest to final customers generally determines the market target price[39]. Therefore, he is the most powerful partner in the chain and thus destined to play the principal's role. There exist two strategies which the principal may follow:

1. A cooperative strategy,
2. A confrontative strategy.

The cooperative strategy is reflected in *"It's got to sell for x. Let's work backwards to make sure we can achieve it"*[40]. This citation assumes a joint effort of the actors in the chain by use of the word "us".

---

[39] This depends on the industry sector though. In the textile industry this is usually the trader whereas in the automobile industry the producer is the one to fix the price.
[40] Worthy (1991), p. 50.

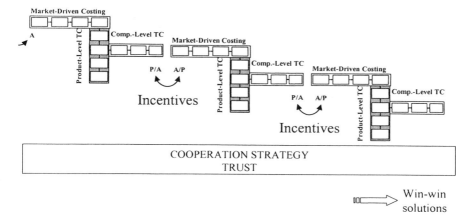

Figure 10: Cooperative Supply Chain Target Costing.

In the cooperative strategy, the principal sets a common objective, determining the allowable costs as usual, and incentives to all his partners including himself. In the case of diverging allowable and standard costs all actors develop cost reduction potentials jointly to solve the difference. Both the principal and the suppliers participate in the effort. Any divergences or related problems are discussed and solved within the supply chain with the objective to adapt to market requirements chain-wide. Responsibility is shared between buyer (principal) and supplier (agent). The entire relationship is based on cooperation and trust, encouraging win-win solutions. This strategy is equally called trust-based supply chain target costing.

The confrontative strategy is characterized by the principal using his power to exploit his partners. *"It's got to sell for x. I'll make the others work to make sure that I can achieve it"*[41]. The principal determines the allowable costs according to the usual procedure. If the standard costs exceed these, he pushes the target through the chain by passing the allowable costs on to his component suppliers. Without undertaking any effort himself to match the two cost positions, he puts his supplier under pressure to fulfil cost targets instead of jointly analysing the origins of higher costs. The entire responsibility is passed on to the suppliers.[42]

The following downstream buyers may behave the same towards their suppliers. The principal tries to control the other chain members' activities by using his power. This provokes win-lose situations. This strategy is called power-based supply chain target costing.

---

[41] Own, based on Worthy (1991), p. 50.

[42] The image of man related to this strategy is rather a tayloristic one which assumes that human beings are stupid, lazy and listless by nature and thus require central guiding and intensive external controls. See McGregor (1960), p. 33ff, 47f.

102   M. Goldbach

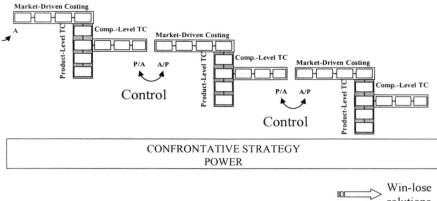

Figure 11: Confrontative Supply Chain Target Costing.

Supply chain target costing is a suitable instrument if the cooperative strategy is applied using coordination mechanisms such as incentives and trust. In the confrontative case, the concept is doomed to fail either because all partners try to pass on responsibility to their supplier which hinders the realization of chain wide cost saving potentials or because the partners in the chain refuse to be patronized and thus collaborate.

4.4 Combining Activity-Based Supply Chain Costing and Supply Chain Target Costing

ABC and target costing are cost management instruments in supply chains which do not have to be applied alternatively, but may complement each other. As displayed in the table below, both activity-based costing and target costing may be based on cooperation, incentive and trust, generating win-win solutions.

In this context, supply chain target costing can be viewed as the shell which takes up market signals and customer requirements through the market price.[43] A certain pressure is built up in the chain, which if exerted to all chain partners at rather equal intensity, may have a positive effect. Activity-based costing serves as a tool that supports each partner as well as the whole of the partners in analysing and optimizing overhead costs jointly.[44]

---

[43] Cooper and Slagmulder attribute activity-based costing to the enabling mechanisms and target costing to the disciplining ones. The disciplining mechanisms translate customer requirements into allowable cost which represent the cost target for the supply chain as a whole as well as on each level throughout the chain. (See Cooper, Slagmulder (1999), p. 10-11).

[44] In this work, jointly shall imply cooperation between the actors. Confrontative constellations in joint approaches may occur, but they are not further investigated in this paper.

	Activity based costing	Target costing
Strategy	Cooperation	Confrontation
Co-ordination mechanism	Incentive	Control
Relationship base	Trust	Power
Solution	Win-win	Win-lose

Table 1: Comparison of Activity Based Costing and Target Costing in Supply Chains.

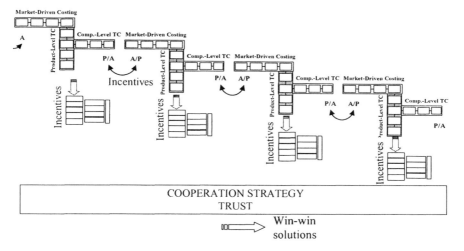

Figure 12: Cooperative Supply Chain Costing.

The combination of both supply chain costing concepts seems to be most appropriate to cooperative supply chain relationships. The cost target which is set by the final customer, who can be characterized as the hidden chain-wide principal, serves as an incentive. The cooperative character of both concepts, assuming that the cooperative and not the confrontative target costing strategy is chosen, feeds trust as the basis of supply chain costing.

So far, the paper pointed out that activity-based costing and trust-based target costing have to be based on cooperative buyer-supplier relationships. Co-operation is not only a prerequisite for supply chain relationships, it also enforces the organizational setting of supply chain costing. Therefore the relation is a circular one. The same applies to the confrontative strategy of supply chain target costing. A confrontative relationship both feeds the functioning of power-based target costing. Confrontative behaviour is fed by the mechanisms of this instrument.

4.5 An Example from the Textile Industry

The theoretical reflections will be illustrated with an example from the textile industry. Two clothing traders want to introduce ecologically optimized clothes to the textile mass market. As ecological optimizations do not add value to the product from the consumers' perspective, the price (as well as design, functionality, etc.) need to be equivalent to the conventional one.

The textile chain of the two traders is designed as follows:

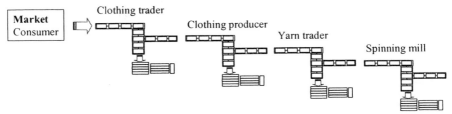

Figure 13: Supply Chain Costing in the Textile Chain.

The traders follow different strategies. Trader A holds regular meetings about three times a year with all partners in the chain. All of the involved actors within the textile chain identify, discuss and classify cost drivers jointly and design cost optimization strategies in order to respond to market requirements. The actors are motivated to cooperate and set internal incentives to achieve the common objective. The relationships are based on a profound basis of trust which generates win-win solutions while achieving the desired market price.

In the chain of trader B, only dyadic meetings along the chain are set up more or less regularly. The chain-wide adaptation to market requirements is therefore impeded. The realization of the target is assured via internal control measures. There exists no sufficient basis of trust between the partners. This constellation generates win-lose solutions without achieving the desired market price.

5 Summary and Perspectives

This paper discussed the question which organizational settings activity-based supply chain costing and supply chain target costing require and provoke. In a first step, the concepts of activity-based costing and target costing were presented and classified according to their functional and institutional implications. The interaction between the actors and the cost management instruments were reflected in the light of organizational settings. From an organizational point of view, activity-based costing is based on the joint discussion and analysis of cost drivers by the involved actors. Target costing aims at the joint realization of a target price set by the market. The implications of the application of the two concepts to supply chains were presented, the major difference in comparison to conventional cost management being the extension of the scope from a single company to the entire supply chain. In order to analyse how these instruments reflect the actors' behaviour, agency theory was introduced as an analytical framework. Using this, activity-based costing was described as cooperative, using incentives and trust as coordination mechanisms, and relying on trust. In target costing though, both a cooperative and confrontative strategy exist. The former is rather similar in its characteristics to activity-based costing, while the latter is characterized by confrontation, uses control as a coordination mechanism and is based on power. In the following step, cooperative or trust-based target costing and activity based costing were integrated. The example from the textile industry illustrated both target costing strategies.

The paper leaves the following aspects and questions open:

- In analysing the agency relationships in supply chains, all partners are considered to be of equal importance. This does not reflect a company's reality as there are always some customers and suppliers who are less or more important than others.[45]
- The work merely focuses on two chosen cost management techniques. Other instruments may be analysed using this framework.
- The integration of transaction costs is a problem in so far as they can hardly be quantified in practice. Thus they merely serve currently as an analytical differentiation.[46]
- This paper only focuses on the action and behavior of the actors but not on the structure which enables or hinders the effects of cost management. This equally leads to the question how cooperative (or confrontative) behavior may actively be induced and influenced.[47]
- Last, but not least, the findings are mainly based on theoretical reflections which have not been tested in practice on a large scale. In order to verify the framework, more intense empirical research needs to be carried out.

The presented work gives an impression of the organizational implications of supply chain costing, spanning at the same time a large variety of future research perspectives.

---

[45] For an example of relationship portfolios see e.g. Sinclair, Hunter, Beaumont (1996), Olsen, Ellram (1997) and Bensaou (1999).
[46] See Seuring (2001); Cooper, Slagmulder (1999).
[47] See Kajüter (1997), (2000).

6 References

Bensaou, M. (1999): Portfolios of Buyer-Supplier Relationships, in: Sloan Management Review, Vol. 40, No. 4 (1999), p. 35-44.

Christopher, M.(1998): Logistics and Supply Chain Management, 2.$^{ed.}$ Edition, Pearson Education Limited, London London.

Coenenberg, A. G., Fischer, T. M. (1991): Prozesskostenrechnung – Strategische Neuorientierung in der Kostenrechnung (Activity Based Costing – A Strategic New Orientation in Cost Accounting), in: Die Betriebswirtschaft (1991) 1, p. 21-38.

Cooper, R. (1988): The Rise of Activity-Based Costing – Part One: What Is an Activity-Based Costing System?, in: Journal of Cost Management, Vol. 2, Summer (1988), p. 45-54.

Cooper, M. C., Ellram, L. M. (1993): Characteristics of Supply Chain Management and the Implications for Purchasing and Logistics Strategy, in: The International Journal of Logistics Management, Vol. 4, No. 2, (1993), p. 13-24.

Cooper, R., Kaplan, R. S. (1991): Activity-Based Costing: Resource Management at Its Best, HARVARDmanager, No. 4 (1991), p. 87-94.

Cooper, R., Slagmulder, R. (1999): Supply Chain Management for the Lean Enterprise - Interorganisational Cost Management, IMA Foundation for Applied Research, Montvale.

Dörnemann, J., Pfitzer, J. (2000): Motivationsförderung durch Anreizsysteme im Target Costing (Motivation Stimulation Via Incentive Systems in Target Costing), Kostenrechnungspraxis, Vol. 44, No. 1 (2000), p. 25-30.

Ebers, M., Gotsch, W. (1995): Institutionenökonomische Theorien der Organisation (Institutional Economic Theories of Organisation), in: Kieser, A. (ed.): Organisationstheorien, Kohlhammer, Stuttgart, Berlin, Köln

Ellram, L. M. (2000): Purchasing and Supply Management's Participation in the Target Costing Process, in: The Journal of Supply Chain Management, Vol. 36, No. 2 (2000), p. 39-52.

Franz, K.-P. (1992): Die Prozesskostenrechnung – Entstehungsgründe, Aufbau und Abgrenzung von anderen Kostenrechnungssystemen (Activity Based Costing – Causes of Emergence, Structure and Differentiation of Other Cost Accounting Systems), in: Wirtschaftswissenschaftliches Studium, Vol. 12, December (1992), p. 605-610.

Franz, K.-P. (1993): Target Costing – Konzept und kritische Bereiche (Target Costing – Concept and Critical Areas), Controlling, No. 3, May/Juni (1993), p. 124-130.

Freidank, C.-Ch. (1993): Die Prozesskostenrechnung als strategisches Instrument des Kostenmanagements, in: Unternehmung, Vol. 47, No. 5 (1993), p. 387-405.

Glad, E., Becker, H. (1997): Activity-Based Costing and Management, John Wiley & Sons, Chichester.

Goldbach, M. (2000): Organisational Impacts On Supply Chain Costing, Paper presented at the 1st PhD Summer Academy at the University of St Gallen, 11th-15th September 2000, St Gallen.

Goldbach, M. (2001): Akteursbeziehungen in nachhaltigen Wertschöpfungsketten (Actors' Relationships in Sustainable Supply Chains), Diskussionsbeitrag Nr. 3, Chair for Production and the Environment, University of Oldenburg, Oldenburg. (Internet-homepage http://www.uni-oldenburg.de/produktion).

Gräfe, Ch. (1997): Kostenmanagement von Produktinnovationen (Cost Management of Product Innovations), in: Kostenrechnungspraxis, Vol. 41, No. 3 (1997), p. 169-171.

Handfield, R. B., Nichols, E. L. Jr. (1999): Introduction to Supply Chain Management, Prentice Hall, Upper Saddle River, New Jersey.

Horváth, P. (ed.): Target Costing – marktorientierte Zielkosten in der deutschen Praxis (Target Costing – Market-Oriented Target Costs in German Practice), Schaeffer-Poeschel, Stuttgart, p. 75-92.

Horváth, P., Seidenschwarz, W. (1992): Zielkostenmanagement (Target Costing), Controlling, Vol. 3, No. 3, Mai/Juni 1992, p. 142-150.

Jensen, M. C., Meckling, W. H. (1976): Theory of the Firm: Managerial Behavior, Agency Costs and Ownership Structure, in: Journal of Financial Economics, No. 3 (1976), p. 305-360.

Kajüter, P. (1997): Unternehmenskultur: Erfolgsfaktor für das Kostenmanagement (Corporate Culture: Success Factor for Cost Management), in: Franz, K.-P., Kajüter, P. (ed.): Kostenmanagement – Wettbewerbsvorteile durch systematische Kostensteuerung (Cost Management – Competitive Advantages Through Systematic Cost Controlling), Schäffer-Poeschel Verlag, Stuttgart, p. 81-98.

Kajüter, P. (2000): Proaktives Kostenmanagement (Proactive Cost Management), Gabler, Wiesbaden.

Lockamy, A., Smith, W. I. (2000): Target Costing for Supply Chain Management: Criteria and Selection, Industrial Management and Data Systems, Vol. 100, No. 5 (2000), p. 210-218.

Mayer, R. (1993): Target Costing und die Prozesskostenrechnung (Target Costing and Activity-Based Costing), in: Horváth, P. (ed.): Target Costing – marktorientierte Zielkosten in der deutschen Praxis (Target Costing – Market Oriented Target Costs in German Practice), Stuttgart, p. 75-92.

Mc Gregor, D. (1960): The Human Side of Enterprise, McGraw-Hill, New York.

Olsen, R. F., Ellram, L. M. (1997): A Portfolio Approach to Supplier Relationships, in: Industrial Marketing Management, Vol. 26, No. 2 (1997), p. 101-113.

Pfaff, D., Weißenberger, B. E. (ed.) (2000): Institutionenökonomische Fundierung (Institutional Economic Foundation), in: Fischer, T. M. (Hg.): Kostencontrolling - Neue Methoden und Inhalte (Cost Controlling – New Methods and Contents), Schaeffer-Poeschel, Stuttgart, p. 109-134.

Pratt, J. W., Zeckhauser, R. J. (1991): Principals and Agents: An Overview, in Pratt, Jo.W.; Zeckhauser, R. J (Hg.): Principals and Agents: The Structure of Business, Harvard Business School Press, Boston, Massachussetts.

Richter, R., Furubotn, E. (1999): Neue Institutionenökonomik, Eine Einführung und kritische Würdigung (New Institutional Economics, An Introduction and Critical Acknowledgement) , Mohr, Siebeck, Tübingen.

Ripperger, T. (1998): Die Ökonomik des Vertrauens (The Economics of Trust), Mohr, Siebeck, Tübingen.

Seuring, S. (2001): Supply Chain Costing – Kostenmanagement in der Wertschöpfungskette mit Target Costing und Prozesskostenrechnung (Supply Chain Costing with Target Costing and Activity Based Costing), Verlag Franz Vahlen, München.

Shank, G. (1993): Strategic Cost Management – The New Tool for Competitive Advantage, Free Press, New York.

Simon, H. A. (1985): Human Nature in Politics: The Dialogue of Psychology with Political Science, The American Political Science Review, Vol. 79, No. 2 (1985), p. 293-304.

Sinclair, D., Hunter, L., Beaumont, P. (1996): Models of Customer-Supplier Relations, Journal of General Management, Vol. 22, No. 2, Winter (1996), p. 56-75.

Vollmann, T. E., Cordon, C., Raabe, H. (1998): Das Management von Lieferketten (The Management of Supply Chains), in: IMD / LBS / Wharton (Hrsg.): Das MBA-Buch: Mastering Management - Die Studieninhalte führender Business Schools, Schäffer-Poeschel Verlag, Stuttgart.

Worthy, F. S. (1991): Japan's Smart Secret Weapon, in: Fortune, August 12 (1991), p. 48-51.

Part 2
Applying Cost Management Instruments

Supply Chain Target Costing – An Apparel Industry Case Study

Stefan Seuring

1	Introduction	112
2	Supply Chain Costing	112
3	Target Costing in Supply Chain Management	114
4	Apparel Industry Case Study	118
5	Conclusion	124
6	References	124

Summary:
The increasing interest in supply chain management needs the development of tools that help companies coordinate their activities starting at the beginning of the product design process, such as target costing. While the integration of suppliers into the target costing process has long been established, it mainly has been limited to setting cost targets to suppliers. The costs of building and maintaining relationships with suppliers have not been taken into account. Hence, it is necessary to develop an approach that integrates target costing and supply chain costing. This paper provides a short summary of target costing methodology and reviews the literature on its connections to supply chain management. Then, the three cost levels of supply chain costing, namely direct, activity-based and transaction costs are integrated into target costing. Finally, a case study from the apparel industry is presented to illustrate the concept of supply chain target costing.

Keywords:
Supply Chain Management, Target Costing, Transaction Cost, Textile Industry

1 Introduction

One of the main reasons for the rise of supply chain management is seen in increased global competition that leads to competition between supply chains. Hence, co-operation between supply chain partners needs tools, that are able to transform market pressure from the end of the chain into managerial objectives along the chain. Among the objectives of supply chain management, the reduction of total costs is a frequently stated objective.[1] Yet, examples are rarely offered on how these objectives are set and how they might be reached.

Target costing is a cost management technique allowing transform of market pressure into product design process inside companies. Furthermore, it has been shown that the methodology of target costing can be applied to other managerial situations, e.g. reducting production cost of existing products by redesigning production.[2] In earlier papers on target costing, the importance of supplier integration was addressed.[3] This makes target costing a suitable instrument for supply chain management.

Furthermore, the issues that are addressed among the term "cost" highlight, that usually only direct costs are taken into account. Within supply chain management, a broader perspective on cost management has to be taken,[4] to integrate all relevant issues, as is done by recent developments in supply chain costing.[5] Hence, within this paper, concept of supply chain target costing will be presented, which merges the supply chain costing and target costing. Its application will be portrayed by a case study from the apparel industry.

2 Supply Chain Costing

2.1 Definition of Supply Chain Management

Within increasingly competitive environments, single companies are not able to survive on their own, but only as part of a supply or value chain, a concept that has gained importance since its introduction by Porter.[6] Together with recent developments in logistics and information technology, it forms the basis for the

---

[1] See e.g. Stevens (1989), p. 3; LaLonde/Pohlen (1996), p. 1; Christopher (1998), p. 25.
[2] See Shank, Fisher (1999).
[3] See Seidenschwarz, Niemand (1994), p. 262.
[4] See LaLonde, Pohlen (1996), p. 1; Smith, Lockamy (2000), p. 68.
[5] See Seuring (2001a); Seuring (2001b).
[6] See Porter (1998).

concept of supply chain management (SCM). "The supply chain encompasses all activities associated with the flow and transformation of goods from raw materials stage (extraction), through to the end user, as well as the associated information flows. Material and information flow both up and down the supply chain. Supply chain management is the integration of these activities through improved supply chain relationships, to achieve a sustainable competitive advantage."[7]

The definition given by Handfield and Nichols highlights that both the management of material and information flows and the management of co-operations along the supply chain have to be taken into account. Hence, the cost associated with this have to be integrated into supply chain costing, which is a cost management technique that allows analysis and control of all costs in a supply chain.[8]

2.2 Cost Levels in Supply Chain Costing

Traditional cost accounting is not prepared to actively manage costs, which has led to the development of cost management techniques that are used to support specific decisions and the overall management of organizations.[9] Still, most cost management techniques look at the internal cost of companies, especially direct and indirect costs. Activity-based costing[10] provides an alternative approach to the allocation of indirect costs among products. Strategic cost management[11] has emphasized the importance of costs within the value chain, but the discussion of cost drivers stays on a general level. Therefore, instruments are needed allowing for the classification of costs within the supply chain, as displayed in Figure 1.

Supply chain costing, defined as a cost management concept, allows analysis and control all costs in a supply chain and takes into account three cost levels:[12]

1. Direct costs, which include such costs as materials, labour and machine costs.

2. Activity-based costs, which arise from the organizational framework and the operational and administrative processes of the company.

3. Transaction costs, which cover the interactions with other companies in the supply chain.

---

[7] Handfield, Nichols (1999), p. 2.
[8] Seuring (2001a), p. 122.
[9] See Franz, Kajüter (1997); Hilton, Maher, Selto (2000).
[10] See Kaplan, Cooper (1997).
[11] See Shank, Govindarajan (1993).
[12] See Seuring (2001a), p. 115; and the paper on supply chain costing in this volume: Seuring (2002), p. 15-30.

114   S. Seuring

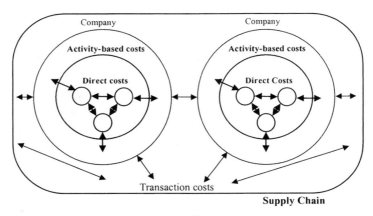

Figure 1: Cost Levels in Supply Chain Costing[13]

The three cost levels provide a basis for the analysis and optimization of costs in the supply chain. For achieving a certain cost level, target costing has been developed. The concepts of target costing and supply chain costing are to be merged with each other.

3 Target Costing in Supply Chain Management

3.1 Target Costing Methodology

Target costing has seen a wide range of applications since it first was developed at Toyota in the sixties.[14] Target costing aims to translate customer requirements into binding competitive constraints that must be met by all processes involved ensuring that future products generate profits.[15] Target costing is rather a management instrument than an accounting technique, so costs are set and not reported. The methodology of target costing can be summarized in three steps, as Figure 2 displays.[16]

---

[13] Seuring (1999), p. 22.
[14] See Tanaka (1993), p. 4.
[15] See Monden (1995), p. 11; Cooper, Slagmulder (1997), p. 8; Ansari, Bell (1997), p. 2.
[16] See Cooper, Slagmulder (1997), p. 11 and 74.

1. Market-driven costing

All products have to satisfy customer demands, which therefore should drive product development. To avoid products that are too costly compared to the customers' willingness to pay, cost targets are deduced. This market-driven costing sets a product's maximum selling price. By subtracting the target profit margin, the allowable costs of the product are obtained.

2. Product-level target costing

Within the product-level target costing, the allowable costs are compared to the current cost, which result from using available design and production technologies. Usually, the current costs will exceed the allowable costs, so cost reductions are necessary.

3. Component-level target costing

For each component of the product, a comparison between its importance to the customer and its costs are made. The component-level target costs can form the basis for contracting with suppliers, hence pushing the cost pressure along the supply chain.

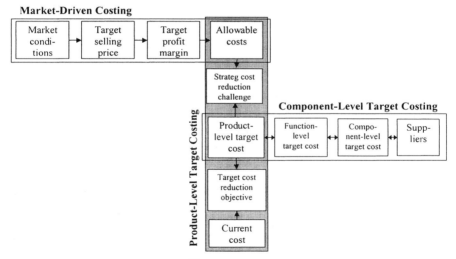

Figure 2: The Target Costing Process[17]

After this description of target costing, the literature concerning the integration of target costing in supply chains or suppliers into target costing is reviewed.

---

[17] Cooper, Slagmulder (1999), p. 162.

3.2 Literature Review

Even in early papers on target costing, the integration of suppliers plays an important role. Four major contributions can be found which will be summarized.

1. Supplier Integration in Target Costing[18]

Seidenschwarz and Niemand show how target costing can be used for supplier management. Component-level target costs are transferred on to them. The more important the part delivered is for the whole product, the earlier the supplier has to be integrated into the product design process. The resulting supplier cost engineering uses a project orientated management to achieve step by step cost reductions until the set target costs are reached.

2. Target Costing in the Extended Enterprise[19]

Ansari and Bell describe target costing in the extended enterprise. They emphasize, that target costing is not about passing on market pressure, but getting involved with supply chain partners so that each company can maintain its profitability. Suppliers are involved in all stages of the design process, so that for example a reduction in lead time from a concurrent supplier engineering can be reached. As in the paper of Seidenschwarz and Niemand,[20] a segmentation of suppliers is presented that is based on the mutual dependence of supplier and buyer. Finally, they point out the importantance of the development of long-term supplier relations is.

3. Chained Target Costing[21]

Cooper and Slagmulder introduce the term chained target costing. Within this concept, target costing is used as a disciplining mechanism helping to keep suppliers on track to reach the function, quality and price goals set jointly. One basic issue discussed is the power distribution among supply chain members. On the distribution side, this might be limited by customers that have little power, on the supplier side, this might be limited by suppliers that are immune to target costing pressure.[22] Regarding so-called function-price-quality trade-offs, it is addressed that target costing is a dynamic process. It might be necessary to relax cost constraints temporarily to allow suppliers to stay in the market. Throughout the book, the close relationship of target costing to other cost management instruments (e.g. kaizen costing, value engineering) is shown where the application of various techniques is needed for an interorganizational cost management.

---

[18] See Seidenschwarz, Niemand (1994), p. 262-270.
[19] Ansari, Bell (1997), p. 79-97.
[20] See Seidenschwarz, Niemand (1994), p. 264.
[21] See Cooper, Slagmulder (1999), p. 181-232.
[22] See Cooper, Slagmulder (1999), p. 210.

4. Target Costing for Supply Chain Management[23]

The framework offered by Lokamy and Smith "combines the two market variables customer requirements and supply chain agility to define strategies for performing target costing".[24] Three strategies are distinguished.[25] The activity-based costing approach serves as an integration tool in stable markets so that an effective collaboration along the chain is ensured. The price-based approach is applied if the supply chain operates in a stable environment with stable value propositions but changing customer requirements. Target costing is used to make certain that market-prices are not exceed at each stage of the chain, but also guarantees that each member of the chain gets a share of the profit. In rapidly changing environments where customer demands are diverse, a value-based approach is taken. A quick reconfiguration of the supply chain is needed to keep up with customer demand. The members of the supply chain that are most capable of performing the required tasks have to be identified. In total, the allowable costs have to be allocated in proportion to the customer value created.

The four different approaches allow taking the market environment into account, but do not allow differentiation of cost levels. While the integration of activity-based cost data is mentioned,[26] the cost of building and maintaining supplier relations as covered by transaction costs is not included.

3.3 Integrating the Three Cost Levels into Target Costing

To allow the separate management of the three cost levels, they must be incorporated into the target costing methodology. Looking at the three steps taken, it is evident that market-driven costing forms the basis for all further cost reduction objectives.

Yet these cost reductions cannot be obtained, by tackling the product level target costs, which mainly focus on the direct costs of the product parts. Suppliers are integrated by setting objectives for them, leaving it up to them how they would achieve these targets. Still, the co-operation with suppliers causes activity-based and transaction costs, so these levels can be used for cost reductions, too (see Figure 3).

---

[23] See Lockamy, Smith (2000), p. 210-218; Smith, Lockamy (2000), p. 67-77.
[24] See Smith, Lokamy (2000), p. 67.
[25] See Lockamy, Smith (2000), p. 215-216; Smith, Lockamy (2000), p. 72-75.
[26] See Seidenschwarz, Niemand (1994), p. 267; Lockamy, Smith (2000), p. 212.

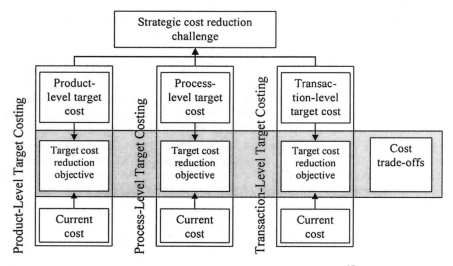

Figure 3: Target Costing on the Product, Process and Transaction Level[27]

While cost reductions can be achieved on all three levels, cost trade-offs between the three levels offer the chance to search for the most appropriate way to reach the target costs set. These cost trade-offs form an important part of supplier relations, as the long term relationship might make it necessary to compromise on short term reduction objectives.[28]

4 Apparel Industry Case Study

4.1 Stages of the Textile Chain

The apparel industry is well known for its competitive environment, where cost reductions are reached by switching suppliers frequently within a few month, as the seasonal cycle of the products dictate. Still, the disadavantages of such a supplier management are increased transaction costs as suppliers have to be audited and certified. Hence, leading companies of the apparel industry have

---

[27] Seuring (2001a), p. 143.
[28] See Cooper, Slagmulder (1999), p. 203f.

introduced programs to reduce the number of suppliers, which often form an important part of supply chain management.[29]

Subsequently, a supply chain for polyester linings will be used to explain the cost influences and the measures taken in supply chain costing. While both fabrics and lining can be made of polyester, the companies involved in the chain first turned to the lining. Polyester lining is used in a wide range of fashion products and accounts for about 70% of all lining used for apparel. The subsequent description will center on the company producing and selling the apparel products to fashion dealers. For the ease of description, this company will be called Fashion Company, while the two suppliers involved will be called Chemicals Company and Textile Company.

In recent years, Fashion company has introduced a program to reduce the number of suppliers. This was also true for polyester linings. One important measure introduced was to shorten the linings supply chain so that only three companies were involved as displayed in Figure 4. This reduces the number of interfaces involved to two. Brief explanations for the activities carried out at each step of the textile supply chain are provided.

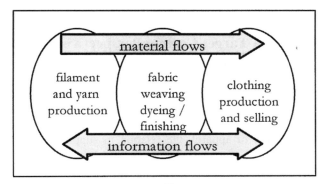

Figure 4: The Polyester Linings Supply Chain[30]

1. Filament and Yarn Production (Chemicals Company)

Polyester is a man-made fiber, produced from limited natural stocks of crude oil. The processing of oil applies to all product groups, so it will not be considered further. The raw material is polymerized and cleaned, leading to polyester chips. Next, filaments (one dimensional) are produced by melting the polyester chips and forcing it through spinneret holes. The extruded filaments are collected into thread forms. Next, they are stretched and drawn to yield polyester yarns.

---

[29] See Vollmann et. al. (1998), p. 380.
[30] See Seuring (2001b), p. 74.

2. Fabric Production, Dyeing and Finishing (Textile Company)

Weaving or knitting the yarn (one dimensional) leads to the creation of fabrics (two dimensional). Textile finishing includes processes that improve the wearing properties of the fabric or modify its look or feel.

3. Clothing Production, Selling and Distribution (Fashion Company.)

The next step is the manufacture of the apparel itself. The finished fabrics and lining are combined with other materials, such as zippers or buttons. The selling and distribution are of great importance as they represent the companies in the chain that decide which fashion is produced in which style and quality. Hence, this step has a major influence on all previous ones since product variety and quality are defined at this level. Selling and distribution can be carried out by a single company or within a tier supplier system of varying depth.

In traditional, market co-ordinated chains, the fashion industry usually does not take into account the single production stages. Apparel is bought in spot markets, where suppliers might change from part to part and even more from season to season.[31] Instead of staying with this kind of "non-management" supply chain target costing can be introduced to overcome the limitations traditionally experienced.

4.2 Introducing a Target Costing Perspective to the Polyester Linings Supply Chain

For the competitive position of Fashion Company, the sourcing of the material plays an important role, as the materials purchased represent about 42% to 47% of the total expenditure of the company. While target costing was applied in the creation and production of apparel, the relation to suppliers was kept at arm's length. The introduction of target costing towards the suppliers created new opportunities for cost reductions. In line with the arguments presented by Smith and Lockamy[32], dynamic customer requirements in the fashion industry compel the companies to join forces to perform value engineering activities. As a consequence, Fashion Company has changed the way they deal with their suppliers.

Still, an additional issue was raised by the power distribution along the supply chain. It is often assumed, that the companies at the end of the chain have the power to set the target prices for their components, so that suppliers must meet theses prices. This assumption does not hold true in the polyester lining chain, as the data in Table 1 shows. The data emphasizes, that the companies are important

---

[31] See e.g. Mariotti, Cainarca (1986).
[32] See Smith, Lockamy (2000), p. 72 and 73.

buyers for the preceding stage of the supply chain if all polyester or linings are purchased at one supplier. Still, the seller is not really dependent on the buyer, so power is almost equally distributed.

Stage of supply chain	Chemicals Company	Textile Company	Fashion Company
Processes	Filament and yarn production	Fabric weaving, dying, finishing	Clothing production and selling
Yearly amount (normalized to polyester linings)	About 500 Mio. m/a	Ca. 40 Mio. m/a	Ca. 4 Mio. m/a
No. of colors	Colorless	About 300 different Colors offered	Reduction to about 50 Colors

Table 1: Some Data on the Polyester Linings Supply Chain

For the success of the target costing process, all three companies had to work together to allow the market introduction of an improved polyester quality that uses a new type of catalyst.[33] First of all, the commitment of the three companies was needed, as each stage had to contribute their share if the target price was to be reached. The target selling price was defined by polyester linings of comparable quality, that can be purchased from various suppliers. At the onset of the project, the target price was exceeded by about 25%. The strategic cost reduction objective was set to eliminate this difference.

The introduction of the improved polyester linings quality made changes in the production facilities both at Chemicals Company and at Textile Company necessary. For the calculation of the current cost, each company evaluated these changes in terms of adjusted technical and additional administrative processes. A major problem was raised by the production of both the old and new polyester quality. Because all subsequent production steps have to be adjusted, it is not possible to change the chemical polyester formulation at Chemicals Company and not inform the following stages of the supply chain.

1. Costs Analysis at Chemicals Company

The dichotomy that arose was bringing the new polyester quality to the market, while continuing to produce the existing quality, a typical problem of new product introduction. Hence, the supply chain of the three companies formed an example allowing testing the new polyester quality and bringing it to the market. The experiences gained are then to be used to spread the polyester to other market

---

[33] See Thier-Grebe, Rabe (2000).

segments. As an example given, Chemicals Company sells only about 10% of its products to Textile Company, because it is one partner in a complex supply network where their polyester ends up in cars, curtains, apparel and more.

In total, the production costs at Chemicals Company rose significantly. The main reason for this was the production of both polyester qualities: the production facilities employed had to be cleaned if the other polyester quality was to be produced next. The next production step, the spinning of the polyester into fibers does not have this problem, as it is carried out in a batch process with much smaller batches and lower setup costs. Only a switch of the complete production to the new quality would eliminate these direct and activity-based costs completely.

2. Costs Analysis at Textile Company

The situation at Textile Company was somewhat comparable. While the weaving as a mechanical process did not lead to significant problem, the dying and finishing processes had to be modified in order to produce the polyester linings in the required quality. The dying process had to be altered as the new catalyst used for the polymerization of the polyester changed the dying properties of the polyester. As a consequence, for each color produced costly preproduction experiments had to be carried out. Furthermore, the logistics, warehousing and adminisitrative costs were rising too, as a higher number of different lots had to be produced and kept on stock.

3. Cost Analysis at Fashion Company

The situation at Fashion Company was quite different. Polyester lining is purchased and used for clothing production. Hence, it has to be cut into the required pieces and sewn to form the final apparel. For this production step, it does not make a difference, which type of polyester is used, so no additional costs occur.

Still, Fashion Company defines the quality and the colors required that have to be produced by the suppliers, so the links in the supply chain are evident.

4.3 Applying Supply Chain Target Costing

After the strategic cost reduction challenge had been defined and the problems addressed previously became visible, all companies tried to optimize their production. Still, the resulting effect was limited for the reasons described above. The partners in the supply chain had to work together to solve these problems behind one factory gate.

1. Joint Reduction of Direct Costs

As the catalyst has some influence on the physical properties of the fiber, all subsequent production steps had to be optimized. Therefore, staff from the yarn producer (Chemicals Company) and the weaver and dyer (Textile Company) worked together to check each production step. The temperature control of the dying had to be changed to lead to high quality dying results. The production steps following the filament production could be adjusted so that they are carried out at the same cost rate. Still, this reduction yielded only a limited decrease in the current cost, so the main part of the cost reduction challenge remained.

2. Joint Reduction of Activity-based Costs and Transaction Costs

The activity-based costs are mainly driven by the processes carried out within the single companies. The lot size has a high influence on these costs, both within the production facility, where it determines the number of set-up processes and administrative processes necessary. By agreeing on lot sizes and production dates, the activity-based costs and the transaction costs were reduced between the Chemicals and Textile Company.

Before the search for supply chain improvements started, Fashion Company (selling and distribution) used more than 300 different colors for polyester lining. In a project, all design and purchasing staff were brought together to evaluate the colors and qualities of the lining. This led to a reduction of the employed colors to about 50, which are checked and updated every season. The reduced color variety did not lead to any major trade-offs in fashion, as this would not be acceptable to the designers.

For this limited number of lining varieties higher amounts are ordered from the suppliers. With the introduction of the new polyester quality, one supplier covering all steps necessary in weaving, dying and finishing the lining was selected to deliver all polyester lining ordered. Furthermore, for some standard colors, e.g. black, at the start of every season (about every six months), the volume ordered as well as the approximate total volume of lining ordered is fixed. Therefore, the supplier guarantees to stock this lining and supply it within two days after an order is placed. These agreements offer the supplier the opportunity to have orders placed well in advance, which allows a better use of production capacities. These colors are produced to stock (push process), so they have a significantly reduced delivery time of two days if they are ordered by the Fashion Compnay. The remaining colors, which are ordered in lower amounts are, are produced after orders are placed, so the lead time is about two weeks. The reduction in color variety led to higher transaction costs at both companies, but reduced the activity-based costs for the polyester lining significantly.

Taking all measures applied along the lining supply chain together, the target costs of "normal" lining could almost be matched. The companies continue to work on these issues.

5 Conclusion

The measures illustrate how increased costs on one level, specially the transaction cost level, help to reduce costs at other levels. So far, transaction costs and activity-based costs created at suppliers and customers' facilities are often not taken into account, as companies tend to focus on their own production facilities. Within the increasingly competitive global environment, supply chains have to consider the competitiveness of the whole supply chain.[34] Cost management will have to form an integrative part of supply chain management on all stages of the supply chain.[35] Further developments in cost management, as presented in this volume, as well will have to be integrated into supply chain management if the full potential of cost management activities in supply chains are to be uncovered.

6 References

Ansari, S. L., Bell, J. (1997): Target Costing – The Next Frontier in Strategic Cost Management, Irwin Professional Publishing, Chicago.

Christopher, M. (1998): Logistics and Supply Chain Management – Strategies for Reducing Cost and Improving Service, 2nd Edition, Financial Times, London.

Cooper, R., Slagmulder, R. (1997): Target Costing and Value Engineering, Productivity Press, Portland.

Cooper, R., Slagmulder, R. (1999): Supply Chain Development for the Lean Enterprise – Interorganisational Cost Management, Productivity Press, Portland.

Franz, K.-P., Kajüter, P. (eds.) (1997): Kostenmanagement – Wettbewerbsvorteile durch systematische Kostensteuerung (Cost Management – Competitive Advantages through Systematic Cost Controlling), Verlag Schäffer-Poeschel, Stuttgart.

Handfield, R. B., Nichols E. L. (1999): Introduction to Supply Chain Management, Prentice Hall, New Jersey.

Hilton, R. W., Maher, M. W., Selto, F. H. (2000): Cost Management – Strategies for Business Decisions, Irwin McGraw-Hill, Boston.

Kaplan, R. S., Cooper, R. (1997): Cost and Effect – Using Integrated Cost Systems to Drive Profitability and Performance, Harvard Business School Press, Boston.

LaLonde, B. J., Pohlen, T. L. (1996): Issues in Supply Chain Costing, in: The International Journal of Logistics Management, Vol. 7, No. 1 (1996), p. 1-12.

---

[34] See Christopher (1998).
[35] See Seuring (2001).

Mariotti, C., Cainarca, G. C. (1986): The Evolution of Transaction Governance in the Textile-Clothing Industry, in: Journal of Economic Behavior and Organization, Vol. 7 (1986), p. 351-374.

Monden, Y. (1995): Cost Reductio Systems – Target Costing and Kaizen Costing, Productivity Press, Portland.

Porter, M. E (1998): Competitive Strategy - Techniques for Analysing Industries and Competitors, 8th Edition, Simon and Schuster Trade Division, New York.

Shank, J. K., Fisher, J. (1999): Target Costing as a Strategic Tool, in: Sloan Management Review, Vol. 41, No. 1 (1999), p. 73-82.

Seuring, S. (1999): Gestaltungsoptionen durch Kostenmanagement – Das Beispiel der Wertschöpfungskette von Öko-Textilien (Improvement Options by Cost Management – The Example of the Supply Chain of Eco-Textiles), in: Umweltwirtschaftsforum. Vol. 7, No. 4 (1999), p. 18-23.

Seuring, S. (2001a): Supply Chain Costing – Kostenmanagement in der Wertschöpfungskette mit Target Costing und Prozesskostenrechnung (Supply Chain Costing with Target Costing and Activity Based Costing), Verlag Franz Vahlen, München.

Seuring, S. (2001b): Green Supply Chain Costing – Joint Cost Management in the Polyester Linings Supply Chain, in: Greener Management International, Issue 33 (2001), p. 71-80.

Seuring, S. (2002): Supply Chain Costing - A conceptual framework for Analyzing and Controlling Costs in Supply Chains, in: Seuring, S., Goldbach, M. (ed.): Cost Management in Supply Chains, Springer Verlag, Berlin, p. 15-30.

Shank, J. K., Govindarajan, V. (1993): Strategic Cost Management - The New Tool for Competitive Advantage, Simon and Schuster Trade Division, New York.

Smith, W. I., Lockamy, A. (2000): Target Costing for Supply Chain Management: An Economic Framework, in: The journal of corporate accounting & finance, Vol. 12, No. 1 (2000), p. 67-78.

Stevens, G. C. (1989): Integrating the Supply Chain, in: International Journal of Physical Distribution & Logistics Management, Vol. 19, No. 8 (1989), p. 3-8.

Tanaka, T. (1993): Target Costing at Toyota, in: Journal of Cost Management, Vol. 7, Spring (1993), p. 4-11.

Thier-Grebe, R., Rabe, M. (2000): Polyester with New Titanium Dioxide Catalyst, in: Melliand International, Vol. 6, No. 4 (2000), p. 4-7.

Vollmann, T. E., Cordon, C., Raabe, H. (1998): Das Management von Lieferketten (The Management of Supply Chains), in: International Institute for Management Development, London Business School, Wharton Business School (eds.): Das MBA-Buch: Mastering Management – Die Studieninhalte führender Business Schools (The MBA-book: Mastering Management), Stuttgart, p. 374-381.

Williamson, O. E. (1998): The Economic Institutions of Capitalism - Firms, Markets, Relational Contracting, Simon and Schuster Trade Division, New York.

Integrating Life Cycle Costing and Life Cycle Assessment for Managing Costs and Environmental Impacts in Supply Chains

Gerald Rebitzer

1	Introduction	128
2	Systems Thinking in Supply Chain and Life Cycle Management	129
3	Life Cycle Costing Based on Life Cycle Assessment	134
4	LCC and LCA in Design for Environment	136
5	Conclusions	143
6	References	144

Summary:
Supply chain management (SCM) has to be seen as one element in the broader contexts of life cycle management (LCM) and sustainable development. Both of these holistic approaches offer the opportunity to apply a systems-thinking approach to the activities of a firm. Within this philosophy a life cycle costing (LCC) concept for estimating the total costs associated with the production, use, and disposal of a product or service is introduced. On an application level this methodology is based on the environmental life cycle assessment (LCA) framework. The methodological background is explained and product design/development case studies demonstrating the advantages and practicality of the proposed LCC method are elaborated.

Keywords:
Cost Drivers, Design for Environment (DfE), Environmental Impacts, Life Cycle Assessment (LCA), Life Cycle Costing (LCC), Life Cycle Management (LCM), Product Design, Supply Chain Management (SCM), Sustainable Development, Systems Thinking

1 Introduction

Supply chain management (SCM) is a concept that expands the bilateral customer - supplier relationship to a more integrated view covering the complete upstream chain. In addition, it is a management approach that focuses on the product itself rather than on divisions of a company such as, purchasing, manufacturing, or logistics. In an even more holistic view SCM can be seen as part of life cycle management (LCM) and sustainable development, concepts which are becoming increasingly important in the business world. This can be prominently exemplified by the quote of William Clay Ford Jr., Chairman and CEO of Ford Motor Company, who noted that "Ford Motor Company once provided the world with mobility by making it affordable. In the 21st century, we want to continue to provide the world with mobility by making it sustainable."[1]

Sustainability, or the synonymous term sustainable development, is defined as a development that "meets the needs of the present without compromising the ability of future generations to meet their own needs".[2] It comprises economic, environmental, and social issues. This broad concept applies to all levels of society. On a business level, it can be expressed in terms of life cycle management (LCM). "LCM is an integrated framework of concepts and techniques to address environmental, economic, technological and social aspects of products, services and organizations. [...] LCM, as any other management pattern, is applied on a voluntary basis and can be adapted to the specific needs and characteristics of individual organizations."[3] Therefore, the environmental and economic performance of products and services are integral parts of LCM and SCM and are important aspects for the long-term success of any business.

Measuring and assessing the economic and environmental supply chain and life cycle performance of products and services are of crucial importance when implementing the concepts mentioned above. Therefore, this paper focuses on the assessment of costs and environmental impacts in the life cycle of products. After a presentation of the underlying concepts, the methodological basis is explained and industrial case studies demonstrating the application of the methods are elaborated.

---

[1] Ford (2000).
[2] WCED (1987), p. 8.
[3] SETAC (2001), p. 4.

2 Systems Thinking in Supply Chain and Life Cycle Management

Essentially, SCM and LCM mark a paradigm shift in management. Rather than focusing on single aspects such as purchasing costs or environmental aspects in a firm's manufacturing, (as is usually done in environmental management)[4], the product and the up- and downstream processes associated with its production, use, and end-of-life are in the focus. It is a shift from thinking in divisions or units of a company or environmental compartments (e.g., air pollution) to a systems thinking approach. The system (product or service system[5]) that has to be built, maintained, operated, and managed in order to provide a product or service is in the center.

This systems thinking enables management and other decision makers, for instance in product development, to find the overall optimum in regards to cost or environmental impacts. Trade-offs between different processes and actors in the life cycle of a product can be determined and resources can be allocated efficiently in order to achieve product improvements and cost savings. This could for example involve utilizing a more expensive material for a product in order to achieve cost savings in later manufacturing or recycling processes, leading to lower overall costs.

For the assessment of environmental impacts caused by a product or service, life cycle assessment (LCA) is an established though evolving methodological framework. Comprehensive international standards have been developed.[6] Life cycle costing, though some building industry-specific standards exist[7], cannot however be called a uniform concept or framework. There are many approaches differing in goal, scope, and methodology.[8] In the following, the fundamentals of both LCA and the LCC methodology are presented.

2.1 The Life Cycle Assessment Concept

Life cycle assessment (LCA) is defined as the "compilation and evaluation of the inputs, outputs and the potential environmental impacts of a product system throughout its life cycle."[9] The basis of any LCA study is the life cycle inventory analysis (LCI), which is the "phase of LCA involving the compilation and

---

[4] See ISO 14001 (1996).
[5] See ISO 14040 (1997).
[6] See ISO 14040 (1997); ISO 14041 (1998); ISO 14042 (2000); ISO 14043 (2000).
[7] See e.g., ASTM E917-99 (1999).
[8] Compare e.g., ASTM E917-99 (1999); Blanchard, Fabrycky (1998), p. 557; Ehrlenspiel et al. (1998); Horváth (1996), p. 8-43; White et al. (1996).
[9] ISO 14040 (1997).

quantification of inputs and outputs for a given product system throughout its life cycle."[10] In this analysis the physical product system with all its processes and material- and energy flows connecting the processes is modeled.

Figure 1 shows the principal model of such a product system with the elements of the supply chain of the end manufacturer (e.g., an automobile manufacturer) shaded. It is clearly visible that the supply chain as commonly referred to in industrial practice is a subset of the life cycle. It has to be noted, however, that on a conceptual level SCM as defined by Handfield and Nichols[11] can also cover downstream processes such as recycling activities. In a product system model all processes are connected via flows of materials or energy. Entering or leaving the system are either products or the so-called elementary flows, which comprise flows that are directly taken out of or discharged into the natural environment[12] (e.g., mineral resources or air emissions from incinerators).

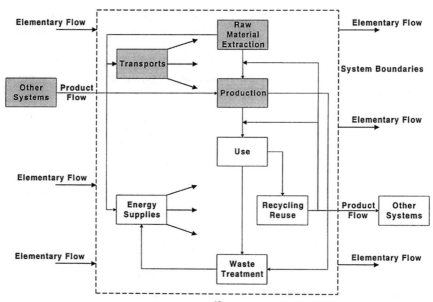

Figure 1: Product System Model of an LCA[13]

In addition, non-flow related environmental interventions, such as land-use or noise may also be accounted for in the LCI. In the LCI all single processes called

---

[10] ISO 14040 (1997).
[11] See Handfield, Nichols (1999), p. 4, 161.
[12] See ISO 14040 (1997).
[13] See ISO 14041 (1998).

unit-processes[14] are identified and analyzed. The flow-related data that are compiled for each unit-process necessary to produce, use and dispose of a defined quantity of the product are shown in Figure 2.

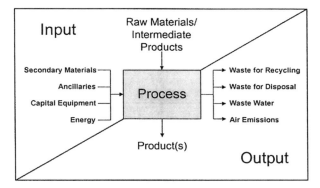

Figure 2: Detailed Inventory of Material- and Energy Flows of a Unit-Process

With such an analysis of the processes, and the corresponding material and energy input and output flows, a detailed model of the complete product system is obtained. One can easily argue that this model and the information contained within is an excellent basis for the analysis and assessment of costs in the supply chain and the complete life cycle if additional elements are added (see Section 3.1). For instance, by analyzing and compiling the energy flows of all processes in the system in regards to different energy carriers as shown in Table 1 for the service of waste water treatment, one can easily allocate the cost of the energy consumption in the system as well as identify cost-drivers due to high consumption or the usage of cost-intensive energy carriers. The energy demand values in Table 1 refer to an example of the treatment of the average amount and composition of waste water per inhabitant (person equivalent) and year (a) in Switzerland (reference flow[15] of the LCA).

To determine environmental impacts, the aggregated flows of the system are assessed in regards to their potential environmental impacts. This subsequent phase of LCA, referred to as life cycle impact assessment (LCIA) leads to environmental indicators such as human toxicity, eco-toxicity, global warming, ozone depletion, or acidification potentials, with which product systems can be assessed and compared and environmental hotspots can be identified.

---

[14] See ISO 14040 (1997).
[15] See ISO 14040 (1997).

Primary energy demand	MJ/pers.equiv/a	
Low-voltage electricity	1.27	⇒ $
Medium-voltage electricity	3.39	⇒ $
Fuel oil	17.17	⇒ $
Natural gas	0.37	⇒ $
Transports	0.03	⇒ $
Calcium Oxide	0.01	⇒ $
Ammonia	0.03	⇒ $
Caustic Soda	0.05	⇒ $
Total	22.352	

Table 1: Energy Flows for a System of Waste Water Treatment (example: for the materials and transports the energy needed to produce and utilize or operate them, respectively, is accounted for)

Recently, these links in the cause-effect chains of impacts (mid-point indicators) have been supplemented by end-point indicators which aim at the final causes of impacts.[16] An example for an end-point indicator is the so-called DALY (disability adjusted lost years), which aims at determining the final impacts on human health caused by factors such as by ozone depletion and global warming. Detailed elaborations concerning LCIA and other aspects of LCA can be found in the literature.[17]

2.2 The Life Cycle Costing Concept

As explained earlier, there is no uniform understanding of the term life cycle costing nor is there a standardized methodological framework that is commonly used in business. The following deliberations of life cycle costing are founded upon the definition by Blanchard and Fabrycky, who state that "life-cycle cost refers to all costs associated with the system as applied to the defined life cycle."[18] In this context, the term life cycle has to be seen analogously to the life cycle as explained in Section 2.1, referring to the processes associated with the production, use, and end-of-life (reuse, recycling, waste treatment) of a product or service.[19]

Figure 3 shows such an economic life cycle. In this LCC system, the costs traditionally accounted for by the manufacturer of a product are supplemented by the costs of the product user, comprising use and end-of-life costs.

---

[16] See Bare et al. (2000).
[17] See e.g., Curran (1996); Guinée et al. (2001); SETAC (1997); SETAC-Europe (1996); Wenzel et al. (1997).
[18] Blanchard, Fabrycky (1998), p. 560.
[19] See Rebitzer (2000), p. 103.

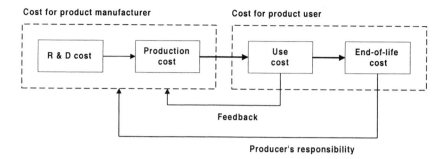

Figure 3: Economic Life Cycle (the bold lines represent the LCI flows)[20]

When considering these costs, products with minimal life cycle cost can be developed and marketed. Less cost for the user leads to advantages on the market, possibly resulting in the achievement of a higher selling price. Lower end-of-life costs are relevant due to the identical reasoning, but also due to existing and evolving regulations concerning take-back of products like those found in the automotive and electronics industries.[21]

In addition to the costs caused by physical processes and their associated material and energy flows (LCI), other costs such as labor costs or costs for utilizing knowledge (e.g., patents) as well as transaction costs (e.g., information flows) must be considered. For example, all costs for research and development which are not linked to material flows have to be integrated.[22]

With this LCC concept all costs caused by the development, production, use, and end-of-life of a product can be determined, thus providing the methodological framework to identify cost-drivers in the life cycle and supply chain and to identify trade-offs in order to achieve minimal total cost. It has to be noted that this life cycle costing methodology is meant to be used for rough cost estimations in product development, marketing analysis, etc. It is not a method to replace traditional detailed cost accounting practices.

---

[20] See Rebitzer (2000), p. 104.
[21] See WEEE (2000) and ELV (2000).
[22] See Rebitzer (2000), p. 103.

3 Life Cycle Costing Based on Life Cycle Assessment

The elaborations in the previous sections show that the information obtained through a life cycle inventory analysis (see Section 2.1) can be efficiently used for life cycle costing assessments. In the following, the common elements of LCA and LCC are analyzed and an LCC methodology based on LCA and tailored to purposes of product design and development is explained.

3.1 Common Elements of LCC and LCA

	Cost for Product Manufacturer	Cost for Product User
R&D	• Market Research • Development costs	
Production	• *Materials* • *Energy* • Machines, plants • Labor • *Waste Management* • *Emission Controls* • *Transports*	
Use	• Maintenance/ Repair (Warranty) • Liability • Infrastructure	• *Transport* • Storage • *Materials* • *Energy* • Maintenance/Repair • Infrastructure
End-of-Life		• *Waste Collection* • *Disassembly/Re-cycling/Disposal*

Table 2: Common Elements of LCC and LCA

Table 2 shows the most relevant elements of life cycle costing and how they are connected to information gained from life cycle assessment. Those costing aspects that can be directly derived from an LCA are written in bold italics. The inventory of an LCA gives the quantities of these flows and the cost can be obtained by multiplying these flows with the respective company costs or market prices (e.g., materials purchasing). Those costing aspects that are written in normal italics can be derived in part or indirectly from the information contained in an LCI. For these aspects additional information, for instance the labor requirements for the operation of a certain process, have to be gathered. If this is done concurrently to the establishment of the LCI model, minimal additional effort is required, since all processes are studied and analyzed in depth for the LCI. Only the costs associated with research and development (R&D) of the product cannot be derived from the LCA model. These have to be determined separately. For a service, the same principals apply; there is no methodological difference to a material product.

Overall, with the exception of the R&D phase, all relevant base data for a life cycle costing assessment can be obtained directly or indirectly from the life cycle inventory analysis of an LCA.

3.2 Methodological Background

As outlined in the previous section, the life cycle costs are either derived directly as in the case of material and energy costs where the costs are a product of physical quantity and price per quantity, or indirectly via identifying the cost issues and allocating costs/prices to it. The identified costs are then aggregated into subcategories, such as costs for research and development (R&D), materials (MAT), transports/logistics (TRNS), manufacturing (MANF), use (USE), end-of-life (EOL), and transaction costs (TC).

These direct life cycle costs are calculated by summing up the categories as shown in Equation 1:

$$LCC = R\&D + MAT + TRNS + MANF + USE_D + EOL_D + TC \quad \text{(Equation 1)}$$

Since some costs such as those for usage and end-of-life can occur over a significant period of time or far into the future, respectively, these costs have to be discounted (denoted with a subscript D in Equation 1).

Other economic aspects such as market risks and opportunities can be integrated intothis model as well, but are not elaborated further in this paper.[23]

This is a straightforward approach building on the inventory analysis of the LCA and available cost data such as materials prices, manufacturing costs (including ancillaries, energy, labor), etc. It depends on the specific case of which cost aspects are relevant and which information has to be gathered in addition to that gained in the LCA model. If no company-specific costs for the materials and processes are available, generic cost databases can be used as well.[24] The application of the outlined LCI-based life cycle costing methodology is demonstrated in the following by two product design case studies.

---

[23] For a complete description of the methodology, see Rebitzer (2001).
[24] See e.g., Granta Design (1999); VDI 2225 (1996).

4 LCC and LCA in Design for Environment

The two case studies presented focus on design for environment (DfE), which is a design approach that aims at integrating environmental considerations into product development. Of course, other design criteria such as technological and market requirements as well as cost constraints and targets are taken into account as well or are merely the basis for the environmental design.

The relevance of addressing environmental issues and life cycle costs from the very beginning of product design is illustrated in Figure 4. Although the research and development phase does itself not cause a great share of the overall costs and environmental impacts (in general between 3-25% of the direct cost of the product manufacturer[25], which itself is only one segment of the total life cycle cost, see Figure 3). It is extremely significant in the determination of the costs and impacts in other phases of the life cycle. The design phase is the key to a cost-efficient product with a good environmental performance.

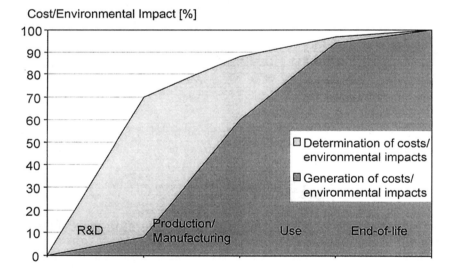

Figure 4: Relevance of LCC and LCA in Product Design

The scope of the two life cycle costing assessments presented is limited to the costs for materials, manufacturing, transports, use and disposal. R&D costs and transaction costs are not determined due to the goals of the studies. The assessment is intended to serve as an estimate for the question whether a substantial effort for R&D and also transaction activities (e.g., establishing new

---

[25] See Ehrlenspiel et. al. (1998), p. 21.

supplier relationships) seems to be beneficial in the case of potential economic and environmental improvements compared to the current state (trade-off estimation).

In the following sections case studies from the automotive and aerospace industries will be summarized.

4.1 Automotive Case Study: Front Subframe System of Ford Mondeo

The results presented in the following section are based on a study by Rebitzer et al.[26], which deals with materials selection in engineering design and the subsequent comprehensive assessment of the different options in regards to technological feasibility, recyclability, costs and risks, as well as environmental and work environmental impacts.[27]

The scope of the LCC and LCA part of the study was the assessment of different material options for the front subframe system of the new Ford Mondeo, a mid-size passenger car. The subframe system is illustrated in Figure 5.

Figure 5: Front Subframe System of Ford Mondeo

The materials selection process for this component, which aimed at a lightweight design, produced among others, the three materials options:

- Glass fiber-reinforced polyamide (PA)
- Hemp fiber-reinforced polypropylene (PP)
- Magnesium

---

[26] Rebitzer et al. (2001).
[27] An overview of the overall results of the comprehensive assessment can be found in the literature, see Schmidt et al. (2000); Rebitzer et al. (2001).

Glass fiber reinforced PA, the currently used material, is already a lightweight solution compared to steel, which is conventionally used for this type of component. The reinforced PA results in a component weight of 4.3 kg, the other two materials 3.5 kg (reinforced PP) and 2.6 kg (magnesium). It is important to note that the application of hemp fiber-reinforced PP, though technologically feasible from the point of material specifications needed to fulfill the use requirements, would require significant additional research and development efforts in order to solve existing manufacturing problems. Manufacturing by injection molding, the desired process for the component, is not at present possible.

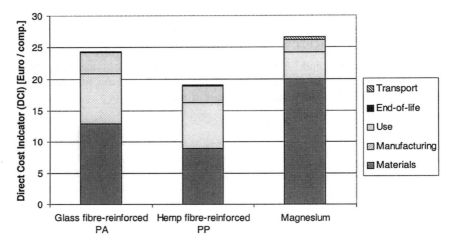

Figure 6: Direct Life Cycle Costs of the Three Material Options for the Front Subframe System

Figure 6 and 7, respectively, show the direct life cycle costs (without R&D) and the environmental performance of the three selected material options. The life cycle costs have been determined based on the life cycle inventory phase of the LCA as outlined in Section 3, with relatively small additional effort needed. For determining environmental performance, global warming potential was chosen as an indicator due to its extreme relevance relevant in automotive applications. Furthermore, it has been identified by other studies as a suitable indicator for measuring the environmental performance of automobiles.[28]

---

[28] See e.g., Schmidt et al. (2001).

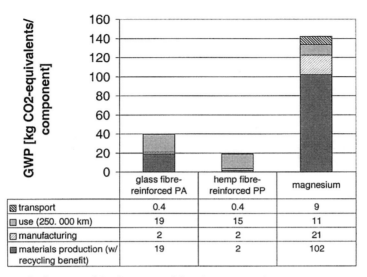

Figure 7: Environmental Performance of the Three Material Options for the Front Subframe System, Expressed in Global Warming Potential (GWP)

The results of these assessments are summarized in the life cycle portfolio (see Figure 8). This portfolio shows that magnesium is clearly not a material that should be preferred for the front subframe system since the life cycle costs, mainly due to the high material purchasing costs, are higher than the currently used material. The global warming potential is higher as well. Therefore, magnesium is not a suitable substitute for the reinforced PA, neither from an economic nor from an environmental point of view.

Hemp fiber-reinforced polypropylene, however, offers significant improvement potentials in both areas. Investing in R&D to solve the manufacturing problems for this material advisable. The recommendation was therefore to keep the current material for the short term and invest in R&D for the natural fiber-reinforced PP. Magnesium should not be considered a further material option. The selection of the most appropriate alternative could also be expressed in terms of the "Return on Environment" (ROE) concept[29], which also points to the direction of recommended development.[30] Therefore, one sees that economic and environmental information can be evaluated using single, application-specific indicators such as global warming potential and life cycle cost, or aggregated indices (e.g., ROE).

---

[29] See Hunkeler (2000); Hunkeler (2001).
[30] See Rebitzer, Hunkeler (2001).

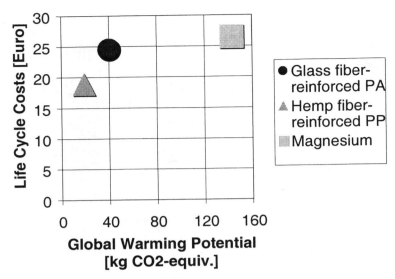

Figure 8: Life Cycle Portfolio for the Front-Subframe System

4.2 Aerospace Case Study: Freshwater Tank for an Airbus Passenger Aircraft

Similar to the aforementioned automotive study, materials for an Airbus freshwater tank (see Figure 9) have been evaluated. The complete study of Lichtenvort et al. can be found in the literature.[31]

Figure 9: Freshwater Tank of Airbus Passenger Aircraft

---

[31] See Lichtenvort et al. (2001).

In this case the materials options were:

- Carbon fiber-reinforced epoxy (EP)
- Polyethylene (PE) fiber-reinforced EP
- Boron fiber-reinforced EP
- Steel

Carbon fiber-reinforced EP is the material currently used for this application.

The results of the life cycle costing and environmental assessment are shown in Figure 10 and Figure 11, respectively.

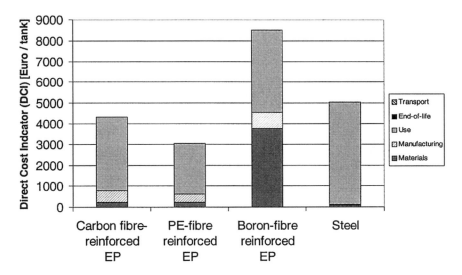

Figure 10: Direct Life Cycle Costs of the Four Material Options for the Freshwater Tank

The environmental assessment is clearly dominated by fuel consumption in the use phase for all impact indicators.[32] Therefore, GWP can be considered a very suitable indicator representing the overall environmental performance in this case, because energy generation and consumption has been shown to correlate highly with this measure.[33]

---

[32] See Lichtenvort et al. (2001).
[33] See Braunmiller et al. (2000).

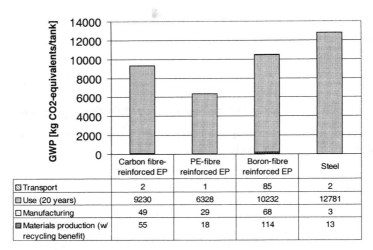

Figure 11: Environmental Performance of the Four Material Options for the Freshwater Tank, Expressed in Global Warming Potential (GWP)

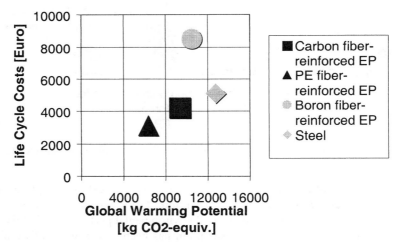

Figure 12: Life Cycle Portfolio for the Freshwater Tank.

Figure 12 shows the life cycle portfolio for this case. Substituting carbon with boron fibers or using steel instead of the plastics composite would create higher costs and environmental impacts and can therefore be disregarded. Substituting carbon fibers by PE fibers, however, seems to be promising because a better environmental performance with decreased direct life cycle costs can be expected.

Therefore, this is the material that should be considered for future research and development activities (necessary because this material has not been used for this application in practice yet). If development costs can be kept at a modest margin, improvements can be realized. On the other hand, this costing assessment can be used to estimate if the direct life cycle costs that could be saved can overcome any development costs, which would also depend on the size of the series to be produced.

However, such an economic and environmental win-win situation cannot be expected in all applications. In cases where these advantages are not observed, such a portfolio analysis can be used to decide to what extent one can afford environmental improvements or how these improvements can be utilized through indirect economic advantages such as an improved image or reputation on the market.

5 Conclusions

In this paper, a life cycle costing method for estimating costs in supply chains, or complete life cycles, was presented. The principal advantage of this method is that – when conducted in an integrated manner with an environmental life cycle assessment (LCA) – only minimal effort is needed to identify cost-drivers and trade-offs in the chain. In addition, the process and product-oriented systems view of LCA allows identification of costs independent from divisions within a firm and thus enables an improved cost allocation to products. Such a method is very well suited for cost estimations in product planning and design as shown in the two industrial case studies. Consequently, economic product planning can be much better integrated into the design process as is commonly practiced today.

Other benefits of such an integrated application of LCA and LCC result from the fact that elements of life cycle management (LCM) and sustainable development can be measured and thus put into practice. The two cases clearly illustrate the advantages of combined environmental and economic evaluations, and point to the need to identify or develop valid environmental indicators (such as GWP in the cases outlined, see Sections 4.1 and 4.2) that are either product or industry specific, depending on the particular case. In this sense, significant research on benchmarking environmental indicators is underway, with some advocating normalized or double-normalized approaches such as Return on Environment[34] or the average cost per environmental impact (E2 Vector[35]). Still others prefer a set of benchmarks which have specific indicators validated for given industries.

---

[34] See Hunkeler (2000) and Hunkeler (2001).
[35] See Goedkoop et al. (2000).

6 References

ASTM (1999): Practice E917-99 Standard Practice for Measuring Life-Cycle Costs of Buildings and Building Systems, American Society for Testing and Materials, West Conshohocken.

Bare, J. C., Hofstetter, P., Pennington, D. W., Udo de Haes, H. A. (2000): Life Cycle Impact Assessment Workshop Summary, Midpoints Versus Endpoints – The Sacrifices and Benefits, in: The International Journal of Life Cycle Assessment, Vol. 5, No. 6 (2000), p. 319-326.

Blanchard, B. S., Fabrycky, W. J. (1998): Systems Engineering and Analysis, Prentice Hall, Upper Saddle River.

Braunmiller, U., Dobberkau, J., Gutberlet, D., Haupt, H.-J., Kunst, H., Rebitzer, G., Schmidt, W.-P., Volkwein, S., Wolf, J. (2000): Horizontale Fehlerbetrachtung (Horizontal Uncertainty Analysis), in: Fleischer, G. (ed.), Becker, J., Braunmiller, U., Klocke, F., Klöpffer, W., Michaeli, W. (co-eds.): Eco-Design – Effiziente Entwicklung nachhaltiger Produkte mit euroMat (Efficient Development of Sustainable Products with euroMat), Springer, Berlin, p. 168-222.

Curran, M. A. (ed.) (1996): Environmental Life-Cycle Assessment, McGraw-Hill, New York.

Ehrlenspiel, K., Kiewert, A., Lindemann, U. (1998): Kostengünstig Entwickeln und Konstruieren – Kostenmanagement bei der integrierten Produktentwicklung (Efficient Design and Development – Cost Management in Integrated Product Development), Springer, Berlin.

ELV (2000): Directive 2000/53/EC of the European Parliament and of the Council of 18 September 2000 On End-of Life Vehicles, European Communities, Brussels.

Ford, W. C. (2000): Speech at the 5th Annual Greenpeace Business Conference in London, 5th October, 2000.

Goedkoop, M., Spriensma, R., Effting, S. (2000): Reducing Environmental Pressure By Dematerialization – An Analysis of the Environmental Load Caused by Dutch Production and Consumption in Relation to the Use of Materials, PRé Consultants B.V., Amersfort.

Granta Design (1999): Cambridge Engineering Selector (CES), Software, Granta Design, Cambridge.

Guinée, J. B., Gorrée, M., Heijungs, R., Huppes, G., Kleijn, R., de Koning, A., van Oers, L., Sleeswijk, A. W., Suh, S., Udo de Haes, H. A. (2001): Life Cycle Assessment – An Operational Guide to the ISO Standards - Final Report, Centre of Environmental Science (CML) - Leiden University, Leiden.

Handfield, R. B., Nichols E. L. (1999): Introduction to Supply Chain Management, Prentice Hall, New Jersey.

Horváth, P. (1996): Produktcontrolling (Product Controlling), in: Eversheim, W., Schuh, G. (ed.): Betriebshütte – Produktion und Management (Production and Management), 7th Edition, Springer, Berlin.

Hunkeler, D. (2000): Return On Environment, in: The International Journal of Life Cycle Assessment, Vol. 5, No. 6 (2000), p. 358-362.

Hunkeler, D. (2001): Return On Environment – Addressing the Need for Normalization and Validation in Ecometrics, in: Proceedings of the Life Cycle Management Conference 2001, Copenhagen, p. 39-43.

ISO 14040 (1997): Life Cycle Assessment – Principles and Framework - ISO 14040, International Organization for Standardization.

ISO 14041 (1998): Life Cycle Assessment – Goal and Scope Definition and Life Cycle Inventory Analysis - ISO 14041, International Organization for Standardization.

ISO 14042 (2000): Life Cycle Assessment – Life Cycle Impact Assessment - ISO 14042, International Organization for Standardization.

ISO 14043 (2000): Life Cycle Assessment – Life Cycle Interpretation - ISO 14043, International Organization for Standardization.

Lichtenvort, K., Bohlmann, B., Borsdorf, R., Dobberkau, J., Horn, S., Hübner, C., Noack, G., Volkwein, S. (2001): Beispiel Airbus-Trinkwassertank (Case Study Airbus Freshwater Tank), in: TU Berlin, C.A.U. GmbH, CTB CAMTEC, Denios AG, FhG ICT, FhG IPT, Ford-Werke AG, MAN Technologie AG, Sachsenring Entwicklungs GmbH, TU Cottbus: Systematische Auswahlkriterien für die Entwicklung von Verbundwerkstoffen unter Beachtung ökologischer Erfordernisse – Abschlussphase (euroMat 2001), Forschungsbericht (Research Report), BMBF-Förderprogramm Sicherung des Industriestandorts Deutschland, Projektträger DLR, p. 522-579.

Rebitzer, G. (2000): Modul Kosten (Life Cycle Costing Module), in: Fleischer, G. (ed.), Becker, J., Braunmiller, U., Klocke, F., Klöpffer, W., Michaeli, W. (co-eds.): Eco-Design – Effiziente Entwicklung nachhaltiger Produkte mit euroMat (Efficient Development of Sustainable Products with euroMat), Springer, Berlin, p. 103-112.

Rebitzer, G. (2001): Modul Kosten (Life Cycle Costing Module), in: TU Berlin, C.A.U. GmbH, CTB CAMTEC, Denios AG, FhG ICT, FhG IPT, Ford-Werke AG, MAN Technologie AG, Sachsenring Entwicklungs GmbH, TU Cottbus: Systematische Auswahlkriterien für die Entwicklung von Verbundwerkstoffen unter Beachtung ökologischer Erfordernisse – Abschlussphase (euroMat 2001), Forschungsbericht (Research Report), BMBF-Förderprogramm Sicherung des Industriestandorts Deutschland, Projektträger DLR, p. 324-397.

Rebitzer, G., Borsdorf, R., Haupt, H.-J., Horn, S., Hübner, C., Schmidt, W.-P., Volkwein, S. (2001): Beispiel Trägermodul Vorderwagen (Case Study Front Subframe System), in: TU Berlin, C.A.U. GmbH, CTB CAMTEC, Denios AG, FhG ICT, FhG IPT, Ford-Werke AG, MAN Technologie AG, Sachsenring Entwicklungs GmbH, TU Cottbus: Systematische Auswahlkriterien für die Entwicklung von Verbundwerkstoffen unter Beachtung ökologischer Erfordernisse – Abschlussphase (euroMat 2001), Forschungsbericht (Research Report), BMBF-Förderprogramm Sicherung des Industriestandorts Deutschland, Projektträger DLR, p. 637-688.

Rebitzer, G., Hunkeler, D. (2001): Merging Economic and Environmental Information in Life Cycle Management, in: Proceedings of the Life Cycle Management Conference 2001, Copenhagen, p. 45-47.

Schmidt, W.-P., Corley, M., Heffels, R., Kortüm, D., Thomanek, R., Rebitzer, G. (2000): Non Stop Use, in: The New Ford Mondeo, Special Edition of ATZ and MTZ, 10/2000.

SETAC (1997): Life Cycle Impact Assessment – The State of the Art (edited by Barnthouse, L. et al.), Society for Environmental Toxicology and Chemistry, Pensacola.

SETAC-Europe (1996): Towards a Methodology for Life Cycle Impact Assessment (edited by Udo de Haes, H.A.), Society for Environmental Toxicology and Chemistry Europe, Brussels.

SETAC-Europe (2001): Life Cycle Management – Definitions, Case Studies and Corporate Applications (authored by Hunkeler, D. et al.), Life Cycle Management Conference 2001, Copenhagen.

VDI 2225 (1996): Technisch-wirtschaftliches Konstruieren – Blatt 2 - Tabellenwerk (Entwurf) (Engineering Design at Optimum Cost, Draft), VDI-Verlag, Düsseldorf.

WCED (World Commission On Environment and Development) (ed.) (1987): Our Common Future ('The Brundlandt Report'), Oxford University Press, Oxford.

WEEE (2001): Directive Proposal on Waste Electrical and Electronic Equipment, European Parliament and Council, Brussels.

Wenzel, H., Hauschild, M., Alting, L. (1997): Environmental Assessment of Products, Chapman & Hall, London.

White, A. L., Savage, D., Shapiro, K. (1996): Life-Cycle Costing – Concepts and Applications, in: Curran, M. A. (ed.): Environmental Life-Cycle Assessment, McGraw-Hill, New York, p. 7.1-7.19.

Transfer Pricing in Supply Chains: An Exercise in Internal Marketing and Cost Management

Messaoud Mehafdi

1 Introduction 148
2 Intra-Firm Trade and the Supply Chain 149
3 An Internal Customer and Marketing Perspective 153
4 Value-Based Performance Management in TP Environments ... 155
5 Conditions for Positive Change 159
6 Conclusion 161
7 References 161

Summary:
Supply chains are, in many industries, dominated by non-market activities in the form of intra-firm trade, often between geographically dispersed subsidiaries of multinational companies. Internal supplier (transferor) - customer (transferee) relationships are governed by internal decisions with transfer prices as the pivotal element. The study of the intra-firm portion of supply chain relationships is a necessity for a proper understanding of cost management throughout the entire supply chain. Transfer prices have usually been driven by subsidiary performance evaluation and international tax consideration, which only seeks a redistribution of accounting income. The actions of the business units involved in internal transactions can affect costs, profits, cash flows, final product customers and competitive position. Practical suggestions are made to ensure that intra-firm trade and transfer pricing are geared towards value creation for all parties.

Keywords:
Transfer Pricing, Internal Supply Chain, Cost Management, Balanced Scorecard

1 Introduction

Creating and sustaining shareholder value, not just accounting profit, top the list of priorities in many modern companies, are pivotal in strategic sourcing decisions and reflect the credibility of corporate governance systems[1]. To effect the shareholder value objective, new concepts and management models such as supply chain management (SCM), relationship management and internal marketing, activity-based management and performance management have emerged in the last decade or so. This paper focuses on SCM from the perspective of transfer pricing (TP), which is reputed as a perennial puzzle for both academics and practitioners[2]. TP is a predominantly management accounting tool used by transnational corporations to facilitate and regulate internal transactions of tangible and intangible property, often between geographically dispersed subsidiaries[3]. The integrative approach of SCM to achieve and sustain shareholder value by delivering products to markets makes management accounting tools indispensable for effective SCM, especially as lowering costs and maximizing net revenues currently preoccupy many leading manufacturing companies[4].

From a managerial perspective, TP has been described as a 'managerial ambiguity by design'[5] but that is the case only when the unitary view of profit maximization, and the 'product out' approach that underlies it, dominates[6]. Companies can no longer afford such an approach, which has at least proven costly to many in the tax courts when profit maximization created the irresistible temptation to use TP for false accounting. In many industries, intra-firm trade is too materially significant and therefore strategically important to be confined to the constrictions of accounting numbers.

A supply chain perspective of intra-firm trade, not just setting tax-driven transfer prices, is necessary to determine whether intra-firm trade, like trade with third parties, creates shareholder value reflecting the opportunity cost of the resources consumed. Intra-firm trade creates both strategic and operational SCM decisions which include not only location, production, inventory and transportation, but also

---

[1] See Quinn, Hilmer (1994); Copeland et al. (1995); Felon et al. (1996); Slater, Olson (1996); Stewart, Ikin (1999).
[2] See Emmanuel, Mehafdi (1994).
[3] For the international tax implications of TP and the arm's length rule that governs transfer price determination, see Emmanuel and Mehafdi (1994); Ernst & Young (1999); Mehafdi (2000).
[4] See Shapiro (2001).
[5] See Vancil (1979).
[6] See Mehafdi (2000).

capital investment and pricing decisions. Despite the global importance of both SCM and TP, there is a noticeable dearth of serious analysis of their relationship[7]. Hence the contribution of this paper to highlight the importance of intra-firm trade and pricing and the management of intra-firm relationships for effective SCM. Since the performance of the chain as a whole is necessary for attaining the objectives of the members of the supply chain, the inclusion of internal customers broadens the purpose of SCM beyond the traditional provision of service to final customers by meeting fixed demand[8]. The remainder of this paper presents a supply chain perspective of intra-firm trade and pricing, focusing in particular on the roles of both transferor and transferee in creating and sustaining value and the necessity of value-based performance management. Suggestions are then made for designing value-based performance measures in the presence of intra-firm trade. This is followed with a discussion of the necessary conditions to pave the way for positive change for better management of TP-based supply chains and for translating improvements into new market opportunities, not just meeting fixed demand.

2 Intra-Firm Trade and the Supply Chain

2.1 Insourcing vs. Outsourcing

There is no internal process typifying intra-firm supply chains better than TP (see Figure 1) which is essentially a preference of a hierarchical governance structure over an external intermediate product market. In strategic terms, it indicates a choice of insourcing over outsourcing, a focus on core competencies, technological differentiation, and the responsible commitment of the company's tangible and intangible assets in a common ownership set-up. The study of intra-firm supply chain relationships is a necessity as evidence suggests that large companies constantly create internal markets or undo them through outsourcing[9]. Thus, the number of players in a supply chain and, consequently, the complexity of the chain and how much direct control a company exerts over it, depend on the two opposite strategies of outsourcing and vertical integration. With outsourcing, the company cedes parts of the supply chain to contract manufacturers. Under full vertical integration, most of the supply chain is owned by a single company,

---

[7] The few works identified as relevant for the purpose of this paper are Adler (1996); Kaplan et al. (1997); Cooper, Slagmulder (1998a,b,c); Shank et al. (1998); Cullen et al. (1999); Holmström et al. (2000); Shapiro (2001).
[8] See Schary, Larsen (1995).
[9] See Quinn, Hilmer (1994); Magidson, Polcha (1992); Cullen et al. (1999); Quinn (1999); Sheridan (1999).

usually through high volumes of intra-firm trade and TP policies[10], making the internal supplier-customer relationship the decisive link in a company's supply chain that affecting the objectives of the external members of the chain.

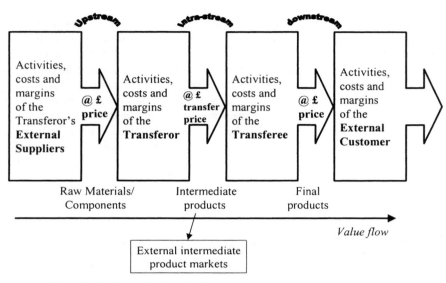

Figure 1: Transfer Pricing in the Supply Chain

Global supply chains now depend heavily on the flow of raw materials and intermediate products, noting that most foreign direct investment flows are intra-firm. Intra-firm trade accounts for more than half of all the trade between OECD member countries and about $1.6 trillion of world trade[11], thus determining the sequence of product flow along the demand-supply chain in scores of manufacturing companies across the globe. As outsourcing strategies have not always lived up to expectations, recently resulting in serious supply chain problems that destroying shareholder value in many leading companies[12], intra-firm trade can be expected to grow as companies re-align their supply chains. Failure to re-align supply chains with strategies can prove costly[13], implying that a

---

[10] Empirical studies show that intra-firm trade varies from negligible amounts to near total vertical integration. The level of intra-firm trade tends to be high in the knowledge-based and capital intensive sectors of electronics, chemicals and pharmaceuticals (see Emmanuel and Mehafdi, 1994; Mehafdi, 2000).

[11] See Cooper (1993); Schary, Skjøtt-Larsen (1995); Mehafdi (2000).

[12] See Lakeman et al. (2001).

[13] See Tamas (2000); McAdam, Brown (2001).

proper co-ordination of intra-firm trade, not just setting tax-driven transfer prices, is necessary for effective SCM.

2.2 Is TP the Weakest Link?

Although the international TP arm's length principle assumes economic growth and wealth creation, it is limited to pricing formulae and rules for profit redistribution by tax authorities and does not provide a mechanism for SCM. A company's transfer prices may be deemed acceptable by tax authorities simply because the prices are "comparable" to those of other companies. However, "market prices" do not necessarily indicate allocative and productive efficiencies or the proper management of demand-supply chains which produce better value and more taxable income. Anecdotal evidence reveals that TP policies create inefficiencies and result in patterns of production and distribution that pile up costs and destroy value for the company as a whole, for example when transferors displace their internal customers in favor of external ones or by simply passing on inefficiencies to internal customers via cost-based 'arm's length' prices[14]. Thus the role of a subsidiary in the effectiveness of a supply chain cannot be underestimated. Moreover, supply chain decisions are influenced by the actions of fiscal authorities to control the TP practices of companies. For instance, the IRS's tough actions on TP issues have been described as "weapons of mass destruction" that have created an anti-competitive business climate for US companies and forced them to shift investments to other countries[15].

Up-stream in Figure 1, the transferor is a customer of external suppliers for raw materials; **in-stream** there is a joint relationship where the transferor is a supplier to the internal customer (the transferee) who in turn is a supplier **downstream** to the final product customer. The ultimate consumer is therefore a customer of a customer and the satisfaction of each is essential for value creation. The transferee may also have external suppliers of input factors used in conjunction to the intermediate product supplied by the transferor. Like with any chain, the strength of the TP chain is defined by its weakest link, implying that proper management of all its links to yield total customer satisfaction is essential for TP to be effective. The weakest link may often be the in-stream activity (see Figure 2) because corporate dictate may not allow the transferor and the transferee to switch to external intermediate markets, thus giving rise to opportunism and other undesirable performance behavior. Opportunistic behavior[16] depends on how much each party to the internal transaction has invested in specific assets and the control mechanisms in operation.

---

[14] See Emmanuel, Mehafdi (1994); Schary, Skjott-Larsen (1995).
[15] See Chip (1999).
[16] See Stump, Heide (1996).

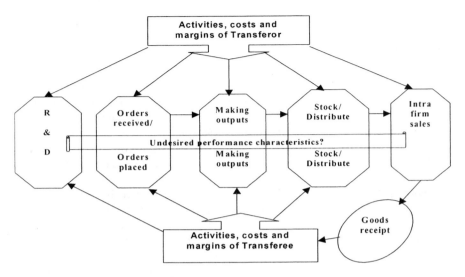

Figure 2: Intra-Stream Supply Chain

The common ownership crosses organizational boundaries and creates (unequal) internal supplier-customer relationships of varying degrees of complexity and impact on value depending on a host of factors, in particular:

- The degree of decision-making autonomy a division manager has over intra-firm trade, TP and capital investment.
- The material significance of the internal trade to the parties involved as well as its ramifications on the supply chain's external links.
- The extent of information asymmetry, for example with regard to TP objectives and cost structures, and the emphasis on accounting numbers as divisional performance indicators.
- The propinquity of the transacting divisions, the trust between their managers and with central management, as well as the willingness to exchange information.
- The position of the TP product on its life cycle curve, the existence of viable outsourcing options and the freedom to choose suppliers.
- Each division's environment. Divisions do not operate in a vacuum, they are affected by the economic conditions (industry, market and the economy in general), as well as organizational structures and strategies, corporate credos and ethical climate.

- The differences between transferors and transferees with regard to objectives, resource mix (e.g. skills, technology, intellectual property), time horizons, cost structures, attitude to risk and perception of value.

These factors indicate that competition for scarce resources, and political control may make the common ownership a tug of war between the internally transacting parties. With each divisional manager having and effecting partial ownership of the assets and processes used in the intra-firm trade, possibly involving irreversible investments, there is the incentive to create hazards along the value chain in order to make and parade the desired accounting results dictated by the performance evaluation system. Political control and competition for scarce resources can incite managers to myopically forsake sound TP practice when under pressure to meet or exceed some crude accounting targets. It is not uncommon for transferor divisions to disadvantage transferee divisions, thus affecting their supply chain decisions[17]. This points to the managerial inability to identify internal weak links and, to avoid such situations, an internal customer and marketing perspective is suggested below.

3 An Internal Customer and Marketing Perspective

Intra-firm trade creates an internal supplier (transferor) - customer (transferee) set along the supply chain, mostly governed by internal decisions under some form of decentralized management. It is evident from the foregoing list of factors that the internal marketing concept which has been in vogue throughout the 1990s[18] is naturally applicable to intra-firm trade which Figure 1 depicts for a two-division company.

3.1 Intra-Firm Partnerships

The concept of partnership which is pivotal for the success of supply chains[19] is absent from the TP literature which is mostly dominated by tax concerns, especially in the wake of tightened arm's length legislation. The transferor and transferee are trading partners and, by making the internal customer concept a pivotal element in this partnership, enables the transferee to be actively involved in the transferor's link of the supply chain and prevents the transferor from creating costs for the transferee. Unilateral actions taken by the supplier that ignore the customer's performance usually waste resources without resulting in

---

[17] See Emmanuel, Mehafdi (1994); Schary, Skjott-Larsen (1995).
[18] See George (1990); Foreman, Money (1995); Hauser et al. (1996).
[19] See Hauser et al. (1996); Stump, Heide (1996); Holmström et al. (2000).

better SCM[20]. Thus, by applying the internal customer concept to TP, managers will not only make the transferor recognize the transferee as a customer, but they will also introduce the necessary mechanisms to guarantee internal customer satisfaction as a product winds its way along the TP supply chain. In other words, the internal customer concept makes the difference between a passive/adversarial association based on transfer price imposition/negotiation pervading the vast TP literature and an active relationship focused on collaboration where the transferee has a say in the transferor's product design and process efficiency. This should lead to more visibility up and down the demand-supply chain, drive efficiencies, create more value and avoid rushing into outsourcing decisions that fail to deliver[21].

3.2 Value Tracking

Under efficient operating conditions, value is added along the TP supply chain as the product develops and traverses from the up-stream stage through to the downstream stage with TP as the regulating mechanism in the intra-stream stage. External prices of input factors regulate the upstream and the external selling price of the final product regulates the downstream. At the end of the TP chain is the margin earned from selling the product to the final customer, calculated after deducting the cost of TP and non-TP activities from the selling price. The effect of intra-stream activities between transferor and transferee on this margin needs to be determined. Although it has been argued that it might be difficult for a firm to establish the value of an intermediate product to the customer of the final product[22], this does not proscribe indirect tracking of value as perceived by the internal customer, the recipient of the intermediate product at the set transfer price. Customer satisfaction can make the difference for a company's success, and the greater the value created by the transferor for the transferee, i.e. the fewer inefficiencies and cavalier attitudes and the more acceptable the transfer price, the greater the margin earned on the final product, and the better the value created for final customers and shareholders. Since competitive advantage is achieved when the difference between the value created and its cost is positive[23], the return from intra-firm trade activities should be in excess of the cost of capital invested in those activities. Otherwise, restructuring the TP supply chain to make it more value-adding, for example by removing and outsourcing ineffective integration, becomes a strategic priority, not just a cost containment exercise.

---

[20] See Holmström et al. (2000).
[21] For current real life examples of failed outsourcing strategies in the electronics sector, see the Booz-Allen report (Lakenan et al., 2001).
[22] See Hergert, Morris (1989).
[23] See Porter (1985).

Failures by the transferor in the joint transferor-transferee relationship reflect poor business risk management with manifest repercussions on the transferee's 'total cost of ownership', as well as tension, conflict, and value loss. The company may end up heaping responsibility and blame on the transferee division which is in the front line to the final customer, yet the transferee's cost differentiation position may be inhibited by the transferor's undesirable actions. The transferor's inefficiencies effectively reduce the number of links in the supply chain that positively contribute to the final margin and the return on TP-specific investments. This may result in rushing into fruitless outsourcing decisions and the disposal of manufacturing assets and skills to contract manufacturers.

It is therefore essential to compel the transferor division to assess its ability to create value for the transferee which in turn must assess its ability to create value for the final customer. This ability depends on whether there is a clear statement of expectations and objectives of the TP system, whether external suppliers of input factors deliver value, and whether performance measures are value oriented. The statement of expectations and objectives serves as a platform for mutual understanding to reach agreement in the joint relationship. Since both transferor and transferee may be customers of and suppliers to external parties, their external contractual relationships could serve as a benchmark for the internal supplier-customer relationship. As both transferor and transferee would only want the best from their external suppliers, they should also form a close partnership to deliver better value. For the internal marketing orientation to be effective, value-based evaluation of TP-related performance is proposed.

4 Value-Based Performance Management in TP Environments

Orientating intra-firm trade towards shareholder value should add to a company's ability to signal positively about its governance structure and management performance and thus strengthen its position in the capital markets. For TP to be part of a company's mission to add value for its shareholders by creating value for its customers and thus remain financially viable, requires the inclusion of TP in strategic planning, not just tax planning, and the design and implementation of the necessary controls to prevent TP from inhibiting value creation which determines competitive position, profits and cash flows. This requires measuring performance in a way to establish whether there is value-maximizing management of all the investments in intra-firm trade or whether intra-firm trade only adds to risk and costs.

4.1 TP and Performance Mismanagement

Performance evaluation and incentive schemes are a key feature of the control apparatus in the large company, and value-based performance measures are not an option if a company wants to successfully implement a supply-chain and internal customer approach to TP. It is well known that traditional performance measures such as return on investment do not support value-based management.[24] As explained above, the prime objective of the internal marketing orientation is to make the transferor aware of the effect of their actions on the transferee in the pursuit of shareholder value. The transferor link in the TP chain may have undesirable performance characteristics which transfer prices, especially cost-based ones, and accounting-based performance measures may not only conceal but also subtly encourage. For example, a full cost-based TP system fully focused on tax matters can lead the transferor to inhibit / destroy value by:

- Behaving irresponsibly with overhead activities since all the costs, direct and indirect, will eventually become a revenue for the transferor and a cost for the transferee.

- Causing delivery delays with repercussions on resource consumption, cycle time and weakening the transferee's position with respect to customer satisfaction and the ability to respond to changing market demands.

- Not properly utilizing capacity, causing capital inefficiency, especially on small amounts of capital expenditure that usually are not subject to scrutiny at higher management levels. A division may easily seek and secure generous capital from central management if TP works in its favor and makes it appear as if it is generating sufficient internal funds. The existing research has not yet studied the possible effects that TP can have on capital structure, cost of capital, gearing and capital investment decisions.

A derivative of the much reviled irrelevance of accounting data for strategic decision-making[25] is that a division's financial report only partially describes its abilities and performance. The price placed by accounting-based cost allocations on an intermediate product may not reflect the effort expended by the transferor (i.e. value delivered) nor match the expectations of internal and external customers to the product (i.e. value perceived). The structure of a transferor division and its portfolio of intangible assets (e.g. skills of its employees, its software development, data bases and management systems) may be its most important value drivers but these are not captured by transfer prices or readily identified in its financial statements and traditional performance measures such as return on capital employed.

---

[24] See Rappaport (1986); Bughin, Copeland (1997).
[25] See Porter (1985); Hergert, Morris (1989).

4.2 Examples of Possible Value-Based Performance Measures for Effective SCM

Below are examples of performance measures that the transferee could use to ensure that the transferor delivers value, not simply pass on accumulated costs through the transfer price. Transaction costs become more apparent through such performance measures and so will the cash flow and finance implications of intra-firm trade, especially in companies with significant levels of internal trade.

4.2.1 Transfer Price Differential Index (TPDI)

$$\text{TPDI} = \frac{\text{Market Price - Transfer Price}}{\text{Market Price}} \text{ or } \frac{\text{Transfer Price - Market Price}}{\text{Transfer Price}}$$

When there is an external competitive market for the intermediate product but company policy requires the transferee to source internally, these ratios can be used to gradually align the transferor's portion of the TP supply chain with the market. A consistently negative price differential from a higher than market transfer price may be due to product design problems, prices of upstream input factors, inefficiencies in the transferor's production process, or the result of notional interest charges from head office when the company practices thin capitalization. A transfer price which is persistently higher than market price can also catch the ever scrutinising eye of tax commissioners, triggering costly tax audits for the company and possible heavy fines that eat into profits and cash flow. On the other hand, a consistently positive price differential from a lower than market transfer price could signal to senior management that the transferor is making the necessary efforts to create value by, for example, simplifying product design and quality assurance programs and passing on the savings to the transferee through the transfer price. It is then for the transferee to demonstrate value creation downstream in the TP supply chain. All cost savings made can then be translated into new market opportunities.

4.2.2 Internal Supplier Quality Performance Index (ISQPI)

$$\text{ISQPI} = \frac{\text{Total Quantity Transferred - Defective Units Received}}{\text{Total Quantity Transferred}}$$

This ratio judges the transferor's operational performance with respect to product quality specifications in the same way as they would apply to products supplied to external customers. Improvements in the ratio would indicate more value created intra-stream. A ratio of 1 indicates total quality and internal customer satisfaction. No improvements or deterioration in the ratio would signal waste of shareholders' funds and the need to reconsider the intra-firm transaction and possibly outsource it. If the transferee also buys from an existing intermediate market, similar calculations can be made to benchmark the transferor's product quality performance. The cost incurred from receiving, handling, using, returning or scrapping the defective units can be captured in the 'total cost of ownership' ratio described below.

4.2.3 Internal Supplier Cost Index (ISCI)

$$ISCI = \frac{\text{Transfer price} + \text{Cost of non-value added activities caused by transferor}}{\text{Transfer Price}}$$

The cost of non-value added activities in this ratio may include opportunity costs from production stoppages caused by late delivery by the transferor or defective units delivered and processed. This measure helps calculate the total ownership cost of intermediate products bought from the transferor, and can highlight product design problems and process inefficiencies at various stages in the TP value chain. If the transferee buys some of the intermediate product from external suppliers, comparisons can then be made and acted upon.

4.2.4 A Balanced Scorecard of Performance Measures

To effect an internal marketing approach, the above performance indicators can form part of a balanced scorecard of measures which distinguishes and compares performance internally and externally (see Figure 3). Such distinction is necessary when intra-firm trade is significant in both quantity and value and transfer prices determining divisional financial results.

Tying the transferor's reward to how well they are evaluated by the transferee through performance measures such as the ones suggested above would force the transferor to constantly ensure that value is being created upstream and intra-stream. Evaluating the transferor's performance in this way would make the transferor recognize and satisfy the needs of the transferee with no or little resource wastage. To avoid opportunism, free rider situations and collusion, central management need to hold the transferee to higher standards that reflect their evaluation of the transferor. In other words, if the transferee gives a highly favorable evaluation of the transferor, the transferee is expected to show how this reflects in their performance to satisfy the final customer. Therefore, certain conditions need to be satisfied to effect the necessary positive change to align intra-firm trade and pricing with shareholder value.

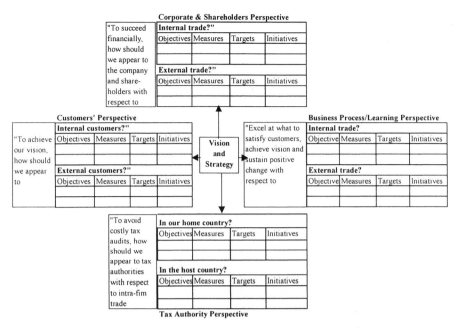

Figure 3: The Transferor's Scorecard of Performance Measures [adapted from Kaplan and Norton's (1996) model].

5 Conditions for Positive Change

5.1 The Essential Role of Proactive Management

The proper functioning of a company's TP supply chain may be influenced by corporate governance systems, or the lack of them, and that determines how much leeway managers have to take an active role in steering TP towards shareholder value. Managers need to ask for their companies whether TP is simply a 'critical mass' factor whereby a certain amount of internalized trade is needed for mere survival, especially in the highly competitive knowledge-intensive industries? The existing TP literature does not answer this question or discuss how a company can use its tangible and intangible resources most advantageously in going to market and reaching its external supplier-customer set via TP activities and its internal supplier-customer set. Nor does it clarify whether TP nurtures in managers a 'laissez-faire' and supercilious attitude towards the investors of funds used in intra-firm trade activities.

By taking an active role in steering intra-firm trade and TP policies away from short-term earnings and gearing them towards value creation, managers would not only financially benefit all of a company's stakeholders (its divisions, shareholders, host countries, etc.) but they would also broaden managerial horizons and remove the temptation to tamper with short-term results which is common with arm's length rule compliance. Managers need to ask and seek answers to the following questions to stimulate positive change:

- Is there a clear strategy for intra-firm trade and TP to create shareholder value, and is this strategy properly communicated and well understood by transferors and transferees?
- Are the decision-making processes at central and divisional levels sufficiently aligned with this strategy, for example through a performance management system that tracks and measures the effect of TP on shareholder value?
- Which activities in the TP supply chain contribute the most to shareholder value, i.e. which activities are most valuable to both internal and external customers? Should the less value creating intra-firm activities be outsourced?
- What are the key drivers or value building blocks in TP activity? Are they the same or different from one division to another and what are the risks that could jeopardize value?
- Are capital and other resources consumed by intra-firm trade allocated to value creating activities? If value is being created, what measures are there to enhance it or what safeguards exist to at least prevent it from being destroyed?

5.2   Mindsets and Education

The above questions call for a thorough self inspection to re-orient TP onto shareholder value which requires a re-molding of mindsets towards positive change. Education and training should not be overlooked in the process[26] to enable managers to express their dissatisfaction with and challenge the status quo. They can then establish through investigation and analysis whether efforts and resources involved in intra-firm trade and pricing are harnessed towards value-creating activities. The status quo may prevent managers from seeing the link between their company's TP system and the rest of the supply chain, first because TP systems can become imbedded routines that are resistant to change and, second, because of the preoccupation with satisfying the burdensome requirements of tax authorities in implementing the arm's length principle. The mindset needed is one

---

[26]   See Drumond (1996).

which makes both transferor and transferee realize that they are entrusted with creating and sustaining value for their individual divisions as well as for their internal and external customers. A transferee division at the front line to the external market cannot accommodate the changing expectations of the final customer unless the transferor does that earlier in the TP supply chain. Hence the need for the type of performance measure suggested earlier.

6 Conclusion

TP systems are important tools for managing intra-firm transactions and should become a focal point in supply chain management analysis. Focusing only on international tax issues and traditional accounting-based performance measures can mask the negative ripple effects that TP activity can have on the supply chain. The way forward in dealing with a business issue as important and complex as TP is by making it an integral part of strategic planning. This involves delimiting and examining the entire TP supply chain, adopting an 'internal customer' perspective in managing the joint transferor-transferee relationship, and supporting that with value-based performance measures and incentive schemes. The topic is rich with opportunities for further research whether through empirical investigation or, if access to essential data is an insuperable obstacle, through theory and model building.

7 References

Adler, R. W. (1996): Transfer Pricing for World Class Manufacturing, in: Long Range Planning, Vol. 29, No. 1 (1996), p. 69-75.

Bughin, J., Copeland, T. E. (1997): The Virtuous Cycle of Shareholder Value Creation, in: The McKinsey Quarterly, No. 2 (1997), p. 156-167.

Chip, B.(1999): Impact of US Tax Rules on International Competitiveness. Testimony of the Chairman of the Tax Committee, European-American Business Council before House Committee on Ways and Means, U.S. Congress, June 30, 1999.

Cooper, J. (1999): Logistics Strategies for Global Businesses, in: International Journal of Physical Distribution and Logistics Management, Vol. 23, No. 4 (1999), p. 12-23.

Cooper, R., Slagmulder, R. (1998a). Cost Management for Internal Markets, in: Management Accounting (USA), Vol. 79, No. 10 (April) (1998), p. 16-17.

Cooper, R., Slagmulder, R. (1998b): Cost Management for Internal Markets, in: Management Accounting (USA), Vol. 79, No. 11 (May) (1998), p. 16-17.

Cooper R., Slagmulder, R. (1998c): Micro Profit Centres, in: Management Accounting (USA), Vol. 79, No. 12 (June) (1998), p. 16-17.

Copeland, T. E., Koller T., Murrin, J. (1995): Valuation: Measuring and Managing the Value of Companies, 2nd edition, John Wiley & Sons, New York.

Cullen, J., Berry, A. J., Seal, W. Dunlop, A. Ahmed, M., Marson, J. (1999): Interfirm Supply Chains: The Contribution of Management Accounting, in: Management Accounting (UK), Vol. 77, No. 6 (June) (1999), p. 30-32.

Drumond, E. J. (1996): Applying Value-Based Management to Procurement, in: International Journal of Physical Distribution, vol. 26, No. 1 (January) (1996), p. 5-16.

Emmanuel, C., Mehafdi, M. (1994): Transfer Pricing, CIMA, London.

Ernst & Young (1999): Global Transfer Pricing Survey: Practices, Perceptions and Trends in 19 Countries for 2000 and Beyond, Ernst & Young, London.

Felon, R. F., Hudnut, A., Heeckeren, J. (1996): Putting a Value on Board Governance, in: The McKinsey Quarterly, No. 4 (1996), p. 170-175.

Foreman, S. K., Money, A. H. (1995): Internal Marketing: Concepts, Measurement and Application, in: Journal of Marketing Management, Vol. 11 (1995), p. 755-768.

George, W. R. (1990): Internal Marketing and Organizational Behavior: a Partnership in Developing Customer-Conscious Employees at Every Level, in: Journal of Business Research, Vol. 20 (1990), p. 63-70.

Hauser, J. R., Simester, D. I., Wernerfelt, B. (1996): Internal Customers and Internal Suppliers, in: Journal of Marketing Research, Vol. 33, No. 3 (1996), p. 268-280.

Hergert, M., Morris, D. (1989): Accounting Data for Value Chain Analysis, in: Strategic Management Journal, Vol. 10 (1989), p. 175-188.

Holmström, J., Hoover JR, W. E., Louhiluoto, P., Vasara, P. (2000): The Other End of the Supply Chain, in: The Mackinsey Quarterly, No. 1 (2000), p. 62-71.

Kaplan, R. S., Norton, D. P. (1996): Linking the Balanced Scorecard to Strategy, in: California Management Review, Vol. 39, No. 1 (Fall) (1996), p. 53-79.

Kaplan, R. S., Weiss, D., Desheh, E. (1997): Transfer Pricing with ABC, in: Management Accounting (USA), Vol. 78, No. 11 (1997), p. 20-26.

Lakeman, B., Boyd, D., Frey, E. (2001): Why CISCO Fell: Outsourcing and Its Perils, in: Strategy+Business, August (2001), p. 54-65.

Lien, J. (1997): Intra-MNC Transactions Dominate Regional Trade, in: Singapore Business Times, 18 November (1997).

McAdam, R., Brown, L. (2001):. Strategic Alignment and the Supply Chain for the Steel Stockholder Sector: An Exploratory Case Study Analysis, in: Supply Chain Management: An International Journal, Vol. 6, No. 2 (2001), p. 83-95.

Magidson, J., Polcha, A. E. (1992):. Creating Market Economics Within Companies, in: Journal of Business Strategy, Vol. 13, No. 3 (May-June) (1992), p. 39-44.

Mehafdi, M. (2000): The Ethics of International Transfer Pricing, in: Journal of Business Ethics, Vol. 28, No. 4 (2000), p. 365-381.

Porter, M. (1985): Competitive Advantage: Creating and Sustaining Superior Performance, Free Press, New York.

Quinn, J. B. (1999): Strategic Outsourcing: Leveraging Knowledge Capabilities, in: Sloan Management Review, Vol 40, No. 4 (Summer) (1999), p. 9-23.

Quinn, J. B., Hilmer, F. G. (1994):. Strategic Outsourcing, in: Sloan Management Review 35(4), Summer (1994), p. 43-55.

Rappaport, A. (1986): Creating Shareholder Value: The New Standard for Business Performance, The Free Press, New York.

Schary, P. B., Skjøtt-Larsen, T. (1995):. Managing the Global Supply Chain, Handelshojskolens Forlag, Copenhagen.

Shank, J. K., Spiegel, E., Escher, A. (1998): Strategic Value Analysis for Competitive Advantage: An Illustration from the Petroleum Industry, in: Strategy+Business, Vol. 10 (1998,) p. 32-39.

Shapiro, J. F. (2001): Modeling the Supply Chain, Duxbury, Pacific Grove, CA, USA.

Sheridan, J. H. (1999): Managing the Chain, in: Industry Week, Vol. 248, No. 16 (September) (1999), p. 50-53.

Slater, S. F., Olson, E. M. (1996): A Value-Based Management System, in: Business Horizons, Vol. 39, No. 5 (September-October 1996), p. 48-52.

Stewart, R., Ikin, D. (1999): Best Practice in Shareholder Value, PriceWaterhouseCoopers Survey, London.

Stump, R. L., Heide, J. B. (1996): Controlling Supplier Opportunism in Industrial Relationships, in: Journal of Marketing Research, Vol. 33, (November 1996), p. 431-441.

Tamas, M. (2000): Mismatched Strategies: The Weak Link in the Supply Chain, in: Supply Chain Management: An International Journal, Vol. 5, No. 4 (2000), p. 171-175.

Vancil, R. (1979): Decentralization: Managerial Ambiguity by Design, Dow-Jones-Irwin, Homewood, Illinois.

The Role of Finance in Supply Chain Management

Lars Stemmler

1	Introduction	166
2	The Role of Finance in the Supply Chain	166
3	Financial Cost Drivers in the Supply Chain	167
4	Solutions for Supply Chain Finance	170
5	Supply Chain Finance: More than Supply Chain Management?	174
6	Supply Chain Finance: Conclusion	175
7	References	176

Summary:
Traditional supply chain management focuses on both materials and information flow. However, considerable cost reductions can also be achieved through optimally designed financial flows within the chain. Savings due to minimized stock levels may easily be offset by the costs to finance the remaining inventory. Inventory carrying costs do not only comprise of financing costs but also of costs associated with taking credit risks upon sale and taking out insurance. Therefore, it is the scope of supply chain management to integrate three flows: product, information and financial. Integrating financial services into supply chain management will not create a new (financial) product. It is however about realizing unused opportunities for cost reductions.

Keywords:
Supply Chain Management, Supply Chain Finance, Inventory Management, Short Term Asset Management

1 Introduction

Traditional supply chain management (SCM) focuses on eliminating waste in the pipeline, i.e. minimizing mass and time. Savings can be achieved through an integrated management of both the physical flow of materials and information along the chain. However, considerable cost reductions can also be gained through optimally designed financial flows associated with the physical movement of goods. While companies tend to target the more tangible cost elements such as handling and transport, the costs to finance products moving through the supply chain are prone to being forgotten. Cost savings due to minimized stock levels may easily be set off by the costs to finance the remaining inventory. Inventory carrying costs do not only comprise of financing costs but also of those costs associated with taking credit risks upon sale, supporting trade credit and taking out insurance. Furthermore, the cash flow and revenue stream generated by successful order fulfillment must be looked at closely. Identifying costs associated with finance which are driven by logistical activities is not an isolated task of the treasury department. On the contrary, it is the role of supply chain management to integrate three flows: product, information and financial. After defining the role of finance in a supply chain the drivers influencing finance related logistics costs are identified. Based on this theoretical framework practical solutions adopted in the logistics industry are explored answering the question of how to integrate financial flows into logistics. This market review will be put back into the theoretical context developed beforehand.

2 The Role of Finance in the Supply Chain

SCM can be defined as a management concept aimed at managing the processes along the supply chain.[1] This definition implies a view limited to optimizing the physical product flow and the information flow and is far too short-minded. By definition, an integrated management concept cannot exclude financial processes from the scope of SCM. Optimizing the finance flows can deliver a yet untapped potential for cost reductions. The length of any supply chain is determined by its cash-to-cash cycle.[2] As investors are interested in a decent return on their invested capital, any supply chain is basically finance related. Cash is turned into goods that in turn are sold to generate more cash. This implies the integration of finance

---

[1] See Weber, Dehler, Wertz (2000), p. 264.
[2] See Chopra, Neher (2001), p. 8.

flows besides information and material. Recent research carried out by Göpfert and Neher suggests that only a fraction of companies regard the management of financial flows as an integral part of supply chain management.[3] The majority of companies surveyed view SCM as incorporating traditional tasks only, e.g. transport and warehousing. Whereas 8 % of the companies see logistics as a transportation-only business, 57 % claim to pursue an all-embracing approach that includes cross-functional planning. However, such planning was meant to be focused on materials and information management.[4] Credit Suisse First Boston (CSFB), a bank, estimates the costs to finance products moving through a supply chain to approach those associated with transportation and distribution.[5] Due to different product values and different interest environments, this estimate can only be a rough guideline. However, it clearly shows the problem and its solution: the study of CSFB suggests that integrating the management of financial flows into a supply chain can deliver substantial cost savings. The aim of this paper is therefore twofold: first, raising awareness for the necessity of a completely cross-functional approach to supply chain management. The paper shall then, secondly, provide for ideas on how to integrate product, information and financial flows. Successful supply chain management goes beyond traditional approaches as it calls for coordinated planning of all those processes associated with moving products through the supply chain.

3 Financial Cost Drivers in the Supply Chain

There is no doubt that a successful business depends on accurate and timely delivery of goods or services to its customers. Supply chain management aims at minimizing mass and time. Needless to say, an efficiently managed supply chain requires the measurement of the costs associated with the physical movement of goods and related information flows.

The financial performance of a company can conveniently be measured by calculating the return on investment (ROI). Defined as the product of two ratios - the margin and the capital turnover - the ROI can be improved by an increase of one or both of these ratios. The cost element within the margin attributable to logistics contains selling and administrative expenses such as order processing, transportation and warehousing costs.[6] Additionally, interest expenses, namely inventory carrying costs and - for ease of reference - lease and rent expenses must be taken into account.

---

[3] See Göpfert, Neher (2001), p. 49-51.
[4] See Göpfert, Neher (2001), p. 49-51.
[5] See Palmieri, Africk (2001).
[6] See Christopher (1991), p. 16.

The logistics impact on the capital element of the ROI is determined - among other factors - by financing options for the inventory and the ownership structure of fixed assets such as plant, depots and warehouses forming the logistics network of the company.

A crucial element of ROI is the revenue stream. This component is central to the liquidity of the organization. Hence, if SCM is about managing the cash-to-cash cycle of this organization, cash flow management forms the backbone of it.

It can be seen from the analysis above that inventory and cash management are the key drivers of finance costs related to logistics. The costs of carrying the inventory associated with finance include inter-alia receivables, taking credit risk upon sale, and supporting trade credit and process costs related to collecting receivables.[7] Most companies have a clear idea of the tangible cost element of their supply chain such as transportation and warehousing costs. Hence, as these costs are easily identifiable, they are a prime target for optimization. However, even this is a tricky undertaking. According to the CSFB analysis, companies were able to cut inventory carrying costs from 5,4 % of GDP in 1990 to approximately 4 % in 2000.[8] Whereas it can be claimed that reduced inventory levels contributed to this cost cutting, a great proportion of the benefits were driven by a reduction in interest rates having a positive impact on the costs to finance inventory.[9] It is very bold to claim that a reduction of finance costs has at least as great an impact on the total logistics costs as savings achieved in transport and warehousing. This argument, however, outlines the problem clearly. In the following chapters a closer look is taken at inventory carrying costs in the supply chain. There are the following basic cost drivers to investigate: Finance costs are kept artificially high not only due to a lack of information sharing and limited co-ordination along the pipeline, but also due to lengthened payment terms. Also, the quality of invoicing must be taken into account.

3.1 Increased Information Sharing

The costs to finance inventory can be reduced by increased information sharing. Finance costs are mainly determined by the interest rate to finance inventory and receivables charged by the company's financiers. The interest rate reflects the cost to fund plus a risk premium the financier considers necessary to cover the credit risk and associated costs such as auditing and inspection expenses. The costs to audit and inspect inventory are influenced by the availability of accurate information about levels and locations of material. Obviously, financiers and logisticians require the same information.

---

[7] See Palmieri, Africk (2001).
[8] See Palmieri, Africk (2001).
[9] See Palmieri, Africk (2001).

Information on inventory levels and status can thus be shared between logistics providers and financiers. From a financing point of view, reliable information of inventory status delivered on a real-time basis reduces the risk associated with financing inventory. A lower risk exposure will be reflected in the costs of credit the company has to shoulder. Hence, the integration of financiers into the information flows along the supply chain is credit enhancing.

3.2 Limited Coordination

In addition to the reduction potential of the costs of credit through optimized information sharing, an improved coordination between supply chain participants to provide finance can result in a lower margin and, hence, lower costs to finance inventory. Typically, each participant in the supply chain arranges its finance independently. Lines of credit to finance products in the pipeline are established by suppliers, manufacturers and retailers separately. Not only does this practice result in costly duplications of processes, but also in higher individual costs to finance as each participant negotiates its own account. Improved coordination in terms of joint negotiating or eliminating duplications provides the opportunity to build a powerful cost saving tool.

3.3 The Payment Terms

The third cost driver turns out to be extended payment terms. The finance costs are pushed up by lengthy payment periods. Very often payment terms of „net 30" become „net 60" or even worse. These terms are often accepted in order not to lose an important customer. The longer the payment terms the higher the interest payable to make available funds financing receivables. These unproductive assets tie up scarce financial resources. Furthermore, longer payment periods might increase the risk of a particular receivable to become a doubtful account, pushing the risk element of the applicable interest rate even higher. As a result, the small supplier bearing relatively high costs of capital subsidizes its customer, probably a large manufacturer or retailer with low capital costs.

3.4 The Quality of Invoicing

This cost driver is closely related to the payment terms. Speed and accuracy of invoicing heavily affects cash flow and accounts receivables management. A short order cycle time requires rapid issuance of the invoice. An inaccurate invoice can deter a customer from paying which results in extended payment lead-time and in turn an unstable cash flow.[10] A cash gap opens requiring additional liquidity in order to be filled.

3.5 Supply Chain Finance as Part of an Integrated Supply Chain Management

The analysis above demonstrates that an efficient supply chain management must be based on an understanding of three critical components, namely:

1. The physical movement of goods
2. The availability of information and the ability to integrate it into the supply chain participant's systems along the pipeline
3. The embedding of financial services into the supply chain.

The aim is to drive shareholder value by combining logistics, IT and finance into a single supply chain management system. How to achieve this? From the above, forming partnerships along the supply chain seems to be one part of the answer. Plentiful voices to form partnerships and cooperations can be heard, particularly in the field of e-commerce, so this suggestion sounds less convincing. However, the difference in our case is the apparent lack of integration in the field of finance that needs to be addressed.

4 Solutions for Supply Chain Finance

4.1 Basic Services

Solutions for supply chain finance are offered by banks and third party logistics providers (3PL) alike. Both see supply chain finance as the opportunity to broaden their respective portfolio. Particularly, 3PLs go beyond traditional logistics. In addition to value-added services such as labeling and packaging, financial services offered by 3PL are part of their strategy to generate extra revenue and position themselves as a one-stop-shop for logistics services. The use of the Internet facilitates such strategies. The connectivity and visibility provided by the Internet allows supply chain integration across company boundaries. Services relating to supply chain finance fall into four broad categories:

---

[10] Christopher (1991), p. 18.

1. Billing, effecting payments and foreign exchange (FX)-transactions,
2. Accounts receivables management,
3. Inventory finance and management of trade credits,
4. Insurance.

Electronic billing delivers invoices electronically, facilitates the dispute resolution process and allows a speedy settlement of invoices online.[11] E-billing is a prime example of how financial services can be integrated seamlessly into the logistical information flow as invoice data is based on order and delivery information provided by the transport provider. E-billing reduces the need to check invoices manually; the ability to establish the relevant IT-based procedures can cut process costs. Banks also provide online settlement and clearing infrastructure for transactions generated for example by exchanges and e-marketplaces. FX-trading and settlement capabilities can be embedded into this infrastructure. Accounts receivables management goes beyond providing simple payment transaction infrastructure. It is not only about trading receivables at a discount on their carrying value, but also - more generally speaking - about enabling the customers to meet their financial obligations. This requires a deeper understanding of the relevant markets only a specialist supply chain finance provider can offer. Providing billing services, payment infrastructure and accounts receivables management in the broadest sense means managing the complete range of financial transactions and the related cash flows along a supply chain.[12] Here, substantial value can be added by offering integrated supply chain financial management. Furthermore, opportunities to add value to a supply chain - from a bank's or 3PL's position - exist within inventory finance. Both work-in-progress and finished goods need to be financed if the supplier has not yet been paid for the material delivered. Again, both banks and 3PLs are active in this field. Insurance services are the icing on the cake of financial services within supply chain finance. Information required and collected by 3PLs to manage the materials flow can be used to facilitate managing the risk exposure when taking out insurance. This applies in particular with regard to information about the status of the inventory to be insured.

Whereas e-billing is a rather straightforward service the complexity of inventory finance is somewhat greater. Due to a higher risk exposure of inventory finance and the need to allocate the risks appropriately to all participants along the supply chain a high level of trust must be achieved in order to implement complex supply chain finance structures successfully.

---

[11] See Citibank (2001).
[12] See Driese (2000).

4.2 Inventory Management as a Core Element of Supply Chain Finance

Inventory has been identified as one of the major drivers affecting a company's ROI. Both the margin and capital turnover of the ROI is influenced by successful inventory management. The question arises of how to integrate inventory finance into SCM. The following example[13] shall exemplify cost-cutting opportunities based on optimized inventory finance within the supply chain. We look at the inbound logistics of a major computer assembler. A logistics provider contracted to supply the assembly line picks up the material from the vendors and delivers it just in time (see Figure 1).

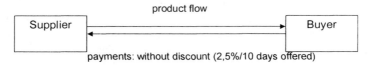

Figure 1: Cash and Product Flows Prior to Optimization

Let us assume that at any given time US-$ 250 Mio. in inventory value is outstanding, i.e. not yet paid for by the assembler. In financing terms this sum represents the average net investment to be financed. According to the trade terms the assembler can make use of a 2.5 %-prompt payment incentive offered by the vendors, which the assembler has chosen to ignore. What solution has been created? A structure has been developed to address the arbitrary opportunities hidden in this supply chain (see Figure 2).

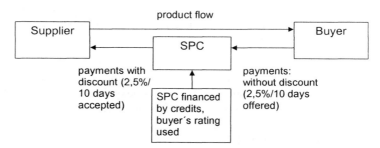

Figure 2: Cash and Product Flows after Incorporation of a Single Purpose Company (SPC)

---

[13] Taken from: Palmieri, Africk (2001).

The 3PL remains responsible for the inbound material and the associated information flow. A special purpose company (SPC) is set up to make and receive payments between the assembler and the supplier. Payments to the supplier are made less the 2.5 %-trade discount. At this stage it is necessary to mention that the SPC owns the inventory; it does not appear on the balance sheet of the assembler. This set-up boosts the assembler's ROI by reducing its exposure to current assets. The assembler in return reimburses the SPC under its normal payment practice. The SPC finances the average net investment by gaining competitive funding based on the credit rating of the computer assembler. According to the bank that initiated this scheme a free cash flow of US-$ 3.3 Mio. is generated annually. After deducting the costs to fund, service risk underwrite and insure (which is also provided) the remaining cash is distributed equally to the assembler, bank and logistics provider.

This example clearly illustrates the basic mechanics of supply chain finance: the logistics provider shares its information management capabilities with financial service providers to arbitrate excess charges between trading partners for financing and insurance. Taking the inbound logistics as an example, arbitration comes in the form of accelerated payments. The economics of accelerated payments are determined by the payment situation and the level of supplier capital costs. Important to note: the assembler's liabilities do not increase as payments are made by a party unrelated to the assembler, in our case the SPC. The prompt payment discount of 2.5 % is used to cover the transaction costs. Of greater importance is, however, how the rating of the transaction partners compares. Being able to use funding cheaper than the supplier can obtain and through this making the scheme commercially viable requires the funding source to have a higher rating than the supplier.

The solution that has been developed in our example is partly based on well-known financial instruments. This might sound not very innovative. However, the most important aim of Supply Chain Finance is showing the necessity of making use of logistics information already available in order to integrate financial flows into the "traditional" supply chain.

4.3 How to Create Value?

Revenue for the participants in this scheme is generated through fees for sharing product status information and asset management services. However, what about generating value cost-wise? The "basic" form of supply chain finance, e.g. billing and effecting payments electronically can see reduced process and transaction costs. Furthermore, substantial cost reduction potential is generated through reduced risk premiums and enhanced credit-worthiness which in effect translates into lower interest expenses.

Product value	The higher the product value, the higher the savings. The product volume is of minor importance here.
Inventory turns	Cost improvement opportunities are also created by faster turn products, i.e. higher cash flows.
Trade terms	Tapping yet unrealized cost saving opportunities by taking trade discounts.
Payment cycle	Elongated payment terms are responsible for unnecessary interest expenses arising from the need to finance receivables.
Cost of capital	Key enabler to make use of arbitrary opportunities exploiting the difference in costs of capital between the seller and buyer.

Figure 3: Value Drivers in Supply Chain Finance

Applying the supply chain finance structure described above to our inbound logistics problem, the supplier receives an immediate payment for the delivered goods subject to the terms and conditions of the sale. Booking a receivable and the related funding requirement can be avoided. As the source of funding is geared to the rating of the assembler, larger credit exposures can be taken. In other words, financing for general corporate purposes can be cobbled together more easily as the credit decision taken by the banks is not only based on the company's financial standing, but also on the relationship with its customers. Generally speaking the value driver can be categorized as follows (see Figure 3):[15]

5 Supply Chain Finance: More than Supply Chain Management?

The key characteristic of supply chain finance is the integration of financial flows into the physical supply chain. It is not a new (financial) product; it can be characterized as an essential part of the management concept commonly known as supply chain management. Supply chain management encompasses all those "activities" associated with the flow and transformation of goods from a raw materials stage through to the end user, as well as the associated information

---

[14] See Palmieri, Africk (2001).
[15] See Palmieri, Africk (2001).

flows. Supply chain management is the integration of these activities through improved supply chain relationships to achieve a sustainable competitive advantage".[16] This rather traditional definition focusing on transport, warehousing and the related IT-processes clearly demonstrates the limited scope of established SCM methodology. In order to accommodate the additional view on financial flows along the pipeline, the scope of supply chain management must be widened. Suitable approaches are already available: "The idea is to apply a total system approach to managing the entire flow of information, materials, and services from raw-materials suppliers through factories and warehouses to the end customer. The focus is on those core activities that a business must operate each day to meet demand. The goals of supply chain management are to reduce uncertainty and risks in the supply chain, thereby positively affecting inventory levels, cycle time, processes, and, ultimately, end-customer service levels."[17] Of interest here is the phrase "services" which includes financial services as well. From a company's point of view however, discussing definitions is only of scientific value.[18] But it illustrates the necessary changes that must take place in the way supply chain management should be approached. What matters is cost savings, regardless of the name of the game. With Cooper/Ellram, "SCM is viewed as lying between fully-vertically integrated systems and those where each channel member operates completely independently. Each player in the channel directly or indirectly affects all other channel members, as well as the ultimate, overall channel performance. This means greater co-ordination of business processes and activities, such as inventory management, across the entire channel and not just between a few channel pairs."[19] The basic idea behind supply chain finance - closer integration and information exchange between the logistics and the finance functions - is of similar nature. It is based on the same key enablers, namely building trust, establishing partnerships and sharing of information. Supply chain finance is a necessary additional element within supply chain management. It is not "more" than supply chain management, but a core element of it.

6 Supply Chain Finance: Conclusion

Managing financial flows related to logistics is a major task within SCM. The scope of SCM is to integrate three flows from sourcing to the customer: product, information and financial. Limiting supply chain management to logistics and information management forgoes plenty of opportunities to tap yet unrealized cost

---

[16] Handfield, Nichols (1999), p. 2.
[17] Chase, Aquilano, Jacobs (1998), p 466.
[18] The difference between logistics and SCM: Weber, Dehler, Wertz (2000).
[19] Cooper, Ellram (1993), p 13.

savings potentials that lie within supply chain finance. Supply chain finance is not a new product. It is about coordinating existing processes in logistics and financing. A prime focus is on information sharing between logistics providers and financiers, particularly with a view to inventory status information. From a financing perspective, accurate and timely delivered information reduces the risk exposure and, hence, the costs to finance the product in the supply chain. Another key issue is the accounts receivables management providing arbitrary opportunities. Banks and logistics providers alike offer a range of packages in varying degrees of scope and complexity. Integrated processes, information sharing and innovative financial structures form the basis for successful supply chain finance.

7 References

Chase, R. B., Aquilano, N. J., Jacobs, F. R. (1998): Production and Operations Management: Manufacturing and Services, 8th edition, Irwin/McGraw-Hill, Boston.

Christopher, M. (1991): The Strategy of Distribution Management, Butterworth Heinemann, Oxford.

Citibank (2001): Financial Services Solutions for Supply Chain Integration. http://ascet.com/documents.asp?grID_133&d_ID=529#, 23.05.01.

Cooper, M. C., Ellram, L. M. (1993): Characteristics of Supply Chain Management and the Implications for Purchasing and Logistics Strategy, in: The International Journal of Logistics Management, Vol. 4, No. 2 (1993), p 13-24.

Driese, W. F. (2000): Wie begleiten Banken die Expansion in der Logistik? (How Do Banks Support the Growth in Logistics), in: Handelsblatt Beilage Logistik, 18.10.2000.

Göpfert, I., Neher, A. (2001): Verbesserungspotenziale (Potential for Improvement), in: Logistik Heute, Vol. 23, No. 5 (2001), p. 49-51.

Handfield, R. B., Nichols, E. L. (1999): Introduction to Supply Chain Management, Prentice Hall, New Jersey.

Palmieri, R. P., Africk, J. (2001): Combining Logistics with Financing for Enhanced Profitability, in: Achieving Supply Chain Excellence Through Technology. http://www.ascet.com/ascet/wp/wpPalmieri.html. 06.03.2001.

Weber, J., Dehler, M., Wertz, B. (2000): Supply Chain Management und Logistik (Supply Chain Management and Logistics), in: Wirtschaftswissenschaftliches Studium, Vol. 29, No. 5 (2000), p. 264-269.

Non-Hierarchical Production Networks – Order Fulfillment and Costing

Tobias Teich, Marco Fischer, Joachim Käschel

1	Introduction	178
2	Cooperation Networks Based on Autonomous Competence Cells	179
3	SME Demands on a Network Costing System	184
4	Costing System in the Network	186
5	Conclusion	192
6	References	192

Summary:
Non-hierarchical regional production networks represent the conceptual vision of a virtual enterprise which is being researched within the framework of a new collaborative research center established at the Technical University of Chemnitz in January 2000. It is intended to improve competitiveness of small- and medium-sized enterprises (SME) through cooperation. In the first part of this study the model of a non-hierarchical production network and its mode of operation are presented. With the demands made on the costing system to be implemented in mind, its applications by SMEs are discussed in the second part.

Keywords: production networks, supply chain management, extended value chain management, cost management.

1 Introduction

Due to rapid globalization and the ongoing emergence of modern communication technologies, the classical image of an enterprise and current economic reality can no longer be matched in many ways. In particular, pressure on SMEs is increasing, and it is the stated purpose of the production network to face this challenge. It is meant to use the potential of close cooperation and unite regionally available capabilities as effectively as possible without relying on an administrative superstructure. To study the potential of networked structures of this type, the collaborative research centre (CRC) 457 of 'Non-Hierarchical Regional Production Networks' was founded in January 2000. The main interest is focused on the development of the model of a virtual enterprise based on very small units of activity, the so-called competence cells (CC). The goal is to improve the competitiveness of SMEs, as they are the economic backbone of Germany, producing more than half of the gross domestic product and account for about 44% of investments.

The approach of our studies differs from that used for previous models, which were mainly developed to restructure cooperation between large-sized enterprises and their dependent partners. Nonetheless, the primary aims of the model are the same as those of earlier ones: reduction of production costs, greater flexibility and agility, higher quality, lowering in administrative overheads and the bullwhip effect.

Previous approaches decompose organizations into smaller units which are equipped with very few and specific core competencies. This top-down strategy aims to link the units into a network to better perform complex tasks in line with the core competencies available. But the concept of small virtual enterprises, following the bottom-up principle, may also be applied to SMEs. Their business is usually centered around a certain core competency, i.e. they fulfill one specific function very well. To them, however, cooperation within the value chain is a necessary prerequisite for handling orders in the same way as large-sized enterprises will, thus generating competitive advantages. Today the pattern of cooperation is typically a hierarchical one, where SMEs are subcontracted by large-sized enterprises as suppliers, which leads to strong economic and existential dependence of SMEs on the focal enterprise. The dominance of single enterprises within the framework of cooperation is to be eliminated by reducing or abandoning hierarchy among partners.

The focus on regional production networks is an important aspect. Because of the lower financial power of SMEs, initial expenditure should be low in order to obtain acceptance. Compared with global networks, regional networks do have various advantages, e.g. all partners have the same basic technical standards, identical law and a common native language, so that it is easier to build up an atmosphere of confidence among partners, thus laying the foundation for cooperation.

2 Cooperation Networks Based on Autonomous Competence Cells

The network model contains the CCs and a decentralized communication and decision-making support system. The latter is implemented by the data-processing model core (DPMC) linking competence cells.

2.1 Competence Cells (CC) as Operative Units

The CC is the fundamental constituent of a non-hierarchical production network. The CC construct can be generally understood as a service unit which is highly specialized, cooperation-dependent, but legally and economically autonomous. It is composed of a combination of production factors and is assumed to yield some economically relevant performance. Human labor is always an indispensable production factor, since only individuals or groups of people may have competence. The term 'economically relevant' implies that the cell is capable of existing on the basis of the performance achieved.

The CC are constituted by existing enterprises according to core competencies. Thus an enterprise may possess one or several CCs and one CC invariably belongs to one enterprise. The subjects of our discussion are cells for marketing, work and production planning, manufacturing, quality assurance, logistics and service, all of which correspond to business processes within the value chain.

The criterion for cell autonomy are required to enable it to make general decisions. These decisions are related to entering into some form of cooperation or accepting the profit share or loss risk from cooperation. Besides, freedom of choice forms the basis for the establishment and development of a cell. To solve a complex task, a cell has two options if the competencies of the cell cover only a partial task: either it grows and evolves the required competencies or it engages in cooperation. The first option presupposes a long period of time and substantial financial resources, which SMEs usually do not have. Therefore the second option seems appropriate.

The CC is so heavily focused on a special kind of performance that cooperation with other units is almost always required to do business. It is this cooperation of highly flexible specialists that offers the chance of building a 'network of excellence' capable of competing with traditional large-sized enterprises regarding quality, price and production time and even outperforming them in satisfying customers' individual needs and demands.

2.2 Data-Processing Model Core (DPMC)

When CCs are assigned to order-essential activities, an inter-enterprise value chain arises accompanied by information (media) discontinuity. This is the consequence of non-existent or incompatible planning instruments. A lack or incompatible concept of interface-management in the process of cooperation affects overall planning of business activities and raises the expense of administration and coordination for any participating CC. An important insight gained from our discussion is that these weaknesses arise with horizontal as well as vertical partners in the cooperation. In contrast, figuring the so-called first supplier, current SCM systems (suppliers such as SAP, i2-technologies, Manugistics)[1] present, at least above the first level of cooperation, a consistent and redundance-free solution to the problem of coordinating the value chain process. Ultimately, however, an instrument for monitoring the exact data of the information and material flow is missing. Yet, it is this instrument that qualifies SMEs to meaningfully and selectively modify the value chain process in order to respond efficiently to disturbances or later wishes by customers.[2] Likewise, the introduction of an overall model of a value chain process reduces planning uncertainties, and the distributed production process becomes more transparent. These tasks are taken care of by the DPMC as a linking element between the CCs.

The value chain units belonging to the non-hierarchical network model can link up with the DPMC and utilize the functionalities it offers. The choice of technologically appropriate CCs to be included in the process variant plan is ensured by the functionality of the DPMC in the CC network. The DPMC functions like a central broker's authority in order to select CCs according to objective criteria and support the genesis of an optimum production network. The functions of the DPMC can be used by any CC of the network. Each CC can consistently initiate the formation of a production net for any customer's order received.[3] The model core provides functionalities for the construction and operation of cooperation networks,[4] evolutionary algorithms for optimization,[5] a neutral controlling authority[6] and the communication infrastructure. In particular,

---

[1] See Knolmayer et al. (2000).
[2] See Fleisch (2001), p. 119.
[3] In contrast to SCM.
[4] See Teich (2001).
[5] See Teich (1998).
[6] See Teich et al. (2001).

decentralized optimization is effected by population concepts, which are known from the field of Genetic Algorithms.[7]

2.3 Operations of a CC Network

The idea of forming a production network from a pool of autonomous CCs is based on the following basic principle: a customer contacts a potential network node, i.e. a CC of the region and signals the demand for production of a certain product. This network node, in turn, has access to a front-end of the DPMC and stimulates the genesis of a temporary network for the production of the product in demand. Thanks to the information stored as rules and factual knowledge on design and manufacture, and deposited into an ontology-based database[8], the DPMC is capable of supporting the decomposition of a production job into a sequence of manufacturing steps. In this process, all sensible manufacturing alternatives of the manufacturing process plan are generated in the form of a graph. First, the different routes are drawn through the graph by means of working plans. The result of this planning stage is the process variant plan. In the next step, the potential CCs are assigned to the nodes of the network according to their suitability for the manufacturing process, i.e. the cell looks out for partners suitable for the partial jobs specified. These partners are mostly other cells from the pool, which, by being contacted, form a cooperation network for the distributed handling of a production order. In the case that a required competency is not available from the pool, it must be purchased from outside.

A cooperation network exists only for as long a time as is necessary for the handling of a customer's order.[9] After the completion of the order the production net decomposes and the cells can participate in new networks to fulfill other orders. Only part of the network, made up of one or several after-sales service cells, continues to exist in order to provide customers with long-term maintenance service, warranty, spare parts and recycling facilities. Figure 1 illustrates the process described.[10]

During the genesis and manufacturing process the storage and exchange of all information is supported by the DPMC of the network, which, in addition, provides tools for distributed controlling, including costing.

---

[7] See Schöneburg (1994), p. 242.
[8] Database which contains in form descriptions of objects and relations of a process chain.
[9] Compare with virtual enterprises, see Schuh et al. (1998).
[10] See Wirth et al. (1999).

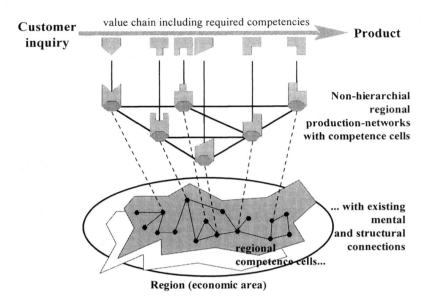

Figure 1: Network Model

2.4 Supporting Instrument: Extended Value Chain Management (EVCM)

For the design and scheduling of the process, the entire information regarding the constitution of the process chain variants is required in one place. This competency is inherently decentralized in the various stages of the value chain. The concept of EVCM allows this decentralized competency to be used. EVCM has been designed as a decentralized device imposed on existing enterprise resource planning (ERP) systems. The concept is displayed in Figure 2. The EVCM system contains the DPMC interface with the ERP system. They communicate on a network level via a common standard. EVCM facilitates the utilization of decentralized CC knowledge and the prevention of information (media) discontinuity.

A customer generates a request to the network system (on the left of Figure 2). Potential suppliers for the final product are identified via one or several marketplaces. These perform the decomposition of the value chain[11] only for the section for which they themselves have the manufacturing and assembling competency.

---

[11] See section 2.3.

For the selection of ABC parts, a decision must be made whether the parts are in stock or can be produced in time. These decisions 'Available to Promise' (ATP) and 'Capable to Promise' (CTP) are supported as functionality in the EVCM system. If both questions turn out negative, further questions regarding other market-places are generated recursively until the leaf nodes of the supply network have been reached. In effect, the same network is generated at the end of the roll out process as in the decentralized approach, but with the advantage that the degree of complexity is reduced.

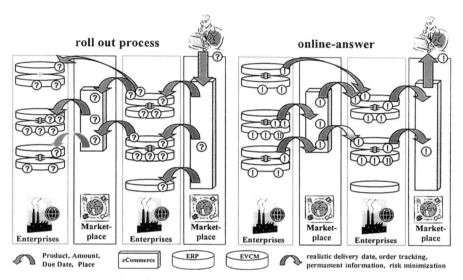

Figure 2: Extended Value Chain Managenment

The right-hand side of Figure 2 illustrates the roll in (online answer) process. The requests generated stimulate corresponding answers to the ability, date, amount, probability and cost of delivery. After their evaluation they are incorporated into the node-specific production process of the value chain and returned to the requesters. The recursion on every level does not stop until the customer has received his answer. The disadvantage is obvious: decisions are made on every level of recursion. However, using this procedure by itself, a global optimum of high probability cannot be attained. Concerning the reduction in complexity and the acquisition of information for costing, this compromise is acceptable with regard to the quick on-line generation of realistic answers.

The technical implementation is currently designed in such a way that the functionality of business logic can be hosted as an add-on to an existing ERP system as an application service providing (ASP) function. The aim of this procedure is to integrate the SMEs into the world of SCM by means of the concept of EVCM and to create economically feasible solutions.

3 SME Demands on a Network Costing System

For the effective and efficient operation of a network the necessity of integrating a network-connecting and network-overlapping costing system arises. In the network model of SFB 457 the DPMC provides a neutral controlling authority with integral costing to generate bids and accounts. The demand on an overlapping costing system results from the interaction and interdependence of the three network elements: the CC as the competence unit, the entire network (including CCs) as a basis for the CC overlapping value chain and the network environment as the habitat and exogenous variable of the network.[12]

Owing to the motivation for membership of SMEs and their integrated CCs in a regional network, a number of costing requirements begin to emerge. The lower capital base of SMEs compared with that of larger companies acts as a bottleneck for both the capacity and competency required. As a consequence of this, SMEs suffer severe disadvantages in fulfilling huge orders that promise a high profit margin. Yet, unused capacities, which, by coupling them with complementary core competencies, promise an additional contribution margin for the CCs and result in cost advantages in contrast to those CCs which act independently on the market. Entry into the network is meant to generate investment and cost advantages by lower initial expenditure. As a consequence of this, CCs of similar or complementary competencies should be included in the network. Fast answer generation with proper cost statements should occur. Another aspect to be considered in the development of network costing is legal independence and autonomy of decisions of network users about the release of confidential cost information. The security of confidential in-company data of users against partners in the network, too, is a precondition for the successful construction of the production network. It cannot be assumed that all the necessary and sensitive cost information is made available to the network. In costing, procedures must be implemented that, despite missing data, make statements regarding the cost of an order in the network. Due to the very nature of the SME target group, it cannot be assumed that these enterprises have any standard business software systems capable of reaching an SAP solution. Rather, a variety of systems with varied costing systems will be available. In addition to the pure cost factors, several soft factors will be listed. CCs cannot be exclusively evaluated by the single parameter of cost. There are other factors such as quality of performance, reliability (delivery according to schedule, abiding by costs) and know-how. Furthermore, important investments by the CCs in the network must also be considered and encouraged. Thus, apart from isolated cost data, a possibility of including soft factors in connection with costing must also be envisaged.[13]

---

[12] See Schweier et al. (1999), p. 84.
[13] See Hess et al. (1999), p. 364.

Network management entails costing requirements too.[14] The specialized distributed, locally separate and customer-oriented value chain in the network is the starting point for this. In this respect, a process-oriented and non-performance or non-function-oriented approach seems reasonable. According to their organizational assignment, the different costs are assigned to the network or CCs level. In this way, the individuality of the network users' costing systems can be taken into account. The issue of overhead on network leveland their integration into costing is closely related to this. Furthermore, competition among CCs is required to achieve marketable performance and output in order to create a domestic market. Thus, CCs will charge adequate prices for their products and services rather than use their information advantages over the network.[15] If there is no competition among CCs, the possibility of disclosing their calculating policies should be considered so that overcharging CCs may be counteracted. It is also essential for costing on a network level to store the appropriate information in a joint database.

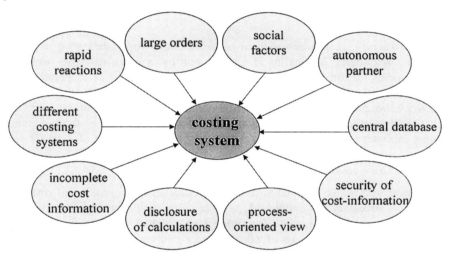

Figure 3: Demands on a Network Costing System

---

[14] See Schweier et al. (2000), p. 259.
[15] See Principal-Agent-Theory in Hess et al. (1999), p. 357.

4 Costing System in the Network

To achieve the degree of customer efficiency desired and, ultimately, competitive ability of the network, detailed cost analysis is imperative.[16] The established requirements on network costing result in different ways of looking at the network. Costs incurred in the network may either be order-neutral or order-related. The latter are, in turn, divided into network layer costs and CC layer costs. Competences as such cannot be used for this. Instead, reference to the concrete order must be made. The costs of a CC, which offers order-neutral as well as order-related performance, must be split. At each layer, various cost elements must be taken into account.

4.1 Order-Neutral Costs

Necessary costs in the network independent of an order are discussed in this section.

IT infrastructure: A process-oriented management of order data such as costs, amounts, due dates or quality is carried out by a joint database with the corresponding infrastructure in the form of DPMC. At the start of cooperation, the installation will cause costs of hardware, software, networking and interfacing. As it cannot be predicted at the start of operation to what extent the network functions, statements about later allocation of costs incurred at the beginning cannot be made. Instead, it seems reasonable to raise some sort of entrance-fee, nominal sum or the like, derived from concrete quotations for these initial installation services and the number of network partners.

CC administration: To respond to the dynamic market environment and customer needs, it is necessary to continuously test the competencies available in the pool for relevance, which means new admission, replacement or exclusion of competencies. This servicing of competencies continues over the duration of single orders and can be viewed as a strategic and permanent task. Because of irregular revenues from the network, it is advisable to introduce a budget for this kind of task, which can be financed by e.g. annual contributions.

IT operation and maintenance: Even if no concrete order is to be processed at any one moment, costs of energy, maintenance and backups as well as rent for the server and work places are incurred. Irrespective of the inflow of orders, these costs must also be budgeted.

Marketing: Marketing and market analysis, just as CC administration, are part of the strategic permanent tasks, which should also be budgeted.

---

[16] See Veil et al. (2000), p. 3.

Order-neutral process chains: After a special customer inquiry, decomposition into smaller partial jobs is required to distribute these to CCs. This splitting process can be performed manually after every inquiry or on the basis of prefabricated, standardized process chains or orders previously completed. For prefabricated order-neutral process chains, costs incurred cannot be assigned to one particular order, because the order is still in the offing. Using this method, it is conceivable to assign standardized machine hour rates derived from preliminary negotiations with the appropriate CCs. This would simplify later calculations on a central level.

The costs just described are to be treated as overhead of network operation. As they are independent of a specific order, it is difficult to include them in the calculation of a concrete order by overhead rates. Furthermore, the plausibility of overhead rates must be questioned against the background of the process-oriented approach in virtual enterprises. Thus, for highly variable production programs, as in the network, rigid overhead rates and the resulting implication of stable relationships between individual costs and overheads cannot be found and lead to wrong costing statements and decisions.[17] The disadvantages of overhead calculation, i.e. the tendency to calculate too low a price for a non-standard product and too high a price for a standard product, are supposed to be avoided by activity-based costing.[18] Therefore, financing by budgets is favored, which is obtained from activity-based costing of CCs. The following cost drivers might be used:

- *IT:* the number of interface adapters, backups and updates
- *CC management:* the number of servicing jobs in the competency database
- *order-neutral process chains:* the depth of decomposition and the number of CCs per low-level code

To obtain cost effectiveness of these jobs, tenders should be invited. Against the background of continuous and permanent performance (network jobs) the disclosure of calculating principles should also be claimed. For the extension and development of the network a profit markup may be added to the calculated price of the order. Thus, at the end of the year, liability accruals can be created for possible future costs of warranty commitments and the remainder can be shared among network users.

4.2 Order-Related Costs

After the costs of the general operation of the network have been discussed, the costs to be directly assigned to orders will be considered in the following section.

---

[17] See Horvath et al. (1993); Cooper et al. (1999), p. 78.
[18] See Horvath et al. (1999).

These differ in the range of the competencies offered in the network. On the one hand, there are network layer costs (coordinating and concomitant competencies) and, on the other hand, CC layer costs (direct partial job on the end-product).

4.2.1 Network Layer Costs

Order-related process chains: If the customer's inquiry is decomposed in relation to a concrete product, the performance can be directly attributed to the object. As the order-overlapping and order-related activities may be performed by one and the same CC, particular attention must be given to cost causation. For calculation, the depth of decomposition and the number of identified CCs might be used as cost drivers.

IT operation: Order-related costs are also incurred by IT operation such as costs of data lines, additional maintenance, including backups, printing of reports and quotations and other manual adaptations. These costs must be calculated by the contributing CCs according to the number of CCs concerned and the size of order.

Acquisition/negotiations: For the close integration of the CCs concerned, incentives for participation must be created and negotiations with customers must be renumerated. (Note: Each and every CC can advertize and attract customers.) To do this, lump sums or percentage markups, which must be agreed upon in advance, must be added to the quoted price and credited to the acquiring CC after completion of the order.

In the absence of competition, value chain overlapping costs should also be disclosed among CCs.[19]

4.2.2 CC Layer Costs

Settlement prices: The illustration of the detailed cost structure of the product manufactured in the network in the form of traditional costing (overhead calculation) in enterprises proves to be difficult. The reason for this is the missing information on thenetwork level with regard to the types of costs of every single CC. An enterprise will disclose its detailed costs to the network only out of self-interest.[20] For this reason, three complementary parallel methods of obtaining cost information will be described here.

As far as possible, prefabricated process chains and machine hour rates previously agreed upon can be easily used in the calculation by assigning the corresponding CCs. The acquisition of cost information and the evolution of cost structure – in as far as prefabricated process chains are at hand – take place on the network level. In this variant, the costs must be negotiated ex ante, i.e. before a customer inquiry,

---

[19] See 4.1.
[20] See Veil et al. (2000), p. 4.

thus accepting additional transactions costs. The calculation of the partial jobs can thus be carried out via the machine hour rates on the central level with any offer of the CC. (The CC must, however, be able to do the job – ATP). The roll out process offers another possibility - calculation by accumulation. When it is used, the quoted price (settlement price in the network) is passed on directly to the requesting CCs in cumulative form, i.e. calculation is carried out on the CC level with the price quoted of the upstream CC in the value chain, their own material and costs, overheads and profit markup. At the end of this process, the network receives the price(s) quoted and possible date(s) from the last CC(s) in the value chain. In addition, the costing module in the DPMC receives settlement prices directly from each CC and the name or identification number (ID) of the upstream CC. In this way, the selection of CCs from the possible upstream CCs can be documented. Since only cumulated prices quoted are passed on, no detailed cost structure of CCs in the network can be provided. The assembly of the cost structure and the acquisition of cost information are decentralized in the CCs. For this possibility, the disclosure of the basics of calculation to CCs should be asked of CCs which do not compete with any others, so that cost disadvantages are avoided due to monopolistic behavior.

In order to enlarge the bargaining room between customer and contractor, it is necessary to know the lowest-price limits of individual CCs – mostly variable costs (profit contribution). This proves to be difficult because, by publishing cost information, the respective CC discloses part of its internal cost structure with the result of facing competitive disadvantages (CCs in the network may well be competitors in the open market). Led by self-protection, no CC will tell a downstream CC its lowest-price limit. To overcome this difficulty, lowest-price limits are published only in central DPMC. CCs in turn utilize, in calculation, settlement prices (variable costs + fixed costs + profit markup) of upstream CCs. This approach, however, requires confidence in the information system of the network and the handling of sensitive data. To ensure this, database and access modes must be encoded. The CC makes the decision on the publication of the lowest-price limit itself, thus influencing its chances to be awarded the contract. The acquisition of cost information is decentralized in the CCs. Using additional lowest-price limits of CCs, decentralized formation of a detailed cost structure is possible. At best, all CCs will disclose their information and promote a maximum of cost transparency in the network.

Logistics costs: Logistics cost of transport between CCs can be dealt with in the same way as prefabricated process chains. Because of the regional character of the network and its limited extent, negotiations on standardized transport services depending on distance and size/weight are less complicated. Thus, calculation of logistics cost may be centrally performed.

4.3 Cost Aggregation

On the basis of the previous discussion on the acquisition of cost information, a calculation scheme for an order in the network can now be devised. Doing this, order-overlapping costs are not included, but, as described in 4.1. on budgets, are financed by entrance fees and annual contributions.

		distributed production			aggregation	
cost information of a single CC	CC-ID	25	36	---		
	upstream CC-ID	20	25	---		
	downstream CC-ID	36	37	---		
	delivery date	20/09/01	15/10/01	---		
	settlement price	1000	1500	---	10500	aggregated price
	variable costs	800	1500	---	10200	variable costs
soft factors of previous orders	quality	8	6	---	8	expected values for the soft factors
	reliability	10	7	---	9	

Figure 4: Costing System Database

Calculation is based on the cost information of the CCs, which have been generated by the EVCM concept. In addition, there is some information on soft factors (reliability and quality) obtained from CCs on previous orders, which is stored in the central database. Simultaneous requests addressed to several potential CCs strengthen the demand for an internal market and, consequently, cost efficiency. As the CCs to be contacted are being selected, the soft factors mentioned above are included. Any previously known performance problems of several CCs that may have occurred in the process can thus be excluded. In the central database, the costs and dates are assigned to the corresponding CCs. If these are CCs having prefabricated process chains and previously negotiated machine hour rates, they can be immediately taken over. The information on other CCs is available in the central database after completion of the roll-in process. Figure 4 shows the content of the database.

Supported by the competence pool and the potential of using various parallel production techniques, a large number of production variants can be derived from the network. To assign the costs calculated to both the CC and the production variant, the upstream and downstream CCs are stored in the data record. Utilizing the predecessor-successor relationship in connection with settlement prices, the proportion of value added by individual CCs is determined. The row 'variable costs', as described above, need not be filled in.

If statements on the cost composition of a product and the aggregate bid price subject to a certain delivery date are to be made, costs can be aggregated with the assignable logistics costs. As a result, for all potential production variants, statements on bid prices, lowest-price limits (as far as variable costs have been published) and dates, related to CC layer performance, are obtained.

Subsequently, network layer costs are added to the calculation. These are calculated on the basis of activity-based costing. Depending on previously made agreements, extra markups for the order-acquiring CC, warranty accruals and a network profit are to be added. By taking into account soft factors on the basis of e.g. Dellmann's[21] network cluster cost model, statements on reliability, quality and exactness of costs of production alternatives can be made.

On the basis of these calculations, customers can be offered various alternatives with respect to costs, delivery dates and technologies. When a decision on a variant has been made, the network is activated.

4.4 Profit Distribution

After the customer's order has been executed, actual accounting of CCs follows for the network, which then does the invoicing with the customer and fixes the all-inclusive price.

If the all-inclusive price is lowered due to conventional penalty for default of delivery date or quality defects, this loss in revenues must be shared by the network according to the principle of causation. For this, the process information transmitted to DPMC by each CC can be used. CCs should document assessments of soft factors (adherence to delivery dates, quality) of upstream CCs, so that they can consult them when warranty claims arise or later orders are executed.

Owing to the procedure used in the calculation of settlement prices in the network, CC profit is normally already included in them. For this reason, possible profit is not distributed to these CCs. CCs receive actual settlement prices provided they have not been reduced. If, on the other hand, an order can be attracted only by using variable costs of one or several CCs, the surplus must be distributed to those CCs for which only variable costs have been fixed, after settlement of other liabilities (settlement prices or variable costs of CCs, profit share of acquiring CCs, accruals, profit reserves as far as agreed upon).

---

[21] See Dellmann (1999).

Profit reserves, if they have been built up, can be dissolved at the end of the year and distributed to CCs according to their involvement. Another way is to reduce annual contributions, the difference being settled by revenue reserves.

5 Conclusion

In the first part of the study, the model of the non-hierarchical regional production network has been introduced. The EVCM concept as a basis for the costing system has been discussed in the second part.

In the latter part, stimulated by demands made on network costing systems, ways of cost aggregation and profit distribution have been presented. In doing so, we have followed very closely the production network and its premises considered in SFB 457.

The approach presented in this paper may be viewed as a starting point for further work. Especially for the extra markups of the different cost components in the network, realistic and applicable parameters must be identified. Another point, which is beyond the scope of this paper, is the question of negotiations after the network is activated. These result from problems during the execution of orders (default of delivery date). For example, multi-agent systems might be employed for negotiations between CCs. A third point is the implementation of the system and the test of the costing system's potential compared with conventional in-company costing systems.

6 References

Cooper, R., Kaplan, R. S. (1999): Integrierte Kostensysteme – Verheißung und Gefahr zugleich (Integrated Costing Systems – promise and risk), in: Harvard Business Manager, Vol. 1, No. 1 (1999), p. 76-86.

Dellmann, K. (1999): Das Netzwerk-Cluster-Kostenmodell – ein allgemeines Modell der Kostenrechnung (The Network-Cluster-Model – A General Costing Model), in: Zeitschrift für Betriebswirtschaft, Vol. 69, No. 11 (1999), p. 1019-1041.

Fleisch, E. (2001): Das Netzwerkunternehmen (The Network Enterprise), Springer-Verlag, Berlin.

Hess, T., Schuhmann, M. (1999): Erste Überlegungen zum Controlling in Unternehmensnetzwerken (First Ideas of Controlling in Networks), in: Engelhard, J., Sinz, E. (eds.): Kooperation im Wettbewerb, Gabler Verlag, Wiesbaden, p. 349-370.

Horvath, P., Mayer, R. (1993): Prozeßkostenrechnung – Konzeption und Entwicklungen (Activity-Based Costing – Conception and Evolution), in: Kostenrechnungspraxis, Sonderheft, No. 2 (1993), p. 15-28.

Horvath, P., Brokemper, A. (1999): Prozeßkostenrechnung als Logistikkostenrechnung (Activity-Based Costing as Logistic Costing), in: Weber, J, Baumgarten, H. (eds.): Handbuch Logistik, Schäffer-Poeschel Verlag, Stuttgart, p. 523-537.

Knolmayer, G., Mertens, P., Zeier, A. (2000): Supply Chain Management auf der Basis von SAP-Systemen (Supply Chain Management Based on SAP-Systems), Springer Verlag, Berlin.

Schöneburg, E. (1994): Genetische Algorithmen und Evolutionsstrategien (Genetic Algorithm and Evolutionary Strategies), Addison Wesley Verlag, Bonn.

Schuh, G., Millarg, K., Göransson, A. (1998): Virtuelle Fabrik (Virtual Factory), Carl Hanser Verlag, Wien.

Schweier, H., Jehle, E. (1999): Controlling logistischer Netzwerke – konzeptionelle Anforderungen und Ansätze zur instrumentellen Ausgestaltung (Controlling in Logistical Networks – Conceptual Demands and Approaches to Instrumental Definition), in: Industrie Management, Vol. 15, No. 5 (1999), p. 83-87.

Schweier, H., Stüllenberg, F. (2000): Netzwerk-Controlling (Network Controlling), in: Controlling, No. 4/5 (2000), p. 259-260.

Teich, T. (1998): Optimierung von Maschinenbelegungsplänen unter Benutzung heuristischer Verfahren (Optimization in Job Shop Scheduling Using Heuristics), Verlag Josef Eul, Lohmar.

Teich, T. (2001): Extended Value Chain Management für Hierarchielose Regionale Produktionsnetzwerke (Extended Value Chain Management in Non-Hierarchical Production Networks), in: Dangelmaier, W., Pape, U., Rüther, M. (eds.): Die Supply Chain im Zeitalter von E-Business und Global Sourcing (Supply Chain in the Age of e-business and Global Sourcing), ALB-HNI-Verlagsschriftenreihe, Paderborn, p. 447-460.

Teich, T., Mehnert, J., Dürr, H. (2001): Planung und Bewertung verteilter Prozessketten in Hierarchielosen Produktionsnetzwerken (Planning and Rating of Distributed Process Chains in Non-Hierarchical Production Networks), in: Zeitschrift für wirtschaftlichen Fabrikbetrieb, Vol. 96, No. 6 (2001), p. 308-313.

Veil, T., Hess, T. (2000): Kalkulation in Unternehmensnetzwerken (Calculation in Enterprise Networks), Arbeitsbericht Nr.3 / 2000 der Abteilung Wirtschaftsinformatik II der Universität Göttingen, Göttingen.

Wirth, S. et al. (1999): Sonderforschungsbereich 1513: Hierarchielose regionale Produktionsnetze. Theorien, Modelle, Methoden und Instrumentarien (Collaborative Research Centre 1513: Non-Hierarchical Production Networks. Theories, Models, Methods and Instruments). Finanzierungsantrag 2000, 2001, 2002 zum Sonderforschungsbereich 1513, Technische Universität Chemnitz, Chemnitz.

Efficient Consumer Response - Increasing Efficiency through Cooperation

Khurrum S. Bhutta, Faizul Huq, Francine Maubourguet

1	Introduction	196
2	Literature Review	197
3	ECR Framework	202
4	Case Study	207
5	Conclusions	209
6	References	210

Summary:

The concept of Efficient Consumer Response was introduced by the Supermarket industry in 1992. Since then, other industries have started their own ECR initiatives. This paper examines the key initiatives surrounding ECR, and discusses a framework that attempts to merge the ECR initiatives with Consumer Centric marketing efforts. A case study is presented illustrating the implementation of the framework.

Key Words:
Supply Chain Management, Efficient Consumer Response, Efficient Frontier, Continuous Product Replenishment.

1 Introduction

The Efficient Consumer Response (ECR) concept was introduced in 1992 as a result of competition from alternative store formats which highlighted major inefficiencies within the supermarket industry and its supply chain. In order to survive, the US grocery industry leaders formed a task force that took an initiative to study how to improve the performance of their supply chain. The results of the study indicated that quick and accurate flow of information through the supply chain enabled suppliers and distributors to anticipate demand requirements far more accurately than current systems.[1] The ECR initiative, therefore, transformed the supply chain from a "push system" to a "pull system" where channel partners form new interdependent relationships and where product replenishment is driven by point of sale (POS) data.

As the grocery industry changed, effects of these aforementioned events accrued and became trends which eventually led to structural change. However, it still took time for a manufacturer to move products from point A to point B. So while manufacturers were able to bypass many of the qualitative functions that channel partners such as wholesalers performed, there still remained physical and temporal activities that needed to be undertaken by someone. This fueled the growth of the "partnership logistics" industry, which comprises third-party logistics providers, transportation service companies, and public warehouses.[2]

To follow up on these initiatives, manufacturers, retailers and wholesalers/distributors attempted to establish a new spirit of cooperation and partnership. The challenge for the distributors and retailers was reestablishing the value of the services they perform and leveraging the volume of their independent customers, as the chain leverages the volume from its stores.[3] Given these conditions, retailers, distributors and manufacturers attempted to maximize the value they offer to the customer – ECR enabled them to do this.

This paper examines the key initiatives surrounding ECR and discusses the primary issues involved in its implementation. A brief literature review is presented in the second section while the third section looks at the background of ECR and its components. The forth section presents a framework and discussion and the conclusions are presented in the fifth section.

---

[1] See Salmon Associates (1993).
[2] See Sherman (1994).
[3] See Sherman (1994), p. 20-24.

2 Literature Review

In traditional supply chains, suppliers, manufacturers, distributors, and retailers work independently to optimize their individual logistics systems, each concerned with their own part of the physical and information flow. As a result, firms inadvertently create problems and inefficiencies for other players in the distribution channel, which creates additional costs within the entire logistical system. Realizing these inefficiencies, firms have begun to form collaborative relationships within and beyond their own organizations in order to optimize the functioning of the entire logistical system. The objective therefore is to have jointly defined areas of cooperation that are derived from the supply perspective, rather than being driven by the products themselves and compelling the distributor or retailer to be a key component in delivering products to the final customer.[4]

Successful adoption of ECR lies in the ability to maintain manufacturing flexibility that enables channel partners to match supply with demand.[5] Key to this flexibility is a process tightly integrating demand management, production scheduling, and inventory deployment. ECR is thus an initiative helping to enhance the flow of information between trading partners.

2.1 ECR Model Components

The primary objective of ECR is to rationalize the distribution chain in order to increase value to consumers. As shown in the figure below, ECR focuses on the customers' actual demand and uses that information to drive the flow of goods through the channel.[6] The frequency and speed of information through the system has a significant effect on inventory levels, efficiencies, costs, and lead times.

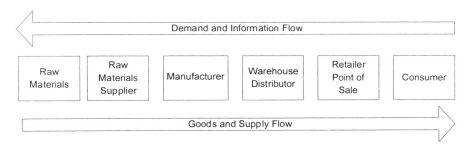

Figure 1: Information Flow in the Supply Chain

---

[4] See Dornier et al (1998).
[5] See Weeks, Crawford (1993), p. 34.
[6] See Weeks, Crawford (1993), p. 3.

ECR simply realigns activities within a common framework to deliver better value to the consumer.[7] In a recent ECR survey, John Harris (1999) notes several key technology-based initiatives that must be undertaken to rationalize the distribution chain and achieve a successful ECR implementation. The initiatives include:

- Integrated Electronic Data Interchange (IEDI),
- Category Management, Continuous Product Replenishment (CPR),
- Computer Assisted Ordering (CAO),
- Flow-Through Distribution,
- Activity-Based Costing (ABC).

Each of these initiatives is described below.

2.1.1 Integrated Electronic Data Interchange (EDI)

EDI is defined as the computer-application-to-computer-application communication of structured, formatted messages based on international standards, using electronic transmission media with no manual intervention.[8] When successfully implemented, EDI allows structured information to be shared among organizations in the supply chain, which results in significant reductions in transaction costs. It is viewed as the essential effective enabler of the ECR management strategy because it focuses on achieving integration across organizational functions along with integration between organizations.[9]

While EDI is viewed as the driver for ECR, many of the efficiencies and benefits expected to be created have yet to be realized. The problem is that EDI requires a significant investment in time and money in order to be implemented, and most companies are unprepared to make the technological and human capital investment.[10]

In addition to the standard EDI, the Internet is forcing companies that intending to fully embrace the ECR concept to look at a much broader set of networked technologies more effective in implementing ECR-type processes. "The state of technology has changed dramatically – especially the explosive growth of the Internet – since ECR was rolled out as an industry-wide cost cutting initiative in 1993. The vision of ECR from a technology perspective has to be completely renewed because the original vision of technology does not represent the environment we're in today."[11] This change will allow companies to leverage Internet-working technologies and EDI standards to create an integrated and data-driven supply chain.

---

[7] See Pearce (1997).
[8] See Brawn (1990).
[9] See Harris (1999), p. 1-5.
[10] See Tosh (1999), p. 8.
[11] See Tosh (1999), p. 10.

2.1.2 Category Management

The focus of ECR, as it relates to category management, is to deliver fact-based information by digitalizing the supply chain.[12] This information leaves little room for interpretation and subjective decision-making throughout the logistics system and ultimately leads to collaborative goal setting and problem solving that didn't exist in the old era of buying and selling. Richard Collins (1999) states that Category Management focuses on four key concepts:

- Matching products and services to the individual store consumer profile,
- The ability of the entire supply chain to react to daily information,
- Putting excitement and convenience into shopping,
- Identifying new opportunities and developing new categories and products to address those opportunities.

Furthermore he believes that the companies in the US have made a big mistake by focusing all their efforts with ECR on reducing costs and not on the idea of effective category management through ECR.

2.1.3 Continuous Replenishment Program (CRP)

An effective continuous product replenishment program is another fundamental platform supporting the overall ECR strategy. Continuous replenishment is a program used to control and monitor the movement of goods from the manufacturer to the warehouse/distributor.[13] In contrast, the traditional demand forecasting techniques and batch ordering processes used today lead to erratic ordering behavior throughout the entire supply chain. This erratic behavior is amplified due to the magnitude of safety stocks covering long lead-time periods as we move downstream in the supply chain. At the same time, these long lead-times contribute dramatically to demand variance and higher costs of holding safety stocks. The overall result of the distorted information from one end of the supply chain to the other leads to tremendous inefficiencies, excessive inventory, dissatisfied customers, lost revenues, and ineffective production schedules.[14] To remedy this situation, companies are utilizing CRP to achieve a more fluid product replenishment system driven by information based on consumer demand. In addition, CRP programs reduce costs in distributors' inventory, but can increase some expenses such as transportation costs if the manufacturer ships smaller truck loads more frequently.[15] Successful CRP implementation, therefore, is dependent

---

[12] See Lewis (1998), p. 27.
[13] See Garry (1994); Grose (1993).
[14] See Grose (1993), p. 3.
[15] See Grose (1993), p. 13.

on effective trade relations, requiring shared business practices and information systems relying heavily on EDI.[16]

2.1.4 Computer Assisted Ordering (CAO)

Computer-assisted ordering, also known as "computer-aided ordering",[17] covers the second half of the overall inventory supply chain - the movement of goods from the warehouse/distribution center to the retail store. The first half, in comparison, is the movement from manufacturer to warehouse/distributor, which many chains are improving through continuous replenishment systems. The aim of CAO is to generate store replenishment orders automatically, with minimal management intervention, based on such things as current and historical Point of Sale (POS) scan data, delivery data and sales forecasts.[18] According to Michael Garry (1994a), President of Inventory Management Technology, CAO is the starting point from which everything else rolls back up the supply chain, all historical and current data is fed into it and the result is an automatically generated store replenishment order.

The benefits of CAO have been identified as labor savings and dependability, warehouse and shipping improvements, and inventory reduction. Traditionally, stores have based their orders on the re-order clerk manually inspecting the store shelves and scanning the shelf-tag barcodes for those items with limited stock on the shelf.[19] The re-order amount entered by the clerk is based on the actual shelf amount and the ideal shelf quantity. At this point s/he does not have information about quantities on hand or of future deliveries. Integrated CAO systems are designed to minimize and even eliminate these problems.[20]

2.1.5 Cross-Docking (Flow-Through Distribution)

Cross-docking and flow-through distribution are frequently cited as key processes in the quest toward ECR implementation.[21] The concept of cross docking was a result of the growth of product customization and product proliferation causing increasing volumes of orders to move through the supply chain. At the same time, competition and slim profit margins were driving manufacturers and distributors to find productivity and customer service improvements through better use of information technology.[22] As a result, new techniques were developed to achieve

---

[16] See Grose (1993), p. 9.
[17] See Thayer (1991), p. 81.
[18] See Thayer (1991), p. 9.
[19] See Anderson (1996).
[20] See Anderson (1996), p. 9.
[21] See Sherman (1995), p. 57.
[22] See Dilger (1997), p. 82.

greater inventory accuracy and closer integration with POS data collection. This data collection process allows retailers to decipher the behaviors and causal factors of demand fluctuations in order to gain insight into what moves a product at the retail level. Through this shipments can arrive at the distribution center as needed to fulfill customer demand.[23]

The purpose of cross-docking is to speed up the flow of products from the supplier to the retail store by reducing storage and handling of products at the distribution center or warehouse. It involves the breaking down of pallets at the distribution center, reassembling them for store delivery and then shipping them to the retail store without storing the product in the warehouse.[24] Cross docking actually skips the inventory process altogether by moving products needed for outbound orders from receiving directly to shipping.[25] This requires significant investment in technologies such as EDI, bar coding and scanning of pallets and cases as well as warehouse design changes such as lower ceilings and less racking. It also requires channel partners to overcome their traditional adversarial relationships and realize how each participant can benefit from sharing information.[26]

While cross docking is frequently cited as a key process in the quest for ECR implementation, few companies have attempted its implementation due to the perceived enormity of the task. Studies conducted[27] by Advanced Marketing Research (AMR) show that less than seven percent of warehouses, both public and private, are automated to any extent. However, results of a Manufacturing Systems survey[28] reveal that individual manufacturers invested approximately $509 million to enhance their cross-docking capabilities, and the numbers are expected to increase in the coming years.

2.2 Activity-Based Costing (ABC)

Activity-based costing provides the cost and operating information necessary to support innovative management improvement initiatives such as ECR. The focus of ABC is to provide information about the true cost of products, services, processes, activities, distribution channels, customer segments, contracts and projects.[29] ABC supplies information about profits (where the money is being made) rather than about costs. Traditional accounting systems use gross margin

---

[23] See Dilger (1997), p. 21.
[24] See Dilger (1997), p. 9.
[25] See Dilger (1997), p. 22.
[26] See Dilger (1997), p. 21.
[27] See Dilger (1997), p. 22.
[28] See Dilger (1997), p. 22.
[29] See Miller (1996).

calculations that spread operating costs across all products based on unit purchase price regardless of the actual value chain through which the product passes.[30]

A growing number of distributors and suppliers are embracing the ABC concept. Proctor and Gamble has gained notoriety for its streamlined logistics programs which use ABC to identify activities that distributors can engage in – such as EDI, faster uploading, and drop and hook – to reduce product costs.[31] Miller and Gary 1996, present another example of a successful ABC implementation at Spartan Stores. In 1996, Spartan rolled out a pricing structure for its retailers that identifies the costs associated with each item. Moreover, manufacturers in the same category that have traditionally charged Spartan the same price will no longer see their products priced identically by Spartan. This is because Spartan's price reflects the cost of moving the product through its distribution center. Jim Swaboda, Director of Grocery/General Merchandise Purchasing for Spartan Stores is quoted as saying that until now, inefficient manufacturers had been subsidized by efficient manufacturers. But under the new approach, markups would be based on the real costs of handling products.

ABC assigns costs to activities in the work environment as a way of both revealing those costs (which have been previously hidden) and finding ways to reduce them. Ultimately, it provides a better understanding of how profits are generated and increases the visibility of costs within the system.[32] Rather than squeezing budgets, ABC focuses management's attention on controlling the source of costs and decisions that create activities. Therefore, ABC analysis as part of ECR can increase the profitability of the supply chain by removing or reducing those cost activities that do not add value. This cannot be done with traditional systems because they do not reflect costs accurately.[33]

3 ECR Framework

The literature refers to several initiatives companies have taken to adopt ECR (Gertler, 1994, Harris 1999, Lewis 1998). In this age of logistics, the final consumer is driving the market and marketing strategies. Plans and investments must be geared to this fact. Consumers are moving from the traditional 4-Ps of the marketing mix (Price, Product, Promotion and Place) to the more recent consumer-centric 5-Cs (Cost, Consumer, Communication, Convenience and Care).[34]

---

[30] See Miller (1996), p. 9.
[31] See Andel (1998), p. 4-8.
[32] See Andel (1998), p. 13.
[33] See Weinstein (1995).
[34] See Kotler (1991); Kurtz, Boone (1989).

The literature on the retail industry comments on consumer-centric organizations tending to be more effective in meeting consumer demands[35] at a lower cost.[36] Frameworks have been proposed in literature to tackle the challenge of consumer oriented supply chains. The following framework attempts to merge the ECR initiatives with consumer-centric marketing efforts in which ECR is used as a facilitator. Collins (1999) believes "In the US, we made a big mistake by focusing all our efforts with ECR on reducing costs". This framework will go a long way in addressing this criticism.

The main features of the proposed framework are:

1. The move from a traditional to consumer-centric approach replacing the 4-Ps with the 5-Cs of a consumer-centric organization.

2. Make use of category management techniques to efficiently introduce, promote, replenish and assort merchandise and to establish a set of criteria to measure goals within primary functions.

3. Leveraging the competitive strengths of an organization enabling it to move to a more efficient level in terms of a consumer satisfaction/service level.

3.1 Replacing the 4-Ps with the 5-Cs of a Consumer-Centric Organization

It is not uncommon to hear statements like "To survive as we move into the twenty-first century, we can no longer rely on a product-centric approach to marketing", or "those who can execute on the promise of customer-centric marketing will be most successful". Executing on customer-centric marketing is not easy. In fact, fundamental changes are required in three key areas: organization, culture and technology. Change management is a difficult practice for even the most savvy of organizations, and executing on customer-centric marketing requires sweeping changes that will impact almost every area of the organization. However, with a focused, evolutionary process to follow, the change to customer-centric marketing can be made with minimum disruption.

One of the first steps is recognizing and accepting the fact that traditional product-oriented marketing can no longer effectively serve the goals and needs of any organization. Product-oriented marketing operates on the principle that customers buy whatever an organization has to offer. Instead, to be successful in the future, organizations must focus on how they can create and increase customer value and long-term loyalty. "Creating value for customers is the foundation for every

---

[35] See Randice (1997); Sansolo, (1993).
[36] See Garry (1993); Matthews (1994); Wood (1993).

successful business system. Creating value for customers builds loyalty, and loyalty in turn builds growth, profit and more value."[37]

Creating real value for customers requires that all marketing and sales initiatives converge at the customer with a true understanding his/her needs. Convergent marketing allows an organization to truly coordinate all activities with a focus on building value for the customer and the organization and achieving greater customer loyalty.

Making the move from product-oriented to customer-centric marketing requires a complete understanding of the key differences between the two approaches. Identifying the main characteristics and impacts of traditional product-oriented marketing makes it easier to see how customer-centric marketing is different in increasing long-term loyalty.[38]

3.2 Establishing a Set of Criteria to Measure Goals Within Primary Functions

The four goals of an efficient ECR initiative, namely efficient store assortment, promotion, product introduction and product replenishment facilitate inventory management within the supply chain along with maintaining the consumer-centered approach. The following is a brief description of each of these goals.

3.2.1 Efficient Store Assortment

The objective of this initiative is optimizing the productivity of inventory and shelf management at the consumer level. Optimal allocation of goods on supermarket shelves (known as "store assortment") maximizes consumer satisfaction by providing the best products and services while at the same time ensuring the most efficient use of available space to increase manufacturer, distributor and retailer profitability. The relationship between manufacturers, distributors and retailers is crucial in achieving efficient store assortment. To streamline business practices in the area of store assortment, manufacturers, distributors and retailers need to adopt a "category management" approach.[39]

3.2.2 Efficient Promotion

Efficient promotion maximizes the total system efficiency of trade and consumer promotions. Efficient promotion attempts to eliminate inefficient trade promotions (forward buying and diverting) by introducing better alternative trade promotions

---

[37] See Reichheld (1996).
[38] See McEachern (1998), p. 485.
[39] See Knill (1997), p. 14.

such as "pay for performance" and "forward commit". In Pay for Performance programs the pay/compensation is linked to measurable outputs of the trade. The better the trade performance the more it is compensated. Forward Commit is basically a commitment to buy at a fixed rate in the future before the products hit the market. This enables the buyer to lock into a price while the producer knows what s/he is guaranteed to sell.

3.2.3   Efficient Product Introduction

The objective of the new production initiative is to maximize the effectiveness of new product development and introduction activities in order to reduce costs and failure rates. This is achieved by the involvement of wholesalers/distributors and retailers and consumers at an early stage of the new product development process. Manufacturers, distributors and retailers must work together as allies to reduce the costs of product development and to produce only products anticipated and demanded by the consumer marketplace. Once again, the "category management" strategy plays a crucial role in achieving this initiative because of its contribution to an understanding of successful existing products. The efficient product replenishment (EPR) system applies to all consumer categories. The ultimate aim is to maintain desired consumer service levels at retailer outlets while minimizing logistics costs[40] including: inventory holding, transportation, warehousing, information acquisition etc. The strategy for EPR is to partner with key accounts and strategic service providers to:

- Explicitly identify desired consumer service levels based on data and scientific methods.
- Explicitly consider tradeoffs among all logistics costs.
- Redesign processes to reduce logistics costs.

3.3   Competitive Strengths of an Organization and More Efficient Consumer Satisfaction/Service Level.

Efficient Frontiers are designed to help measure and improve the performance of organizations. The quest for greater efficiency is never ending as managers are always under pressure to improve the performance of their organizations. Today, managers must cope with and make sense of an enormous amount of data relating to their organization. The challenge is to somehow derive useful insights from all these numbers that will lead to improvements in the performance of the organization. All attempts to measure performance may however produce no overall clear picture as considerable variation depending on the performance

---

[40] See Knill (1997), p. 39.

indicators chosen. This is where Efficient Frontier helps as it provides a more comprehensive measure of efficiency by taking into account all the important factors affecting an organization's performance. It is seldom the case that a unit has only a single input and output. There are usually a number of factors, determining the operational efficiency of a unit. The higher the ratio of output to input the more efficient an organization is in producing that output. The Efficient Frontier's Graph is a method of resolving this graphically by plotting, for example, overall costs to the outlet service levels. This is shown in the following 'frontier graph':

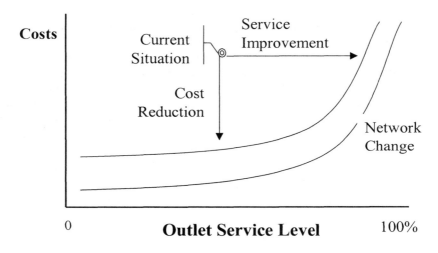

Figure 2: Working at the Efficient Frontier

Figure 2 shows the cost-service relationship. Higher service levels can be attained using proportionately lower costs by leveraging the process changes to move to a new cost-service curve, resulting in lower costs for the desired service level. A company can leverage its "strengths" and move its cost-service curve outward to gain better service levels at proportionally lower costs.

When more than two outputs and one input or one output and two inputs are active the problem becomes 'multidimensional' and is no longer suitable to be represented graphically.

4 Case Study

The Alpha-Delta[41] Company is one of the world's largest computer hardware manufacturers. The company produces more than 10,000 products used by both individual and industrial consumers. The company had a net revenue in excess of $20 billion in its 1997 fiscal year.

Traditional Approach [4-Ps]	Consumer-Centric Approach [5-Cs]	Response of a Consumer-Centric Organization
Product	**Customization**	Meet category needs Use of category product management system to tailor products/services to meet retail buyer and channel partner needs
Price	**Cost**	Consumer relationship management system Provide efficient consumer support in pre- and post-sales environment to minimize a buyer's time investment and create loyalty Facilitate differentiation
Place	**Convenience**	Shelf Replenishment System Ensuring information on product availability to facilitate inventory management Key account management system to successfully manage and retain alliances
Promotion	**Communication**	Consumer relations management Processes in place to facilitate feedback
	Care	Putting in place processes that ensure customer satisfaction

Table 1: Consumer-Centric Initiative at Alpha-Delta

---

[41] The name and figures used in the case are disguised to protect the identity of the company.

A substantial amount of its business comes from overseas operations. Headquartered in the US, it has major sites in Europe, Latin America and Asia. It sells its products and services through over 500 sales and support offices and distributorships in more than 120 countries by means of resellers and retailers.

The Alpha-Delta Company has adopted a consumer-centric approach to its product management and has processes to ensure compliance with this new initiative. Table 1, reflects the response of the company to the changes.

Assets	Functions	Process Goals	
		Goals	Measures
Consumer Relationship Management System	Image of the brand Customer service and support	Premium image in the selected market. Loyalty of customers	Brand equity Consumer satisfaction, loyalty retention, advocacy, & profitability
Information Network	Information management	Information at the right place & time	Quality & speed of decisions
Category Product Management System	Use of Category Management to manage products	Dominant market share	Share of category
Shelf Replenishment System	POS data SKU Forecasting at all levels Dynamic Computer Assisted Ordering Electronic Warehouse Receiving	Production to consumer same day Supply & demand balanced throughput	Total order fill rates Information, inventory & cash to cash cycle times. Costs
Store Support System	In-Store Merchandising In-Store Data Collection	Winning the shelf war Keeping the diagnostic & predictive data in focus	Share of shelf In-Store Hours

Table 2: Process Goals and Measures

Along with the consumer centric initiative, Alpha-Delta has also initiated "Category Management" approach to managing products and organize them as business units. Category management provides a more effective way to cater to customer demands and managing supply-chain relationships because it has a more broad-based interest. Coupled with the recent ECR initiative at the company, Alpha-Delta has reaped promising benefits.

Two forces are driving ECR: awareness of the cost structure and understanding the consumer mindset.[42] New measurement systems that track performance and mask non-value added costs are essential. Goals and respective measures need to be set up to ensure greater control and smooth functioning of the ECR initiative. Table 2 lists the core assets developed through "Category Management" and the different measures that could be used in tracking progress along with the process goals.

While EPR looks at the processes, Alpha-Delta is also using the theory of Efficient Frontier to help lower its costs while maintaining the desired service levels. Table 1 shows the cost-service relationship. Higher service levels can be attained using proportionately lower costs by leveraging the process changes to move to a new cost-service curve, resulting in lower costs for the desired service level.

5 Conclusions

This paper has presented the key initiatives surrounding ECR, discussing the primary issues involved with ECR implementations, and has described how ECR is being applied within the computer hardware industry. Both the Consumer Centric approach and ECR initiatives have greatly affected the way companies look at their business. The benefits derived from these in monetary terms are great and well documented. The dry grocery retail industry, which was one of the first to adopt ECR in its business practices, has according to one estimate reaped over $30 billion in savings.[43] Another study by Mckinsey estimates that dry grocery consumer prices were reduced by 10.8 percent by the adoption of ECR industry wide.[44] Other companies are only now coming even with the grocery industry.

Most companies in the past have invested in optimizing production or in optimizing the selling process. More recently, companies have channeled their investments into optimizing the purchasing process. The inexpensive nature of web-based EDI and its connectivity to ERP systems has enabled purchasing

---

[42] See Harran (1994), p. 7.
[43] See Wood (1993), p. 39.
[44] See Jenkins (1993), p. 147.

processes to migrate from an out of control activity to a more organized set of transactions. The procurement process is a front office activity in the supply chain. In the new paradigm of the consumer-centric approach a reverse process has taken place with the front office receding into the back office and vice-versa. Customer-centric has come to mean supplier-centric for the flow of information.

The Alpha-Delta Company, one of the benchmarks for ECR in the computer industry, has adopted ECR and benefited both in monetary terms and also in increasing the awareness and brand loyalty of its products. Specific measures have ensured a scientific approach to this initiative and brought about acceptance within the company.

6 References

Andel, T. (1998): Get in Shape for the Millenium, in: Material Handling Engineering, Vol 53, No. 2 (1998), p. 4-8.

Anderson, B. (1996): The Art and Science of Computer Assisted Ordering: Methods for Management, Quorum Books, Westport, Connecticut.

Brawn, D. (1989): EDI Developments Abroad and How They Impact Australia, in: IDC Conference, EDI – The Key to Profitability in the 1990s, IDC Conferences, Sydney.

Collins, R. (1997): ECR – Breaking China in the US Supermarket Industry, in: Supply Chain Management, Vol. 2, No. 3 (1997), p. 5-6.

Cross, G. J. (1993): Continuous Replenishment Planning: An Untapped Gold Mine, in: Transportation and Distribution, December, Vol. 34, No. 12 (1993), p. 49.

Dornier, Ph.-P., Ernst, R., Fender, M., Kouvelis, P. (1998): Global Operations and Logistics – Text and Cases, John Wiley & Sons Inc., New York, New York.

Dilger, K. A. (1997): Warehouse Wonders, in: Manufacturing Systems, Vol. 15, No. 2 (1997), p. 80-2.

Facenda, V. L. (1998): Let Us Entertain You., in: Discount Merchandiser, Vol. 38, No. 12 (1998), p. 14.

Garry, M. (1993): Efficient Replenishment: The Key to ECR, in: Progressive Grocer, Vol. 72, No. 12 (1993), p. 5-8.

Garry, M. (1994a): The Stepping Stone to ECR, in: Progressive Grocer, Vol. 73, No. 6 (1994), p. 59-60.

Garry, M. (1994b): Is there Life After CRP?, in: Progressive Grocer, Vol. 73, No. 9 (1994), p. 73-8.

Garry, M. (1996): ABC in Action., in: Progressive Grocer, Vol. 75, No. 2 (1996), p.71.

Gertler, P., Phipps, J. (1994): Category Management, in: Discount Merchandiser, Vol. 34, No. 7 (1994), p. 68-70.

Harran, J. (1994): The ECR State of Mind, in: Progressive Grocer, Vol. 73, No. 1 (1994), p. 7-8.

Harris, J. K. (1999): Efficient Consumer Response (ECR): A Survey of the Australian Grocery Industry, in: Supply Chain Management. Vol. 4, No. 1 (1999), p. 1-5.

Hofler, R. (1996): Glossary of Grocery Terms, in: Progressive Grocer Associates, Stamford, Connecticut.

Jenkins, D. B. (1993): Jenkins Leads EDI Effort, in: Chain Store Age Executive, March (1993), p. 147.

Knill, B. (1998): How Efficient is Efficient Consumer Response? Material Handling Engineering, in: Supply Chain Management and Warehousing Supplement, July Issue, (1998) p. 13-15.

Kurt Salmon Associates, Inc. (1993): Efficient Consumer Response: Enhancing Consumer Value in the Grocery Industry, Food Marketing Institute, Washington, DC.

Kotler, P. (1991): Marketing Management: Analysis, Planning, Implementation and Control, Prentice-Hall (1991), Englewood Cliffs, N.J.

Kurtz, D. L, Boone, L. E. (1989): Contemporary Marketing, Dryden Press, 6th ed, Chicago.

Lewis, L. (1998): Hanging Up the Gloves, in: Progressive Grocer. Vol. 77, No. 10 (1998), p. 27.

McEachern, C. E. (1998): Convergent Marketing: Executing On the Promise of 1:1, in: Journal of Consumer marketing, Vol. 15 (1998), p. 481-490.

Mathews, R. (1994): A New Look at ECR, in: Progressive Grocer, Vol. 73, No. 6 (1994), p. 29-32.

Miller, J. (1996): Implementing Activity-Based Management in Daily Operations, John Wiley & Sons, New York, New York.

Pearce, T. (1997): Lessons Learned from Birds Eye Wall's ECR Initiative, in: Supply Chain Management, Vol. 2, No. 3 (1997), p. 99-106.

Reicheld, F. F. (1996): The Quest for Loyalty: Creating Value Through Partnership, Harvard Business School Press, Boston, MA.

Radice, C. (1996): Perceptual Realities, in: Progressive Grocer, Vol. 76, No. 8 (1996), p. 24-32.

Sansolo, M. (1993): Don't Forget the "C", in: Progressive Grocer, Vol. 72, No. 12 (1993), p. 4.

Sherman, R. J. (1994a): PRWs and Wholesalers: Turf Battle Ahead?, in: Frozen Food Age., Vol. 43, No. 3 (1994), p. 20-26.

Sherman, R. J. (1994b): From Vision into Action, in: Beverage World, Vol. 155, No. 1599 (1994), p. 56-60.

Thayer, W. (1991): Computer Aided Ordering is Ready, Should You Care?, in: Progressive Grocer, Vol. 74, No. 3 (1991), p. 81-86.

Tosh, M. (1998): What's Up With ECR - ECR '99 Supplement, in: Progressive Grocer, Vol. 27. December Issue (1998), p. 8.

Weeks, D., Crawford, F. A. (1994): Efficient Consumer Response: A Mandate for Food Manufacturers?, in: Food Processing, Vol. 55, No. 2 (1994), p 34.

Wood, A. (1993): Efficient Consumer Response, in: Logistics Information Management, Vol. 6, No. 4 (1993), p. 38-40.

Weinstein, S. (1995): On the Cutting Edge, in: Progressive Grocer, Vol. 74, No. 8 (1995), p. 34-40.

Improving Supply Chain Productivity Through Horizontal Cooperation
– the Case of Consumer Goods Manufacturers

Kourosh Bahrami

1	Introduction	214
2	Distribution Networks	214
3	Horizontal Cooperation as a Means to Optimize Joint Distribution Networks	218
4	The Case of Two Consumer Goods Manufacturers	223
5	Conclusion	230
6	References	230

Summary:
This paper turns the perspective from the popular vertical to the less discussed horizontal cooperation within supply chains. The analysis is driven by the hypothesis that horizontal cooperation in a supply chain may contain undiscovered potentials to increase productivity. This hypothesis is confirmed through theoretical and practical considerations. Horizontal cooperation is a means of logistical optimization within a joint network. The case of two manufacturers collaborating in distribution reveals savings with respect to overall distribution costs of 2,4% through process and 9,8% through structure optimization.

Keywords:
Consumer Goods Manufacturer, Distribution Network, Horizontal Cooperation, Supply Chain, Synergy

1 Introduction

The integrated perspective of supply chain management concentrates on *vertical* cooperation. Popular examples are the vertical cooperation between suppliers and manufacturers in the automobile industry (e.g. Just-in-Time)[1] or between consumer goods manufacturers and retailers (e.g. Efficient Consumer Response).[2]

This paper shifts the perspective to *horizontal* cooperation within supply chains. The goal is to verify whether this complementary view could help find undiscovered potentials to improve productivity of supply chains. Therefore, in a first step the theoretical background of horizontal cooperation in supply chains is developed. This is done in an application context of distribution networks[3] of fast moving consumer goods in the German market. In a second step the generated theoretical framework is applied to the case of two collaborating fast-moving consumer goods manufacturers. It serves as an example of a qualitative and quantitative illustration of increased supply chain productivity through horizontal cooperation.

2 Distribution Networks

2.1 Distribution Networks as Subsystems of Supply Chains

In general, the term *supply chain* represents the inter-linked sequence of the subsystems raw material suppliers, production facilities, distribution services and customers by the flow of goods and information.[4] This image of a chain has a *linear-vertical perspective*.

In the practical environment, the combination of all flow and transformation activities does not just consist of one hub per subsystem. For instance, in the case of consumer goods the supply chain usually encompasses several suppliers of raw

---

[1] For the general development of cooperation in supply chains see Laarhoven, Sharman (1994), p. 39.
[2] For examples of vertical cooperation see Österle, Fleisch, Alt (2001), p. 111.
[3] The following considerations are not limited to distribution. Due to the fact that networks are analyzed, the results of this paper could also be transferred to other parts of the supply chain.
[4] See Towill, Naim, Wikner (1992), p. 3.

materials, several manufacturers of consumer goods and several warehouses (of the manufacturer or/and logistics service provider or/and retailers) and outlets. Out of this complementary horizontal perspective the term supply chain could be understood in the sense of a *supply network*.[5] Using the image of a network *distribution* could be defined as a network of interrelated production sites, warehouses, transshipment points and outlets (see Figure 1).

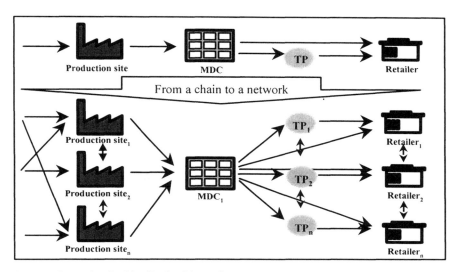

Figure 1: Example of a Distribution Network

The design of distribution networks is determined by two factors: structure and process.[6] The structural design contains decisions about the number of different steps taken through a network from production to the retailer (vertical structure) and the type as well as number of hubs used per step (horizontal structure). The process design is inter-linked with the structure of the network. On the one side the type of transportation mode has to be defined, on the other side decisions about the transportation process must be taken. In the case of fast moving consumer goods there are basically two different transportation processes. The first represents a two-stage delivery from the production site to a manufacturer distribution center (MDC) and from there directly to the retailer. The second process called three-stage delivery contains the transshipment point (TP) as an

---

[5] See Delfmann, Albers (2000), p. 33, who formulate: "(...) real world relations of a company show a network structure which increases the complexity of supply chain management by a considerable factor"; also Pfohl, Buse (2000), p. 395.

[6] See Ballou (1992), p. 26.

additional interface between the MDC and the retailer (see Figure 1). The transshipment point serves as a consolidation point.

2.2 Productivity Indicators of Distribution Networks

The productivity of distribution networks is the *ratio between the input and its output*.[7] All input factors are represented by process costs and all output factors by service measures. This paper concentrates on process costs which implies that a potential increase in productivity is based on process costs reduction while sustaining at least a constant service level. The service level is evaluated in a more qualitative way by measuring the impact on lead time and delivery reliability.

Process costs contain the resources used for warehousing, transportation and order processing activities. From the perspective of consumer goods manufacturers, these activities are more and more fulfilled by logistics service providers.[8] Thus they are measured by cost rates such as €/ton. In the case of transportation the prices of the logistics service providers are calculated on the basis of a specific weight-distance combination. Figure 2 illustrates the correlation of the price (in €/ton) and the delivery size (in tons) with a constant distance. The negative correlation relies on the fixed cost digression. The switch from the three- to the two-stage delivery process creates an additional price decrease based on the disappearance of the interface-related transshipment point costs.

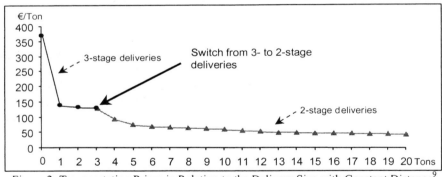

Figure 2: Transportation Prices in Relation to the Delivery Size with Constant Distance[9]

---

[7] For a detailed concept of productivity indicators in distribution see Amstel, D'hert (1996), p. 73.

[8] See Laarhoven, Berglund, Peters (2000), p. 425, for an overview of the development of third-party logistics in Europe within the last five years.

[9] This curve is based on the cost rates of the German GFT at an average distance of 350 kilometers. The 'Güterverkehrsferntarif (GFT)' contains the legal rates for 2- and 3-

2.3 Current Developments in the Context of Distribution Networks

The context of distribution networks is characterized by several changes such as the liberalization of the markets (European Union and the transportation markets), higher restrictions regarding the use of transportation infrastructure, an intensifying application of information technology, and concentrating activities of the main retailers in their supply logistics.[10]

The last point could be interpreted as a central threat for the consumer goods manufacturers due to the risk of significant cost increases. The *retailer activities in supply logistics* could be seen as an intensifying takeover of the manufacturers' distribution logistics.[11] One of the key drivers for this development is the high complexity at the retailers' reception points. This is basically caused by a low capacity use of the transportation vehicles. Through a retailer driven consolidation, the capacity use could be increased and consequently the number of trucks fulfilling the same volume could be reduced. Some of the main retailers have started these kinds of actions by taking over outlet deliveries. They are fulfilled from a retailer distribution center or a cross-docking station. The second step could be to pick up the consumer goods at the manufacturer's central warehouse or directly at the manufacturer's production site. On one hand this would result in increasing costs per unit for the remaining distribution volume for retailers without supply logistics activities. On the other hand the compensation demands of the retailers for their transportation services could be used as a new area of discount negotiations. Current examples confirm this projection.[12]

In fact, one central reason for the low capacity use and subsequently the retailers' activities in supply logistics could be seen in the insufficient results of the logistics service providers' productivity. Their core competence in creating synergies through adequate pooling of goods in order to optimize the use of transportation capacity is not yet sufficiently developed. Overall transports are done with more than 45% free capacity.[13] The high relevance of the logistics service providers' inactivity becomes even clearer in the context of growing restrictions concerning the use of transportation infrastructure.

---

stage deliveries, which were legally binding until the transportation market's liberalization in January 1st, 1994; see GFT (2000). The GFT still has an orientation function for current rates.

[10] See Faller (1999), who concentrates on the developments in Austria, but which could be transferred to Germany; also Karp (2000), p. 295.
[11] See Bretzke (1999), p. 81, who discusses the issue of a takeover of the manufacturers' distribution logistics by the retailers due to comparative system advantages.
[12] See Bretzke (1999), p. 93.
[13] See Erdmann (1999), p. 4.

Summing up, it can be said that current developments in the context of the manufacturers' distribution networks create a need for further productivity increase. Horizontal cooperation could be one strategy to cope with those developments sufficiently.

3 Horizontal Cooperation as a Means to Optimize Joint Distribution Networks

3.1 Cooperation in Supply Chains

The term *cooperation* is defined in a diversified way by scholars. Cooperation can be specified by the use of criteria. In the criterion coordination system, cooperation can be differentiated from market and hierarchy.[14] The coordination system in markets is the price mechanism, in hierarchies it is instruction and in cooperation it is negotiation. Thus, in cases of market and hierarchy failure the cooperation symbolizes an alternative.[15] The consideration of further criteria affirms on the one hans these cases. On the other hand it becomes obvious that - depending on the context - cooperation also includes market- or hierarchy-specific elements. Examples for these criteria are the dependency of the parties, the intensity of opportunism or the allocation of decision-making competence.[16] Concerning the first criterion the parties are independent in markets, in hierarchies mono-directional dependent and in cooperation bi-directional dependent. This mutual dependency requires an atmosphere of trust and, consequently, the level of opportunism is low. In the opposite, scenario markets are characterized by a high level of actors' opportunism. In hierarchies according to the principal-agent-phenomenon the level of opportunism is situated between these extremes. Regarding the allocation of decision-making competence - depending on the context - cooperation could be more on the side of hierarchies with a central or on the side of markets with a decentral decision-making competence.

A further specification of the term cooperation can be achieved by the distinction of different *cooperation types*. For this purpose a variety of different criteria can be used. A popular and accepted criterion is the distinction based on the direction of the cooperation within the value chain.[17] In this typology the collaboration

---

[14] See Powell (1990), p. 301. In this context cooperation and networks synonymous.
[15] For the explanation of market and hierarchy failure the transaction cost concept could be used; see Williamson (1975), p. 40.
[16] See Child, Faulkner (1998), p. 17, who illustrate the issue of cooperation in discussing the contributions of the main perspectives in economics.
[17] See Backhaus, Meyer (1993), p. 330.

between partners of different levels of the value chain is called *vertical cooperation*. An example in the context of supply chains is the collaboration of manufacturers, logistics service providers and retailers to achieve a more efficient reaction to consumer needs (ECR). The *horizontal cooperation* is complementary to this type. In this case, partners on the same level of the value chain collaborate. Horizontal cooperation is not yet as developed as vertical. They are both however regarded as "(...) one of the newest and most complex formats for an alliance."[18] A key reason for this view is the possibility that the collaborators simultaneously belong to the same sector.

The issue of *'competitive atmosphere of the collaborators'* has not yet been pointed out clearly in the literature. This is illustrated by the so-called diagonal type of cooperation.[19] These are cooperation of partners on the same level of the value chain but from different sectors. This further specification of cooperation types contains two defects. First, the criterion is only applied for horizontal cooperation. In the case of vertical cooperation it is assumed that the partners do not belong to the same sector. But in reality, vertical cooperation between partners of the same sector can also be observed. For instance, IBM and Intel belong to the Information Technology sector. At the same time IBM serves as a supplier of micro-processors for Intels' PC-production.[20] The second defect could be seen in the insufficient preciseness of the criterion 'sector'. For instance, the collaboration of two consumer goods manufacturers in distribution could mean both collaborative transports of two cosmetics mass-producers aa well as the cooperation of a cosmetics producer with a detergents manufacturer. Both belong to the fast moving consumer goods sector but in the first situation they are direct competitors and in the second they are not.

The distinction of cooperation according to the criterion 'competitive atmosphere' appears to be nevertheless fruitful, because obviously the cooperation among competitors is much more problematic than among non-competitors. Particularly the realization of an atmosphere of trust is much more difficult in these situations. Therefore, this paper offers a proposition for the use of this criterion without the existing defects. Regarding this, in a first step the criterion 'sector' is concretized by the use of the criterion 'competitor'. As a result the two types of cooperation are competitive- and non-competitive cooperation. Second, the differentiation is done for both horizontal and vertical cooperation. Consequently, four types of cooperation can be differentiated: competitive-horizontal, competitive-vertical, non-competitive-horizontal and non-competitive-vertical cooperation.

These criteria can also be applied on *cooperation in supply chains*. In this context the first criterion could be specified by the level of value creation within a supply

---

[18] Bowersox et al. (1992), p. 143.
[19] See Backhaus, Meyer (1993), p. 332.
[20] See Dowling, Lechner (1998), p. 88.

chain. Figure 3 illustrates this for the case of distribution logistics as the level of value creation within a supply chain. In addition, it offers for each of the four cases one example. The above mentioned cooperation of two cosmetics manufacturers serves as an example for competitive-horizontal cooperation and the distribution of a competitor`s goods by a manufacturer symbolizes an example of competitive-vertical cooperation. This can often be observed in the context of internationalization activities. For example, in a rather fragmented market of cleaning products a 'foreign' competitor would use the facilities of another cleaning products manufacturer to distribute its own products. The 'foreign' competitor overcomes easily market entry barriers such as investments for a new distribution network; the 'domestic' cooperation partner realizes cost degressions due to the higher volume. ECR is a popular example of non-competitive vertical cooperation. Finally, cooperation between small and medium-sized transportation service providers with the objective of higher or full geographical coverage of a region might serve as an example of non-competitive horizontal cooperation.

	Same Logistical Level of Value Creation (here distribution logistics)	
	yes	no
Competitor for products with same necessity fulfillment — yes	**Competitive horizontal cooperation** (e.g. cosmetic producers cooperation in distribution)	**Competitive vertical cooperation** (e.g. distribution of a competitor's goods)
Competitor for products with same necessity fulfillment — no	**Non-competitive horizontal cooperation** (e.g. small and medium transport service provider cooperation)	**Non-competitive vertical cooperation** (e.g. efficient consumer response)

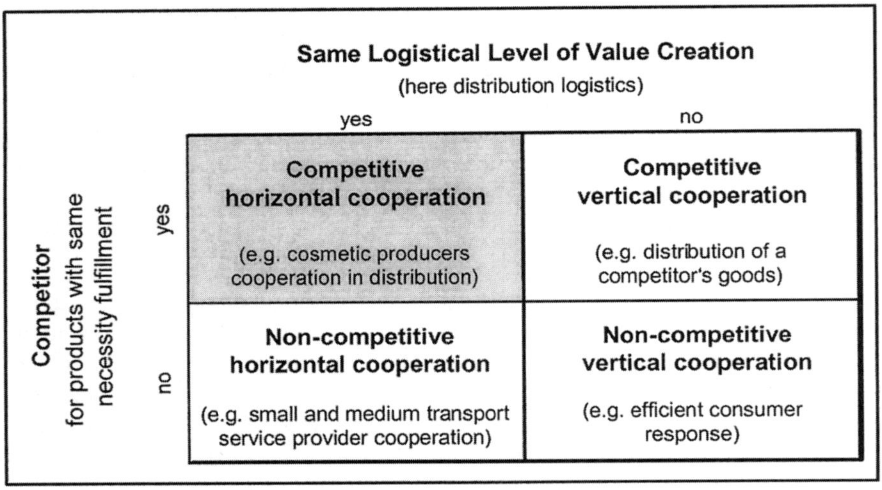

Figure 3: Typology of Cooperation within Supply Chains

3.2 Understanding of Horizontal Cooperation in Distribution Networks

The following passage specifies in a two step approach the understanding of horizontal cooperation in distribution networks of consumer goods manufacturers.

First of all, horizontal cooperation is interpreted as *a means of process and structure design* of distribution networks.[21] For instance, the transportation process could be improved through a pooling of orders of different collaborating manufacturers in the way that a three-stage delivery could be transformed into the more efficient two-stage delivery. This implies simultaneously a change in the structural dimension of the distribution network, for example when joint manufacturer distribution centers would be constructed.

Following this interpretation of horizontal cooperation as a mean of process and structure design, the attendance of the individual manufacturer implies a modification of its distribution network.[22] Thus the horizontal cooperation creates a change of the existing hubs and their interrelation as well as causes the creation of new ones. In other words: the hubs of the different collaborating manufacturers start to interact. This means that the separate distribution networks could be understood as one *joint distribution network*. From a logistical point of view, it does not make a difference to whom a hub belongs. The important fact is that the joint distribution network offers new opportunities of improvement such as a more intensive use of existing infrastructure or the elimination of redundant elements. Furthermore, with this understanding all existing theoretical tools concerning the optimization of supply chains could be applied to horizontal cooperation due to the fact that it represents a distribution network. Consequently the optimization can be realized – as is the case in distribution logistics – on *two levels of intensity*. *Process improvements* (first level) through cooperation changes within existing structures. Their effects are in general smaller than *optimization in structure* (second level), because a modification of the hubs also signifies a change of processes.

3.3 Realization of Synergies as the Goal of Horizontal Cooperation in Distribution Networks

The motivation of the manufacturers to cooperate could result from additional increases in productivity. However, the growing pressure on their distribution networks created by current developments pushes the manufacturers towards innovative action.[23] Both are reflected in the aim to realize synergies. Thus the

---

[21] See Bahrami (1998), p. 27.
[22] See Bahrami (1998), p. 27.
[23] This reflects also a possible reaction to hierarchy and market failures. After outsourcing all operative and parts of the strategic distribution logistics activities due to the higher productivity of the market instead of the 'make alternative' (hierarchy failure), the horizontal cooperation of manufacturers would symbolize a re-integration due to insufficient productivity of the service providers (market failure); see also La Londe, Powers (1993), p. 4.

goal of horizontal cooperation could be the *realization of synergies by pooling resources*.[24] In general, synergies are realized by economies of scale and scope.[25]

Economies of scale characterize in the context of this paper the effect that with an increase of the (transportation) volume the costs per unit decrease. A precondition for is the cost's subadditivity. This implies that the costs for transportation of a specific volume fulfilled by two or more manufacturers is higher than the fulfillment by one manufacturer. In a mathematical form this can be illustrated in the following way:

(F.1) Cost's subadditivity: $$\sum_{i=1}^{n} C(x_i) > C\left(\sum_{i=1}^{n} x_i\right)$$

with C = transportation costs
with x_i = transportation volume of manufacturer (i), and $x_i > 0$

The explanations concerning economies of cale reflect an increase of the volume of one transportation good or a type of good. In contrast, *economies of scope* symbolize the effect of the volume increase by different transportation goods or types of goods. In addition to the precondition of cost's subadditivity in this case, the precondition of cost's complementarity must exist. This implies that the marginal costs of delivery of one transportation good decrease in the case of an increase in the other transportation goods (types) when a joint use of resources generally serving for different needs is given. In a mathematical form this could be illustrated in the following way:

(F.1) Cost's complementarity: $$C(x_1, 0) + C(x_2, 0) > C(x_1, x_2)$$

with C = transportation costs
with x_1 and x_2 = transportation volume of good 1 and 2,
with $x_1 > 0$ and $x_2 > 0$

In general, economies of scale and scope are the result of several effects such as fixed cost digression, learning or statistical compensation effects. Fixed cost digression represents the main reason for the digressive curve of the transportation costs per ton illustrated in Figure 2. But the shift from a three- to a two-stage delivery is neither fully described by fixed cost digression nor by learning or statistical compensation effects. The central reason is the change in process, which implies a shift in effectiveness. Taking the example of the officially proposed rates of GFT this point of shift is about three tons. From this point onwards the cost-intensive activities of transshipment do not exist due to the fact that it pays to distribute the goods directly.

---

[24] See Mitchell et al. (1992), p. 19, who formulate: "(...) two (or more) dissimilar organizations have essentially pooled resources in an attempt to realize benefits not available to the parties individually."

[25] See Ansoff (1998), p. 23.

The demonstration of the cost effects in Figure 2 could be used for both economies of scale and scope. Taking into account the application context of this paper, which is that the goods of different manufacturers are pooled together, the synergy effects of the cooperation could be understood as economies of scope.

The pooling of goods of different manufacturers represents the means to realize economies of scope. This can be done by minimizing transportation distances or *maximizing the unloading volume per stop*.[26] The first target was recently analyzed by different studies particularly in combination with alliances of logistics service providers.[27] The second target has not yet been the focus of analysis. Therefore, the following case demonstrates the application of this target. This intention is also confirmed by the fact that the maximization of the unloading volume per stop does not only offer a decrease in costs but also reduces the complexity at the retailer's unloading point, which could be interpreted as a service increase. Consequently, a maximization delivery size established through horizontal cooperation would increase the productivity of the supply chain not just due to a cost decrease, but also because of an improvement in service. In the following, these theoretical considerations are applied in the context of a case study. The results are generated in qualitative and quantitative form.

4 The Case of Two Consumer Goods Manufacturers

The case of Henkel Cosmetics and Schwarzkopf represents an example for competitive-horizontal cooperation (see Figure 3). The cooperation concentrates on joint transportation. The two levels of cooperation intensity are simulated and evaluated separately. This is done in a three-step approach (see Figure 4).

In the first step (situation S.I) the separate distribution networks of the two companies are described and the total costs of the two networks calculated. In the second step (situation S.II) a cooperation with the target of process optimization is simulated, costs are calculated and compared to S.I. The third step (situation S.III) illustrates a cooperation on the structural level. The results of the simulation are compared to S.I and S.II. Finally, the key findings are presented.[28]

---

[26] This is also called vehicle consolidation and terminal consolidation; see Hall (1987), p. 58 and 63. Inventory consolidation is not considered in the following due to the fact that in this case, lead time is examined; see Hall (1987), p. 58 and 61.
[27] See Erdmann (1999) and the literature overview given there.
[28] The simulations are based on real figures of the two companies but represent hypothetical scenarios. In reality Schwarzkopf was integrated into the Henkel Cosmetics business due to its acquisition by the Henkel Group; this also changed the production landscape.

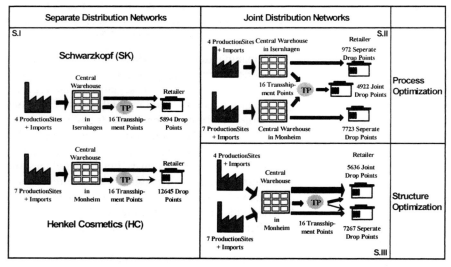

Figure 4: Distribution Networks in Overview

4.1 The Separate Distribution Networks (S.I)

As mentioned in section 3.3 the preconditions of economies of scope are cost subadditivity and cost complementarity. The first condition is given due to the fact that an increasing delivery size implies lower costs per ton (see section 2.2). The cost's complementarity shows that it is possible to transport the goods of different manufacturers on the same vehicle. This is basically dependent on the kind of products transported but also indirectly affected by the production and client structure.

Concerning the *kind of product*, Schwarzkopf and Henkel Cosmetics produce both cosmetics asfast-moving consumer goods. These products are characterized by light weight per unit volume. As they can be piled and shipped in cardboard boxes according to the standard size of the Euro-pallet (800mm x 1200mm) and underlie strict regulations (like maximum temperature), these products could be easily transported together. The *production structure* illustrates the high significance of national production. In both cases just about 15% of the total volume is produced outside of Germany. The domestic production is fulfilled by four factories in the case of Schwarzkopf and seven in the case of Henkel Cosmetics. The *customer structure* of cosmetics consists of wholesalers, retailers (such as supermarkets), self-service shops, ordinary department stores and drug stores. The customers are represented by about 100 purchase organizations with 5.894 drop points for Schwarzkopft and 12.645 for Henkel Cosmetics. (Figures for Henkel Cosmetics will be shown from here on in parenthesis.) High concentration implies that the ten biggest purchase organizations generate more than 90% of total turnover.

Due to the significant homogeneity in the dimensions product, production and customer the two cosmetics manufacturers have for the most part similar distribution networks. By concentrating on their core competences, the two companies have out-placed all operative logistic tasks through *outsourcing measures*. Therefore, the main logistic tasks of the cosmetic producers are concentrated on strategic issues like the conceptualization of the structure and the determination of the process types of distribution logistics, the selection of the logistics service providers and the controlling of process activities within the distribution logistics.

Concerning the conceptualization of the *vertical warehouse structure* Schwarzkopf and Henkel Cosmetics practice a combination of two- and three-stage distribution network (see also Figure 4, S.I). First, the cosmetic products are transported from the production sites to the central warehouse. About 51% (36%) of total tonnage of cosmetics are supplied directly from the central warehouse to the customers (two-stage distribution). The remaining 49% (64%) is distributed via transshipment points (three-stage distribution). Regarding the costs of transportation the three-stage distribution is about three times more cost intensive than the two-stage case.

Key Data	SK	HC	S.I
Vertical warehouse structure (as % of total volume)			
1-stage structure: exline	0%	0%	0%
2-stage structure: direct deliveries	51%	36%	44%
3-stage structure: deliveries via transshipment point	49%	64%	56%
Horizontal warehouse structure			
# production sites	4	7	11
# of central warehouses	1	1	2
# of regional or field warehouses	0	0	0
# of transshipment points	16	16	32
Delivery size in gross tons (gt)	0,524	0,182	0,287
Distribution costs as index	46	54	100

Table 1: Key Data in Overview

On the *horizontal dimension*, the warehouse structure is characterized by four (seven) production sites [three domestic and one abroad (five domestic and two abroad)], one (one) central warehouse and 16 (16) transshipment points.

The transportation process of cosmetic products is divided up into the supply to the central warehouse and to the customers. In the pre-stage cosmetic products are transported daily by full trucks from the production sites to the central warehouse (i.e. with an average delivery size of 17 tons per truck). Depending on the customers' premises and on the delivery size, all shipments exceeding 2,5 gross tons are directly delivered (two-stage) by trucks. The rest is sent via transshipment points (three-stage). In the main stage, the products of all shipments that are transported through the same transshipment point are collected on one truck. At the transshipment point the products are reloaded on a number of vehicles for regional transportation to fulfill the final stage of delivery. As one of the key measures for transportation (implicitly also for warehousing and administration) the delivery size of Schwarzkopf is 0,524 gross tons, Henkel Cosmetics 0,182 gross tons. Thus, from the total costs of the two networks Schwarzkopf has a lower part even though it has a higher total volume (see Table 1).

Looking at the separate distribution networks as a whole, (this represents situation S.I), the total number of production sites is eleven. In addition, the networks contain two central warehouses, one for Schwarzkopf in north central Germany at Isernhagen and one for Henkel Cosmetics in the mid west of the country at Monheim. Furthermore, the two separated distribution networks count 32 transshipment points of two different service providers. As a logistical result the two networks have an average delivery size of 0,287 gross tons. The total costs (transportation, warehousing, administration) are represented by an index of 100, which help to compare with the scenarios of joint distribution networks.[29]

4.2 Process Optimization As a Result of a Joint Distribution Network (S.II)

As the preconditions of economies of scope are fulfilled, a potential cooperation promises to be fruitful. In the following, the joint distribution network is optimized. Starting with the assumption that the two distribution networks should not be changed significantly and each company should preserve the highest possible level of autonomy, the potential of optimized processes through a collaborative approach was analyzed. The highest savings potentials with the condition of at least one constant service level represented a cooperative transportation for deliveries via transshipment points.[30]

This is illustrated in Figure 4 as situation S.II. Instead of two different service providers with different transshipment point networks (16 for Schwarzkopf and Henkel Cosmetics alike), only one service provider will distribute the total volume of the two companies in this transportation segment. Consequently, the service provider has the opportunity to consolidate the transshipment point deliveries of the two companies to the same drop point. As the prices for the transportation

---

[29] The calculation of the costs is done by the multiplication of the deliveries with the same price matrix in order to eliminate price effects between the two companies.

[30] City logistics concepts or a two central warehouse solution were analyzed but implied smaller savings potentials than a collaborative transportation for the deliveries via transshipment points.

service are directly negatively correlated to the delivery size, each combined delivery (one delivery of Schwarzkopf and one of Henkel Cosmetics to the same drop point) creates a lower price and savings as a result.[31]

In order to identify the saving potential of this collaborative approach the situation of a joint distribution network with two central warehouses and joint transshipment point network (S.II) is *simulated*. The simulation consists of four steps. In the first step, the measures of the two data bases (orders, delivery size, location of the transshipment points, location of the customers/drop points, delivery dates) are harmonized. In the second step, the potentially combined deliveries are identified by matching deliveries to the same delivery point from the same transshipment point within one calendar week.[32] The new data base with the combined deliveries along with the rest is evaluated by a price matrix. The deviation between the total costs of the joint transshipment network solution and the sum of the costs of the two separate transshipment networks represents savings.

Key Data	S.I	S.II
Vertical warehouse structure (as % of total volume)		
1-stage structure: exline	0%	0%
2-stage structure: direct deliveries	44%	44%
3-stage structure: deliveries via transshipment point	56%	56%
Horizontal warehouse structure		
# production sites	11	11
# of central warehouses	2	2
# of regional or field warehouses	0	0
# of transshipment points	32	16
Delivery size in gross tons (gt)	0,287	0,345
Distribution costs as index	100	97,6

Table 2: Comparison of the Separate and the Process Optimized Joint Distribution Network

The results of the simulation are illustrated in Figure 4, S.II and Table 2. Concerning the drop points, Schwarzkopf and Henkel Cosmetics have 4.922 similar customer addresses. This implies that 84% of Schwarzkopf drop points are congruent to Henkel Cosmetics (39%). Implementing the time restriction of one calendar week has the effect that in 54,8% (24,3%) of all deliveries a combined shipment is

---

[31] The second component of the transportation price 'distance' is not significantly tackled by the collaborative transportation due to the reason that the location of the central warehouses and the drop points will not change.

[32] The time window of one week is an assumption and reflects a higher amount of combined deliveries as in the case of totally random combinations. In this case the time window would be narrowed to the same delivery day.

possible. The total number of deliveries decreases by 16,8% and consequently the average delivery size increases by 20,3% from 0,287 to 0,345 gross tons. This increase effects a cost reduction of 15,3% for the deliveries from the transshipment points to the customers or a total cost savings of 2,4% from 100 to 97,6 in the index scale. This cost savings represents the effects of the economies of scope.

4.3 Structure Optimization As a Result of a Joint Distribution Network (S.III)

In addition to the process optimization-based cooperation in S.III, the total joint distribution network is seen as an arena of optimization. The scenario with the highest savings potential is presented in the following. In this distribution network the two companies use the same service provider and thus have access to the same transshipment point network. Additionally, one central warehouse is eliminated. All goods are shipped to the central warehouse in Monheim.[33] From there the transports *to* the transshipment points can be fulfilled together. Furthermore, the two-stage transports are distributable in the same truck. Up to this point, the optimized structure of the joint distribution network creates economies of scope. In addition to this, we have economies of 'shift' from the cost intensive three-stage to the two-stage transportation process. Deliveries via transshipment point that have a delivery size of >1,25 gross tons before cooperation could have in case of a joint distribution a delivery size higher than 2,5 gross tons, assuming that two deliveries of >1,25 gross tons are transported together. In this case we have a shift from the three- to the two-stage transportation process, which implying that the costs per gross ton will decrease significantly (see also Figure 2).

Key Data	S.I	S.III
Vertical warehouse structure (as % of total volume)		
1-stage structure: exline	0%	0%
2-stage structure: direct deliveries	44%	54%
3-stage structure: deliveries via transshipment point	56%	46%
Horizontal warehouse structure		
# production sites	11	11
# of central warehouses	2	1
# of regional or field warehouses	0	0
# of transshipment points	32	16
Delivery size in gross tons (gt)	0,287	0,349
Distribution costs as index	100	90,2

Table 3: Comparison of Separate and Structural Optimized Joint Distribution Network

---

[33] Monheim is identified as the warehouse with the smallest extra costs in transportation taking into account all incoming and outgoing transportation costs.

The simulation is done with the similar logic of the case of the process optimization. The results are illustrated in Figure 4, S.III and Table 3.

The number of joint drop points could be increased by the destinations served via a two-stage distribution process with an additional 714 drop points. Consequently, the number of orders declined by an additional percentage point to 17,8% and the average delivery size increases slightly to 0,349 gross tons. The shift of joint deliveries of the previous three- to the two-stage segment has the effect that the part of two-stage deliveries in terms of percentage of the total volume increases from 46% to 54%. As an effect of all changes the transportation costs decrease by 26,3%. In contrast the replenishment costs due to the elimination of the central warehouse in Isernhagen increase by 2,4%.[34] Including this negative effect the index notes a net total cost reduction of 9,8 points.

In comparison to S.II (the process optimization) the structural improved joint distribution network creates a four times higher saving potential (see Figure 5). This is basically driven by the following two factors:
1. The scope of the cooperation is enlarged to the deliveries from the central warehouse to the transshipment points and the direct deliveries to the drop points.
2. The structural change allows a shift of a joint 3-stage delivery with a joint delivery size higher than 2,5 gross tons to the significantly less cost-intensive two-stage transportation.

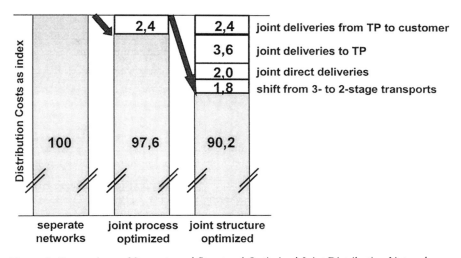

Figure 5: Comparison of Separate and Structural Optimized Joint Distribution Network

---

[34] Concerning the warehousing it is assumed that the costs will not change, although here as well economies of scope could be possible.

The first effect of the higher collaboration intensity basically creates supplementary economies of scope due to a larger scope of cooperation. In addition, the structure optimization enables the distribution network to take a step towards higher productivity due to a shift from three- to two-stage deliveries. This savings potential is original to the cooperation concerning the structural dimension.

5 Conclusion

The hypothesis of this paper - that horizontal cooperation in supply chains could encompass undiscovered potentials for productivity increase - is confirmed. This is demonstrated on the basis of theoretical and practical considerations. Horizontal cooperations are understood as a means of logistical optimization within a joint network. The case of two collaborating manufacturers in distribution reveals savings with respect to overall distribution costs of 2,4% through process and 9,8% through structure optimization. A constant level in service is regarded as a precondition. Thus, the horizontal cooperation effects a significant increase in productivity.

But horizontal cooperation does not represent a one-size-fits-all. For example, the case shows an increase of the delivery size from 289 to 345 kg which represents just a slight improvement of the ill-optimized capacity use within the fast-moving consumer goods sector. Thus, horizontal cooperation should be understood as a complementary means to the popular vertical cooperation or other supply chain management activities which target productivity optimization. The considerations of this paper could motivate further analysis of horizontal cooperation.

6 References

Ansoff, H. J. (1998): Synergy and Capabilities, in: Campbell, A., Luchs, K. S.: Strategic Synergy, 2nd ed., International Thomson Business Press, London et al. (1998), p. 21-40.

Amstel, R. P. van, D'hert, G. (1996): Performance Indicators in Distribution, in: The International Journal of Logistics Management, Vol. 7, No. 1 (1996), p. 73-82.

Backhaus, K., Meyer, M. (1993): Strategische Allianzen und strategische Netzwerke (Strategic Alliances and Strategic Networks), in: Wirtschaftwissenschaftliches Studium (WiSt), Vol. 22, No. 7 July (1993), p. 330-334.

Bahrami, K. (1998): Herstellerkooperationen in der Distriubtionslogistik (Production Cooperations in Distribution Logistics), unpublished diploma thesis, University of Cologne.

Ballou, R. H. (1992): Business Logistics Management, 3rd ed., Prentice Hall, Englewood Cliffs, New Jersey.

Bowersox, D. J. (1992): Logistical Excellence. It's Not Business As Usual, Digital Press, Burlington.

Bretzke, W.-R. (1999): Industrie- versus Handelslogistik: Der Kampf um die Systemführerschaft in der Konsumgüterdistribution (Industrial versus Retailer Logistics), in: logistik management, Vol. 1, No. 2 (1999), p. 81-95.

Child, J., Faulkner, D. (1998): Strategies of Cooperation. Managing Alliances, Networks, and Joint Ventures, Oxford University Press, Oxford et al.

Dowling, M., Lechner, C. (1998): Kooperative Wettbewerbsbeziehungen: Theoretische Ansätze und Managementstrategien (Cooperative Competitive Relations), in: Die Betriebswirtschaft, Vol. 58, No. 1 (1998), p. 86-102.

Delfmann, W., Albers, S. (2000): Supply Chain Management in the Global Context, Working Paper No. 102, Dept. of General Management, Business Planning and Logistics of the University of Cologne, Cologne.

Erdmann, M. (1999): Konsolidierungspotentiale von Speditionskooperationen. Eine simulationsgestützte Analyse (Consolidation of cooperations among freight forwarders), Gabler, Wiesbaden.

Faller, P. (1999): Transportwirtschaft im Umbruch: Strukturwandel, Anpassungserfordernisse, Gestaltungsaufgaben (Transport in Transition: Structural Change, Adaptation, Configuration), Linde, Wien.

GFT (2000): Güterfernverkehrstarif (Stückgut und Ladungssatz) gültig ab 01.01.1992 (Tarif of Long-Distance Hauling), Sydow, Aichtal.

Hall, R. W. (1987): Consolidation Strategy: Inventory, Vehicles and Terminals, in: Journal of Business Logistics, Vol. 8, No. 2 (1987), p. 57-73.

Karp, P. (2000): Logistik in der Konsumgüterindustrie (Logistics for Consumer Goods), in: Klaus, P;,Krieger, W.: Gabler Lexikon Logistik. Management logistischer Netzwerke und Flüsse (Gabler Encyclopedia Logistic), Gabler, Wiesbaden (2000), p. 293-297.

Laarhoven, P. van, Sharman, G. (1994): Logistics Alliances: The European Experience, in: The McKinsey Quarterly, Vol. 31, No. 1 (1994), p. 39-49.

Laarhoven, P. van, Berglund, M., Peters, M. (2000): Third-Party Logistics in Europe – Five Years Later, in: International Journal of Physical Distribution & Logistics Management, Vol. 30, No. 5 (2000), p. 425-442.

La Londe, B. J., Powers, R. F. (1993): Disintegration and Re-Integration: Logistics of the Twenty-First Century, in: The International Journal of Logistics Management, Vol. 4, No. 2 (1993), p. 1-12.

Mitchell, M.A. et al. (1992): Symbiotic Logistics, in: The International Journal of Logistics Management, Vol. 3, No. 2 (1992), p. 19-30.

Österle, H., Fleisch, E., Alt, R. (2001): Business Networking. Shaping Collaboration Between Entprises, 2nd, Revised and Extended Ed., Springer, Berlin et al.

Pfohl, H.-C., Buse, H. P. (2000): Inter-Organizational Logistics Systems in Flexible Production Networks. An Organizational Capabilities Perspective, in: International Journal of Physical Distribution & Logistics Management, Vol. 30, No. 5 (2000), p. 392-408.

Powell, W. W. (1990): Neither Market Nor Hierarchy: Network Forms of Organization, in: Research In Organizational Behaviour, Vol. 12, Cunnings, L.G. (ed.), Staw, B. M. (1990), p. 295-336.

Towill, D. R., Naim, M. M., Wikner, J. (1992): Industrial Dynamics Simulation Models in the Design of Supply Chains, in: International Journal of Physical Distribution and Logistics Management, Vol. 22, No. 5 (1992), p. 3-13.

Williamson, O. E. (1975): Markets and Hierarchies: Analysis and Antitrust Implications, Free Press, New York.

Cost Efficiency in Supply Chains – A Conceptual Discrepancy? Logistics Cost Management between Desire and Reality

Herbert Kotzab, Christoph Teller

1	Starting Point Considerations	234
2	Cost Efficiency in Supply Chains from SME Trade Company's Point of View– Theoretical Notions	234
3	Empirical Validation	239
4	Synopses of the Results and Outlook For Further Research	246
5	References	248

Summary:
Logistics managers usually properly define logistics costs and services in order to generate necessary information to support logistics management decisions. Beyond the supply chain perspective, one could presume the equal ability to manage logistics costs and services within all involved organizations. However, there are differences referring to the size and position of the supply chain members. Small and medium sized trade companies often lack basic cost accounting tools which could be used to manage their logistics costs and service centers. This paper presents the state-of-the-art in logistical cost accounting and cost management of Austrian small and medium-sized trade companies and portrays three discrepancies between logistical cost management theory and practice.

Keywords:
Supply Chain Management, Logistics Cost Systems, Performance Measurement, SME

1 Starting Point Considerations

The dynamics in many supply chains force members to shape their logistical profile. Kotzab/Schnedlitz determine four arguments for the growing importance of performing logistics in an efficient manner[1]:

1. Logistics influences all business areas and cannot be determined as a sole function
2. Innovative logistics solutions can help improve the profitability of companies by lowering total costs to a stable sales volume
3. Logistics is *the* competitive advantage either in terms of cost leadership or differentiation strategie
4. Beyond the global perspective in any supply chain, logistics influences positively and negatively the firm's success

These notions clearly point out the important relation between logistics and cost management. However, most of the published results in terms of the level of logistics costs and the degree of logistics cost management topics bring limited results[2]. This is especially true when the research focus is drawn to the customer side of a supply chain consisting of retailers, distributors and wholesalers[3]. We therefore concentrated our research to these supply chain members and investigated their cost management capabilities to manage efficient supply chains.

2 Cost Efficiency in Supply Chains from SME Trade Company's Point of View– Theoretical Notions

2.1 Logistics, Cost Management and SME Trade Companies

1. Logistics – Definition and Understanding

The German scientific community in the field of business administration developed a logistics theory in the last forty years, which is considered as "the

---

[1] See Kotzab, Schnedlitz (1997), p. 1.
[2] See e.g. Schnedlitz et al. (1999); Weber (1987/1996).
[3] Kotzab, Schnedlitz (1999).

managerial business logistics conception"[4]. Based on this understanding, Klaus distinguishes between an operative understanding (simple transportation/ inventory/handling processes), a tactical managerial understanding (management of the total flow of goods and related services within a company and between their customers and vendors) and a strategic network perspective (value-added inter-organizational flow management)[5]. Particularly the third definition would be seen as the contemporary concept of Supply Chain Management by many researchers, which can be defined as an end-user oriented, cooperative, inter-organizational strategic management philosophy with a positive effect on the overall performance for the total supply chain[6].

2. Cost Management – Definition and Understanding

Cost management is more than a simple cost accounting system. The goal of a cost accounting system is capturing certain cost categories and locate them to certain cost units[7]. Cost accounting systems deliver the necessary information to perform cost management which is the purposeful influence of costs. As a result, cost management suggests steps to be taken to control the costs of products, processes and resources and consequently improve the competitiveness of the firm[8]. Franz/Kajüter suggest that cost management actively influences the level, structure and direction of the costs within a company[9]. Cooper/Slagmulder expand this view by introducing the concept of strategic cost management, which could be seen as an inter-organizational approach[10]. Due to this inter-organizational element, the adaptation of strategic cost management could be helpful in managing SCM- or logistics costs.

3. Small and Medium Sized Trade Companies - Definition and Understanding

A small and medium sized enterprise (SME) is typically determined by the number of employees, sales volume, involvement of the owner or entrepreneur, market presence and capital resources[11]. Eurostat applies the following typology: companies with up to 9 employees (micro enterprise), companies with 10 to 99 employees (small enterprise), companies with 100 to 499 employees (medium enterprise) and companies with more than 500 employees (large enterprise). Small and medium sized enterprises (SME) have an enormous impact on the national economy of a country, where companies with less than 100 employees account for

---

[4] See e.g. Pfohl (2000) or Göpfert (1998).
[5] See Klaus (1993/1999).
[6] See Otto, Kotzab (2001), pp. 157.
[7] See Seicht (1999), p. 16.
[8] See Franz, Kajüter (1997), p. 8; Cooper, Slagmulder (1998a), p. 14; Reiß, Corsten (1990), p. 390.
[9] See Franz, Kajüter (1997), p. 9.
[10] See Cooper, Slagmulder (1998b), p. 16.
[11] See Mugler (1995), p. 29.

99 % of all companies and employ 50 % of the total workforce[12]. This is also true for commercial companies in the European economy. About 75 percent of all European retailing companies are small to medium-sized companies with sole proprietorships[13]. Schnedlitz/Waidacher examined the situation of SME within the Austrian trade sector and could identify a rate of 99 % of trade companies as SMEs employing on average 12 people[14].

2.2 Logistical Cost Management

2.2.1 Efficiency Thinking and Total Cost Perspective and Consequences for Logistical Cost Management

The interaction between cost management and logistics is very well known[15]. Logistics is recognized as an important business process, where costs certainly can influence performance and where logistics managers must find the 'optimum' between sales and logistics costs levels (logistics efficiency thinking, where input and output must be equally measured)[16]. Pure attention towards the cost side or the sales side will lead to sub-optimal profits. However, the registration and evaluation of logistics costs and services is very difficult not only due to the complexity of these cost and service categories[17], but also due to the lack of logistics-oriented accounting systems[18]. Thus, it is not surprising that during the last thirty years, logistics cost has been presented as being in a range from 10 to 30 percent either from sales or total costs[19]. The level of logistics costs is driven by the overall logistics understanding[20] and by the ability to apply the logistics' relevant total-cost principle[21]. In order to influence logistics costs in a certain direction, Schulte suggests three alternatives to converting the company's cost accounting system into a logistics-oriented one[22]: a) keep the existing system and refine it for logistics, b) expand the existing system with special logistical calculations and c) include an additional – separately organized – logistical cost accounting system. Recently, Keebler et al. introduced activity-based costing systems as a suitable and successful approach for managing logistics costs in

---

[12] See Mugler (1995), p. 99.
[13] PriceWaterhouseCooper (2000).
[14] Schnedlitz, Waidacher (1995).
[15] See e.g. Lambert, Stock (2001).
[16] See Pfohl (2000), pp. 41.
[17] See Weber (1996), p. 158.
[18] See Ihde (1987), p. 705.
[19] See e.g. Schulte (1999); Pfohl (2000); Stock, Lambert (2001).
[20] See e.g. Seicht (1999), pp. 566.
[21] See Pfohl (2000), pp. 30.
[22] See Schulte (1999), p. 9.

desired directions[23]. This is particularly necessary in a supply chain setting where cross-boundary logistics processes determine the profitability of the total chain. Here, the notions of Cooper/Slagmulder regarding strategic cost management seem to be a fruitful alternative[24], as it does not "limit itself to either the four walls of the factory or the boundaries of the firm"[25].

2.2.2 Logistical Cost Management in SME Commercial Companies

Although nominally dominating the market, Austrian SMEs in the trade sector are in a managerial dilemma. More than two-thirds of all Austrian trade companies are in the loss zone and most of them face dramatic competitive pressures by larger competitors (concentration in the trade sector). Most SMEs have deficits in their cost accounting and cost management systems. These deficits also impact the efficiency of their logistics operations. Kotzab/Schnedlitz have presented empirical data on the logistics cost situation for Austrian retailers, who claim to face an average of 19.6 % of total costs (with a range of 0.3 % to 100 %)[26]. Another empirical study by Schnedlitz/Kotzab within the Austrian DIY-retail and wholesale sector indicates an average logistics cost level of 14 % of total costs (with a range of 1 % to 70 %)[27]. Both studies showed that these numbers are only estimates due to lacking cost management systems and logistics know-how. Thus, these SMEs compete against "high rationalized selling machines"[28] which are large retail corporations operating mainly with hyper-market outlets at very low costs. These competitors apply certain activity based costing approaches such as DRP (direct product profitability) and are fully aware of their logistics cost and service situation[29].

2.3 Identified Problem Areas

Although all these notions have been published for many years, SME-specific gaps between science and business practice can be identified, whose problem areas can be summarized as presented in Figure 1:

- *Diverging Logistics Understanding:* Baumgarten presents empirical evidence that 86 % of managers interviewed rate inventory management as being part of logistics, while information and communication issues are only rated by

---

[23] See Keebler et al. (1999).
[24] See Cooper, Slagmulder (1998b).
[25] Cooper, Slagmulder (1999), p. 16.
[26] See Kotzab, Schnedlitz (1997), p. 21.
[27] See Schnedlitz, Kotzab (1997).
[28] See Schnedlitz, Kotzab (1997).
[29] See Müller-Hagedorn (1999), pp. 729.

25 % as a typical logistical activity[30]. Kotzab/Schnedlitz showed that a majority of SME managers recognize logistics as the management of the product flow and a minority interprets logistics as an inter-organizational network management approach[31].

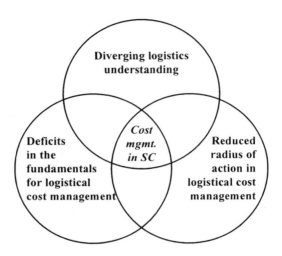

Figure 1: SME-Specific Problem Areas in the Field of Logistical Cost Management

- *Deficits in the Fundamentals for Logistical Cost Management:* Many commercial SMEs do not have the necessary cost accounting tools to generate relevant information for logistics purposes. There is a dominant tendency to apply full cost principles[32] and approximately calculating logistics activities. In such cases, logistics costs are then considered as the costs for maintaining inventory, transportation and selected handling processes[33]. Activity-oriented cost driver analysis does not belong to the cost management tool box of SMEs.
- *Reduced Radius of Action In Logistical Cost Management:* Logistics requires the holistic integration of value adding processes within value-chain systems. The pure concentration on logistics costs results in limited effects due to the service dimension being neglected[34].

---

[30] See Baumgarten (1996), p. 3.
[31] See Kotzab, Schnedlitz (1997), pp. 17.
[32] See Witt (1992), p. 95.
[33] See Kotzab, Schnedlitz (1997), pp. 24.
[34] See Schulte (1999), p. 9.

3 Empirical Validation

The described problem areas build the starting point for the empirical research endeavor presented in this section. After a short description of the research approach and methodology, the results of the project are presented and critically discussed.

3.1 Research Approach

The primary goal of this project was to evaluate the following issues:

- What is the specific logistics and/or Supply Chain Management understanding at this stage of a supply chain?
- Are these supply chain members ready to measure supply chain efficiency?
- What are the logistics costs and service levels at this stage of a supply chain?
- Are there any differences in terms of size, retail category or main activities in terms of the perceived logistics understanding and the embedding of logistics cost systems within the organization?

These four elements represent the various sections of the questionnaire.

3.2 Methodology

To examine the research questions, we developed a four-page questionnaire consisting of 22 logistics and supply chain efficiency related questions and nine general questions regarding the company background of the responder. Figure 2 summarizes the methodological parameters of our research.

The questionnaire was mailed to all relevant companies with more than one employee. We eliminated all micro-companies[35] in order to minimize bias and to generate an 'economic' return rate. Experience showed that such companies return ineffective information either through incomplete answers or not returning the questionnaires at all. For the purpose of the research question at hand, we limited our analysis to the following four heterogeneous retail categories where we experienced the highest return rate: office supply/equipment, electronics, groceries and textile/apparel.

These categories probably face 'hyper-competition' where most of the SMEs are embedded in highly concentrated markets. For example, ten companies generate

---

[35] We define micro enterprises as companies having less than one employee.

99 % of the grocery business[36]. Furthermore, we considered all companies with a sales volume of less than EUR 1.82 million and less than 16 employees as SMEs. By applying this segmentation, we could generate two even sub-samples.

Type of survey	Mail survey
Population	3,767 members of the Vienna Chamber of Commerce and Trade
Targeted respondent	The logistics manager or the person responsible for logistics in the company
Duration of the data collection and analysis	November 1999 – March 2000
Total return rate	5 % within all categories
Return rate in selected categories	- electronics: 18% - textile, apparel: 14% - office supply/equipment: 12% - groceries: 10%
Number of returned questionnaires	187
Number of analyzed questionnaires	109
Analysis software and applications	SPSS Win 10.0 uni- and bivariate analysis

Figure 2: Research Design

3.3 Results and Discussion

3.3.1 General Information On the Sample

The relevant sample (109 analyzed questionnaires) consisted of 22 office supply/equipment companies (20.2 %), 37 electronics dealers (33.9 %), 19 grocers (17.4 %) and 31 textile/apparel companies (28.4 %). Considering their main trade functions, 41.3 % were mainly wholesalers (45 total), 45 % mainly retailers (50 total) and 11 % were active on both levels. The remaining companies did not indicate their main field of trade activity. From the perspective of size, we could observe the typical pattern of Austrian economy. 82.1 % of all companies have less than EUR 7.27 million sales volume. Three out of four companies employ less than 20 people. Taking our discrimination criteria for SMEs, we could

---

[36] See Schnedlitz, Waidacher (1995).

consider 46.8 % as SMEs and 53.2 % as large companies. Looking at the legal status of the companies involved, we observed mainly limited companies (71.6 %) and a small number of partnerships (28.4 %).

3.3.2   Perceived Understanding of Logistics

We confronted the targeted person with the basic notions of Klaus' three meanings model of logistics (see section 2.1.)[37]. 93.5 % of our sample referred to logistics as the sum of operative transportation, inventory and handling issues (first meaning of logistics). Consequently, logistics is seen as a means to overcome distances in space and time. 77.5 % recognized logistics as a management function (second meaning). The Supply Chain Management perspective (third meaning) was acknowledged by only 56.6 %. The results showed a very traditional understanding of logistics and we could see a lack of comprehension regarding the integrated view. Less than 2 % of the respondents indicated no knowledge about logistics being the sum of all material-related activities, while 19.8 % were unaware of the integration meaning of logistics. In comparison with the total results we could identify significant differences between perceived logistics understanding in terms of size of the companies, retail category or main trade function ($p<0.05$)[38]. The identified differences cannot be explained by these variables.

3.3.3   Market Opportunities By Logistics

Figure 3 highlights the basic results of this special analysis. Certainly 94 % of those questioned (n=107) saw the potential of logistics as a cost-saving tool. Less than 90 % of the sample evaluated logistics as a chance to increase sales volume, while 80 % could imagine the positive effects of inter-organizational logistics operations in terms of Supply Chain Management. However, only two-thirds of the respondents assessed logistics as a means for establishing competitive advantages in the market place. Looking at company sizes, SMEs neglected this issue ($p<0.05$): 57.5 % of all SME-members agreed on this special characteristic, while nearly 80 % of all respondents of large corporations recognized this issue as an important one. Again, we found an increasing lack of knowledge about the chances and business opportunities offered of logistics, particularly when the more complex characteristics of this business function are taken into account. In our case, logistics is seen rather as an operative cost driver – a tool to minimize costs -

---

[37]   See Klaus (1993/1999).
[38]   As these variables were examined on a nominal scale level, we checked our findings for the presence of a significant relation between the variables by applying the chi-square test.

than a strategic management philosophy. According to Kent/Flint, these results had been typical for logistics understanding between the 1960s and 1980s![39]

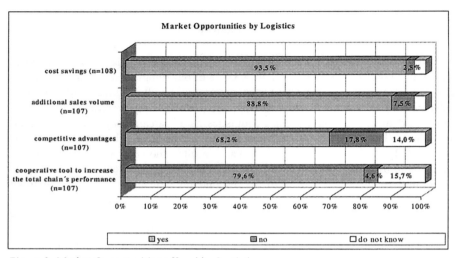

Figure 3: Market Opportunities offered by Logistics

3.3.4 Measuring Supply Chain Efficiency

- *Logistical Cost Accounting Systems*

Here we examined the fundamentals of cost accounting systems which could be used to determine logistics costs within the company. The overall results are summarized in Figure 4. More than two-thirds (n=74) of all respondents indicated having a separate cost accounting system.

In our case, larger companies significantly run more frequently a separate cost accounting system (80.7 %) than SMEs (54.9 %; p<0.05). This result supports our notion that SMEs do not possess the basics to capture their logistics costs. When stating the person for having a cost accounting system, almost 50 % indicated application of contribution margin accounting approaches, while 24 % indicated the use of full costing principles. The usage of variable costing systems with a rate of 14 % could be judged as very low. In terms of more recent cost management approaches, only 4 % indicated employing of activity-based costing systems. Our results confirm Witt's assumptions of a domination of overhead-oriented costing systems within commercial companies[40].

---

[39] See Kent, Flint (1997), p. 22.
[40] See Witt (1992), p. 95.

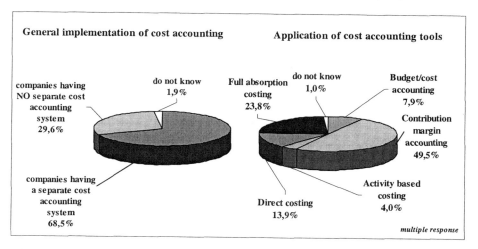

Figure 4: State-of-the-art Cost Accounting Systems and Their Applications

- *Determination and Calculation of Logistics Costs*

In the next step we concentrated our analysis on the methods of capturing and calculating logistics costs (see Figure 5). We tried to identify whether the respondents apply typical cost accounting systems such as cost category accounting, cost location accounting or cost unit accounting.

Although having the requirements for a logistics-oriented cost accounting system, the majority of the respondents indicated not using the typical cost accounting methods for such an issue. Less than half of the sub-sample (n=74) indicated forming logistical cost categories. Less than a third of the respondents reported forming logistical cost locations. Considering logistical calculation issues, 44 % of the respondents pointed out that they had performed logistical cost unit accounting. However, the number of valid answers for describing logistical cost categories, logistical cost centers or special units of logistics output was very low. We could not observe any significant differences in these results in terms of size of the company, retail category or trade activity.

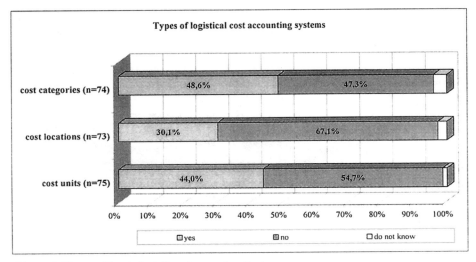

Figure 5: Types of Logistical Cost Accounting Systems

- ***Self Assessment of the Logistical Cost Accounting Systems and Confrontation With Alternative Approaches***

Results of the Self Assessment Process

After detecting the state-of-the art logistical cost accounting systems in our sample, we asked the respondents based on a five point Likert scale (anchored by 1, 'very well capable', to 5 'absolutely not capable'), to self-evaluate their own approach. 15.5 % of all respondents having cost accounting system said that they do not know whether their system is able to capture logistics costs or not. Within the remaining respondents, we could identify a cautious assessment behavior where they chose the possibility of making the median the highest (mode with 40 %, n=60). Only 5.6 % thought that their approach is best suited for logistical cost accounting issues, while 8.5 % evaluated their cost accounting system as not suited at all.

Alternate Approaches

In the next step, we confronted the respondents with Schulte's (1999) three options for setting up an optimal logistical cost accounting system. The results were surprising. It seems that the respondents were aware of their need to generate logistical cost information. Furthermore, they were conscious about the problems they would face while applying such systems. 50.7 % of the sample (n=74) showed tendencies towards the more sophisticated alternatives by either expanding the existing system or applying an additional cost accounting system. 21.5 % of the respondents decided to 'postpone' the decision by choosing the answer category 'I do not know'. One out of five respondents would stay with the existing system and refine it for logistical issues.

- **Estimated Level of Logistics Costs**

The level of logistics costs can be based on total costs or sales[41]. We chose both alternatives for our research and differentiated between those companies with and without a cost accounting system (see Figure 6).

Share of logistics costs	with cost accounting system (n=74)	without cost accounting system (n=32)[42]
own average logistics costs in % of total costs (Std.dev)	16.7 (16.4)	22.1 (26.2)
own average logistics costs in % of total sales (Std.dev)	6.4 (5.9)	8.7 (9.2)
competitors' average logistics costs in % of total costs (Std.dev)	14.3 (14.5)	-
competitors' average logistics costs in % of total sales (Std.dev)	7.3 (8.0)	-

Figure 6: Estimated Logistics Cost Levels

Our results show certain trends. All our respondents estimated their logistics costs compared to other empirical studies as being very high. The individual approximations ranged between 1 % and 70 % of total costs. We could observe that those respondents having a cost accounting system estimated their costs lower than the others. We then asked the respondents to compare their costs with their estimation of the rest of the industry. Only a small number of respondents answered our request. Interestingly, they judged the cost level of their industry lower than their own level. This implies that – in their perception – their competitors perform logistics more efficiently than they do. The opposite picture was presented while looking at the ratio between logistics costs and sales volume, where they rated their costs lower than their competitors. We do not have an explanation for this. However, it emphasizes the 'confusion' within SMEs while calculating logistics costs[43]. Overall, the evaluation of logistics costs is more

---

[41] See e.g. Schulte (1999), p. 9; Pfohl (2000), pp. 52.
[42] We did not calculate the values for logistics costs as a percentage of the sales volume due to a lack of suffient valid answers.
[43] For this question we faced a high non-response rate. Therefore any distinction between retail category and logistics cost level which brought some significant results

driven by poor impressions rather than managerial accounting ability. Drucker's way to see logistics in the 60s is still valid for our respondents: "We know it is there, and we know it is big, and that's about all."[44]

- *Measuring Logistical Performance Indicators*

The final section of our research design dealt with the issue of measuring logistical performance indicators. The measurement of supply chain efficiency includes the combination of effective cost management and customer oriented service measurement. We used two open questions to let the respondents describe what kind of performance indicators they apply and how they measure them. However, only 6 of the 109 respondents gave valid answers! These results certainly show the gap between the leading edge and the 'average punter' in this field[45]. Our respondents did not even measure the traditional service components such as order cycle, fill rates, etc.

4 Synopses of the Results and Outlook For Further Research

4.1 Identification of Certain Discrepancies

Based on our results, we could discover the following three discrepancies between logistics cost management theory (desire) and its reality when it comes to the customer side of a supply chain:

Discrepancy 1: Logistics is the integrated management of the product and related information flow

Commercial companies, independent of size, retail category and main trade activity, show a divergent knowledge about logistics and Supply Chain Management. The dominant perception of logistics within these companies is that of operative transportation, warehousing and handling activities. The information character of logistics and the power of inter-organizational business process management were not recognized. The view is rather one-dimensional. Although the respondents were familiar with the cost effects of logistics, the marketing side of logistics were not realized. However, from a cost management point of view,

---

(grocery representatives indicate with 39 % the highest logistics costs!), or SME and larger company, were not applied due to an insufficient number of valid cases.

[44] Drucker (1962), p. 103.
[45] See e.g. Keebler et al. (1999).

one could positively remark that at this stage of a supply chain, the cost issue was also seen as a sensitive one.

Discrepancy 2: Logistics costs are visible

We identified different practices in cost accounting systems between SMEs and larger companies. The bigger the company, the more cost accounting systems were in practice. Although we deducted that size would determine the quality of a logistical cost accounting system, our results did not confirm this expectation. Logistics costs are intuitively apparent but not visible in terms of cost categories, cost centers or units of output. As in our case, the respondents indicated their subjective 'impression', which led to higher costs in comparison with competitors.. Beyond the perspective of increased importance of cost transparency in order to exchange relevant cost information between supply chain members, SMEs will be forced to close this gap in the future.

Discrepancy 3: Logistics is a competitive weapon

Logistics is rather seen as a cost savings tool than a means to generate additional sales volume. Consequently, the majority of the analyzed companies do not evaluate their logistical activities to include the perspective of generating competitive advantages. Although the driving forces in today's global business setting (Just In Time, global sourcing, 365x24x7, lean logistics) should influence these types of companies, nearly all of them do not evaluate the simplest forms of logistics performance indicators such as delivery time or inventory turns. As Supply Chain Management forces the supply chain members to inherently improve their performance, our analyzed companies risk a so-called 'efficiency myopia', where only the cost side gets attention.

4.2 Outlook For Further Research

There is no doubt that the importance of interorganizational management topics will increase in the field of cost management as well as logistics and Supply Chain Management. The members of the supply chain we analyzed will be forced to close the identified gaps in order to survive in a dynamic business environment. Although our research was limited to the members of a supply chain in a specific geographic area in Austria, we could offer some insight into the field. We suggest further topics of research:

- The reasons for the low implementation of logistical cost accounting systems among small and medium sized commercial companies
- The effects of lacking cost management systems on the concentration processes in the retail sector

5 References

Baumgarten, H. (1996): Trends und Strategien in der Logistik 2000 - Analysen-Potentiale-Perspektiven (Trends and Strategies in Logistics 2000 – Analysis, Opportunities, Perspectives), Springer Verlag, Berlin.

Cooper, R., Slagmulder, R. (1998a): Strategic Cost Management: What Is Strategic Cost Management, in: Management Accounting, No. 1 (1998), p. 14-16.

Cooper, R., Slagmulder, R. (1998b): Strategic Cost Management: The Scope of Strategic Cost Management, in: Management Accounting, No. 2 (1998), p. 16-18.

Drucker, P. (1962): The Economy's Dark Continent, in: Fortune, No. 4 (1962), p. 103, p. 265-270.

Franz, K.-P., Kajüter, P. (1997): Proaktives Kostenmanagement als Daueraufgabe (Proactive Cost Management as Continuous Challenge), in: Franz, K.-P., Kajüter, P. (eds.): Kostenmanagement. Wettbewerbsvorteile durch systematische Kostensteuerung (Cost Management – Competitive Advantages through Systematic Cost Controlling), Schäffer-Poeschel, Stuttgart, p. 5-27.

Göpfert, I. (1998): Stand und Entwicklung der Logistik - Herausbildung einer betriebswirtschaftlichen Teildisziplin (State of the Art and Developments in Logistics), in.: Logistikmanagement, No. 1 (1998), p. 19-33.

Ihde, G.-B. (1987): Stand und Entwicklung der Logistik (State of the Art and Developments in Logistics), in: Die Betriebswirtschaft, Vol. 47, No. 6 (1987), p. 703-716.

Keebler, J. S., Manrodt, K. B., Durtsche, D. A., Ledyard, M. D. (1999): Keeping Score – Measuring the Business Value of Logistics In the Supply Chain, Council of Logistics Management, Oak Brook.

Kent, J. L., Flint, D. J. (1997): Perspectives on the Evolution of Logistics Thought, in: Journal of Business Logistics, Vol. 18, No. 2 (1997), p. 15-29.

Klaus, P. (1993): Die dritte Bedeutung der Logistik (The Third Meaning of Logistics), Nürnberger Logistik Arbeitspapier Nr. 3, Wirtschafts- und Sozialwissenschaftliche Fakultät der Universität Erlangen-Nürnberg 1993.

Klaus, P. (1999): Logistik als Weltsicht (Logistic as „World View"), in: Weber, J., Baumgarten, H. (ed.): Handbuch Logistik. Management von Material- und Warenflussprozessen (Handbook Logistic), Schäffer-Poeschel, Stuttgart, p. 15-32.

Kotzab, H., Schnedlitz, P. (1997): Status quo und Entwicklungsperspektiven der Distributionslogistik. Ergebnisse einer empirischen Untersuchung in ausgewählten österreichischen Unternehmungen (State of the Art and Perspectives for Developments in Distribution Logistics), in: Schnedlitz, P. (ed.): Schriftenreihe Handel und Marketing, Vol. 15, Wien.

Kotzab, H., Schnedlitz, P. (1999): The Integration of Retailing to the General Concept of Supply Chain Management Concept, in: Journal für Betriebswirtschaft, No. 4 (1999), p. 140-153.

Lambert, D., Stock, J. (2001): Strategic Logistics Management, 4th Edition, McGraw Hill-Irwin, Boston et al..

Otto, A., Kotzab, H. (2001): Der Beitrag des Suppy Chain Management zum Management von Supply Chains – Überlegungen zu einer unpopulären Frage (The Contribution of Supply Chain Management to the Management of Supply – Thoughts on an Unpopular Question Chains), in: Zeitschrift für betriebswirtschaftliche Forschung, Vol. 53, No. 3 (2001), p. 157-176.

Pfohl, H.-Ch. (2000): Logistiksysteme - Betriebswirtschaftliche Grundlagen (Logistics Systems), 6. Auflage. Springer, Berlin et al..

PriceWaterhouseCooper (2000): European Retailing 2010, http://www.ideabeat.com/ResLib/pricewaterhouse/euroretail2010/page1.htm, accessed April 4, 2000.

Reiß, M., Corsten, H. (1990): Grundlagen des betriebswirtschaftlichen Kostenmanagements (Foundations of Cost Management), in: Wirtschaftswissenschaftliches Studium, Vol. 19, No. 8 (1990), p. 390-396.

Schnedlitz, P., Kotzab, H. (1997): Die Effizienz der Distributionlogistik in Österrreich - Eine empirische Bestandsaufnahme (Efficiency of Distribution Logistics in Austria – An Empirical Investigation), in: der markt, No. 3-4 (1997), p. 148–160.

Müller-Hagedorn, L. (1999): Bausteine eines Management Informationssystems: Balanced Scorecard, Benchmarking, Betriebsvergleich (Contributions to a Management Information System: Balanced Scorecard, Benchmarking), in: Beisheim, Otto (ed.): Distribution im Aufbruch: Bestandaufnahme und Perspektiven (Distribution in Breakup), Vahlen, Munich, p. 729-753.

Mugler, J. (1995): Betriebswirtschaftslehre der Klein- und Mittelbetriebe (Management of SMEs), 2nd Edition, Springer, Vienna/New York.

Schnedlitz, P., Kotzab, H., Teller, Ch. (1999): Die Effizienz der Distributionslogistik in Österreich (The Efficiency of Distribution Logistics in Austria), Teil 1, in: Schnedlitz, P. (Ed.): Schriftenreihe Handel und Marketing, Vol. 22 (1999), Vienna.

Schnedlitz, P., Waidacher, E.-M. (1995): Retail Trade In Austria, in: The European Observatory for SMEs. Third Annual Report. Report submitted to

Directorate-General XXIII of the Commission of the European Community by ENSR – European Network for SME Research. Brussles.

Schulte, Ch. (1999): Logistik: Wege zur Optimierung des Material- und Informationsflusses (Logistics – Optimization of Material and Information Flows), 3rd Edition, Vahlen, Munich.

Seicht, G. (1999): Moderne Kosten- und Leistungsrechung: Grundlagen und praktische Gestaltung (Modern Accounting), 10th Edition, Linde, Vienna.

Weber, J. (1987): Logistikkostenrechung (Logistics Accounting), Springer, Berlin.

Weber, J. (1996): Logistik-Controlling (Logistics Controlling), in: Schuh, G., Weber, H., Kajüter, P. (eds.): Logistik-Management – Strategische Wettbewerbsvorteile durch Logistik (Logistics Management – Strategic Competitive Advantages through Logistics), Schaeffer-Poeschel Verlag, Stuttgart, p. 151-179.

Witt, F.-J. (1992): Handelscontrolling (Retail Controlling), Vahlen Verlag, Munich.

Part 3
Building Cost Management Models

Interdependencies between Supply Contracts and Transaction Costs

Stefan Voß, Gabriele Schneidereit

1	Introduction	254
2	Supply Contracts	255
3	Transaction Costs and IT Requirements	260
4	Some Game Theoretic Approaches to Supply Chain Management	266
5	Conclusions	269
6	References	270

Summary:
Supply contracts facilitate relationships between partners within supply chains and networks. While contracts allow to make terms of relationships explicit they also allow a closer look at transaction costs related to information and communication as well as coordination issues for designing and managing supply chains and networks. In this paper we provide a classification scheme for supply contracts and consider interdependencies with transaction cost economics. Insights are provided by means of exemplifying selected avenues of research that have been undertaken or might be useful to be undertaken.

Keywords:
Supply Chain Integration, Supply Contracts, Transaction Costs, Supply Chain Planning

1 Introduction

Supply chain integration refers to connecting at least two parties within a supply network. In addition to activities associated with supply chain management, integration refers to the fact that the parties have to agree upon the way they interact with each other. Especially in the economics literature there is a long history of analysis of the contractual treatment of relationships. Within the modern supply chain discussion the importance of the topic has not diminished but is gaining even more prominence, especially when system-wide optimization is taking place and the incentives discussion as well as concepts like transfer pricing are considered. Supply chains are, by their very nature, based on partnerships. Products as well as information necessary for an optimization must be exchanged between partners. What a *supply contract* may add to this is the explicit specification of a relationship especially by articulating efficiency measures or metrics that are direct input to supply chain planning models such as, e.g., lead times or capacity bounds.

Supply contracts may contain, e.g., clauses concerning decision rights, pricing strategies, transportation, buyback/return policies and allocation rules. In addition, financial and organizational regulations need to be included. The latter refer especially to the use of information technology and the distribution of information in supply chain organization and control. While this distribution allows for efficient integration it leads to *transaction costs*. In general these costs are defined for coordinating transactions, i.e., a regulated distribution of goods and rights, such as information. Therefore, transaction costs do not only refer to distributing information, but also to contracting, several decisions and their realization and control. Since the overall goal of supply chain management is to increase the value of the whole supply chain, the amounts of transaction costs have to be considered. In this paper we consider centralized versus decentralized coordination of a supply chain as well as supply chain integration by means of appropriate supply contracts.

In Section 2 we provide a brief survey on the discussion of supply contracts. While these contracts provide one side of the building blocks for successful supply chain management another side refers to integration by means of, especially, information as well as information and communication technology (IT) and the corresponding cost considerations (see Section 3). Obviously, interdependencies with transaction costs have to be observed. As an example, one may investigate the impact which a certain means of IT may have regarding transaction costs, legal aspects and contractual agreements.

Besides transaction cost economics one may also investigate game theoretical approaches. In Section 4 we provide some thought provoking ideas regarding the interplay of incentives and transaction costs. The idea of fairly distributing costs naturally leads to basic concepts from game theory. While this is common knowledge within the literature on cost allocation we go one step further by proposing to link these concepts with the Steiner tree problem in graphs and respective generalizations. We conclude with some final remarks.

2 Supply Contracts

Supply chain management (SCM) rose to prominence as a major management issue in recent years.[1] The ability to instantaneously exchange information together with increased computational power has enabled the use of sophisticated optimization software. Still, one has to admit that appropriate planning functionality has not yet come to its full extent despite the advertisements of most SCM software vendors. While the focus of managing a supply chain has undergone a drastic change as a result of improved information technology, supply chain planning and integration remains a critical issue.

Supply chain integration refers to the connection of at least two parties within a supply network. Different means of integration subdivide vertical versus horizontal integration. In any case different parties have to agree upon the way they interact with each other. Especially in the economics literature there is a long history of analysis of the contractual treatment of relationships[2]. Supply contracts have the function to regulate the cooperation between several enterprises or parts of them and to prescribe related conditions. When considering the literature it should be noted that the various contributions mainly take one of two important directions that need to be distinguished. First one can investigate the contract design itself and second one can analyze the implication of certain contractual agreements.

2.1 A Classification Scheme

While contract design has been an important topic within economics throughout the last decades important parts of the business administration literature has neglected integration and planning concerns based on contractual relations. One of the most important early steps to overcome these deficiencies is to develop and to establish classification schemes as a basis for further discussion. Based on

---

[1] See, e.g., Chopra, Meindl (2001) for a comprehensive presentation of SCM.
[2] See, e.g., Tirole (1988) or Katz (1989).

common sense considerations various aspects come to mind when dealing with contracts. In the literature there is only one comprehensive classification scheme which mainly focuses on quantitative models for supporting the design of supply contracts.[3] Therefore, as this may turn out to be a somewhat limited approach it seems necessary to propose and discuss a modified classification scheme.

While the classification could be solely developed along the lines of timing, pricing, quantity, and quality we follow the idea of having contract clauses in the foreground. Therefore, we modify and extend the classification scheme of Tsay et al. (1999) by adding regulations on information, transport, and legal concerns. Beside that, bounds on purchase commitments also subsumes minimum purchase commitments as well as quantity flexibility, as such regulations are closely related to each other.

In addition to the clauses presented below a number of parameters have to be kept in mind (or specified) such as the number of partners, the number of products or services involved as well as the intended duration of a contract (in terms of validity). Simplified, the latter aspect asks for short-term versus long-term contracts. Furthermore, the level of completeness has to be determined. While incomplete contracts allow for certain degrees of freedom they might make some renegotiation processes necessary in case of unanticipated events. In addition one has to decide upon eventual terms of renewal of already up and running contracts, e.g., in case of recurrent contracts.

1. Specification of Decision Rights

Decision rights have to be defined in order to make a contract executable. A determination of who is allowed to make decisions and within which range of action is based on different types of data and information. This may also include rules for (re-)negotiation processes. Control mechanisms may be centralized or decentralized as well as global or local.

2. Information

Supply partners have to mutually agree about which data and information have to be exchanged at what time and through which channels.[4]

3. Pricing (including Incentives)

Pricing refers to the specification of financial terms of the supply partners. Commitments have to be made regarding most aspects of the contract such as production costs or retail prices but also the interplay of cost functions (e.g.,

---

[3] For further reading we refer the reader to Tsay et al. (1999) as well as the literature given there. For additional references and surveys on supply contracts see, e.g., Schneidereit, Voß (2001a) and Zimmer (2001). For a practical example regarding a subset of clauses see ICC (2000).

[4] See Voß, Gutenschwager (2001) for information logistics and information management considerations.

allowing for discounts in certain cases, having modified pricing on different lead times based on alternate routings). We include also the implementation of mechanisms to divide profits based on cooperation as well as the arrangement for incentives. Additionally, reservation prices have to be determined in cases where options may be purchased. Options refer to the agreed upon possibility to purchase specified amounts of goods or products without the obligation to do so.

4. Bounds on Purchase Commitments

Upper and lower quantity bounds for the purchase of goods or products have to be specified. This also includes terms of flexibility, e.g., regarding early or late delivery as well as deviations from previously planned quantity estimates.

5. Allocation

Defines distribution mechanisms especially for cases of limited availability of goods, resources and capacity.

6. Timing (including Lead Times)

The time of delivery of items or parts has to be specified. The lead times have to be determined and controlled. When linked with transportation clauses, this includes possible definition of push or pull mechanisms for the ordering processes.[5]

7. Transport

The contract can include clauses on how the delivery is performed (e.g. by using third party logistics provider) including transport mode selection and the definition of penalties for modifications or late arrivals as well as items damaged during transport. This is related to the implementation of rules for having various transport possibilities enabling, e.g., expedited delivery in cases of necessary adjustments in the lead times.[6]

8. Quality

Thresholds for the quality of the parts or items as well as allowable modifications like possibilities for upgrades or price reductions in case of unavailability of desired items are articulated in the contract.

9. Buybacks or Return Policies

Responsibilities and cost implications for unsold inventory or products with a different quality than agreed upon have to be determined.

---

[5] Note the distinction between lead time and flow time as well as that of lead times being data or variable, e.g., when considering load dependent lead times; cf. Voß, Woodruff (2000) as well as Domschke et al. (1997) and the references given there.

[6] See also Schneidereit, Voß (2001b).

10. Legal Concerns

Legal concerns have to be observed and degrees of freedom have to be envisaged by appropriate agreements. For multinational companies this also refers to transfer pricing between companies and their subsidiaries (transfer prices are prices or payments for intra-firm transactions of goods), tax and duty requirements and the treatment of exchange rate risks.

2.2 Discussion

Supply contracts may contain several clauses as described above. Especially, financial and organizational regulations refer to the use of information technology in supply chain organization and control. For determining which kind of clauses should be taken, the contract parties need a wealth of data and information. In this respect not only the quantity and quality of information before contracting is important, as some clauses need considerable information during the whole supply chain and logistics processes, e.g., complex quantity clauses where the quantity of purchased goods become more concrete during time depending on the information about future demands.

The distribution of such information leads to transaction costs (see Section 3). Influences on cost values for a certain transaction are in particular the kind of coordination between the parties of the transaction and the range of use of information technology, which both can be determined by supply contracts. For coordinating a supply chain there are two main possibilities; cf. Figure 1.

On the one hand, a central coordinating instance can carry out all planning processes for the whole supply chain. In this case, all supply parties have to share their information with this central coordinating instance.[7] After the planning process the central instance spreads the planning information, e.g., on prices, quantities, and dates, around the supply parties. Therefore, each supply partner only distributes his/her own information (regarding demands, costs, etc.) to one institution and receives all other necessary information from this institution.

On the other hand, there is a decentralized approach for coordinating the supply chain. In this case, every supply partner is able to plan his/her own activities mainly based on local information. The goal of increasing the value of the whole supply chain can only be achieved by taking into account the plans of other parties, especially of those directly connected to each other within the chain. Consequently, each supply partner has to distribute (several parts of) his/her

---

[7] Sometimes such an instance is referred to as intermediary. Examples are manifold; see, e.g., data and communication service provider in major seaports (such as http://www.dakosy.de in Hamburg, Germany) even if they only provide coordination support and do not serve as an instance in the broad sense as defined above.

information to several other supply parties, in particular to his/her direct predecessors as well as direct successors in the supply network.

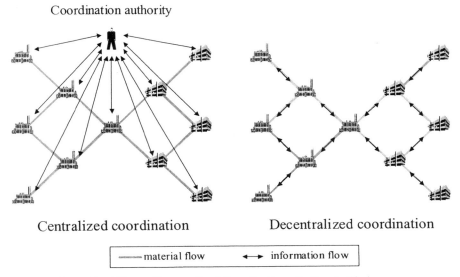

Figure 1: Centralized Versus Decentralized Coordination of a Supply Chain

Usually, the amount of distributed information and the costs for distribution are higher in decentrally coordinated supply chains. However, a centralized coordination often seems to be impossible, in particular in the case of suppliers involved in more than one supply chain or in case of supply chains including competing enterprises. Hence, the problem of choosing the most effective and acceptable coordination form arises and has to be solved.

Owing to the developments in information technology distributing information became less cost intensive over the last years. Therefore, clauses concerning information technology may also influence the amount of transaction costs. In particular, using the same software (not only for information distribution between different supply partners but also for planning succeeding elements of the supply chain), e.g., electronic data interchange for information distribution or special supply chain management software for the planning processes, may decrease transaction costs. However, fixing the technology within supply contracts is associated with several problems, too, in particular within supply chains with suppliers involved in more than one supply chain. In Section 3 we exemplify these issues in some more detail by means of simple examples.

It should be noted that the qualitative exposition above may only provide a framework and needs to be filled appropriately according to the specifities in certain supply networks. A more normative examination of contracts is provided in the operations research literature. For example, Barnes-Schuster et al. (2000) examine optimal ordering policies for a buyer where there is a pre-specified annual minimum order quantity. Vidal, Goetschalckx (2001) present an optimization model to maximize after tax profits of a multinational corporation that includes transfer prices as well as the allocation of transportation costs as explicit decision variables. Incentives schemes may reward to stay within contractual boundaries which may have an effect on reducing information asymmetry as noted, e.g., by Lee, Whang (1999) and Lim (2000).[8]

3 Transaction Costs and IT Requirements

Over the years, transaction cost economics has become a major asset regarding the discussion how markets and hierarchies are chosen. Influencing factors are issues such as coordination, specifities and, most important at least in our respect, contractual relations[9]. That is, transaction costs are considered as one of the main motives for coordination. They encompass all informational activities with partners within a supply network and include, among others, interaction, motivation and coordination costs.

Below we introduce transaction costs and briefly evaluate costs and benefits of *electronic data interchange (EDI)* as a well-known example within the field of transaction cost economics. While EDI requires certain IT means they may be part of legal concerns and contractual agreements. On the other hand one may have to check contract clauses and technology whether they fulfill given legal requirements. Once the basic conditions are set one may proceed to planning as we do by providing an appropriate reference model.

3.1 Transaction Costs

Following Williamson (1985) transactions occur when a good or service is transfered across a technologically separable interface. In a figurative sense transaction costs may be interpreted as an economic equivalent to friction within physical systems. In general transaction costs are defined as costs for coordinating a transaction, which is a regulated distribution of goods or rights, such as information. Therefore, transaction costs are not only costs for distributing information, but also costs with respect to contracting, several decisions and their realization and control. Since the overall goal of supply chain management is to

---

[8]   For an extended discussion see also Tsay et al. (1999).
[9]   Cf. Williamson (1979, 1985).

increase the value of the whole supply chain, the amounts of transaction costs have to be considered, too. Enabling better IT usage to reduce transaction costs alone does not suffice as better communication is also based on and also enables a restructuring of organizational means and the processes within a supply network.

It should be noted that transaction costs may occur on various time scales (i.e. on the strategic as well as on the tactical and operational level).[10] While contracting, in a certain sense, may be referred to as a special form of planning, it is well-known that not everything could or should be pre-planned by means of detailed contracts. Examples are coordination and communication issues especially in unanticipated cases where, e.g., due to actual changes of a prespecified plan or disturbances in the running proceeding, immediate actions need to be taken (i.e. coordination in case of exceptional behaviour and eventually the start of re-negotiation processes). While many of these actions may be performed within the boundaries of given contract clauses one might have to think about degrees of freedom in contracts. On the other hand, this is in line with the arguments of the incentives literature which proposes not to overregulate, hence leaving room to establish feasibility within the limits of given contract conditions. For instance, incomplete contracts may bring us back to the topic of integration, as motives for this phenomenon arise from an inability to write comprehensive contracts.[11]

It should be noted that we have not treated the well-known discussion of the agency theory and property rights. Here we might have to consider information asymmetry as well as certain cost means such as monitoring costs, bonding costs and residual loss costs, or sunk costs in case of incomplete contracts.[12] Finally, to the best of our knowledge most normative approaches in the literature refer to transaction cost models in a bilateral setting or a multilateral setting where only two stages are considered.

3.2 Example 1: Electronic Data Interchange

Nowadays, the awareness of up-to-date information technology enables communication within supply networks and improves the possibility of efficient electronic data interchange integration. Depending upon the costs and benefits of different EDI-systems, the options for an appropriate integration vary.[13] Recent trends such as WebEDI and XML/EDI may enable an intensifying EDI-penetration throughout the supply chain. One may suggest a modular architecture

---

[10] Principal dimensions for describing transactions and related costs are asset specifity (non specific, mixed or higly specific), uncertainty and frequency (one time, occasional or recurrent).
[11] See, e.g., Bolton, Whinston (1993).
[12] See, e.g., Voß, Gutenschwager (2001) for an introduction and further references.
[13] See, e.g., Jones, Beatty (1998), Lee et al. (1999) and Chwelos et al. (2001) for some related material. For an extended overview we refer to Voß and Reiners (2000).

for an EDI-front-end that combines different technologies with a traditional EDI-system. The advantage of such a system is the flexibility, scalability, and reusability to support, especially, the integration of small and medium-sized enterprises in the EDI-communication and business processes.

Obviously, there are investment and operating costs that are (directly or indirectly) associated with an EDI-system. Depending on the current status of the IT of a company as well as the requirements of an EDI-system to be installed, the investment costs can vary considerably. The software costs concern operating systems, application software, converter, administration tools, and network software to connect to other networks or companies. In case that only few transactions are made a substantial reduction of software costs (and probably hardware costs, too) may be realized by using a clearing center (combined with value added networks). Additional costs concern personnel, e.g., when implementing the system or during its use.

The benefits of the introduction of an EDI-system can be classified in quantifiable benefits (e.g. cost reductions due to improved business processes and workflows), those that are hard to quantify (e.g. improved interaction capabilities with customers and suppliers), and non-quantifiable benefits (e.g. the opening to new market segments). However, a comprehensive projection on any company cannot be generally performed, but the presented aspects allow an argumentation for or against an EDI-system by weighting each aspect for the total benefit. It is almost impossible to estimate the savings implied by using EDI in particular or to calculate the return on investment.[14]

Last not least (hidden) costs and benefits may arise from the reorganization of workflows and business processes. To summarize, it seems, that one natural way to achieve integration and reduce transaction costs at the same time is the use of EDI and its recent extensions and modifications.

3.3 Example 2: Barcode Technology

IT has a profound impact on SCM and appropriate planning. Given the recent trend to allow for tracking and tracing we recognize opportunities for monitoring and control. This also enables dynamic information management especially in case of short-term changes over usual workflows which make immediate reactions necessary and possible (with transaction costs applicable on different time horizons). As an example consider a supply chain where the status information of a container or box is needed on various levels. Whenever a transfer of the box

---

[14] Approaches like activity-based costing try to estimate the benefits using specialized systems or simulation-based methods. See, e.g., Hoogeweegen et al. (1996). Furthermore, measurements for the technological and operational compatibility (or complexity of integration) should be mentioned; cf. O'Callaghan et al. (1992).

between technologically separable interfaces or adjacent systems occurs, besides information processing, one has to ensure sufficient status checks to fulfill legal concerns. IT including transponder or barcode technology provides the background for respective logistics provider; cf. Figure 2. An important question refers to whether the applied technology fulfills contractual agreements and legal concerns. That is, in which way do we have to apply IT options and contract design to suffice legal concerns[15] so as to minimize transaction costs.

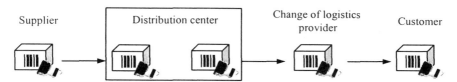

Figure 2: Schematic View on Using Barcode Technology within a Supply Chain

3.4 Supply Chain Planning within Contractual Boundaries

EDI enables supply chain planning. While mathematical modeling in this respect is well-known one has to bridge the gap to appropriate philosophies that are used without an explicit connection to those models (such as *"Produce everything as late as possible, but not too late"* as we know from early *mrp* (materials requirements planning) and *MRP II* (Manufacturing Resources Planning) which can easily be modeled mathematically[16]). Similarly we may rethink vendor managed inventory or product data management, just to mention some concepts that may easily be backed up with appropriate models. For supply chain planning within the boundaries of contractual agreements (eventually given as constraints) and given IT one may coordinate, exchange and use data and information on, e.g., forecasting or collaborate planning.

Certainly, logistics remains as a backbone of SCM. Based on the level of actuality and quality of data provided for planning purposes the better may be decisions. When appropriate IT means provide actual data on a timely basis this may even lead to the necessity to solve so-called online optimization problems.

Similar to the general proceeding of configuring distribution networks in Böse et al. (2001) we may develop a reference model for supply chain planning using the above components; cf. Figure 3. Here, supply chain planning is embedded in a modeling cycle, where based on the overall design of a supply network incorporating results from strategic design decisions (e.g., choice of IT

---

[15] See Schneidereit, Voß (2001b) for details.
[16] Cf. Voß, Woodruff (2000).

infrastructure) as well as agreed upon contractual clauses a simulation model may evaluate the possible outcome of certain policies and prerequisites (e.g., stochasticity regarding variable demand).[17]

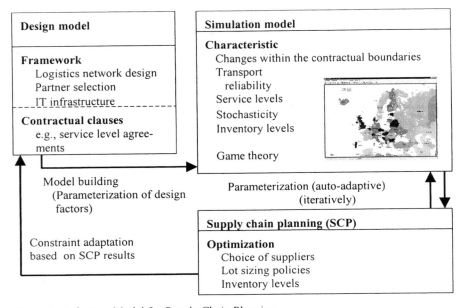

Figure 3: Reference Model for Supply Chain Planning

The first step of the modeling cycle consists in designing the contractual base for supply chain planning, i.e., the framework of the supply partnership. This especially contains the design of the logistics network, the selection of the supply partners, i.e., the parties of the supply contract, and agreements on the IT infrastructure. In addition, general contractual clauses are specified, e.g., clauses on service level agreements or buyback possibilities.

Subsequently, a (simulation) model for testing the parameters resulting by supply chain planning has to be developed. The benefits of this procedure arise from the possibilities of comparing different parameter specifications with respect to their consequences on the objective (e.g. minimizing the overall costs), evaluating

---

[17] Using simulation models has become quite a fashion in SCM. For instance, Anderson, Morrice (1999) investigate the dynamic behaviour of a simple service oriented supply chain in the presence of non-stationary demand using simulation. Also the beer distribution game, which is closely related to the well-known bullwhip effect has been studied using simulation; cf. Simchi-Levi et al. (1999). See also Hicks (1999) and Mylonopoulos et al. (1995). The latter suggest a simulation model for evaluating the costs and benefits of EDI.

several policies within the contractual boundaries (e.g. lot sizing or buyback policies) and considering the stochasticity of data. Therefore, one may not only determine specific parameters once by using optimization approaches and operations research methods but also iteratively or auto-adaptively during an interplay between supply chain planning and simulation.

As a result of supply chain planning and simulation of the planning parameters and their consequences an adaptation of the constraints of the supply chain could be necessary to obtain the overall goal of increasing the efficiency of the supply chain. In this case, the iteration process of supply chain contracting, planning and simulation restarts based on these adaptations.

An important aspect of this reference model is finding an appropriate balance between coordination and cooperation. The interplay between contract design, supply chain planning and simulation of the consequences of the resulting specifications may help finding this balance since various degrees of freedom in contracts and the resulting benefits and problems of supply chain planning can be investigated.

Decentrally coordinated supply chains are characterized by several decision instances instead of only one as in centralized supply chains. Therefore, the problem of interdependencies between the decisions of the various supply parties arises. Usually, these interdependencies cannot be considered by supply chain planning alone. To overcome this deficiency the above-presented reference model with the possibility of simulation was introduced.

The investigation of such interdependencies between several decisions (e.g., the decision of the seller regarding the pricing policy and the following decision of the buyer regarding quantities ordered at this price) is one of the main topics of game theory. Therefore, in addition to simulation also game theoretic approaches may be used to investigate the consequences of selecting specific supply parameters. That means, game theory is one methodological concept for supporting supply chain planning as well as supply contract design.

Game theoretic approaches are often used in principal agent relationships. These relationships are characterized by a cooperation between different individuals or organizations, which are divided in principals and agents, where principals are those institutions which delegate processes to agents.[18] The main aspects of these relationships are information processes between principals and agents, especially processes to overcome the usually existing information asymmetry which leads to transaction costs. The agency theory then investigates problems arising from the control of these information processes and incentive mechanisms. One of the main goals in this respect is the minimization of transaction costs.

---

[18] Cf. e.g. Voß, Gutenschwager (2001).

That is, besides other concepts supply chain relationships can be interpreted as special principal agent relationships. As game theoretic approaches, among others, analyze those principal agent relationships and may help to solve several problems occurring there these approaches may also support the design of supply contracts and supply chain planning.

Therefore, game theory may be incorporated within different planning stages indicated in Figure 3. For instance, it could become part of the design phase, in particular when choosing partners and building (strategic) alliances. Similarly, one has to choose suppliers from a given set of possible enterprises throughout the planning phase. For this reason, the next chapter introduces some special game theoretic approaches to illustrate the possibilities and benefits of game theory within supply chain contracting.[19]

4 Some Game Theoretic Approaches to Supply Chain Management

Practically, any situation where multiple agents (i.e. players, rational self interested agents, or, to be more specific, supply partners) affect an outcome and value it differently is bound to be considered with game theoretic approaches. The two most important fundamental areas addressed in this respect are the following:

- Cooperative game theory

    Issues are the allocation, e.g. of costs or surplus, resulting from a cooperative endeavor such as the joint operation of a communication network, a transportation network, or a supply (chain) network.

- Non-cooperative game theory

    Here players or agents are allowed to independently choose their strategy where equilibria refer to joint strategy choices that no player wishes to leave or deviate from under the assumption that all players have chosen their strategies, respectively.

---

[19] For instance, Granot, Sosic (2001) study the formation of alliances in internet-based supply exchanges. As an important issue they study supply partners that may have certain degrees of substitutability. Real-world concerns in this respect refer to the choice of partners within electronic marketplaces as can be seen especially in the automotive industry. Another example for an application of game theory in supply contracting can be found in Spinler et al. (2001) who investigate the benefits of options in spot markets using game theory.

Game theoretic concepts may be applied to provide useful means for cost allocation within networks.[20] Based on given supply contracts one may try, e.g., to select transfer prices that must be charged by and to individuals within a network. Obviously, ideas from cooperative game theory may be applied to define reasonable allocations. Following an axiomatic approach one may use the Shapley value and the nucleolus as traditional methods. Here allocations are determined based on reasonable properties that any of these allocations should have. On the other hand one may follow so-called coalition rationality requirements, especially when prices of regulated supplies of services within a network, e.g. according to a specification of the frame of contracts, are based on allocations in the light of competition with rival producers. Practical examples for both cases may easily be found in supply networks with third party logistics providers involved.

When defining games this may circumvent important issues such as cost allocation, resource allocation and incentives. Famous early examples are the linear production games defined by Owen (1975) and the issue of cost allocation on spanning tree networks by Claus and Kleitman (1973). Refering to cost allocation and incentives issues a major avenue of research distinguishes centralized planning with a planner having complete information (so that in cooperative game theory each player is assumed to have full information) and cases where players have local or private information so that the incentives discussion arises (cf. Fig. 1 above). A detailed survey on cost allocation on networks can be found, e.g., in Sharkey (1995).[21]

A cooperative game may consist of a set $N = \{1,\ldots,n\}$ of players and a function $v: 2^N \rightarrow R_+$ which assigns a value to every coalition (i.e. subset) of players.[22] Then a solution of a game (N,v) consists of a set of vectors x which assign a payoff x_i to every player $i \in N$.

Here we focus on minimum cost spanning tree games before we extend them with respect to, e.g., more realistic questions regarding paragraphs 3 (pricing) and 7 (transport) of Section 2 by means of transportation/distribution networks. The cooperative game approach to respective problems is to find a stable cost allocation which, to a certain extent, ensures that everyone is going to stay in the partnership (called coalition) and does not give any, at least monetary, incentive for any subset of users to secede and build their own competing subnetwork.

Given a set $N = \{1,\ldots,n\}$ of customer nodes with an additional node 0 specified as the root node. For any subset S of N define $V_S = S \cup \{0\}$, and consider a graph $G_N = (V_N, E)$ with edge set E and a symmetric nonnegative cost matrix $C = \{c_{ij}\}$ with

---

[20] Of course one has to distinguish between games and game theory but, nevertheless, both may help to visualize, analyze and explain certain effects in SCM (see the discussion of the beer distribution game to visualize the bullwhip effect).
[21] See Inderfurth, Minner (2001) for some additional references.
[22] Usually, the value of the empty set is required to be 0.

$c_{ii}=0$.[23] Assume that any coalition S of customers may be provided with a certain service by a connected graph including the nodes from V_S. That is, for any $S \subseteq N$ let $T_S=(V_S,E_S)$ represent a minimum cost connected graph such that $E_S \subseteq E$. For nonnegative cost values there is an optimal solution that is a tree and the respective game is called the minimum cost spanning tree game for coalition S of customers. Here a spanning tree may only use nodes from V_S.

The use of additional nodes leads to the monotone minimal cost spanning tree game and to the Steiner tree game. In the latter additional nodes from V–S (e.g. called transshipment nodes in the SCM context) may be used to achieve a tree T_S connecting the nodes from S which may allow additional cost reductions while making the problem more difficult to handle.[24] A comprehensive collection of results regarding Steiner tree games can be found in Skorin-Kapov (1995, 2001).

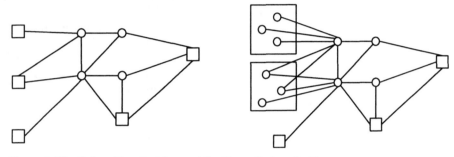

Figure 4: The Steiner Tree Problem and the Group Steiner Problem

An extension of the Steiner tree game may provide given subsets of nodes from V_N (e.g. possible suppliers that may provide the same material or service) where at least one of the nodes of a given subset needs to be chosen (and not necessarily all nodes of a subset). That is, as a variant on the classical Steiner tree problem in graphs the interest is growing for a generalization that considers a number of vertex sets $V_k \subset V$, say for indices $k \in K$. The *Group Steiner Problem* requires a minimum cost tree that spans at least one vertex from each group. Furthermore, the set of vertices that do not lie in any of the given groups may be non-empty. With each group containing only one vertex the problem specializes to the Steiner

---

[23] For different situations certain additional assumptions need to be made; see, e.g., Sharkey (1995).

[24] The left hand side of Figure 4 shows a graph where nodes indicated as squares (set S) have to be connected at minimum cost while nodes indicated as circles (set V–S) may be used to achieve this goal.

problem in graphs.[25] The main motivation for using this generalization is the appropriate *substitutability* within groups.

Skorin-Kapov (2001) also considers a capacitated version of the Steiner tree game which may be adapted for our purposes. Here the set of nodes requires a certain service that can be provided by connecting them (eventually by using other nodes or switching points) to capacitated facilities, yet to be constructed.

5 Conclusions

In this paper we have investigated interdependencies between supply contracts and transaction costs. Based on the fact that we deal with contracts for integration within supply chain management it is only natural to combine our efforts with disciplines and research areas which put contracts into the foreground, i.e., transaction cost economics and game theory.

While we have provided a classification of supply contracts one must admit that the literature still mainly analyzes contracts where two partners, or partners on at most two stages, either one upstream or one downstream from a given company, are considered. Furthermore, it is still open how much information companies are willing to share if more partners are included. Empirical analysis will eventually allow new implications that can stand the test of time. A major concern of future research, however, refers to the extension of normative approaches for cases where more than two stages are involved.

In the spirit of more general situations we may deviate from existing concepts and allow more influences from, e.g., (cooperative) game theory. Reducing transaction costs in this respect can be achieved by means of efficient ways for communication and information exchange. However, better cooperation according to frames provided from respective contracts married with some game theoretic concepts may reach even further. As an example we have formulated a generalized Steiner tree game. Future research has to ensure that such a game is further analyzed theoretically. As our connection of these different streams of research, i.e. supply contracts, supply chain planning and game theory, is still not

---

[25] We may call the respective game theoretic extension the *Group Steiner Game* following the appropriate graph theoretic problem considered in the literature even if it may be reduced to the original Steiner problem; cf. Duin et al. (2001). The right hand side of Figure 4 shows a graph where the nodes indicated as squares have to be connected at minimum cost while nodes indicated as circles may be used to achieve this goal. Furthermore, the figure shows two sets or groups of nodes (indicated as large squares) where at least one from each set has to be connected to the resulting connected graph, too.

fully explored, we may have to put some effort in finding additional arguments whether this connection is valid as well as useful.

6 References

Anderson, E.G., Morrice, D.J. (1999): A Simulation Model to Study the Dynamics in a Service-oriented Supply Chain, in: Farrington, P.A., Nembhard, H.B., Sturrock, D.T., Evans, G.W. (eds.): Proceedings of the 1999 Winter Simulation Conference, IEEE, Piscataway, pp. 742-748.

Barnes-Schuster, D., Bassok, Y., Anupindi, R. (2000): Coordination and Flexibility in Supply Contracts with Options, Working paper,
http://kaizen.kellogg.nwu.edu/anupindi/options.pdf. Last check on 1.10.2001.

Bolton, P., Whinston, M.D. (1993): Incomplete Contracts, Vertical Integration, and Supply Assurance, in: Review of Economic Studies, Vol. 60 (1993), pp. 121-148.

Böse, J., Fink, A., Gutenschwager, K., Reiners, T., Schneidereit, G. (2001) Konfiguration von Distributionslogistiknetzwerken unter Berücksichtigung kundenorientierter Lieferserviceanforderungen (Configuration of Distribution Networks under Customer-oriented Service Level Agreements), in: Sebastian, H.-J., Grünert, T. (eds.) Logistik Management, Teubner, Stuttgart, pp. 337-350.

Chopra, S., Meindl, P. (2001): Supply Chain Management: Strategy, Planning, and Operation, Prentice-Hall, Upper Saddle River.

Chwelos, P., Benbasat, I., Dexter, A.S. (2001): Research Report: Empirical Test of an EDI Adoption Model, in: Information Systems Research, Vol. 12 (2001), pp. 304-321.

Claus, A., Kleitman, D.J. (1973): Cost Allocation for a Spanning Tree, in: Networks, Vol. 3 (1973), pp. 289-304.

Domschke, W., Scholl, A., Voß, S. (1997): Produktionsplanung (Production Planning), 2nd ed., Springer, Berlin.

Duin, C.W., Volgenant, A., Voß, S. (2001): Solving Group Steiner Problems as Steiner Tree Problems on Graphs, Working Paper, University of Amsterdam.

Granot, D., Sosic, G. (2001): Formation of Alliances in Internet-Based Supply Exchanges, Working Paper, University of British Columbia, Vancouver.

Hicks, D.A. (1999): A Four Step Methodology for Using Simulation and Optimization Technologies in Strategic Supply Chain Planning, in: Farrington, P.A., Nembhard, H.B., Sturrock, D.T., Evans, G.W. (eds.): Proceedings of the 1999 Winter Simulation Conference, IEEE, Piscataway, pp. 1215-1220.

Hoogeweegen, M.R., Wagenaar, R.W. (1996) A Method to Assess Expected Net Benefits of EDI Investments, in: International Journal of Electronic Commerce, Vol. 1 (1996), pp. 73-94.

ICC (International Chamber of Commerce; ed.) (2000): Incoterms 2000: ICC Official Rules for the Interpretation of Trade Terms, Paris.

Inderfurth, K., Minner, S. (2001): Spieltheorie in Produktion und Logistik (Game Theory in Production and Logistics), Working Paper No. 12/2001, Otto von Guericke University Magdeburg.

Jones, M.C., Beatty, R.C. (1998): Towards the Development of Measures of Perceived Benefits and Compatibility of EDI: A Comparative Assessment of Competing First Order Factor Models, in: European Journal of Information Systems, Vol. 7 (1998), pp. 210-220.

Katz, M.L. (1989): Vertical Contractual Relations, in: Schmalensee, R., Willig, R.D. (eds.), Handbook of Industrial Organization, Vol. 1, New York, pp. 656-721.

Lee, H.G, Clark, T., Tam, K.Y. (1999): Research Report: Can EDI Benefit Adopters? in: Information Systems Research, Vol. 10 (1999), pp. 186-195.

Lee, H.L., Whang, S. (1999): Decentralized Multi-Echelon Supply Chains: Incentives and Information, in: Management Science, Vol. 45 (1999), pp. 633-640.

Lim, W.S. (2000): A Lemons Market? An Incentive Scheme to Induce Truth-telling in Third Party Logistics Providers, in: European Journal of Operational Research, Vol. 125 (2000), pp. 519-525.

Mylonopoulos, N.A., Doukidis, G.I., Giaglis, G.M. (1995): Assessing the Expected Benefits of Electronic Data Interchange through Simulation Modelling Techniques, in: Doukidis, G., Galliers, R., Jelassi, T., Krcmar, H., Land, F. (eds.) Proceedings of the 3rd European Conference on Information Systems, pp. 931-943.

O'Callaghan, R., Kaufmann, P.J., Konsynski, B.R. (1992): Adoption Correlates and Share Effects of Electronic Data Interchange Systems in Marketing Channels, in: Journal of Marketing, Vol. 56, No. 2 (1992), pp. 45-56.

Owen, G. (1975): On the Core of Linear Production Games, in: Mathematical Programming, Vol. 9 (1975), pp. 358-370.

Schneidereit, G., Voß, S. (2001a): Vertragsgestaltung in der Supply Chain (Contract Design for Supply Chains), in: Dangelmaier, W., Pape, U., Rüther, M. (eds.) Die Supply Chain im Zeitalter von E-Business und Global Sourcing, ALB-HNI, Paderborn, pp. 421-433.

Schneidereit, G., Voß, S. (2001b): Rechtliche Aspekte des Supply Chain Managements (Legal Aspects of Supply Chain Management), Working paper, TU Braunschweig, to appear.

Sharkey, W.W. (1995): Network Models in Economics, in: Ball, M.O., Magnanti, T.L., Monma, C.L., Nemhauser, G.L. (eds.): Network Routing, North-Holland, Amsterdam, pp. 713-765.

Simchi-Levi, D., Kaminsky, P., Simchi-Levi, E. (1999): Designing and Managing the Supply Chain, McGraw-Hill, Boston.

Skorin-Kapov, D. (1995): On the Core of the Minimum Steiner Tree Game in Networks, in: Annals of Operations Research, Vol. 57 (1995), p. 233-249.

Skorin-Kapov, D. (2001): On Cost Allocation in Steiner Tree Networks, in: Cheng, X., Du, D.-Z. (eds.): Steiner Trees in Industries, Kluwer, Boston, to appear.

Spinler, S, Huchzermeier, A., Kleindorfer, P.R. (2001): Optionen auf Kapazität: Anwendungen für e-Transportplattformen (Options on Capacity: Applications for e-Transportation Platforms), in: Sebastian, H.-J., Grünert, T. (eds.), Logistik Management – Supply Chain Management und e-Business, Teubner, Stuttgart, 2001, pp. 305-314.

Tirole, J. (1988): The Theory of Industrial Organization, Cambridge.

Tsay, A.A., Nahmias, S., Agrawal, N. (1999): Modeling Supply Chain Contracts – A Review, in: Tayur, S., Ganeshan, R., Magazine, M. (eds.), Quantitative Models for Supply Chain Management, Kluwer, Boston, 1999, pp. 299-336.

Vidal, C.J., Goetschalckx, M. (2001): A Global Supply Chain Model with Transfer Pricing and Transportation Cost Allocation, in: European Journal of Operational Research, Vol. 129 (2001), p. 134-158.

Voß, S., Gutenschwager, K. (2001) Informationsmanagement (Information Management), Springer, Berlin.

Voß, S., Reiners, T. (2000): Costs and Benefits of EDI Integration in Supply Chains and Networks. Working Paper, Technische Universität Braunschweig.

Voß, S., Woodruff, D. (2000): Introduction to Computational Optimization Models for Production Planning in a Supply Chain, Manuscript, Braunschweig und Davis.

Williamson, O.E. (1979): Transaction-cost Economics: The Governance of Contractual Relations, in: Journal of Law and Economics, Vol. 22 (1979), pp. 233-261.

Williamson, O.E. (1985): The Economic Institutions of Capitalism, Free Press, New York.

Zimmer, K. (2001): Koordination im Supply Chain Management (Coordination in Supply Chain Management), Gabler/DUV, Wiesbaden.

Decision Support by Model Based Analysis of Supply Chains

Michael Kaczmarek, Frank Stüllenberg

1 Supply Chains and Supply Chain Management 274
2 Modeling of Supply Chains with a Process Chain Approach 275
3 Simulation as an Instrument for Decision Support 278
4 Performance Management Using Simulation 283
5 Conclusion 286
6 References 287

Summary:
The paper presents an evaluation concept of different possible supply chain configurations. A concept for modeling and simulation of supply chains based on process chains is described. The results of the simulation can be used to measure the technical and economic performance of different possible configurations of the supply chain. The performance measures derived from the simulation model have to be integrated in the toolbox of the network management. In order to evaluate the performance and to design supply chains effectively, a concept for a network controlling is needed. The authors present a conceptual framework for the network controlling and a performance measurement of supply chains.

Keywords:
logistic networks, modeling, simulation, process chain model, supply chain management, network controlling, performance measurement

1 Supply Chains and Supply Chain Management

The environmental conditions for enterprises have changed. Global supply and sales markets as well as increased customer requirements concerning costs, time, quality and service levels, require an interorganizational planning, control and regulation of the material-, information- and finance-flows. For this purpose enterprises cooperate with their suppliers and customers in a supply chain, in order to establish the required goals jointly. The collaborative research center 559 "Modeling of large logistics networks" at the University of Dortmund intends to describe, analyse and optimize logistic networks in order to develop a theory and a method toolbox for the control of such networks.[1]

A supply chain represents a special type of a large network in logistics, which "encompasses all activities associated with the flow and transformation of goods from raw materials stage (extraction), through to the end user, as well as the associated information flows."[2] The definition of a supply chain is extended by the inclusion of the redistribution and the after sales service.[3] The supply chain is a complex system consisting of nodes (participants) and relations. The complexity of the supply chain makes it difficult to detect the system behavior and interdependencies between the nodes resp. participants. The complexity is essentially determined by number of the participants and their networking. Further criteria for the complexity are structural changes caused by joining and withdrawing participants and the heterogeneity of the enterprises. This heterogeneity expresses itself in different positions and roles of participants within the supply chain as well as in varying resource configurations.

The interorganizational processes in the supply chain must be planned, managed and controlled in accordance with a generally accepted target system. The participants "have realized that the real competition is not company against company but rather supply chain against supply chain."[4]

---

[1] See http://www.sfb559.uni-dortmund.de
[2] Handfield, Nichols (1999), p. 2.
[3] See Jehle (2000), p. 216; Buxmann, König (2000).
[4] Christopher (1998), p. 16.

2 Modeling of Supply Chains with a Process Chain Approach

Organizational parameters need to be known for an effective and efficient supply chain management. These are provided, so far research has been presented, in the form of empirical studies and specific case studies. However, the information found there is rather general. Reliable predictions about a successful conversion of the own enterprise cannot be made. A manager must therefore make decisions in a situation, which is determined by uncertainties and risks, without having complete information on the effects of the decision.

This problem is to be solved in the collaborative research center by means of a model supported procedure on the basis of a process chain model.[5] Organizational alternatives are illustrated and analyzed, so that quantitative result data are obtained. This data can be used for the decision support of a network controlling which aims at an entire performance measurement.

A model supported methodology is appropriate and necessary, since experimenting at the real system can meet with opposition of the participants, because the expected results may be uncertain due to the complexity of the supply chain.

The advantages of a model supported procedure are:

- saving of time, because the experiments do not have to take place in real time,

- minimizing the risk, because the determined effects in the model are limited and have no direct influence on the real system and

- a higher transparentness by simulating different scenarios e. g. with diverging system loads.

The requirements for a model based proceeding is the existence of suitable process models to describe the supply chain.

During the planning phase no real system is existing. Thereby the modeling and the simulation are the only possibility to generate statements concerning the system behavior.

Today predictions concerning logistic networks can be generated by model based descriptions. Often these illustrations of logistic networks are descriptive at first.

---

[5] See Kuhn (1995). An alternative instrument to model supply chains is the Supply Chain Operations Reference-Model (SCOR-Model) of the Supply Chain Council (SCC). This model is commonly used in practice. The SCOR-Model focusses on providing standard processes to describe supply chains and on ratios to carry out benchmark studies. (http://www.supply-chain.org)

The substantial advantage of such description forms exists in the support of communication among the network partners, without limiting it by restrictive (formal) conditions due to their modeling.[6] More formalized models are necessary for a model supported analysis, whose target is the generation of quantitative results.

The so-called process chain model is used to enable a verbal description of supply chains to logistics experts. In addition, suitable specifications of the models have to be supported, in order to receive the necessary information regarding the system dynamics for model supported quantitative analyses.

The process chain model enables a visualization and analysis as well as the organization of processes within the supply chain. "The process chain is defined as a set of chronological and logical related activities performed to achieve a defined business outcome."[7] Central constituent of the process chain model is the process chain element (Figure 1).

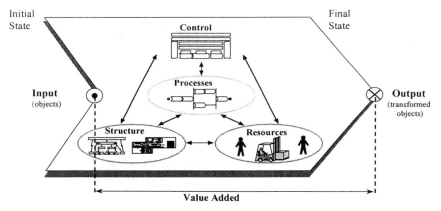

Figure 1: The Process Element[8]

Each process in the supply chain can be represented with the help of the parameters input, output, resources, structures, processes and control deposited in the process chain element. The process chain element is linked with the enviroment by its input, which describes the system load, and output. The process chain element transforms a defined input in accordance with the deposited process chain map into a defined output. The processes contained in this process chain

---

[6] See Bause, Kaczmarek (2001).
[7] Beckmann (1999), p. 27.
[8] Beckmann (1999), p. 28.

map are described by means of process chain elements on a lower level (Figure 2). Thus a "self similarity" between model and sub model results.[9]

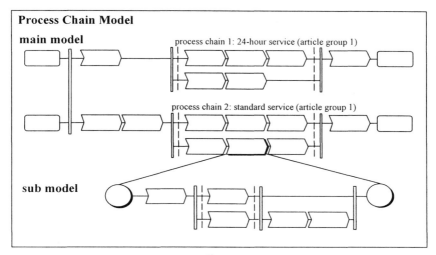

Figure 2: Example of a Process Chain Map[10]

In order to receive quantitative results, a more precise description of the supply chain is necessary. For this a model formalism was developed by *Beilner*[11], which is based on the process chain model. This model formalism represents a part of the process chain model. This formalism is so far specified that a description and an automatic analysis are enabled.[12] This analysis is not only limited to analysis by simulation. Furthermore queuing network analysis and Markov chain analysis of process chains are possible.[13]

---

[9] See Bause, Beilner, Kemper, Schmitz, Wenzel (2001), p. 19.
[10] Bause, Beilner, Kemper, Schmitz, Wenzel (2001), p. 19.
[11] See Bause, Beilner, Kemper, Schmitz, Wenzel (2001).
[12] See Bause, Kaczmarek (2001).
[13] See Bause, Beilner, Kemper, Schmitz, Wenzel (2001), p. 27-36.

3 Simulation as an Instrument for Decision Support

3.1 Simulation of a Supply Chain

A simulation is defined as the imitation of a system with its dynamic processes in a model in order to get knowledge for designing supply chains, which are portable to reality.[14]

An alternative to the use of simulations are analytical (mathematical) methods. The possibility of mathematical models to picture issues is indeed limited.[15] Many systems, as in particular the supply chain, are in reality so complex "that models of these systems are virtually impossible to solve mathematically."[16] The simulation allows the evaluation of complex systems.

The simulation represents a suitable method for the analysis of supply chains.[17]

For the analysis of supply chains the discrete-event simulation is used. „Discrete-event simulation concerns the modeling of a system as it evolves over time by a representation in which the state variables change instantaneously at separate points in time."[18]

A (discrete-event) simulation is executed not as self purpose, but effected on the background of a concrete objective.[19] The most important supply chain objectives for simulation studies are:

- the improvement of supply chains regarding service times and costs,
- the reduction of logistics costs,
- the reduction of stocks without reducing the customer service level,
- the analysis of demand changes and the development of strategies for adaption,
- the visualization of the benefits of a collaboration with partners in the supply chain,
- the sensitization of own staff for the importance of cooperation in a supply chain.[20]

---

[14] See Banks, Carson, Nelson (1999), p. 3.
[15] See Law, Kelton (2000), p. 91.
[16] Banks, Carson, Nelson (1999), p. 4.
[17] See Milling, Größler (2001), p. 61.
[18] Law, Kelton (2000), p. 6.
[19] See Heinzl, Brandt (1999), p. 393.
[20] See Scholz-Reiter (2000), p. 141-142.

Simulation studies must be economical. The benefits and costs must be set in relation to each other in order to evaluate the economy of modeling and simulation. The expected results must justify the cost of model creation and model analysis. The precise determination of the relevant costs and benefits measures is difficult. So far, no method exists, that helps in predicting the benefits achieved.

Simulation studies are carried out as follows:[21]

1. Determination of the relevant supply chain topology.
2. Providing of data concerning the interorganizational processes and the available resources by the autonomous participants.
3. Illustration of the supply chain part on the basis of the provided data by making use of a suitable descriptive language in a simulation model.
4. Determination of varying parameters regarding the particular aim.
5. Realization of simulation runs.
6. Documentation and interpretation of the technical and logistic results.
7. Execution of a cost evaluation on the basis of the technical and logical results.
8. Depending on the results' quality, they are either transferred to the real supply chain or a modification of the simulation model and further simulation runs are carried out.

The main problem domain on conducting simulation studies is the provision of information from the participants within the supply chain regarding the processes and the available resources. The companies have to provide the data. The process and simulation models are established on the basis of the delivered data. The quality of the result data depends mainly on the precision and the correctness of the provided data during this step.

3.2 Cost Simulation

The cost simulation extends the classical simulation of economical cost measures, so that apart from the technical and logistic performance measures, like stocks, turn-around times, throughputs and extents of utilization, also appropriate economical measures can be determined. Because of that, it results in a qualitative improvement of the simulation which is a condition for an efficient and effective decision supporting process. The cost measures, which are the basis of the decisions, must be integrated into the simulation model. By this the accuracy of the cost data determines the quality of the attainable results.[22]

---

[21] See Kuhn, Rabe (2000), p. 10-12.
[22] See VDI 3633 (2000), p. 1.

There are two approaches existing for the software-technical implementation of the cost simulation: the on-line cost simulation and the off-line cost simulation (Figure 3).[23]

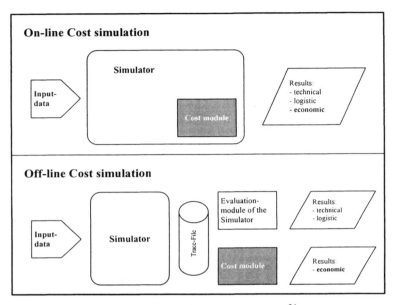

Figure 3: Alternative Software Solutions for the Cost Simulation[24]

The on-line cost simulation is characterized by a cost module which is integrated in the simulator. This enables a cost allocation during the simulation. In this case the costs for the use of resources are distributed directly by cost rates on the objects (unit of costs) as for instance orders. The advantages of the on-line cost simulation are the permanent availability of cost measures and the possibility to control the processes during the simulation on the basis of cost measures. The disadvantage of these cost simulations is distinguished by the necessity of two simulation runs. The first simulation run is needed to determine the cost rates whereas the second simulation run allocates the costs to the objects with the help of cost rates.[25]

With the off-line cost simulation the simulator and the cost module are separated. The simulator produces a "trace file" during the simulation. In this trace file the technical and logistic performance data of the simulation are deposited. It

---

[23] See Jehle (2000), p. 211; VDI 3633 (2000); Schäfer-Kunz (1997), p. 276-277.
[24] See VDI 3633 (2000), p. 3-4.
[25] See VDI 3633 (2000), p. 3; Schäfer-Kunz (1997), p. 277.

represents the basis for a subsequent cost evaluation. On the basis of the technical data, cost rates are calculated in the cost module and the costs are assigned to the individual objects (unit of costs). In contrast to the on-line cost simulation there is no need for two simulation runs. The independence of the cost module from the simulation tools is profitable, since thereby the flexibility is increased regarding the coupling with simulators. The disadvantage of the off-line cost simulation is the lack of cost-supported decision making during the simulation.

The cost simulation enables an economical evaluation of alternative supply chain configurations. To support the management decisions the information supplied with the cost simulation can be processed in the context of a network controlling.

3.3 Example for an Analysis by Using Simulation

Subsequently, an exemplary simulation study of a supply chain is presented.[26] The subject of the study is the comparison of a traditional order handling strategy by an order point system and a Vendor Managed Inventory (VMI) strategy.

In the traditional order handling strategy by an order point system the repeat order is placed by the retailer when his defined reorder level is achieved. The order quantity is fixed.

The VMI strategy is characterized by a wholesaler who gets the sales data from the retailers. On the basis of these data he undertakes the retailer's warehouse refil. The wholesaler also admits the responsibility for the delivery process and the material disposability.

To achieve the comparison, descriptive models were developed. They describe a part of a supply chain, which contains an original equipment manufacturer, wholesaler and retailer. The participants of the supply chain follow individual aims and try to maximize their own profit. In the framework of simulation studies simple models are developed. Based on them the single participant's benefit of the chosen strategy can be analysed.

For this the characteristic features of the strategies were considered in the model. Afterwards these models with the illustrated method were transferred into formalized models.

The screenshot (Figure 4) displays a high level model of a supply chain. The lower part illustrates the participants of the supply chain and the upper part the processes. These processes trigger activities by the participants, which execute the transformation. Therefore resources are assigned to the process chain elements.

---

[26] See Bause, Kaczmarek (2001).

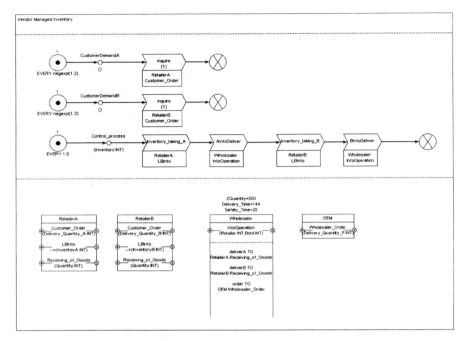

Figure 4: Model of a Supply Chain

To conduct the simulation, further information was needed, especially the specification of system load data that allows to imitate the system behavior. The system load of the supply chain is determined by the retailer´s incoming customer demand.

The following two requirements guarantee the comparability of the resulting data: On the one hand models with an identical system load are simulated and on the other hand the retailers are supposed to have a customer service level at a hundred percent.

The technical result data are supplied by the simulation with the varying parameters "order quantity" and "reorder level" (order point system) as well as "order quantity" and "delivery quantity" (VMI). We concentrated on the warehouse inventory of the wholesaler and retailer, whose average values and standard deviations were determined. Furthermore the utilization of resources and the number of calls of individual processes were analyzed. Figure 5 provides an overview of the ascertainable results which can be achieved by simulation.

Traditional Order Handling Strategy (Order Point System)

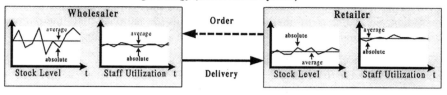

Vendor Managed Inventory (VMI) Strategy

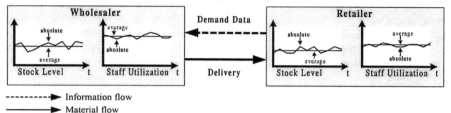

----▶ Information flow
——▶ Material flow

Figure 5: Exemplary Trend of the Stocks and Utilizations

The strategies in this example were exclusively evaluated on the basis of these technical measures. In order to be able to determine the costs and the proceeding effects of the strategy alternatives, these technical results must be transformed in a second step into economical measures by cost evaluation. This is necessary due to a different number of orders or deliveries and a different utilization of resources result in varying costs.

4 Performance Management Using Simulation

Given the data of the supply chain simulation, the controlling has to evaluate different strategic alternatives. In particular the technical measures already evaluated with costs, for example the inventory carrying costs, including costs of the bounded capital, transprot costs and orders handling costs, can be used by the network controlling.

The decision making process of the management is only effectively supported, if, besides the directly visible technical measures, the management also gets the interpretation and the derived advice for the corporate policy. In the context of supply chain management three different levels for an entire approach to manage these systems have to be differentiated.[27]

---

[27] See Arns, Bause, Kemper, Schmitz, Schweier, Stüllenberg, Völker (2000), p. 34.

Strategic organization measures are basic nature. They affect primarily on a long-term basis. Organization object is the structure of the supply chain, for example regarding the number of the participants involved, national and international aspects or the supplier structure influenced by the selected sourcing strategy.

A medium-term effect is indicated by tactical modification measures. Activities and processes have to be arranged and optimized. To ensure the availability of the resources the necessary capacities have to be provided.

Operational modifications with short-term effects follow the target to control daily processes allocating scarce resources.

The network controlling has to ensure decision support on all three levels. It is clearly visible, that financial indicators are not sufficient to plan and control complex systems like supply chains. "There is increased recognition that companies compete on a wide range of dimensions whose evaluation cannot be confined to narrow financial indicators."[28] Using supply chain simulation important cost measures can be extracted for the performance management.

Logistics costs can be reduced by eliminating non-value-added processes. They can be discovered by supply chain simulation. Using the words of *LaLonde* and *Pohlen*: "Supply chain management has a particularly critical need to link performance measurement with cost. "[29] Existing approaches to determine the costs of supply chain activities lack the evaluation of different 'what-if-scenarios'.[30] The activities of all partners participating in the supply chain are made visible by simulation. On the basis of this knowledge the structure of the supply chain can be redesigned.

Different supply chain strategies are formulated after establishing supply chain objectives (see Figure 6). This is usually a common process. These strategies are evaluated with the help of the simulation. The results of the simulation have to be interpreted and visualized. The relevant technical and cost performance measures are derived from the simulation. They are an important part of the performance measurement process.

Non-simulated data, like measures concerning the firms' environment, marketing data or information affecting the firms' staff, have to be added to the simulated data to establish an entire interpretation of different supply chain strategies including time, quality, cost and flexibility measures. The interpretation of this information is the task of the network controlling. Therefore, network controlling prepares the decision of the management in a sense of decision making support by using the simulated and non-simulated data.

---

[28] Fitzgerald, Moon (1996), p. 9.
[29] LaLonde, Pohlen (1996), p. 9.
[30] An example of an approach using the transaction cost analysis and the systems approach can be found in Ellram, Feitzinger (1997).

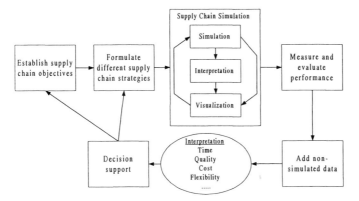

Figure 6: Using Simulation to Evaluate Supply Chain Performance[31]

In the context of the collaborative research center 559 a controlling concept for planning, controlling and regulating large networks in logistics has been developed.[32] The aim is the development of business management methods and tools. This enables the successful and effective design of large networks in logistics, for example supply chains.

The basic component of the network controlling concept is the information supply. An important question is how the data, derived from the simulation of supply chains can be used for this purpose and how the decision makers are supplied with relevant information. So far, controlling goals have been formulated and controlling tasks as well as activities have been deducted after formulating the requirements on controlling of large networks in logistics and the development of a controlling concept structure. A conceptual framework with five different controlling subsystems ensures the entire approach to a network controlling (see Figure 7).

The simulated data are an input for the process and the resources subsystem of the network controlling. Important measures, e.g. lead times and levels of capacity utilization are directly derived from the technical results of the simulation. Whereas cost measures for the finance subsystem of the network controlling are the output of the cost simulation.

---

[31] Adapted from LaLonde, Pohlen (1996), p. 9.
[32] See Schweier, Stüllenberg (1999).

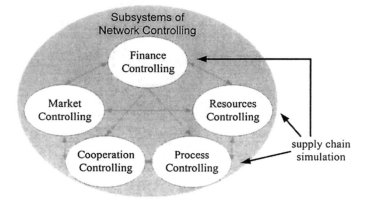

Figure 7: Five Subsystems of Network Controllig and Supply Chain Simulation

Especially the cooperation controlling and the market controlling need additional nonfinancial measures. The executives participating in a study noticed an increased trust within a cooperation comes along with more shared information, ideas and technology. The information sharing resulted in reduced costs or improved efficiency.[33]

Current research acitivities deal with the question, which specific performance management system can be used to ensure an entirely network controlling approach. The Balanced Scorecard concept from *Kaplan* and *Norton*[34] seems to be a valuable basis, which can be useful to evaluate supply chain strategies. Other performance management systems are evaluated, how far specific methods can be integrated.

5 Conclusion

Process chains are a useful tool to support the communication between logistics and simulation experts, offering the possibility to describe and evaluate logistics systems. Simulation studies have shown, that a modell based analysis is suitable to determine technical and economical measures. The simulation is therefore an important preliminary system to ensure an entire approach to performance measurement of supply chains. But it has to be mentioned, that the decision support of the network controlling can only be assured, if additional data besides the technical measures is derived from the used simulation.

---

[33] See Mentzer, Foggin, Golicic (2000), p. 57.
[34] See Kaplan, Norton (1996).

Acknowledgements

The research work presented is supported by DFG collaborative research center 559 "Modeling of Large Logistics Networks".

6 References

Arns, M., Bause, F., Kemper, P., Schmitz, M., Schweier, H., Stüllenberg, F., Völker, M. (2000): Gestaltung von Beschaffungsnetzwerken auf Basis einer prozeßkettenorientierten Modellierung (Design of Procurement Channels Based upon Process Chain-Oriented Modeling), in: Industrie Management, Vol. 16, No. 3 (2000), p. 33-36.

Banks, J., Carsonn, J. S. II., Nelson, B. L. (1999): Discrete-Event System Simulation, 2nd Edition, Prentice Hall, Upper Saddle River, NJ.

Bause, F., Beilner, H., Kemper, P., Schmitz, M., Wenzel, S. (2001): Modelling and Evaluation of Logistic Systems, International Multiconference on Measurement, Modelling and Evaluation of Computer-Communication Systems. 11.–14.09.2001 in Aachen.

Bause, F., Kaczmarek, M. (2001): Modellierung und Analyse von Supply Chains (Modelling and Analysis of Supply Chains), in: Wirtschaftsinformatik, Vol. 43, No. 6 (2001).

Beckmann, H. (1999): Method Handbook Supply Chain Management: the Systematic Search for Exellence, Praxiswissen, Dortmund.

Buxmann, P., König, W. (2000): Inter-Organizational Cooperation with SAP Systems: Perspectives on Logistics and Service Management, Springer, Berlin.

Christopher, M. (1998): Logistics and Supply Chain Management – Strategies for Reducing Cost and Improving Service, 2nd Edition, Financial Times, London.

Ellram, L. M., Feitzinger, E. (1997): Using Total Profit Analysis to Model Supply Chain Descisions, in: Journal of Cost Management, Vol. 11, No. 4 (1997), p. 12-21.

Fitzgerald, L., Moon, P. (1996): Performance Measurement in Service Industries: Making it Work, CIMA Publishing, London.

Handfield, R. B., Nichols, E. L. (1999): Introduction to Supply Chain Management, Prentice Hall, Upper Saddle River, NJ.

Heinzl, A., Brandt, A. (1999): Simulationsmodelle (Simulation Models), in: Weber, J., Baumgarten, H. (ed.): Handbuch Logistik: Management von Material- und Warenflußprozessen, Schäffer Poseschel, Stuttgart, p. 392-411.

Jehle, E. (2000): Steuerung von großen Netzen in der Logistik unter besonderer Berücksichtigung von Supply Chains (Management of Large Logistic Networks especially Supply Chains), in: Wildemann, H. (ed.): Supply Chain Management, TCW, München, p. 205-226.

Kaplan, R. S., Norton, D. (1996): The Balanced Scorecard: Translating Strategy into Action, Harvard Business School Press, Boston.

Kuhn, A. (1995): Prozeßketten in der Logistik: Entwicklungstrends und Umsetzungsstrategien (Process Chains in Logistics: Future Trends and Implementation Strategies), Praxiswissen, Dortmund.

Kuhn, A., Rabe, M. (2000): Simulationseinsatz in der Logistik (Using Simulation in Logistics), in: Baumgarten, H., Wiendahl, H.-P., Zentes, J. (ed.): Logistik-Management: Strategien – Konzepte – Praxisbeispiele, Springer, Berlin, p. 1-30.

LaLonde, B. J., Pohlen, T. L. (1996): Issues in Supply Chain Costing, in: The International Journal of Logistics Management, Vol. 7, No. 1 (1996), p. 1.-12.

Law, A. M., Kelton, W. D. (2000): Simulation Modeling and Analysis, 3rd Edition, Mc Graw Hill, New York.

Mentzer, J. T., Foggin, J. H., Golicic, S. L. (2000): Collaboration – the Enablers, Impediments and Benefits, in: Supply Chain Management Review, Vol. 4, No. 4 (2000), p. 52-58.

Milling, P., Größler, A. (2001): Simulationsbasierte Analysen von Wertschöpfungsnetzwerken: Erfahrungen aus der virtuellen Realität (Simulation Based Analysis of Value Added Networks: Experience from the Virtual Reality), in: Bellmann, H. (ed.): Kooperations- und Netzwerkmanagement : Festgabe für Gert v. Kortzfleisch zum 80. Geburtstag. Duncker & Humblot, Berlin, pp. 55-81.

Schäfer-Kunz, J. (1997): Perspektiven der simulationsgestützten Kostenrechnung (Perspectives of Simulation Supported Accounting), in: krp, Vol. 41, No. 5 (1997), p. 276-280.

Scholz-Reiter, Chr. (2000): Supply Chain-Simulation für kleine und mittlere Unternehmen (Supply Chain Simulation for Small and Medium Sized Companies), in: Lawrenz, O., Hildebrand, K., Nenniger, M. (ed.): Supply Chain Management – Strategien, Konzepte und Erfahrungen auf dem Weg zu E-Business Networks, Vieweg, Braunschweig/Wiesbaden, p. 133-144.

Schweier, H., Stüllenberg, F. (2000): Netzwerk-Controlling (Network Controlling), in: Controlling, Vol. 12, No. 4/5 (2000), p. 259–260.

VDI-FML (ed.) (2000): Simulation von Logistik-, Materialfluss- und Produktionssystemen – Kostensimulation (Simulation of Systems in Material Handling, Logistics and Production - Simulation of Costs), VDI 3633 Blatt 7, Beuth, Düsseldorf.

A New Customer-Oriented Methodology to Evaluate Supply Chain Lost Sales Costs Due to Stockout in Consumer Goods Sectors

Marco Perona

1	Introduction	290
2	Background	290
3	The Lost Sales Cost Computation Methodology	292
4	Empirical Evaluation	299
5	Concluding Remarks	303
6	Appendix: List of Abbreviations	304
7	References	306

Summary:
This paper presents a new methodology to compute costs arising in consumer goods sectors when a purchase intention is lost due to stockout of the searched good. This occurs only at the final tier of a consumer good supply chain, yet it can affect any upstream tier. Thus, the methodology proposed here encompasses all the relevant tiers within a consumer goods supply chain: the retailer, the producer of the final good, and the producer of components within the final good. The paper also provides a practical application of the proposed methodology to the Italian fashion sector, through which it is shown that, within the investigated branch of industry, a relevant amount of sales is lost due to stockout, that the corresponding costs affect upstream stages even more seriously than downstream ones, and that companies tend to seriously underestimate this phenomenon at all stages.

Keywords:
Supply Chain Management, Lost Sales Cost, Stockout, Fashion Industry

1 Introduction

The main function of stock within a supply chain is to face the uncertainties existing within its tiers and between the chain and served market. Stock can ensure flexibility, elasticity, capacity and time margins among the supply chain actors and toward the final customer, allowing the chain to be effective even when facing a disruption in one of its actors or an unexpected behavior by the final market. Nevertheless, any amount of stock is connected to certain costs. For instance, consider a retailer managing a stock of finished products in order to face the uncertainties characterizing its final customer demand and/or procurement process by its suppliers. The retailer has to suffer some stock carrying costs connected to running capital, warehousing and handling operations and obsolescence. Yet, stocks kept at the point of sale can ensure benefits both to the retailer and its supply chain. In fact, a greater availability of the products on the shelf can increase the probability of satisfying a greater amount of final customers. This in turn can reduce the risk of lost sales on the final market and the impact of lost sales costs.

It is important to find a correct trade-off between the benefits and costs of stock by considering the full range of costs suffered by the actors at any level of the supply chain as well as the global amount of benefits connected to stockkeeping. In fact, the loss of sales that might occur at retail depends on the stocks located at virtually any level of the supply chain. The connected costs affect not only the retailer, but the upstream tiers too. Therefore, any decision regarding the stock location and sizing is a supply chain matter if a global optimization is sought.

This paper deals with the problem of how to evaluate costs connected to lost sales. The objective pursued is to present a methodology useful for estimating the lost sales costs suffered by each actor within a supply chain due to stock out on the final market; consumer goods, as opposed to investment goods, are specifically addressed.

2 Background

The problem of defining the lost sales effect and assessing its influence on the cost structure of a supply chain does not seem to have received all the attention it deserves, both at the level of academic research and corporate practice. In particular, several disciplines of management deal with the lost sales phenomenon, but no one deepens the assessment of the opportunity costs suffered by a firm and its supply chain when a purchase intention for one brand belonging to that firm is lost. The effects of lost sales are relevant for at least three areas of corporate management and the corresponding scientific and managerial communities:

Operations & Logistics, Cost Accounting, and Marketing. All three communities agree that the opportunity cost suffered when a customer explicitly wanting to purchase a specific good gives up the purchase consists of the contribution margin attached to the mentioned good[1].

As regards *Operations & Logistics*, an analysis of the literature shows that the problem of lost sales is addressed when dealing with two specific aspects. In materials management models[2], safety stocks are often set by using an *ex ante* approach: a certain amount of accepted lost sales is set, in terms of a minimum service level to assure customers. Then, these models compute the safety stocks that can ensure achieving this fixed service level, often under the hypothesis that customers' demand be distributed after a Gauss normal curve. Thus, an optimization of the total relevant costs is not achieved as proposed in section 1, because the formulation is not structured as a cost optimization. Furthermore, these models tend to consider the costs of each single firm individually, rather than the costs suffered by the firms of a supply chain as a whole.

Another domain in which lost sales are dealt with by the Operations Management theory is in aggregate production planning models[3]: these models often overcome some of the limitations highlighted above, in that the amount of sales lost is directly computed as an effect of the stock level maintained. A cost optimization (yet, still limited to a single tier of the supply chain), takes into consideration that a cost trade-off is actually put into place. Nevertheless, these models assume that each time a stock-out situation is encountered at a manufacturer's finished product's warehouse a loss of sales takes place corresponding to all the demand that cannot be satisfied in the considered period: yet, this might not be the case if some stock is also kept by the retailer, or if the final customer can wait.

A more articulated nature of lost sales phenomenon is highlighted by *marketing* literature because it starts from another point of view. More specifically, marketing researchers have focused on modeling the customer behavior and studying the reasons affecting the final customers' purchasing intentions. In order to avoid losing market shares, branding has been recognized as the tool to attract and retain final customers. For this purpose, we can recall all the literature about the brand equity issue[4]. Following this path, researchers have developed the issue of the final customer loyalty to the brand or store, particularly topical nowadays if we consider the harsh conflict that goes on in a wide spectrum of industries between manufacturers and large distribution companies in order to conquer the

---

[1] Miller, Buckman (1987).
[2] Buffa, Miller (1979); Ferrozzi, Shapiro, Heskett (1985); Marini (1983); Plossl, White (1967); Chase, Aquilano (1977).
[3] Karni, Roll (1982).
[4] Aaker (1991); Kapferer, Thoenig (1989); Shocker, Srivastava, Ruekert (1994); Vicari (1995).

customer's loyalty[5]. Yet, none of the reviewed sources in marketing literature encompass any effort to assess the cost effects connected to the different customer behaviors highlighted.

Finally, the *Cost Accounting* systems typically adopt an *ex post* approach: the control loop typically consists of a results measurement, an analysis of the results deviation from the planned objective and finally, a definition of corrective actions[6]. More specifically, traditional cost accounting systems measure costs affecting the firm on the basis of recorded transactions: when a transaction occurs, a document registers it, so providing the information needed to close the control loop. Nevertheless, this very nature of accounting systems prevents them from easily controlling and evaluating lost sales costs, since a lost sale does not cause any transaction and, indeed, it occurs typically when a potential purchase transaction does not take place at all. In such a case there is no registration of the lost sales event and any traditional cost accounting system is therefore unable to consider its impact. This means that managers cannot check effectively on the basis of traditional cost accounting systems if their decisions, aimed at avoiding lost sales, are the right ones or not, because the control loop cannot be closed.

3 The Lost Sales Cost Computation Methodology

This section presents the new methodology proposed to compute the cost incurred by various actors within a supply chain due to the loss of purchase intentions by final customers, motivated by the unavailability of the searched good. To this purpose, we considered a generic consumer goods supply chain consisting of three tiers, namely components suppliers, final goods manufacturers and retailers. We assumed the final good manufacturer to own the considered brand, which is the most common case even though some significant cases of strong component brands (e.g. Gore-Tex or Intel), as well as retailer brands (e.g. private labels) exist as well. Since the following discussion encompasses a large amount of abbreviations, a complete list of their meaning is provided in the appendix.

3.1 Data Collection and Processing

Since the cost connected to one lost sale event arguably corresponds to the connected contribution margin, to compute the overall sales costs lost by a specific firm, it is necessary to estimate the rate at which loss of sales events take

---

[5] Pellegrini (1996); Zaninotto (1991).
[6] Azzone (1994).

place for that firm within its supply chain. For this purpose, it is necessary to carry out interviews with an adequate sample of final customers in order to find out which percentage of customers adopt which kind of behavior when the searched brand or good is not available at the considered point of sale. Each interview must single out the events taking place once inside the shop: the main possible choices are described by the events tree depicted in Figure 1 explaining what happens when the searched good is not available.

Once a suitable amount of interviews have been carried out, the gathered data can be arranged as required by the specific cost computation needed. Refer to the appendix for further detail on the various amounts computed.

3.2 Cost of Sales Lost By the Whole Supply Chain

By using data referred to in section 3.1 and defined in the appendix, it is possible to approximate an expected probability of finding a searched product later if the

search is not given up. We can define this Later Purchase Probability (LPP) as the sum of the probability that the final customers find (and hence, purchase) the desired product / brand later, in the same or another point of sale if they do not find such a product in the shop at whose exit they have been interviewed. LPP can be estimated by using the collected data as follows: if H is not equal to 0%, then we are dealing with goods that satisfy unnecessary needs, since only the satisfaction of necessary needs would force 100% unsatisfied customers to continue searching. In such a case, the whole supply chain can lose sales if it is unable to satisfy the final customer need immediately. If the final customers do not find what they are looking for and try again later at the same or another point of sale, we can assume that they can find the searched product/good later with a probability that matches the overall ratio of the number of final customers that actually purchase to the number of final customers willing to purchase. Thus, in this case we have:

$$LPP = (B+C)/A \qquad (1)$$

By using the computed LPP probability, and the I' factor (see § 3.1.), it is possible to estimate the percentage I of customers that actually buy the searched good in the same point of sale, later, not finding it immediately due to it being out of stock.

$$I = I' * LPP \qquad (2)$$

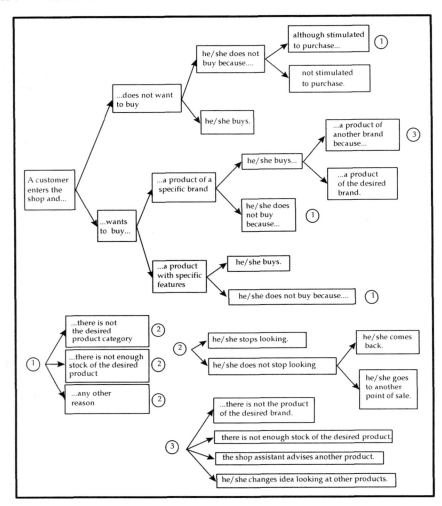

Figure 1: Outline of the Purchase Event Tree Used as a Data Collection Pattern

Moreover, by using I, it is possible to achieve the percentage M of customers that do not buy after looking for alternative brands or goods in the same point of sale where they did not find the originally searched good or brand because it was out of stock.

$$M = I' - I = I' * (1 - LPP) \qquad (3)$$

The same way as for I and M, and starting from J' (see § 3.1), it is possible to compute the dual values of I and M when another point of sale is considered, namely J (percentage of customers that actually buy in another point of sale, not finding the searched good or brand because of logistic reasons) and N (the percentage of customers that do not buy after looking for the searched brand / good in other points of sale, and after not finding the originally serached good / brand because of logistic reasons).

With a probability (1 - LPP) we evaluate the percentage of final customers that do not find the product and decide to stop looking for it, giving up the purchase process, simply because the product is unnecessary. As a consequence, logistic lost sales can be divided into *first order* and *second order* lost sales. The first order lost sales are those due to final customers that do not look for the product later (H, see § 3.1.). The second order logistic lost sales are those due to final customers that stop looking for the product because they have not found the product even if they have searched another time. These final customers are represented by the data M and N. If H is equal to 0%, then LPP = 100%. In facts, this is the case for goods fulfilling necessary needs, and therefore it is not likely that a customer gives up his or her purchasing process. In such a case, even if the searched product or brand is not available in the first visited point of sale, the final customer will not stop looking for it.

The same process can be replicated to take into consideration customers that do not find what they want for reasons different from the product being out of stock. In this case, we only want to compute the percentage of customers that will buy later in the same point of sale (K) and in another one (L). All of these percentages are computed by using LPP as an estimator, in the two cases defined above (H>0% and H=0%).

After having computed I, J, K, L, M and N by using LPP, let us define the overall rate of final customers that purchase (FCP) and that do not purchase due to the product being out of stock (FCNP). Notice that both percentages are computed on the overall sample of interviewed customers, and that the sum of FCP + FCNP does not equal 1, since customers that do not buy for reasons other than logistic are not taken into consideration.

$$FCP = B + C + G + I + J + K + L \tag{4}$$

$$FCNP = H + M + N \tag{5}$$

Finally, it is possible as follows to compute the amount of sales lost by the whole supply chain (LSSC) because of unavailability of the searched good or brand.

$$LSSC = FCNP/FCP \tag{6}$$

3.3 Sales Lost By the Retailer

Consider final customers that have not been satisfied in a certain point of sale and decide not to stop looking for the desired article. These customers can decide to visit later the same point of sale or another one. Now, let us define the percentage of final customers that purchase in the same point of sale visited (or in another one of the same distributor) as FCPVS, and the percentage of final customers that purchase in another point of sale (belonging to another retailer), because of logistic reasons as FCPAS. These percentages can be computed as follows, with regard to the whole set of interviewed customers:

$$FCPVS = B + C + G + I + K \tag{7}$$

$$FCPAS = J \tag{8}$$

Finally, it is possible to compute the amount of sales lost by the retailer because of substitution effect due to logistic reasons (unavailability of the searched good or brand) and connected to store loyalty behaviour (LSDS).

$$LSDS = FCPAS / FCPVS \tag{9}$$

3.4 Sales Lost By the Producer

In order to estimate the lost sales for the producer due to substitution effect, it is first needed to define *specific* and *generic* lost sales. A specific lost sale for a producer due to substitution effect occurs when the final customer searches a specific brand but buys another, regardless of where this event takes place or why. Yet, final customers do not always look for a specific brand, but simply for a product with specified characteristics without expressing any preference about the brand (functional purchase). In this case, all the products matching the customer's requirements available at the chosen point of sale and in the chosen time have a chance of being purchased. Thus, any product fitting the requirements but not currently available loses this chance. This is a generic lost sale. Both these categories of lost sales for the producer, can be split according to the reason triggering the loss of sale. Again, only lost sales due to logistic reasons are considered here.

Let's first compute the impact of the specific lost sales for producer substitution due to logistic reasons (SLSPS) on all the specific sales, that is on the actual sales due to the intentions of purchasing a specific brand. For this purpose it is possible to define a later purchase probability for final customers looking for a specific brand (SBLPP). SBLPP has the same meaning as LPP (see § 3.2.): the only difference is that SBLPP refers only to brand-conscious customers, while LPP refers to all customers. Like LPP, SBLPP is computed on the basis of first order lost sales and is used to estimate the second order lost sales.

$$\text{SBLPP} = O / (B + E) \tag{10}$$

It is now possible to compute the brand substitution probability BSP, and the impact of logistic reasons for doing so (LRP).

$$\text{BSP} = P/O \tag{11}$$

$$\text{LRP} = Q/P \tag{12}$$

At this point, it is possible to compute R (percentage of customers that look for a specific brand and buy in another shop, regardless of the specific brand purchased and the specific reason for their behavior) and S (percentage of customers that look for a specific brand and buy another brand in another shop due to unavailability of the searched brand at the considered point of sale) by using SBLPP, BSP and LRP as follows:

$$R = R' * \text{SBLPP} \tag{13}$$

$$S = R * \text{BSP} * \text{LRP} \tag{14}$$

Now, based on the computed percentages, it is possible to define and compute the overall percentage of brand-conscious final customers that actually purchase, regardless which brand they buy (FCSBP), and the percentage of brand-conscious final customers purchasing another brand because of stock out (FCPAB). Notice that each percentage is expressed with regard to the overall amount of brand-conscious customers interviewed.

$$\text{FCSBP} = (O + R) / (B + E) \tag{15}$$

$$\text{FCPAB} = (Q + S) / (B + E) \tag{16}$$

Finally, it is possible to compute the overall percentage of specific sales lost by a producer due to brand substitution effect (store loyalty behavior) after a product runs out of stock, as follows. Notice that SLSPS is expressed as a percentage of overall brand-conscious sales of one producer.

$$\text{SLSPS} = \text{FCPAB} / (\text{FCSBP} - \text{FCPAB}) \tag{17}$$

Notice that equation 17 holds true only if there are not sales lost due to reasons other than an item being out of stock. In other cases, FCPAB should be divided by the actual value of the considered producer's sales that can be obtained by considering FCSBP and subtracting FCPAB, and another term that considers other lost sales not due to stockout. As regards the generic sales lost by a generic producer for substitution effect, it is not possible to single out an equation such as

(17), due to the nature of this second type of purchase. Thus, we hypothesize that their impact on the generic sales is exactly equal to SLSPS: this hypothesis seems likely, at least for lost sales due to logistic reasons, because the probability of stockout for a certain product does not depend on the customer's purchasing intention. Thus, generic brand substitutions due to stockouts will likely affect the generic sales of a producer exactly the same way as specific lost sales affect its specific sales. As a consequence, SLSPS can be considered the overall percentage of sales lost by a producer due to stockouts at points of sale that sell its products.

3.5 Sales Lost By the Components Supplier

Once sales lost by the producer of the final goods have been computed, it is possible to compute the sales lost by components suppliers as an effect of the loss of sales suffered by the producer. More specifically, if the average producer loses a percentage of its actual sales equal to SLSPS (see equation 17 in § 3.4.), each of its average suppliers of raw material and/or components run the risk of suffering a corresponding loss of sales: the amount of this risk depends on SLSPS and the probability (PSBNE) that the good / brand chosen by the final customer not be equipped with the considered raw material / component. The objective of this section is to developing a method to estimate this second probability.

First, let us consider that PSBNE depends on two aspects: the first is the probability that any supplier must be connected to each producer (PSCP). This in turn depends on two factors: the level of concentration of the producer's industry, and the strategic choice of each supplier in terms of the number of customers with which they are connected. Thus, we can express PSCP as follows:

$$PSCP = (NCS - 1) / NPM \tag{18}$$

In equation 18, NCS is the number of customers served by the average components supplier within the considered industry. NPM is the overall number of producers of the considered sector operating in the considered market.

The second element affecting PSBNE is the average number of suppliers each producer keeps for each purchased item. In fact, in the majority of industrial sectors it is common that each item be supplied by two or more different companies. Thus, the probability that the new product is equipped with that component (PNPEC) depends on the average number of suppliers managed for that component type by the producers of the final good (ANS), expressed as follows:

$$PNPEC = 1 / ANS \tag{19}$$

Now it is possible to compute PSBNE, or the probability that the new product purchased will not be equipped with the considered brand of components, as a combination of the PSCP and PNPEC effects, as follows:

PSNBE = 1 − (PSCP * PNPEC) (20)

Finally, by means of PSNBE it is now possible to compute the percentage of sales lost by the average components supplier (SLCS) as follows:

SLCS = SLSPS * PSNBE (21)

4 Empirical Evaluation

The new methodology proposed in this study was developed as a secondary result of a larger research program intended to evaluate the supply chain integration achieved in Italy by companies within three relevant branches of industry: home appliance, fashion and book publishing[7]. Some results of this research, in particular those of the home appliance industry have already been published[8]. Real data gathered from the fashion industry within this research was used to implement the new methodology into practice with the objective of assessing its practical value. Data were gathered in 1998 and 1999 from a range of almost 20 apparel points of sales, selected to be representative (in terms of type, dimension and geographical positioning) of the Italian fashion sector retailing system[9]. We interviewed more than 500 customers.

First, let us analyze the results concerning the supply chain lost sales (see also § 3.2.). The survey showed that the Italian fashion industry as a whole actually loses sales due to logistic reasons. Results are presented in Figure 2.

As shown in Figure 2, all actors within the average fashion supply chain lose around 12% (LSSC = 9.5/77.5) of their turnover because customers stop looking for the desired product or brand if they cannot find it immediately at the visited point of sale.

---

[7] Adani, Angellara, Chessa (1998).
[8] Perona, Cigolini, Adani, Angellara, Chessa, Jenna (2001).
[9] Moda Industria (1997); Moda Industria (1997).

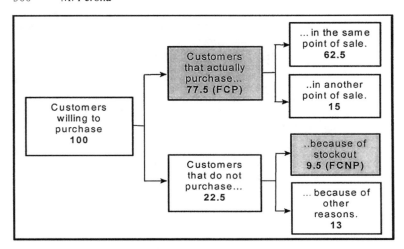

Figure 2: Empirical Findings Regarding the Lost Sales for the Whole Supply Chain

As for retailers, let us consider Figure 3 that presents the connected lost sales empirical findings. As shown, the average retailer loses potential sales worth about 13% of its turnover (LSDS = 8/62,5) due to substitution effect by its competitors in connection with stockout events.

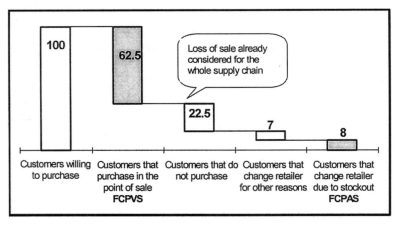

Figure 3: Empirical Findings Regarding Lost Sales for the Average Retailer

For the same reason, a clothes producer may be substituted at a point of sale by other producers as a consequence of stockout (see § 3.4.). For this purpose, let us consider Figure 4 that summarizes empirical data needed to assess the producer lost sales as described in § 3.4. Notice that in this picture the overall amount of customers that do not purchase is greater than 22.5% because Figure 4 only considers specific lost sales, that is sales lost when a brand-conscious purchase is in progress. As shown in Figure 4, the average clothes producer loses potential sales worth about 29% of its turnover due to stockout (SLPS = 14/(48.5). The empirical data presented in Figure 4 supports two further concepts: first, the amount of sales lost by the average Italian clothes producer for logistic reasons (29%) is more than twofold that one of the average retailer (13%). Despite the fact that Italian consumers tend to be considered very brand-conscious when it comes to fashion, the power of the average point of sale to affect the purchase process and thus retain sales turns out to be much stronger than that of producers that in most cases own brands. Moreover, the stockout of goods at points of sale explains almost two-thirds of sales lost by producers, while it is worth "only" half of those lost by retailers. This finding reinforces the remark made in § 1 of this paper that lost sales cost must be a supply chain issue since it occurs at the retail tier but influences costs on all tiers of the chain.

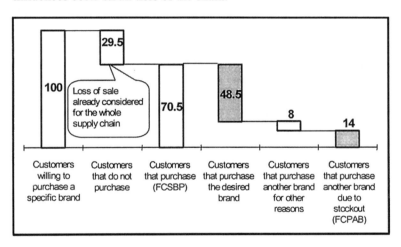

Figure 4: Empirical Findings Regarding Lost Sales for the Average Producer

Figure 5 presents the empirical findings regarding lost sales for the average fabric supplier (SLCS).

The resulting probability of incurring a loss of sales due to a stockout at the point of sale for the average fabric supplier equals 26% of its current sales due to the fact that: a) the average fabric supplier tends to focus on a rather limited number of clothes producers (PSCP = 20%) rather than serving all of them, and b) on average, clothes producers decide to allocate each fabric type to two different suppliers (ANS = 2) rather than concentrating all their purchases with the same fabric manufacturer.

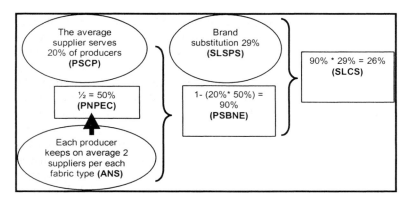

Figure 5: Empirical Findings Regarding Lost Sales for the Average Fabric Supplier

Figure 6 summarizes the total lost sales costs due to stockout computed from lost sales figures presented above as percentage values of actual sales by multiplying these values by the percent contribution margin of each actor (respectively: 53% of sales for suppliers, 46% for producers and 45% for distributors). In darker color, we reported the average estimation of the same costs as directly supplied by the interviewed companies. As shown in Figure 6, in this branch of industry the cost of lost sales due to logistic reasons is rather large for all types of actors within the fashion supply chain, and it increases with the distance from the final customer. Moreover, companies seem to seriously underestimate the lost sales cost they incur: this effect also increases with the distance from the final customer.

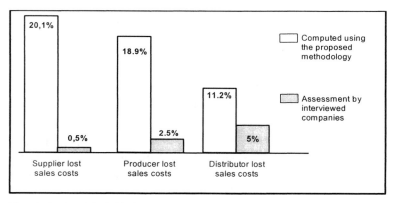

Figure 6: Empirical Findings Regarding Supply Chain Lost Sales Costs for the Italian Fashion Industry

5 Concluding Remarks

The proposed methodology deals with a phenomenon whose magnitude is often underestimated if not completely overlooked both by researchers and managers: the costs suffered by each member of a supply chain when a lost sale occurs. The methodology described in detail in Section 3 of this paper fills this gap by providing a thorough formulation to compute the opportunity costs arising with virtually any actor within a supply chain that experiences lost sales due to stockout at the point of sale. It is argued that, depending on the motivations driving the final customer's purchase intention, a loss of sale occurring at one point of sale could affect all of the actors within the connected supply chain, just one, or some of them. Hence, this paper provides managers with a framework to compute the cost affecting each type of actor as a consequence of various types of events following a stockout. More specifically, an *a posteriori* method of assessing this amount is proposed, based on field interviews, especially directed to final customers. Hence, a major aspect of this methodology is that it can be applied to a specific company or to a whole sector, depending on the sample of customers interviewed and the specific questions directed to them. The objective pursued while developing the method regards in particular lost sales due to stockouts, so this specific apect is specifically investigated. However, the same methodology could be used as well to compute lost sales costs due to incorrect pricing or unfit design for example, provided the appropriate questions are posed to final customers.

Section 4 of this paper provides an empirical test of the proposed methodology by means of data gathered in the field and regarding the Italian fashion sector. Outcomes underline some remarkable findings. First it is shown that, provided a sufficiently broad sample of customers is interviewed, the methodology proposed in this paper is actually able to supply thorough and reliable results with a limited computational effort (all computations required were carried out through a rather simple spreadsheet). Moreover, at least in the considered branch of industry, costs suffered by companies as a consequence of losses of sales are actually very relevant as compared to actual sales. Thus, it can also be deduced that a conceptual and operative tool supporting managers in evaluating this effect is also relevant. Finally, it was also shown that all companies within the considered sector tend to underestimate their lost sales costs, which demonstrates that they actually do not care much about this aspect, or at least that they tend to be missing a suitable tool to support their evaluation efforts. Since the quantitative results highlighted in Section 4 match similar results achieved within this research in other branches of industry, a strong suggestion is produced regarding the fact that above considerations could be generalized to all sectors involving consumer goods, thus setting a very high relevance on the method developed and presented here.

6 Appendix: List of Abbreviations

- A: percentage of customers that actually entered the point of sale with the intention of buying something, referred to all the interviewed sample.
- ANS: average number of suppliers managed for a specific component type by final goods producers within a specified industry.
- B: percentage of customers that, after entering the point of sale with the intention to buy a specific brand, actually carry out a purchase (regardless of the brand purchased), referred to all the interviewed sample.
- BSP: Brand Substitution Probability.
- C: percentage of customers that actually carry out a purchase (regardless of the brand purchased) after entering the point of sale with the intention to buy a good of a generic brand, referred to all the interviewed sample.
- E: percentage of customers that entered the point of sale with the intention to buy a specific brand and did not buy anything, whatever reason for this behavior. Referred to all the interviewed sample.
- FCNP: percentage of customers that do not purchase due to logistic reasons.
- FCP: percentage of final customers that purchase, regardless which product or brand they purchase, and regardless where they purchase.
- FCPAB: percentage of brand-conscious final customers purchasing another brand because the desired brand is out of stock, regardless where they purchase.
- FCPAS: percentage of final customers purchasing in another point of sale (belonging to another retailer) because of logistic reasons, regardless which product or brand they purchase.
- FCPVS: percentage of final customers that purchase in the same point of sale visited (or, in another one of the same distributor), regardless which product or brand they purchase.
- FCSBP: overall percentage of brand-conscious final customers actually purchasing, regardless which brand they purchase.
- G: percentage of customers that entered the point of sale without the intention to buy, but actually purchased within that point of sale, regardless of the specific brand they purchased referred to all the interviewed sample.
- H: percentage of customers that stop looking for the searched brand or good after not being satisfied at the considered point of sale because the brand or good they are looking for is out of stock.

- H': percentage of customers that continue looking for the searched brand or good after not finding it at the considered point of sale.
- I: percentage of customers that actually buy the searched good later in the same point of sale after not finding it initially due to it being out of stock.
- I': Percentage of customers that will look later for the searched good / brand in the same point of sale after not finding it initially due to it being out of stock.
- J: Percentage of customers that actually buy in another point of sale after not finding the searched good or brand because of logistic reasons in the point of sale previously visited.
- J': Percentage of customers that will look later for the searched good / brand in another point of sale after not finding it initially due to it being out of stock.
- K: percentage of customers that will buy later in the same point of sale, after not finding the searched brand or good initially, due to logistic reasons.
- L: percentage of customers that will buy later in another point of sale, after not finding the searched brand or good initially, due to logistic reasons.
- LPP: Late Purchase Probability. Expected probability of finding a searched product later if it is not found immediately and the search not given up.
- LRP: percentage of brand substitutions due to logistic reasons.
- LSDS: percentage of sales lost by the retailer because of substitution effect due to logistic reasons.
- LSSC: percentage of sales lost by the whole supply chain because of logistic reasons.
- M: percentage of customers that do not buy after looking for alternative brands or goods in the same point of sale, where they did not find the originally searched good or brand because of logistic reasons.
- N: percentage of customers that do not buy even after looking for the searched brand / good in other points of sale, and after not finding the originally searched good / brand at the original point of sale because of logistic reasons.
- NCS: number of final goods producers served by the average components supplier within the considered industry.
- NPM: overall number of final goods producers of the considered industry that operates in the considered market.
- O: total percentage of customers that actually buy in the visited point of sale, regardless which brand they buy.

- O': total percentage of customers that actually don't buy in the visited point of sale, regardless whether they stop searching for the required brand or not, and regardless which brand they eventually buy afterwards.
- P: percentage of customers that buy, in the same point of sale initially visited, another brand from that one originally searched, regardless of the reason for this change of brand.
- PNPEC: probability seen by an average components supplier within a specified industry that a final product chosen at random within that industry will be equipped with its own components.
- PSBNE: probability that one finished product within a specific sector will be equipped with a specific raw material / component.
- PSCP: probability within one specific industry that the average components supplier has to supply the average final goods producer.
- Q: percentage of customers that buy, in the same point of sale initially visited, another brand from that one originally searched because of logistic reasons.
- R: percentage of customers that look for a specific brand and buy in another shop, regardless of the specific brand purchased and the specific reason for their behavior.
- R': percentage of customers that continue to look for the searched brand in another point of sale, regardless whether they will actually buy it or not, and regardless what reason caused them to do so.
- S: percentage of customers that look for a specific brand and buy another brand in another shop due to unavailability of the searched brand at the considered point of sale.
- SBLPP: later purchase probability for final customers looking for a specific brand.
- SLCS: percentage of sales lost by the average components supplier.
- SLSPS: percentage of the specific lost sales for producer substitution due to logistic reasons on all the specific sales.

7 References

Aaker, D. A. (1991): Managing Brand Equity, Free Press, New York.

Adani, M., Angellara, S., Chessa, M., (1998): The Supply Chain Management: A Conceptual Framework and an Empirical Evaluation, Master thesis, Politecnico di Milano.

Azzone, G. (1994): Innovare il sistema di controllo di gestione (Cost Accounting System Innovation), Etaslibri, Milano.

Buffa, E. S., Miller, J. G. (1979): Production-Inventory Systems Planning and Control, Richard D. Irwin Inc., Homewood, Illinois.

Chase, R. B., Aquilano, N. J. (1977): Production and Operations Management, A Life Cycle Approach, Richard D. Irwin Inc., Homewood, Illinois.

Ferrozzi, C., Shapiro, R. D., Heskett, J. L. (1985): Logistics Strategy: Cases and Concepts, West Publishing Co., St. Paul, Minnesota.

Karni, R., Roll, Y. (1982): A Heuristic Algorithm for Multi-Items Lot Sizing Problem With Capacity Constraints, in: IIE Transactions, Vol. 14, n° 4 (1982).

Kapferer, J.-N., Thoenig, J.-C. (1989): La Marque. Moteur de la competitivité des entreprises et de la croissance de l'economie (The Brand : Engine of Firms' Competitiveness, and of Economic Growth), Mc Graw Hill, Paris.

Marini, G. B. (1983): Logistica Industriale e Commerciale (Industrial and Commercial Logistics), Franco Angeli, Milano.

Miller B. L., Buckman A. G. (1987): Cost Allocation and Opportunity Costs, in: Management Science, May (1987).

Moda Industria (1997a): L'abbigliamento esterno maschile in Italia: consuntivo anno 1996 (Male Apparel Market In Italy: 1996 report), Trade fair "NOMI-Moda Milano", Milan, October 3rd-7th.

Moda Industria (1997b): L'abbigliamento esterno femminile in Italia: consuntivo anno 1996 (Female Apparel Market In Italy: 1996 report), Trade fair "NOMI-Moda Milano", Milan, October 3rd-7th.

Pellegrini, L. (1996): Marche e insegne: valori e ruoli (Brands and Signboards: Values and Roles), in: Economia & Management, N. 2 (1996).

Perona, M., Cigolini, R., Adani, M., Angellara, S., Chessa, M., Jenna, R. (2001): The Integrated Management of Logistic Chains in the White Goods Industry. A field Research in Italy, in: International Journal of Production Economics; Vol. 69 (2001), p. 227-238.

Plossl, G. W., Whight, O. W. (1967): Production and Inventory Control, Prentice-Hall, Englewood Cliffs, NJ.

Shocker, A., Srivastava, R. K., Ruekert, R. W. (1994): Challenges and Opportunities Facing Brand Management: An Introduction to the Special Issue, in: Journal of Marketing Research, May (1994).

Vicari, S. (1995): Brand equity. Il potenziale generativo della fiducia (Brand Equity: The Generative Power of Trust), Egea, Milano.

Zaninotto, E. (1991): Store loyalty e brand loyalty: differenziazione e informazione nel marketing del produttore e del distributore (Store Loyalty and Brand Loyalty: Differentiation and Information in Producer's and Distributor's Marketing), in: Commercio: rivista di economia e politica commerciale, N.13 (1991).

Global Supply Chain Management: Extending Logistics' Total Cost Perspective to Configure Global Supply Chains

Rolf Krüger

1	Introduction	310
2	Challenges of Supply Chain Management: Cost Management for Globalization	310
3	The Importance of Product Characteristics for the Global Supply Chain's Configuration	314
4	The Influence of a Product's Logistics Reach on the Configuration of a Global Logistics Network	319
5	Conclusion	323
6	References	323

Summary:
Due to highly integrated purchasing, manufacturing and distribution activities over long distances, global supply chain management is challenged to combine the ideas of just-in-time and of global sourcing in order to configure an efficient global logistics network. Referring to the logistics' total cost perspective, the attributes of a product in terms of value, weight and volume influence significantly the supply chain's design. All three variables can be concentrated in a ratio which is called "logistics reach". The logistics reach gives information about a product's suitability for different means of transportation and, furthermore, about an adequate configuration of the global logistics network. A high logistics reach indicates a network configuration related to the idea of just-in-time. A low logistics reach leads to a configuration according to the idea of global sourcing.

Keywords:
Global Supply Chain Management, Just-in-Time, Sourcing, Configuration of a Global Logistics Network, Total Cost Perspective, Products' Attributes and Logistics Reach

1 Introduction

During the last decades there has been a profound development towards the globalization of production and operations. Therefore an effective and efficient global supply chain management becomes more and more important. Significant cost drivers of global supply chains are the logistics activities. While e.g. production costs decline due to global sourcing and economies of scale, logistics costs increase because of longer distances, rising inventory levels and growing uncertainties. Only if the advantages of globalized procurement and production exceed the additional logistics costs, a global supply chain management will turn out profitable. Thus, logistics cost management is the hidden success factor of global supply chain management. Extending logistics' total cost perspective to the entire supply chain is one of the main challenges of global supply chain management.

2 Challenges of Supply Chain Management: Cost Management for Globalization

2.1 The Globalization of Supply Chain Management

Supply chain management can be defined as inter-organizational integration of value-adding processes and activities from the first supplier to the final customer.[1] Referring to Porter's value chain model[2], these processes encompass logistics and operations as core activities and can be expanded to procurement, marketing and sales, services or research and development. Thus ever, the overall objective of establishing an integrated supply chain management is the reduction of costs and time-to-market as well as the improvement of quality and flexibility in order to achieve a sustainable competitive advantage for all members. The characteristic key to successful supply chain management is close inter-organizational cooperation, which includes tangible components, particularly the integration of information systems, and intangible components, e.g. confidence-building measures.[3]

---

[1] See Lambert et al. (1998), p. 2-3; Handfield, Nichols (1999), p. 2.
[2] See Porter (1985).
[3] See Lambert et al. (1998), p. 10.

The scope of the functional and organizational integration of supply chain management complies with the principles of effectiveness and efficiency: Scarce resources should be allocated to realize maximum improvement. As a consequence, the realization of an overall integrated supply chain has some obvious restrictions:[4]

1. Several case studies show that even the integration of a single function along the supply chain requests a huge amount of temporal, financial and personnel resources. Therefore a simultaneous integration of all functions or processes is not practicable – though it would be desirable. Instead, a step by step procedure should focus on functions which are crucial for cost reduction or service improvement.

2. Since not all processes and activities in a supply chain are equally important to the overall output, the required level of integration varies among the supply chain's links. Comparable to the functional integration, scarce resources should also be allocated to those business links, which are critical to create value in the supply chain. Integration from the first supplier to the final customer is normally not feasible.

Referring to these conclusions, this article focuses on logistics of an international supply chain with procurement, manufacturing and distribution spread across different countries. Logistics management is defined as the part of the supply chain management process that is responsible for the strategic configuration and implementation as well as the operative planning and control of material flows and related information.[5] Especially in the international context, logistics activities are regarded as significant cost drivers.[6] The logistics' objectives of supply chain management are the stabilization of material flows, the reduction of inventories, the reduction of lead-times and the improvement of flexibility and reliability.[7] While logistics' tasks and objectives are not altered by internationalization, the profound change of the relevant environmental circumstances forces logistics to find new ways to fulfill both tasks and objectives. A very important role for the internationalization of logistics plays the general internationalization strategy.[8] Setting up a strategy to gain a maximum internationalization advantage from purchasing, manufacturing and distribution has to take into account the sectoral, local and product-specific characteristics of a particular industry. These advantages can be derived from two groups "access to resources" and "economies of scale". Both influence logistics in different ways.[9]

---

[4] See Lambert et al. (1998), p. 5.
[5] See Council of Logistics Management (1998).
[6] See Cooper (1993), p. 12; Dornier et al. (1998), p. 1.
[7] See Handfield, Nichols (1999), p. 6-11.
[8] For examples of different strategies see Bartlett, Ghoshal (1995), p. 14.
[9] See Schary, Skjøtt-Larsen (1995), p. 23-24; Bowersox, Closs (1996), p. 126-140; Dornier et al. (1998), p. 224-227; Delfmann, Albers (2000).

1. *Access to resources:* Internationalization offers companies' access to resources, which are not available nationally, or in a specific sense only. The access to resources, e.g. access to foreign markets or to locational advantages, determines the dispersion and location of value-adding activities and the distances between them. Availability of resources increases companies' interests in bridging high spatial and temporal distances. However, for logistics long *distances* result in longer lead-times and growing uncertainties for planning and processing. As consequences the inventory level in the international supply chain rises, flexibility and reliability of logistics services decline. Besides, long distances typically cause intermodal transports using different means of transportation with unequal capacities. Thus intermodal transports impair the stabilization of material flows.

2. *Economies of scale:* Internationalization bears the opportunity to reap high economies of scale, if an activity is concentrated on one or only a few locations for serving the company plants worldwide. This allocation of activities allows a high degree of specialization on the one hand and needs a high level of integration on the other. Here, the level of integration affects the logistics' situation in terms of demand level and demand patterns as well as delivery times or delivery flexibility. From a logistic point of view a high integration level leads to a frequent crossborder exchange of materials among purchasing, manufacturing and distribution locations requiring short delivery times and high flexibility. The efficient management of these complex and intensive material and related information flows assumes high specific investments in the logistic infrastructure and an elaborated planning and controlling of logistics' activities.

During the last years there has been a profound development towards the globalization of purchasing, manufacturing and distribution. Globalization is considered qualitatively different from internationalization.[10] While internationalization describes the geographic extension of economic activities across national borders, globalization additionally characterizes the integration of the crossborder activities. The logistics of such a global supply chain have to face two challenges simultaneously: Long distances and a high level of crossborder integration.

2.2 Costs of Global Supply Chains

Distances and integration in global supply chains affect logistics' costs. The cost driver "distance" can be regarded as a traditional source of global logistics costs due to any kind of international trade. However, as long as only a limited number of companies was involved in the international trade of exclusive goods, logistics'

---

[10] See Dicken (1998), p. 5; Porter (1986), p. 20.

costs were merely of minor importance. The rising understanding of international trade as a way to gain comparative cost advantages changed the way of dealing with logistics' costs, which have become a critical part of a product's total cost. Up to the present decade of global sourcing, declining logistics' costs and low product prices drive international logistics' activities and overcompensate sometimes their poor reliability. Efficient global sourcing bases on the realization of cost degression effects by ordering big lots to reduce the costs per unit. A significant impact of the second cost-driver "integration" on the logistics costs characterizes a global logistics process. While in the international context aspects of integration are quite new for logistics, there are lots of examples in a regional context, how the integration of suppliers and customers changes a logistics system to a just-in-time system. Comparable to the just-in-time principle, global supply chain logistics have to cope with supposedly short delivery times and high delivery flexibilities which cannot be achieved just by high inventory levels. Therefore the reduction of lead-times is inevitable to enable economies of speed.

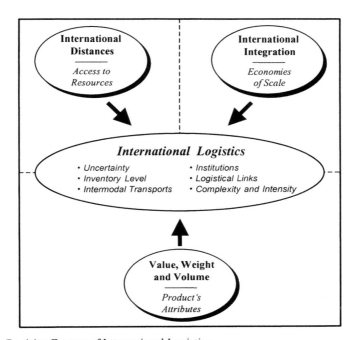

Figure 1: Decisive Factors of International Logistics

In general, global supply chain management faces the challenge to configure logistics by merging the principle of global sourcing with the principle of just-in-time.[11] Cost degression and lead-time reduction must be combined in a way that on the one hand the increasing costs of global logistics do not overcompensate the advantages of globalization e.g. declining costs of procurement and manufacturing. On the other hand, logistics should be able to provide the necessary customer service. The adjustment of logistics towards cost degression or reduction of lead-time has to start with the configuration of the logistic network underlying a supply chain. Among the stated circumstances (a highly integrated network with long distances) the physical attributes of a product, as value, weight and volume, are crucial for the logistics network configuration. Thus three factors have to be considered for the configuration of an international logistics network: The international distances, the international integration and the product's variables value, weight and volume (see Figure 1).

3 The Importance of Product Characteristics for the Global Supply Chain's Configuration

3.1 The Total Cost Perspective

Main characteristics of logistics goods are their value, weight, and volume.[12] A product's value on the one hand and its weight and volume on the other hand influence the costs of logistics and determine the efficiency of a logistics process. Reflecting the total cost perspective, an analysis of logistics costs should include all costs necessary to fulfill logistic requirements[13]. Overall logistics costs consist of transportation costs and inventory costs (see Figure 2).

The weight (W) and the volume (V) influence the transportation costs (TC): In order to establish a transportation cost unit ratio, two groups of cost-drivers can be distinguished. The first group forms the freight rate (α) which is a time-sensitive measure, related to a single unit of volume or weight. The second group, weight and volume, builds the physical attributes which are of particular importance for the calculation of transportation costs. The transportation costs increase with growing weight or volume or freight rate.

(1) $\quad TC = f(W, V, \alpha) \quad$ with $\quad \dfrac{\partial TC}{\partial W} > 0, \ \dfrac{\partial TC}{\partial V} > 0, \ \dfrac{\partial TC}{\partial \alpha} > 0$

---

[11] See Fawcett, Birou (1992), p. 3.
[12] Other characteristics of goods not relevant in this context are risk criteria as perishability or obsolescence.
[13] See Bowersox, Closs (1996), p. 10-12; Lewis et al. (1956).

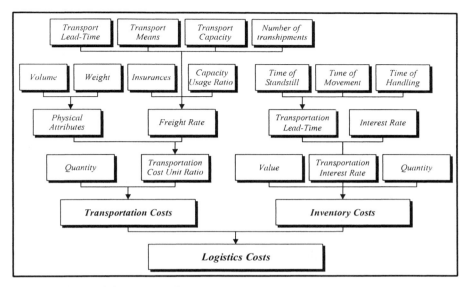

Figure 2: The Total Cost Perspective

However, inventory costs (IC) depend on the product's value (PV) and the transportation interest rate (β) which consists of an interest rate related to the tranportation time. An increase of value or interest rate (β) leads to higher inventory costs:

(2) $IC = f(PV, \beta)$ with $\dfrac{\partial IC}{\partial PV} > 0$, $\dfrac{\partial IC}{\partial \beta} > 0$

Globalization influences both transportation costs and inventory costs. Longer distances make freight rates rise, longer transportation times cause more stock in transit. Hence, the globalization of logistics activities intensifies the effects of value, weight and volume. Particularly those goods with high value and low weight and volume are predestined for global logistics processes. In the logistic literature several examples show how to express the complex and wide-ranging interdependencies between value, weight and volume of a product and its suitability for global logistics' processes in a simple ratio.[14] This ratio is called value-volume-ratio, value-weight-ratio or value density. In this article the term logistics reach (LR) is used. The logistics reach of a product rises with increasing value or with declining weight or volume:

---

[14] See e.g. Heskett et al. (1973), p. 45-50; Cooper (1993), p. 14-15; Pfohl (1994), p. 128; Ballou (1999), p. 63-64.

(3) $LR = f(PV, W, V)$ with $\dfrac{\partial LR}{\partial PV} > 0$, $\dfrac{\partial LR}{\partial W} < 0$, $\dfrac{\partial LR}{\partial V} < 0$

Obviously the logistics reach is a term putting the product's value into relation to its weight and volume. The main problem is to find an adequate mathematical function reflecting the relation of weight and volume. First, volume and weight show different dimensions, what makes it necessary to transform one factor into the other. Second, volume and weight have basically different influence on the freight rate: The influence depends on the underlying system of shipping rates, e.g. for the calculation of an air cargo rate the weight has a substantial higher influence while smaller changes of the volume probably will not affect the cargo rate. Besides, the volume-weight-relation very often cannot be mapped in a steady mathematical function. Because of these problems the less important factor sometimes is neglected in the logistic literature. For example, the value-weight ratio is concentrating on the weight, what is likely appropriate to cover the situation of air transportation. The value-density introduced by Cooper[15] tries to solve that deficit and considers explicitly the weight as well as the volume. But Cooper provides no details how to combine volume and weight. Following the definition of physical density, "density" implies the weight divided by volume. Consequently the value density would indicate an improvement of a product's suitability for global logistics' processes with increasing volume, which of course does not fit the mathematical definition of the logistics reach. To avoid these problems the following working definition of logistics reach does not base on a specific function:

(4) $LR = \dfrac{PV}{f(W, V)}$

3.2 Logistics Reach and Logistics Costs

A high logistics reach indicates low transportation costs, compared to the product's value.[16] But the transportation costs per value unit are just a part of the overall logistics costs per value unit. These relative logistics costs per piece (rLC) are equivalent to the absolute logistic costs per piece (LC) divided by the product's value:

(5) $rLC = \dfrac{LC}{PV} = \dfrac{TC + IC}{PV}$

Similar to the logistics reach the mathematical formulation of the transportation costs has to consider the influence of weight and volume. Both cases can be

---

[15] See Cooper (1993), p. 14.
[16] See Ballou (1999), p. 64.

attributed to the same system of shipping rates. The freight rate (α) is related to a single volume or weight unit and therefore allows a multiplication:

(6) $\quad TC = f(W, V) \cdot \alpha$

The inventory costs are the product's value and the transportation time-related interest rate (β):

(7) $\quad IC = PV \cdot \beta$

Thus the relative logistic costs amount

(8) $\quad rLC = \dfrac{TC + IC}{PV} = \dfrac{f(W, V) \cdot \alpha + PV \cdot \beta}{PV}$

Between the logistics reach and the relative logistics costs exists the following relation:

(9)
$$\begin{aligned}
rLC &= \frac{LC}{PV} = \frac{f(W, V) \cdot \alpha + PV \cdot \beta}{PV} \\
&= \frac{f(W, V) \cdot \alpha}{PV} + \beta \\
&= \frac{\alpha}{\dfrac{PV}{f(W, V)}} + \beta \\
&= \frac{1}{LR} \cdot \alpha + \beta
\end{aligned}$$

The examination of the second and the third derivation of the logistics reach reveals a strict monotonously declining function.[17] The parameters α and β determine the shape of the graph, which runs steeper with an increasing freight rate α. However, an increase in the interest rate β moves the graph away from the origin. In both cases the logistics reach must rise to realize the same relative logistics costs again. With increasing logistics reach the graph approximates to the parameter β, which can be interpreted as the minimum relative logistics costs. For the evaluation of the logistics costs different standards of comparison are

---

[17] This calculation stands in contradiction to a cost hypothesis which is presented in several logistics books. Heskett et al. (1973), p. 48, and Ballou (1999), p. 63, suppose increasing relative inventory costs and declining relative transportation costs due to a rising logistics reach. Presumably they divide the logistics costs by the product's price and regard the price and the product's value as independent from each other. Therefore the graph of the relative logistics costs shows a U-form with an unambiguous minimum. But in almost every case rising value leads to rising prices and in several cases value and price are identical, e.g. in procurement processes. Besides, logistics reach, increasing because of a reduction in weight or volume, does not effect the inventory costs. Thus the relative logistic costs also decline.

available, e.g. the average logistic costs per product unit of a particular industry or product-specific upper limits of logistics costs. A common limit is the condition that products produced abroad should not be higher in price - inclusive logistics costs - than products manufactured in the home country.

The idea of logistics reach bases on the consideration that with rising value of a product the relative logistics costs decline. Hence, with increasing value a product can be charged higher logistics costs at the same level of relative costs. Vice versa the same level of relative logistic costs can be obtained by different logistics reaches depending on the parameters α and β. Both parameters reflect the cost structure of different means of transportation. The choice between two alternatives, in the global context e.g. the choice between air and sea transportation[18], can be supported by the logistics reach. This is shown in the following example: While a function representing the option of air transportation includes a higher freight rate α, the option of sea transportation is characterized by a higher interest rate β due to longer transportation times. For sea transportation a freight rate $\alpha_1 = 20$, and a transportation time-related interest rate $\beta_1 = 0,016$ (equivalent to an interest rate p.a. of 10% and a transportation time of 60 days) is assumed. The air transportation distinguishes a freight rate $\alpha_2 = 50$ and an interest rate $\beta_2 = 0,001$ (interest rate p.a. 10%, transportation time 4 days). Figure 3 shows the shapes of the function for sea and air transportation.[19] The logistics reach for the intersection of both functions can be identified in the following way:

$$(10) \quad LR = \frac{\alpha_2 - \alpha_1}{\beta_1 - \beta_2} = \frac{50 - 20}{0,016 - 0,001} = 2000$$

This results in relative logistics costs of 2.6% of the product's value. Above and below the intersection point, the respective parts of the functions represent the favourable cost situation, which combines the logistics reach with the lower relative logistics costs. Thus, in the example, air transportation is preferred for goods with a logistics reach of at least 2000. Sea transportation is suitable for goods having a logistics reach of less than 2000.

For logistics management of global supply chains, the conducted cost analysis giving advice for the choice between air and sea transportation has not only operative relevance. Sea or air transportation stand for the decision between the principle of cost degression and the principle of lead-time reduction and its strategic implication for the network configuration. For example, the advantages of air transportation can only be taken, if a centralization of inventory and an adequate design of facilities and processes are implemented. In this context, the principle of lead-time reduction is more important than the principle of cost degression. Instead, cost degression is the decisive principle for logistics processes

---

[18] See Lewis et al. (1956).
[19] For this example value and weight are combined: $f(W,V) = W + V$.

basing on sea transportation. Therefore the physical attributes of logistics goods take influence on the entire configuration of the global supply chain's logistics network.

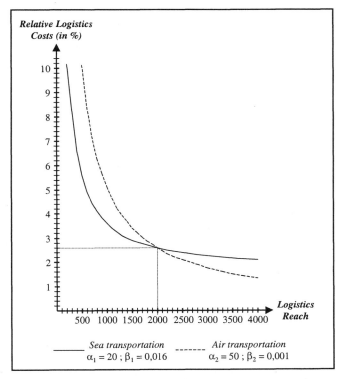

Figure 3: Logistics Reach and Logistics Costs of Sea and Air Transportation

4 The Influence of a Product's Logistics Reach on the Configuration of a Global Logistics Network

4.1 The Centralization of the Logistics Network

The configuration of a logistics network bases on three interdependent decisions, all influenced by the logistics reach of its products: the degree of centralization, the segmentation of the network by postponement strategies and the structure of the logistics processes as direct or indirect processes.[20]

Its vertical and horizontal dimension can describe the degree of a network's centralization. While the vertical dimension encompasses the number of logistic tiers across the network, e.g. a central warehouse, regional warehouses, distribution warehouses, the horizontal dimension describes the number of logistic facilities located within each tier, e.g. the number of distribution warehouses. Provided that the range of products is similar for every logistics facility, a reduction of the facilities in form of vertical centralization as well as in form of a horizontal centralization leads to lower inventory costs.[21] But at the same time the transportation costs increase: A vertical centralization prevents the utilization of those means of transportation that can convey high transportation volumes at low transportation costs to a warehouse close to the customer. A horizontal centralization, e.g. the reduction of the number of distribution warehouses, rises the distances between supplying and ordering facilities. However, preconditions for the centralization of a logistics network are sufficient delivery flexibilities and short delivery times responding to the customer's demands. So not only the costs of means of transportation play an important role, but also their performance. If the demanded delivery time is within the range of the feasible delivery time, a centralization might be possible. Demanded delivery times which are not feasible for technological reasons force the network's decentralization, e.g. by establishing warehouses close to the customer.

Both aspects, costs and performance, are of great importance for the configuration of a global supply chain's logistics network. Products with a high logistics reach allowing an efficient transportation by air freight lead to a centralized logistics network. But also with products of high logistics reach, increasing requirements for delivery time and delivery flexibility can affect the network's decentralization. Products with low logistics reach are actually excluded from a centralized stock keeping due to low flexibility and high delivery times of sea transportation. Here, decentralization by establishing distribution warehouses close to the customer is unavoidable.

4.2 Segmentation of the Logistics Network

The segmentation divides the logistics network into a number of sections. For each section a different approach of logistics planning and control can be implemented suiting exactly the requirements of a particular section. A very important approach for the segmentation is the principles of postponement. Postponement principles refer to the close relation between the costs of risk and

---

[20] Pfohl (1994), p. 139.
[21] Pfohl (1994), p. 142-143.

uncertainty and the differentiation of products by attributes, time and region.[22] On the condition, that production or logistics processes can be postponed until a specified order is available, the number of faults due to uncertainty, e.g. material shortages or surplus transportation capacities, can be reduced.

The postponement of logistics processes replaces forecast-related activities by order-related activities. A storage or transportation activity should only be launched at a point of time, when the underlying order is known in its specific qualitative and quantitative attributes. Starting with the point of consumption, an utmost number of logistic tiers should work order-related. The interface between order-related and forecast-related processes is called the order-penetration point. The farther away the order-penetration point is located from the point of consumption, the lower will be the amount of inventory which can be concentrated in one or a few facilities of the logistics network. Order-related processes should be highly responsive, leading to higher transportation costs especially in the case of long distances. Besides, with a rising number of transports the volume of each transport declines. Thus, the postponement of logistics processes is primarily suitable for products with high logistics reach.

Strategies of production postponement strive to shift the specification of products and materials to the latest possible point in time. Compared with the logistics postponement, the postponement of production processes has an impact on the location of the order-penetration point in the opposite way. The closer the order-penetration point is located to the point of consumption, the lower the level of inventory will be, because less specified and in case of order cancellation obsolete material has to be kept in store. Thus, postponement allows a reduction of stocks even if a low logistics reach of a product causes long delivery times. However, the postponement of production reduces production's economies of scale, so that this postponement strategy is not profitable under all conditions.

4.3 The Structure of the Logistics Processes

Logistics processes can be established as single-tier or as multi-tier processes. A single-tier process enables a direct material flow from the point of origin to the point of consumption without additional warehousing. However, if it is necessary to interrupt the material flows for consolidation purposes, the material flows between supplier and customer will be ensured by multi-tier logistics processes. The tendency to either a direct or indirect structure of logistics processes refers again to a product's logistics reach and the efficient means of transportation. For products with high logistics reach, which can be shipped efficiently in small transportation lots by airfreight, consolidation activities have little relevance, whereas sea transportation requires both temporal consolidation activities and

---

[22] See Pagh, Cooper (1998), p. 13-14, Bowersox, Closs (1996), p. 472-475.

spatial consolidation activities. Temporal consolidation is crucial in order to gather the necessary transportation volume, spatial consolidation ensures an efficient operation of precarriages and onward-carriages.

Between the direct, air freight related structure of material flows on the one hand and the indirect sea freight related structure on the other hand exist some intermediate structures:

1. Combined structures: In the global context, for products with low logistics reach only a combination of direct and indirect material flows is conceivable: Long lead-times make a global logistics network vulnerable to any kind of disturbance, e.g. delivery delays, planning mistakes or fluctuations in demand. Therefore, in particular cases aircraft transportation is inevitable also for a low logistics reach in order to prevent production shortfalls.

2. Air transportation with consolidation: Creative solutions may lead to currently uncommon ways of air transportation for products with low logistics reach beside the traditional mixed air cargo. Using chartered freight aircrafts reduces transportation costs per unit and lead-times decline tremendously, compared with sea transportation. Normally, this approach needs the cooperation of several suppliers in order to realize an efficient loading. Therefore, consolidation processes and indirect material flows become more important.

All in all, two fundamental ways of configuring a global logistics network can be distinguished. Products with high logistics reach indicate a central configuration: The order-penetration point is located as far as possible from the final customer. Direct material flows operated by fast and expensive means of transportations connect the internal and external customers in the global supply chain. In these logistics networks, the just-in-time concept with its principle of lead-time reduction dominates in order to achieve the logistic objectives of global supply chain management. For products with a low logistics reach a decentral network configuration is more likely. Material flows are organized indirectly, stocks, being partially in transit due to slower transportation, are dispersed among the several network facilities. Here, for the configuration of the logistics network, the principle of cost degression known from global sourcing is more important than lead-time reductions to attain economies of scale. The logistics objectives, the stabilization of material flows, the reduction of inventory, the reduction of lead-times and the improvement of flexibility and reliability, are more difficult to achieve. For example, inventory can only be reduced to the level that still guarantees logistics efficiency and the fulfillment of the customer's requests.

5 Conclusion

The integration of global sourcing and just-in-time is a challenge for global supply chain management. Important factors for the efficient configuration of the global supply chain's logistics network are the value, the weight and the volume of a product. All three factors form a ratio, called the logistics reach, which explains a product's suitability for global logistics processes. A high logistics reach indicates good ability for global logistics: Here, fast but expensive means of transportation can be used leading to centralized networks with direct material flows. The order-penetration point is located far away from the final point of consumption, so that most processes work order-related. Contrarily, a low logistics reach indicates a more difficult situation: The necessary reduction of transportation costs requires cheap but slow means of transportation. Therefore the logistics network should be decentralized with indirect material flows utilizing consolidation advantages.

6 References

Ballou, R. H. (1999): Business Logistics Management – Planning, Organizing, and Controlling the Supply Chain, 4th Edition, Prentice Hall, Upper Saddle River (New Jersey).

Bartlett, Ch. A., Ghoshal, S. (1995): Transnational Management – Text, Cases, and Readings in Cross Border Management, 2nd Edition, Irwin, Chicago.

Bowersox, D. J., Closs, D. J. (1996): Logistical Management – The Integrated Supply Chain Process, McGraw-Hill, New York.

Cooper, J. C. (1993): Logistics Strategies for Global Businesses, in: International Journal of Physical Distribution & Logistics Management, Vol. 23, No. 4 (1993), p. 12-23.

Council of Logistics Management (1998): CLM's Definition Of Logistics, URL: http://www.clm1.org.

Delfmann, W., Albers, S. (2000): Supply Chain Management in the Global Context, Working Paper No. 102, Dept. of General Management, Business Planning and Logistics of the University of Cologne, Cologne.

Dicken, P. (1998): Global Shift – Transforming the World Economy, 3rd Edition, Chapman, London.

Dornier, Ph.-P., Ernst, R., Fender, M., Kouvelis, P. (1998): Global Operations and Logistics – Text and Cases, Wiley, New York.

Fawcett, S. E., Birou, L. M. (1992): Exploring the Logistics Interface between Global and JiT Sourcing, in: International Journal of Physical Distribution & Logistics Management, Vol. 22, No. 1 (1992), p. 3-14.

Handfield, R. B., Nichols, E. L. (1999): Introduction to Supply Chain Management, Prentice Hall, Upper Saddle River (New Jersey).

Heskett, J. L., Glaskowsky, N. A., Ivie, R. M. (1973): Business Logistics – Physical Distribution and Materials Management, 2nd Edition, Ronald, New York.

Lambert, D. M., Cooper, M. C., Pagh, J. D. (1998): Supply Chain Management: Implementation Issues and Research Opportunities, in: International Journal of Logistics Management, Vol. 9, No. 2 (1998), p. 1-19.

Lewis, H. T., Culliton, J. W., Steele, J. D. (1956): The Role of Air Freight in Physical Distribution, Harvard University, Boston (Massachusetts).

Pagh, J. D., Cooper, M. C. (1998): Supply Chain Postponement and Speculation Strategies: How to Choose the Right Strategy, in: Journal of Business Logistics, Vol. 19, No. 2 (1998), p. 13-33.

Pfohl, H.-Chr. (1994): Logistikmanagement – Funktionen und Instrumente (Logistics Management – Functions and Instruments), Springer, Berlin.

Porter, M. E. (1985): Competitive Advantage – Creating and Sustaining Superior Performance, Free Press, New York.

Porter, M. E. (1986): Competition in Global Industries: A Conceptual Framework, in: Porter, M. E. (ed.): Competition in Global Industries, Harvard Business School Press, Boston (Massachusetts), p. 15-60.

Schary, Ph. B., Skjøtt-Larsen, T. (1995): Managing the Global Supply Chain, Handelshøjskolens, Copenhagen.

Managing Stocks in Supply Chains: Modeling and Issues

Layek Abdel-Malek, Giovanni Valentini, Lucio Zavanella

1	Introduction	326
2	Background	326
3	Considerations of Environment Uncertainty	330
4	Evaluating the Performance of CS Policy	331
5	Conclusions	334
6	References	334

Summary:
The paper presents a policy for inventory management in simple supply chains consisting of one buyer and a single vendor. The method is based on consignment stocks. A model is developed and a performance satisfaction indicator is introduced. In its development, the Consignment Stock model considers the uncertainty stemming from demand fluctuation and the unpredictability of lead times. Experiments were conducted to compare the performance of the Consignment Stock policy to some of those existing in literature.

Keywords:
Inventories, Stock Management

1 Introduction

Recent research showed how optimal production and transport quantities might be calculated for the most common Supply Chains consisting of a single-buyer and a single-vendor[1]. The results are interesting because they give the optimal solution to the problem and as a consequence practical situations may be addressed. Nevertheless, in the previous models two basic assumptions were made: first the demand is deterministic and second the supply lead times are predictable. When these hypotheses do not hold, the model must be adapted to the more realistic situation of fluctuating market demand and stochastic transport times.

In this paper, we analyse a Supply Chain management technique that considers the aforementioned randomness in both demand and transport times. The technique is designated as "Consignment Stock". Earlier, Valentini and Zavanella (2000) analyzed this concept in a case study in the area of manufacturing of automotive components, where considerable performance improvement has been obtained. This policy can be regarded as the equivalent of the classical (s, S) policy in the well-documented inventory control literature. Extending this policy to supply chain environment seems to provide benefits in containing stock costs as well as promptness in responding to market demand.

The work highlights the main advantages and features of the technique, with reference to the aforementioned industrial case study. To show the advantages of the technique, an experimental comparison is carried out with the single-buyer single-vendor situation. The experiments render necessary insights into the applicability of this technique and how the different variables affect the performance of the entire company-supplier system.

2 Background

The Consignment Stock management of inventory requires a continuous collaboration between the company and its suppliers. The agreement between the two parties is based on the supplier ability to maintain for the company a stock level ranging between a minimum level s and a maximum level S. This fact presents a significant impact on the information available to the vendor, as shown in Fig.1. The company picks up raw materials daily, according to market demand, and the picked up materials are paid to the supplier according to the agreement

---

[1] See e.g. Goyal, Gupta (1989); Hill (1997).

arranged, hypothetically determined by daily frequency. The information concerning the consumption trend is constantly refreshed and immediately transferred to the vendor-supplier.

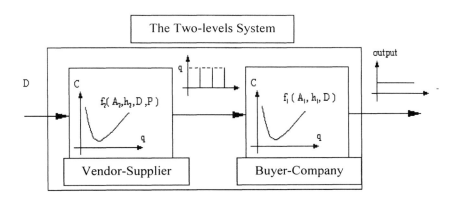

Figure 1: The Buyer-Vendor Situation

As Fig.1 describes, the Consignment Stock allows the supplier to receive directly market demand D, without the filter usually introduced by the buyer. To illustrate this point, let us consider the situation of a non-collaborative relationship between the buyer and its supplier. In this case, the buyer organises its orders according to the classical economic Order Quantity (EOQ), i.e. on the basis of its order emission cost (A_1), its holding cost (h_1) and under the assumption of constant market demand D. As a consequence, the order quantity q presents the well known optimal value (q_1) which is a function of A_1, h_1 and D. Likewise, the supplier identifies its Economic Production Quantity (EPQ) according to its machine set-up costs (A_2) and holding costs (h_2). Also the production quantity (i.e. the batch size) presents an optimal value (q_2). In comparison with the buyer situation, the supplier must also take account of its production rate P, which should obviously be larger than D.

The situation is different when the entire two-level system is considered, i.e. when the vendor and the buyer are regarded as a whole. In such a case, the minimum of the total costs (set-up, ordering and holding) may differ from both q_1 and q_2. In the literature, Hill's model (1997) develops the optimal production quantity q' for such a system and its minimum cost C(q'):

$$q' = \sqrt{((A_2 + nA_1)\frac{D}{n})/(h_2(\frac{D}{P} + \frac{(P-D)n}{2P}) + \frac{h_1 - h_2}{2})}$$

$$C(q') = (A_2 + nA_1)\frac{D}{nq} + h_2(\frac{Dq}{P} + \frac{(P-D)nq}{2P}) + (h_1 - h_2)\frac{q}{2}$$

In further contributions by Hill, the optimal solution is also searched according to some variables defining the quantities to deliver to the supplier, i.e.

$$q_i = q \cdot k^{i-1}$$

where i is the index for the i-th delivery and:

q: size of the first delivery of the batch produced by the vendor;

n: number of deliveries in which the batch produced is divided to transport it to the buyer;

k: coefficient introduced to determine the ratio between the successive quantities delivered and, of course, for $k = 1$ all deliveries are identical sized.

From this brief description offered, one can see Consignment Stock approach still works in the direction of a renewed and reinforced collaboration between producers and their suppliers. This collaboration is necessary for acquiring competitive advantages in a dynamic and selective market[2]. Also it is typically implicit in several managing techniques such as Quality Insurance, Co-Makership and Just In Time manufacturing[3].

Because of the common agreement described before, the company inventories are continuously supervised and replenished by the supplier, up to the situation where the company-buyer does not control its own inventory levels anymore. In addition, costs determined by eventual stockout may be reversed to the vendor-supplier, because of contract penalties. In this case, the supplier gains a better perception of its customer requirements: less stocking costs are incurred and the continuous evolution of market demand is directly received due to Electronic Data Interchange (EDI) interface[4]. The most evident benefits induced by Consignment Stock are summed up in Table 1.

The reduced stock represents an advantage to the vendor only from the warehousing cost point of view, as items are not stored in its own premise. As far as investments are concerned, it should be highlighted that the capital invested in items production remains charged to the vendor up to the utilisation time. Basically, this fact may be positive for the entire system, as it allows "freeing" the capital of the last ring of the chain (the buyer-company). On the other hand, the position of the vendor-supplier may be safeguarded by imposing a time limit to the payment of items delivered, regardless of their utilisation in production cycles.

---

[2] See Dyer, Ouchi (1993).
[3] See e.g.: Donovan, Maresca (1998), pp.21.1-21.27.; Clark (1989); Hay (1988).
[4] See Lee, Padmanabhan, Whang (1997).

Aspect Considered	Vendor-Supplier	Buyer-Company
Inventory	Reduced stock	Guaranteed availability of the raw material; inventory control carried out by the supplier
Production	Possibility of organising production in different ways (e.g. to satisfy other buyers' demand)	
Capital	Immediate payment at item utilization	Payment limited to material utilized
Holding Costs	Reduction due to the decreased occupation of space in warehouses	Reduction due to lower invested capital, mainly charged to the supplier
Others	Increased collaboration between the chain actors; EDI interface	

Table 1: Benefits Induced by Consignment Stock Policy

The reduced stock represents an advantage to the vendor only from the warehousing cost point of view, as items are not stored its own premises. As far as investments are concerned, it should be highlighted that the capital invested in items production remains charged to the vendor up to the utilisation time. Basically, this fact may be positive for the entire system, as it allows "freeing" the capital of the last ring of the chain (the buyer-company). On the other hand, the position of the vendor-supplier may be safeguarded by imposing a time limit on the payment of items delivered, regardless of their utilisation in production cycles.

Consignment Stock performance is also linked to the selection of some critical parameters, as s and S levels are, and to the reliability of the data electronically exchanged. As far as the former parameter is concerned, opposite tendencies may emerge during the bargaining phase: they are summed up in Fig.2.

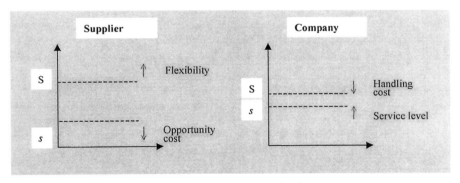

Figure 2: Different "Pressures" on (s; S) Levels Determination

Using the notation of Fig.2, the buyer will be inclined to consider s level as a safety stock, essentially paid by the vendor who, on his turn, will try to keep it as low as possible (in limiting conditions, $s = 0$). Opposite positions refer to S level, as the vendor will ask for a larger space to store the material produced (theoretically, the upper limit is represented by the vendor-supplier EPQ), while the buyer will try to limit the holding costs incurred while storing material in its own warehouses. It is evident that the negotiation on levels represents a critical phase, during which the relative strength of the two actors should be laid aside, favouring the search for the maximum benefit of the entire system.

3 Considerations of Environment Uncertainty

In the previous section, we described some of the benefits related to Consignment Stock adoption. The model by Hill gives optimal results under the EOQ and EPQ hypotheses already mentioned, i.e. constant demand, order and holding costs assigned. In such an environment, it is clear that Consignment Stock cannot outperform Hill's model results, because inventories are moved downstream in anticipation. Furthermore, it should be mentioned that when Consignment Stock is adopted:

1. The vendor maintains the property of the goods stocked in the buyer's warehouse up to their utilisation time (this determines a reduction of the buyer's holding cost, as payments are delayed).
2. EDI is used (this reduces drastically the fixed order costs).

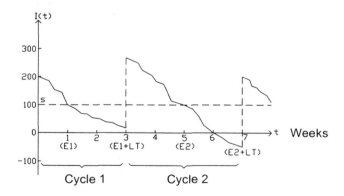

Figure 3: Stockout Event

In our analysis of the Consignment Stock, we will focus on situations where the deterministic conditions necessary for applying Hill's model do not prevail and the two aforementioned point effects are not pronounced. We will, therefore, be comparing the performance of CS model to that of Hill's in a stochastic environment. Generally speaking, the major effect determined by these uncertain conditions is represented by stockout, i.e. the buyer's inability to promptly satisfy demand because of stock absence. This fact is usually described as in Fig.3, which makes reference to a reorder point s = 100 [items] and a lead time LT = 2 [weeks].

It should be mentioned that the larger the market demand during the lead time LT, the larger the stockout probability. To solve this problem, the ordinary approach is to increase the reorder point s, which can be regarded as a safety stock. Safety stock is kept by the companies to face stockout events. One can see that an increased safety stock leads to the downstream movement of inventories. This is similar to the CS approach.

4 Evaluating the Performance of CS Policy

In the following, we shall compare Hill's model performance to the CS one. To compare these two approaches, we introduce S_L as a level of service indicator. The level of service is determined by $B_{ss,i}$, the number of items in stockout during the i-th cycle. Consequently, during one year, the expected number of item in stockout per cycle will be $E(B_{ss,i})$. Therefore, the total number of items in stockout per year will be $E(B_{ss,i}) \cdot C_y$, where C_y is the number of cycles per year.

Thus, the level of service is expressed by:

$$S_L = 1 - \frac{E(B_{ss,i})}{E(D)} \cdot C_y$$

where $E(D)$ is the mean of the annual demand.

The following Tables 2 and 3 show data obtained through a large set of simulation experiments carried out for different values of variance of the yearly demand. Other parameters are extracted from Goyal (1995) and Hill's (1997 and 1999) examples, i.e.:

A_2 = 400 [$/set-up] and A_1 = 25 [$/delivery];

h_2 = 4 [$/item/year] and h_1 = 5 [$/item/year];

P = 3200 [item/year] and D = 1000 [item/year].

Demand variance	Hill's model		Consignment stock		Cost difference
	Safety stocks	Costs	Safety stocks	Costs	
0	0,000	1903	0,000	1963	-60
10	2,601	1916	0,977	1968	-52
40	5,685	1932	2,277	1974	-43
90	8,87	1948	3,676	1981	-34
160	12,21	1964	5,132	1989	-24
250	15,57	1981	6,646	1996	-15
360	19,00	1998	8,18	2004	-6
490	22,54	2016	9,75	2012	4
640	26,09	2034	11,33	2020	14
810	29,64	2051	12,95	2028	24
1000	33,25	2070	14,56	2036	34

Table 2: Service Level Equal to 98%: Safety Stocks and Related Costs.

It should be emphasized that a preliminary simulation analysis allowed the identification of the optimal shipment policy, under the hypothesis of identical quantity delivered per transport, i.e. q. For both Hill's model ($q = 110$) and Consignment Stock policy ($q = 107$), the optimal number of deliveries n is equal to 5. In particular, the minimum obtained for the Consignment Stock approach refers to the condition where the last three deliveries are postponed, so as to maintain the buyer's stock at a maximum level of 181 items. Of course, the batch produced by the vendor will be $Q = n \cdot q$.

Demand variance	Hill's model		Consignment stock		Cost difference
	Safety stocks	Costs	Safety stocks	Costs	
0	0,000	1903	0,000	1963	-60
10	2,213	1914	0,699	1966	-52
40	4,929	1928	1,757	1972	-44
90	7,80	1942	2,930	1978	-35
160	10,82	1957	4,184	1984	-27
250	13,90	1973	5,490	1990	-18
360	16,99	1988	6,83	1997	-9
490	20,19	2004	8,17	2004	0
640	23,41	2020	9,57	2011	9
810	26,62	2036	11,03	2018	18
1000	30,00	2053	12,43	2025	28

Table 3: Service Level Equal to 94%: Safety Stocks and Related Costs.

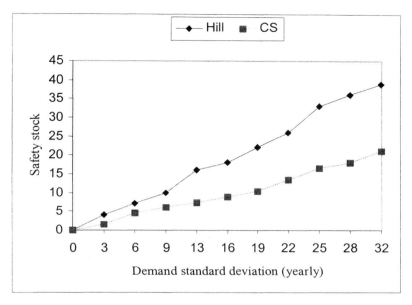

Figure 4: Safety Stock to be Introduced to Guarantee $S_L=100\%$

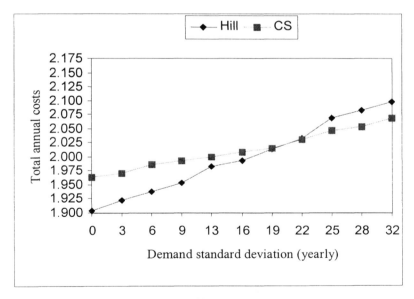

Figure 5: Costs Charged to Guarantee $S_L=100\%$

The results show that as the variance in the demand increases, the service level S_L obtained by applying the CS policy is higher than that of Hill's model. As shown in Fig.4, for a service level of 100%, the CS policy requires less safety stock than that needed for the same level as determined by Hill's model. Further, Fig.5 exhibits the behaviour of the cost versus the randomness in demand, as expressed by the variance. The threshold for the standard deviation in the demand is identified. As can be seen, as the standard deviation of the demand increases, the CS policy presents a lower cost than Hill's approach (data offered for the Consignment Stock approach refer to the condition where the last three deliveries are postponed).

5 Conclusions

In this paper, we presented an inventory policy for Supply Chain designated as Consignment Stock methodology. A model for the Consignment Stock policy was developed for the single buyer and single vendor case. The model takes into account the random nature of the demand. We compared the results of applying the introduced model to the existing deterministic approaches. The conducted experiments showed that the application of the CS policies reduces the system's cost and lead time stockout in most situations. The CS performance is particularly remarkable when the variance in the demand is large.

Acknowledgements.

Study supported by the Italian National Council for Research (CNR) by grant #11516/2001. The research assistantship of Antonio Nicolis, graduated at the Università di Brescia, is gratefully acknowledged.

6 References

Clark, K. B. (1989): Project Scope and Project Performance: The Effects of Part Strategy and Supplier Involvement on Product Development, in: Management Science, Vol. 35, No. 1 (1989), p. 247-263.

Donovan, J. A., Maresca, F. P. (1998): Supplier Relations, in: Juran J. M., Godfrey, A. B. (ed), Juran's Quality Handbook, 5th ed., McGraw Hill, New York, p. 21.1-21.27.

Dyer, J. H., Ouchi, W. G. (1993): Japanese-Style Partnerships: Giving Companies a Competitive Edge, in: Sloan Management Review, Vol. 34, Fall (1993), p. 51-63.

Goyal, S. K. (1988): A Joint Economic Lot Size Model for Purchase and Vendor: A Comment, in: Decision Sciences, Vol. 19 (1988), p. 236-241.

Goyal, S. K., Gupta, Y. P. (1989): Integrated Inventory Models: The Buyer-Vendor Coordination, in: European Journal of Operational Research, Vol. 41 (1989), p. 261-269.

Goyal, S. K. (1995): A One-Vendor Multi-Buyer Integrated Inventory Model: A Comment, in: European Journal of Operational Research, 82 (1995), p. 209-210.

Hay, E. J. (1988): The Just-in-Time Breakthrough: Implementing the new Manufacturing Basics, John Wiley & Sons, New York.

Hill, R. M. (1997): The Single-Vendor Single-Buyer Integrated Production-Inventory Model with a Generalised Policy, in: European Journal of Operational Research, Vol. 97 (1997), p. 493-499.

Hill, R. M. (1999).:The Optimal Production and Shipment Policy for the Single-Vendor Single-Buyer Integrated Production-Inventory Model, in: International Journal of Production Research, Vol. 37 (1999), p. 2463-2475.

Lee, H. L., Padmanabhan, V., Whang, S. (1997): Information Distortion in a Supply Chain; the Bullwhip Effect, in: Management Science, Vol. 43, No. 4 (1997), p. 546-558.

Valentini, G., Zavanella, L. (2000): The Consignment Stock Management of Inventories: an Industrial Case", Proceedings of the 11th Int. Symposium on Inventories, Budapest (H), August 20-25th.

Some Optimization Tools to Improve Manufacturing and Supply Chain Performance

Riurik Skomorokhov

1	Introduction	338
2	Traditional Production Management Approaches	340
3	Sequencing Products and Structuring Workstations	342
4	Efficiency of Better Sequencing Products and Structuring Capacities	345
5	Conclusion	346
6	References	348

Summary:
This paper portrays a new approach to manufacturing and supply chain management for low and mid-volume machine-building manufacturing companies based on system optimization. The objectives are to achieve the minimum possible costs and best possible deliveries. Therefore, the supply chain is treated as related job shops, so the existing models of job shop scheduling can be applied to improve supply chain performance.

Keywords:
supply management, manufacturing management, manufacturing management technology, system optimization, manufacturing and supply chain performance

1 Introduction

Supply chains are formed by connected companies. Often as a starting point for improving supply chain management and supply chain performance, optimization techniques are applied.[1] Therefore, it is necessary to identify the varying parameters that influence supply chain performance. From there, supply chain efficiency and flexibility can be determined.

The main idea of supply chain management is a system approach covering all related processes. To realize a supply chain wide optimization of all processes, the most effective optimization criterion (the objective function), the appropriate optimization problems and the most effective tools for solving the problems derived this way must be identified. The supply chain is therefore treated as a single manufacturing entity, comparable to connected job shops within a single company.

To provide system wide and coordinated optimization in supply management, a single objective function for optimization during all the stages of supply management should be used. Without such an objective function (goal) it is almost impossible to determine the most effective techniques in achieving this goal in manufacturing systems and supply chain management.

A general goal of manufacturing and supply management is meeting demand with minimum possible costs, on time and at minimum possible (short) cycle times. To meet demand during the first stage of manufacturing management, i.e. aggregate planning, the desired capacities need to be determined. Several variables can be altered to change the medium range production capacity from month to month. Among these variables are: (1) size of work force, (2) use of overtime, and (3) use of inventories, backlog, subcontractors, and leaving demand unfilled to buffer the difference between production capacity and variations in demand.[2]

To meet demand within aggregate manufacturing planning we should determine not only the desired capacities values, but their balance along the supply chain. An ideal balance of capacities can be expressed as the following correlation for each used process r: $E_r = F_r$, where - F_r available time for production at the process r, r $\in l = \{1, ..., l\}$; E_r - labor requirements (sum of labor and machine standard times) for all products scheduled for manufacturing within this time period.

---

[1] See Shapiro (2001).
[2] See textbooks on operations or supply chain management, e.g. Chase, Aquliano, Jacobs (2001); Slack, Chambers, Johnston (2001).

At the same time, existing methods, especially synchronous manufacturing, optimized production technology (OPT)[3] and Theory of Constraints (TOC)[4] state that unbalanced capacities would be preferable. Yet, for which specific r should we have the unbalance, and what is the best possible value of a general unbalance? What kind of the unbalance is preferable for a specific r; $U_r < 0$ or $U_r > 0$, where $U_r = E_r - F_r$? Therefore, we suppose that there is not enough theoretical and empirical data confirming the position that unbalanced capacities are preferable to a balance of the time available and the time needed.

Considering synchronized manufacturing, Optimized Production Technology (OPT) other contradictions can be observed which do not allow realization of a strong system approach to optimization in manufacturing and supply management. Definitions of the synchronous manufacturing are: 1. system of production planning and control in which all parts of an organization work together to achieve the organization's goals;[5] 2. the entire production process working together in harmony to achieve the goals of the firm. Synchronous manufacturing logic attempts to coordinate all resources so that they work together, are in harmony, or are synchronized.[6] These definitions do not provide a clear analytical expression. Having this, we would be able to estimate basic features of the effectiveness and the efficiency of synchronized manufacturing.

Rather than balancing capacities, the flow of products through manufacturing and supply chain systems should be balanced. However, flow or schedule parameters depend on capacities and, as will be demonstrated below, on the structure of capacities available.

There is evidence that when the desired time for production and common labor requirements of products are given, scheduling the minimum value of common manufacturing lead time (CMLT) in manufacturing for all the products allows obtaining minimum costs.

At the same time, in aggregate planning and master production scheduling (MPS) a time function is not taken into account explicitly. Traditionally, it is assumed that the manufacturing lead time (MLT) both of any single product and CMLT do not exceed the length of the planned period. In other words, the length of the planned period covers MLT for all the products and CMLT. If CMLT depends on a sequence of manufacturing different products, we must take into account all possible sequences (when available time for production is given). This leads to different CMLT and idle times of workstations, and as a result, different cost, productivity, inventory, and even delivery times. However, it is assumed

---

[3] See Goldratt, Cox (1992).
[4] See Dettmer (1997).
[5] See Gaither (1992).
[6] Chase, Aquilano, Jacobs (2001).

subsequently, that all relevant costs are included and no idle times or other waste of related resources are part of the initial data for manufacturing planning.

Hence, a time function needs to be included at the aggregate planning stage to obtain effective unbalance values $\forall\, r \in 1$. This would allow creating the necessary conditions for obtaining minimum CMLT during all stages of manufacturing in the supply chain.

2 Traditional Production Management Approaches

Traditional objectives of master production scheduling (MPS) are:

1. Scheduling end items (products) to be completed as promised to customers.
2. Avoiding overloading or underloading the production facility so that production capacity is efficiently utilized and low costs result.

Tools such as MRPII and related software are based on backward scheduling. This scheduling approach does not allow varying the manufacturing sequence of different products. Synchronous manufacturing and OPT are based on forward scheduling, but they are not aimed at obtaining the minimum value of CMLT in the explicit form and determining the optimum sequence of manufacturing different products.

Hence, there is evidence that an objective function for system optimization in manufacturing and supply chain management aiming at the simultaneous improvement of the stated objectives has to based on the minimum CMLT, which is not done explicitly in existing approaches.

Dates of beginning and finishing the manufacture of different products at all stages of manufacturing allow to determining real dynamics of inventory and are the basis for decision making in supplying, manufacturing and delivering. The exactness of determining the dates stipulates efficiency both of using manufacturing resources and meeting demand decisions on the whole.

The problem of effective manufacturing planning in a supply chain demands taking into account that there are different manufacturers in the chain and that their capabilities are different. Several tools for coordination in the supply chain exist.[7] Still, it is proposed that improving coordination and supply chain performance can be reached through a different approach in manufacturing scheduling. A major problem of supply chain management for low and mid-volume machine-building companies is the number of different end items delivered to final consumers.

---

[7] See Handfield, Nichols (1999); Chopra, Meindl (2001).

To create necessary conditions for better supply chain performance at the stage of manufacturing management, the focal manufacturer determines the manufacturing dates for all end items. This implies the desired time interval for supplying raw materials, the dates for beginning assembly of each end item and the time interval for supplying parts, components and units bought.

The main optimization problem for operations scheduling in low and mid-volume machine-building manufacturing is the job shop scheduling problem. It is devoted to scheduling jobs only, i.e. to scheduling the processing stage of manufacturing. Yet, it is necessary to schedule processing and assembly stages jointly. Also, the job shop scheduling problem does not fit the goal of obtaining the minimum CMLT for all end items which would allow achieving the minimum manufacturing lead time for a single "end item.

There is another related shortcoming of job shop scheduling . The existing methods for solving it deal with a single function of operations (jobs) scheduling, specially the jobs sequencing, taking not into account other essential scheduling functions,[8] such as the allocation of jobs among interchangeable (parallel) workstations. Usually, parallel workstations are employed in manufacturing to allow fulfilling several orders and thus reducing manufacturing lead times.

After making the basic decisions to make or buy, choosing suppliers, aggregate manufacturing and capacities planning for each period, a model for job scheduling can be formulated. A certain number p of different products (end items) a, a $\in$ p = $\{1,..., p\}$ is given, each of which requires a different number m of original jobs i, i $\in$ m = $\{1,..., m\}$. Each job is successively processed by y technological operations g, g $\in$ y = $\{1, ..., y\}$, and the number of processing operations y_i is usually different for different jobs. Also given is a certain number of non-interchangeable processes (machines) l. Each process r, r $\in$ l = $\{1, ..., l\}$ comprises a different number n of interchangeable (parallel) workstations j, j $\in$ n = $\{1, ..., n\}$; each job may have its individual processing route (a different sequence of r for g) and the process r may repeat after a certain y. Furthermore, the processing time (labor and machine standards) $t_{a,i,g}$ $\forall$ a $\in$ p, $\forall$ i $\in$ m, $\forall$ g $\in$ y is given.[9] Finally, is the lot size of each product and job is given.

In the stage of manufacturing scheduling it is necessary to sequence all products p, into frameworks of any next single product a to sequence all jobs m_a and allocate them among interchangeable workstations $\forall$ a $\in$ p, $\forall$ g $\in$ y in a way to obtain the minimum value of CMLT. We can consider the formulation as a new and wider

---

[8] See Blazewich, Domschke, Pesch (1996).
[9] In a more common and complicated case, where differences in individual productivities of interchangeable workers engaged in some kinds of processes exist, the time to process a job is usually different for different interchangeable workstations.

statement of the job shop scheduling problem and call the problem a multi-step job shop.

The described model represents a typical situation in operations scheduling of low and mid-volume machine-building manufacturing as there are two basic and interrelated functions of scheduling, which we should take into account: sequencing and allocation. However, as noted above, the job shop scheduling problem takes into account the sequencing function only. The problem of sequencing and allocating jobs among interchangeable (parallel) workstations is the object of aother optimization problem – the problem of scheduling parallel machines.

For more effective operations scheduling in frameworks of multi-stage job shop we need to determine the best possible scheme for combining functions of jobs sequencing and their allocation among parallel workstations, particularly when taking into account (for some processes) different productivities of interchangeable (parallel) workstations stipulated by different individual productivities of workers engaged at them. In this case, we could use for some sequencing and primarily for allocating jobs, the so-called analytical (the Hungarian or the Mack's) methods of the assignment problem.[10] When taking into account different productivities of interchangeable (parallel) workstations the assignment problem is a multi-criteria one. Hence, the main objective function results by aiming at minimum total labor requirements for fulfilling jobs E' and minimum lead times within T', i.e., the maximum completion time.

Despite this multi-criterion nature of the assignment problem, analytical methods solve the problem as an uni-criterion and allow obtaining the optimal solution of the problem by the criterion of minimum E' or common costs of allocated jobs. This is true for a particular case only, when m ≤ n, where m - number of jobs, n - number of parallel workstations. However, the case of minimizing T' is rather complicated and relevant for operations scheduling at low and mid-volume machine-building companies. Finally, the analytical methods of the assignment problem are insensitive to changing precedence conditions, which play a very important role in real manufacturing and scheduling practices.[11]

3 Sequencing Products and Structuring Workstations

Low and mid-volume machine-building companies produce within each scheduled period different products. Yet, from a managerial viewpoint the most important issue is the different structure of their labor requirements. The structure of labor

---

[10] Skomorokhov (1991).
[11] Skomorokhov (1991).

requirements is much more variable for different products than the structure of workstations. Within a constant (given) scheduled period it is evident that there is a difference (imbalance) between the individual structure of labor requirements of any single product and the given (constant) structure of workstations. Our research demonstrated this situational incompatibility (sometimes quite significant) was one of the main reasons for potential wastes (bottlenecks, idles, etc.) in manufacturing and supply chain management, which led to increased costs, inventory, and delivery times. As a result, to organize both within a company and within a supply chain effectively, we need to obtain compatibility among the structure of workstations and labor requirements for all products.

The required compatibility can be achieved primarily through a simultaneous solution of the following optimization problems: the problem of determining an optimal (effective) manufacturing sequence of different products and the problem of determining an optimal (effective) structure of workstations. In general, not depending on the above, a varying sequence of manufacturing different products provides the opportunity for optimization.

Considering this, the optimal solution for the optimization problem is achieved by the criterion of the minimum CMLT for given (constant) E and N, where E = common labor requirements of all the products. However, the formulation and methods for solving the job shop scheduling problem aim at obtaining $T_a = T_{a,\,min}$, but this is clearly inadequate to obtain the minimum value of CMLT.

The interrelationship and interdependence between the structure of workstations (capacities) and products sequencing stipulate the necessity for solving the problems jointly. Such research addresses the following: 1. how does the sequencing influence CMLT; 2. what does variation of the structure of capacities or workstations allow to obtain concerning the minimum value of CMLT for given E and N and 3. what are the best possible values of balance for each r and $\forall\, r \in l$?

These questions can be answered only based on building operations schedules for different products depending on the above. Such schedules were built for four real products, when using scheduling schemes and methods aimed at achieving the minimum value of CMLT.

We will now consider the scheduling for four different end items (products). During scheduling we examined a large number of reasonable alternative structures for given (constant) E and N, and for each alternative structure we built operations schedules for all (p = 4! = 24) variants of the sequence of manufacturing the products and determined for each sequence the value of CMLT.

The parameters of the workstation structures investigated were closest to the labor requirements structure of all the products. Some of the simulation results are presented in Table 1, where T_g, T_s and T_a respectively are the greatest, the smallest, and the average values of the performance criterion (CMLT), in time units. These were chosen and calculated for all (p = 4! =24) values of CMLT obtained, and Δ and $\Delta(\%)$ are the minimum possible, for the given case, values of common absolute and relative difference (im balance) between structure of workstations and structure of labor requirements of all products. T_{min} is the exact analytical estimation of the minimum value of CMLT.

№ str.	T_g	T_a	T_s	T_{min}	T_g/T_s	T_a/T_s	Δ	$\Delta(\%)$
1	123.4	107.2	87.4	77.0	1.41	1.23	1.60	7.27
2	174.0	126.1	100.4	96.8	1.73	1.26	1.70	7.72
3	110.6	100.3	84.5	72.1	1.31	1.19	1.70	7.72
4	129.8	102.6	89.6	77.1	1.45	1.15	2.20	10.0
5	127.7	105.8	94.8	78.5	1.35	1.12	2.34	10.64
6	174.0	130.2	105.3	96.8	1.65	1.24	2.38	10.82
7	112.3	101.7	91.0	78.2	1.23	1.12	2.46	11.18
8	124.7	107.8	87.4	77.0	1.43	1.23	2.68	12.18
9	174.0	125.0	100.4	96.8	1.73	1.25	2.78	12.64
10	130.0	108.4	88.9	77.1	1.46	1.22	2.88	13.09
11	174.0	127.0	100.4	96.8	1.73	1.26	2.98	13.54
12	125.7	110.0	94.8	78.5	1.33	1.16	3.02	13.72
13	174.0	127.9	100.8	96.8	1.73	1.27	3.12	14.18
14	172.6	162.4	158.6	154.0	1.09	1.02	3.14	14.27
15	129.9	103.4	89.5	77.1	1.45	1.12	3.28	14.91
16	131.2	104.8	94.8	78.5	1.38	1.11	3.42	15.54
17	117.7	109.4	102.0	95.0	1.15	1.07	3.54	16.09
18	134.2	107.5	95.4	78.5	1.41	1.13	3.62	16.45
19	150.5	127.8	118.6	115.6	1.27	1.08	3.74	17.00
20	111.1	101.8	87.7	77.1	1.27	1.16	3.74	17.00

Table 1: Influence of Sequence of Manufacturing Different Products and Structure of Workstations on CMLT

4 Efficiency of Better Sequencing Products and Structuring Capacities

The results obtained demonstrate the strong influence of solving these optimization problems on CMLT and, as a result, on manufacturing and supply chain performance. They confirm the position that unbalanced capacities are better. At the same time, accordingly to the given values of T_g, T_s and T_a, the best values of the common unbalance value are about zero. For example, when $\Delta = 0$ (obtained in a special way) we obtained $T_g = 123.2$, $T_a = 108.2$ and $T_s = 86.7$. There is no strong correlation in increasing the values of T_g, T_s, T_a when increasing the unbalance values.

The results given will now be used to estimate the potential increase in efficiency of manufacturing performance due to the effective solution of the optimization problems. The parameters of structure No. 12 confirm the structure parameters of the basic manufacturing. Since the smallest T_a, T_g, T_s were obtained for the structure No. 3, it is reasonable to regard this structure as optimal.

Assuming a normal distribution, the probability of choosing the best (allowing to obtain T_s) and the worst (allowing to obtain T_g) sequence of manufacturing different products is at the minimum possible level, yet it is approximately the same for both extremes. Therefore, it is reasonable to use the average value of CMLT - T_a for estimating the efficiency of the manufacturing performance

Determining the ratio $T_{a,e}/T_{a,o}$ (where $T_{a,e}$ corresponds to the existing workstation structure and $T_{a,o}$, to the optimal structure), the potential of reducing CMLT by means of determining the optimal structure of workstations is estimated. Determining the ratio $T_{a,1}/T_{a,2}$ for any two variants of structure of workstations, the potential of reducing CMLT by means of improving the structure of workstations is estimated. From the ratio T_a/T_s for any variant of workstations, the structure is assessed towards the potential improvement in manufacturing performance due to determining the optimal (effective) sequence of manufacturing different products. Finally, from the ratio $T_{a,e}/T_{s,o}$ we can estimate the potential of increasing the efficiency of manufacturing performance due to a simultaneous solution of both optimization problems.

Successively comparing T_a for alternative No.12 with T_a and T_s for alternative No. 3, we obtain the following estimates for a potential increase in efficiency of the manufacturing performance:

(110,0 - 100,3)/100,4×100% = 9,7%; and

(110,0 − 84,5)/84.5 ×100% = 30,2%.

Nevertheless, the best obtained value of T = 84.5 is not minimal. Hence, applied to T_{min} index, this formula allows estimating the minimum value of CMLT and is directly connected with the underlying criterion (objective function) devised, and aimed at achieving the minimum value of CMLT.

Based on the research carried out, an analytical criterion for the problem of optimal manufacturing management is formalized that allows obtaining its extreme value. The main peculiarities of the criterion devised consist of the following: obtaining an extreme value of the criterion yields the minimum value of CMLT. Using the criterion appropriately allowed mathematically grinding a principal way for increasing efficiency of manufacturing and supply chain performance. Still, further problems arise. For example, we have grounds to suppose that a proper usage of this criterion allows explaining one of the main features of efficiency of lean manufacturing.

Using the criterion confirmed that by means of solving the above optimization problems we could not provide the best solution, as all the values of T_{min} are less then all the values of T_s obtained during the simulation. This is not accidental, as we did not vary other parameters. As an example, by means of varying parts lot size we obtained $T = 72.5$ (the best obtained variant of sequence of manufacturing the products for the variant of structure of workstations No. 3).

As you can see from the data in Table 1, when obtaining extreme value of the criterion, the theoretical minimum of $T = 72.1$. This demonstrated, that this value of T was practically impossible to obtain accepting existing regularities of machine-building processing technologies. Taking into account this fact for the cases investigated, we found that the minimum value of $T = 72.2$. This value of T was obtained by a simple revision of the operations schedule for one job only. We consider this fact as possessing a certain luck, as other results obtained confirm the possibility of obtaining subextreme value of the criterion.

Nevertheless, in this concrete case, when the criterion is used properly, by building on the optimum variant of the workstation structure and effectively sequencing products and a proper lot size variation, we managed to obtain the minimum value of CMLT.

5 Conclusion

Taking into account the managerial side of the results presented, it is not difficult to see opportunities for improving existing systems, including most advanced ones for manufacturing and supply chain management.

As mentioned, an important goal of supply chain management is system optimization, which aims at achieving minimum costs and optimal (on-time) fulfillment of customer orders . To meet demand with minimum possible costs, increase efficiency of supplying, provide on-time and generally fast deliveries, achieve subextreme value of the criterion devised, and provide more effective system manufacturing and supply management optimization, we developed new manufacturing management technology for low and mid-volume machine-building manufacturing based on a joint solution of the following and new knowledge-based optimization problems:

1. The problem of aggregate planning in the form of an original model of integer linear programming taking into account unbalanced capacities explicitly and allowing organization of effective precedence conditions. Using the model developed, the model obtained creates necessary conditions for meeting demand and achieving subextreme value of the criterion devised in this stage of manufacturing.

2. The problem of determining the effective structure of workstations (capacities) was addressed. A method was developed that proves to be more effective than traditional ones.

3. The problem of determining the effective sequence in manufacturing different products was tackled. A method developed is based on using rational levels of aggregated initial data and a proper accounting of precedence conditions when determining the effective sequence.

4. The problem of determining, organizing and scheduling effective precedence conditions was taken into account. The effective solution of the problem provides one of the main necessary initial conditions for obtaining subextreme value of the criterion.

5. The problem of sequencing and allocating jobs among parallel workstations, including their different individual labor productivities was addressed. The method developed is based on a proper usage of an analytical condition for simpler and more effective operations scheduling. A more effective method (in comparison to the analytical methods of the assignment problem) for solving the problem of jobs sequencing and allocation was obtained. Using the analytical condition, a method of proper sequencing and allocating jobs provides final conditions for obtaining subextreme value of the criterion devised.

On the whole, if each manufacturer in the supply chain when manufacturing management obtains the subextreme value of the criterion devised, it might mean obtaining minimum possible cost, inventory and a new possibility for faster deliveries. At the same time, to obtain it, any manufacturer in the supply chain should have some time interval for necessary scheduling optimization. To achieve it and have additional possibilities for better coordination in the supply chain it is necessary to combine more effectively timing and optimization aspects in manufacturing and supply chain management.

6 References

Blazewicz J., Domschke W., Pesch E. (1996) : The Job Shop Scheduling Problem: Conventional and New Solution Techniques, European Journal of Operational Research, Vol. 93 (1996), p.1-33.

Chase, R. B., Aquilano, N. J., Jacobs, F. R. (2001): Operations Management for Competitive Advantage, 9. edition, McGrawHill, Boston.

Chopra S., Meindl P. (2001): Supply Chain Management: Strategy, Planning and Operation, Prentice-Hall, Upper Saddle River, NJ.

Dettmer H.W. (1997): Goldratt's Theory of Constraints: A System Approach to Continuous Improvement, Milwakee, ASQC Quality Press.

Gaither N. (1992) Production and Operations Management, Dryden Press, Orlando, FL.

Goldratt, E. M., Cox J.(1992): The Goal: Excellence in Manufacturing, North River Press, Croton-on-Hudson.

Handfield, R. B., Nichols E. L. (1999): Introduction to Supply Chain Management, New Jersey: Prentice Hall, 1999.

Shapiro, J. F. (2001): Modeling the Supply Chain, Duxburg/Thomson Learning, Pacific Grove, CA.

Skomorokhov R.V.(1991): Some Features of Solution of Multicriterion Job Allocation Problem. Doklady AN SSSR, Vol. 318, No.1 (1991), p. 55-59.

Slack, N., Chambers, S., Johnston, R. (2001): Operations Management, 3. edition, Financial Times Prentice Hall, Upper Saddle River, N.J.

An Options Approach to Enhance Economic Efficiency in a Dyadic Supply Chain

Stefan Spinler, Arnd Huchzermeier, Paul R. Kleindorfer

1	Introduction	350
2	Literature Review	351
3	The Market Model	351
4	Welfare Properties	357
5	Cost Management to Enhance Efficiency Gains	357
6	Conclusion	359
7	References	360

Summary:
In this article we present a framework to analyze the efficiency-enhancing impact of contingency contracts. At the beginning of the contract, market session in period 0, the seller announces a two-part tariff applicable to obtaining options on slots of his capacity. This entitles the buyer to a non-storable good or dated service provided by the seller. The buyer in turn decides how many options to purchase. Both parties act under state-contingent uncertainty concerning demand, costs, and spot price. In the spot market in period 1, with uncertainty resolved, the buyer determines his optimal contract and spot consumption portfolio, while the seller offers potentially remaining capacity at the prevailing spot market price. The opportunity of long-term capacity trading and planning provides the seller with an instrument of efficient cost management resulting in lower marginal cost related to long-term capacity allocation as opposed to those associated with allocation on short-notice. Economic efficiency is enhanced in the options scenario as compared to the one obtained in a pure spot market.

Keywords:
Supply Chain Management, Capacity Options, Cost Management, Cost Differential Long-Term vs. Short-Term Allocation

1 Introduction

Options have attracted tremendous attention not only in the context of financial markets, fueled by the seminal article by Black and Scholes[1] who were first to provide a method to value this derivative instrument, but also recently as so called real options. Real options serve to *quantify* managerial and operational flexibility with regard to an investment project whose inherent expansion, termination or down-sizing opportunities are considered options and priced according to the Black-Scholes framework. Exogenous risks such as demand and exchange rate uncertainty can thus be modeled more accurately than traditional discounted cash-flow would allow[2].

Our article is concerned with an extension to the theory of real options by considering capacity options on non-storable goods or dated services. The introduction of options with respect to supply chain contracts aims at making both trading partners more flexible in responding to uncertain future market environments and at providing a hedging instrument against pronounced spot market volatility. As we demonstrate in the following, establishing a market scheme consisting of a long-term contract market and a short-term spot market also provides the seller with a key to exploit cost savings generated through early demand discovery in the options market enabling long-term planning. Welfare created in this market scenario grows with an increasing gap between marginal costs associated with short-term vs. long-term allocation, thus yielding an incentive for both parties to engage in this novel market set-up.

The remainder of this paper is organized as follows: in section two, the related literature is briefly presented. We go on in section three to introduce the market model and state the results for the buyer's and seller's strategy. Welfare properties are discussed in the subsequent section, linking the options scenario to the possibility of applying cost management, as is further highlighted in section five by examining an example in the air cargo business. Section six concludes with remarks on future research opportunities.

---

[1] Black, Scholes (1973), p. 637 – 654.
[2] See Huchzermeier, Cohen (1996), p. 100 – 114.

2 Literature Review

The starting point for our analysis is Wu, Kleindorfer and Zhang[3], who determine buyer and seller strategies in a similar framework, however limited to pure spot price uncertainty. A comprehensive overview of methods and applications with regard to real options is given in Dixit and Pindyck[4]. Tsay, Nahmias and Agrawal[5] provide a synopsis of current research on modeling of supply chain contracts, where contracts with quantity flexibility are analyzed via a multi-stage newsboy model rather than via a game-theoretic as is done here. A number of papers on yield management[6] illustrate an efficient method to cope with demand uncertainty when total capacity is limited. Oren, Smith and Wilson[7] study the issue of optimal pricing for services with a specified total capacity and date of delivery. Capacity fees are demonstrated to be an important component of a tariff. Harris and Raviv[8] derive an optimal pricing scheme for a monopolist facing demand uncertainty. Newbery[9] models similar contracts as the one analyzed here, consisting of a forward and a spot market for electricity. He focuses on issues of competivity in the British electricity market. In Spinler, Huchzermeier and Kleindorfer[10] implications of an options market scenario for electronic transportation platforms are discussed. The Extension of the model from a two-state to a continuous state space is undertaken in Spinler, Huchzermeier and Kleindorfer[11].

3 The Market Model

We consider a two-period von Stackelberg game to model the market interactions between the seller and the buyer. In period 0, the contract market, the seller as the Stackelberg leader first announces a two-part tariff consisting of an immediately payable reservation fee r and an execution fee e, which is due if the buyer exercises the option later in period 1. A single option entitles the buyer to a fixed portion of the total available capacity. The option is assumed to be a *European* call option. This is a standard assumption within the real options literature and it reflects reality rather well whenever high costs of repositioning, e.g., in air freight

---

[3] Wu, Kleindorfer, Zhang (2001).
[4] Dixit, Pindyck (1994).
[5] Tsay, Nahmias, Agrawal (1999), p. 299 – 336.
[6] See for example Gale, Holmes (1992), p. 413 – 437.
[7] Oren, Smith, Wilson (1985), p. 545 – 567.
[8] Harris, Raviv (1981), p. 347 – 365.
[9] Newbery (1998), p. 726 – 750.
[10] Spinler, Huchzermeier, Kleindorfer (2001a), p. 305 – 315.
[11] Spinler, Huchzermeier, Kleindorfer (2001b).

transportation, or reconfiguration, in manufacturing environments, are incurred. The buyer then decides on the number of options Q to be purchased in the contract market. Both decisions are taken under uncertainty. The seller's marginal costs $\tilde{b}$ as well as the buyer's demand $\tilde{D}$ are state-contingent. All parameters marked by a tilde are random variables. Moreover, the spot price $\tilde{P}^s$ prevailing in period 1 is uncertain, too, and considered to be influenced neither by the buyer nor the seller, thus stemming from a competitive fringe in the spot market.

In practice, the time span between the contract market and the spot market or actual day of use would vary depending on the underlying good or service. As the day of use draws closer, the uncertainty resolves and the buyers would use a secondary market to trade options that may have turned out to be of no use in the meantime. We do not model this intermediate stage here. Rather, we directly proceed with the spot market in period 1.

The buyer now determines his optimal contract and spot market consumption portfolio, where he decides on how many options $\tilde{q}^e$ ($\leq Q$) to execute and what quantity $\tilde{q}^s$, if any, to purchase in the spot market. The seller in turn allocates the capacity that has been contracted for in period 0 and that is now called upon, while attempting to find buyers for the remaining capacity in the spot market.

The von Stackelberg game structure enables an analysis via dynamic programming, starting with the determination of the buyer's consumption portfolio in period 1. Then expectation is being taken to compute the number of options Q the buyer contracts for in period 0 as a function of e and r. In our analysis, we use the information on $Q(e,r)$ to maximize the seller's profit by appropriately setting the execution fee e and the reservation fee r.

3.1 The Buyer's Optimal Consumption Portfolio

We make the following assumptions in modeling the buyer's behavior.

1. There are two states of the world ω in Ω, $\Omega = \{L,H\}$, with corresponding probabilities π^L and π^H, which are known to both the buyer and the seller. The state of the world may indicate the state of the economy, L representing poor conditions while H representing good ones, or a physical parameter such as temperature.

2. The spot price $\tilde{P}^s$ is state-contingent, with $\tilde{P}^s = p\,\tilde{\Psi}(\omega)$, where p is positive and accounts for a multiplicative non-state-contingent price component. $\tilde{\Psi}$ represents price uncertainty, with $\Psi^L < \Psi^H$. Thus the spot price increases with improving economic conditions. As mentioned previously, the spot price cannot be influenced either by the buyer or the seller.

3. The buyer's utility $\tilde{U}$ is affine-separable. For ease of notation, let $\tilde{U} = a\,D^\alpha \tilde{\Phi}(\omega)$ with demand D and the parameters $a > 0$, α in $(0,1)$. The results

would hold for any increasing and concave function of D, as long as separability is conserved. $\tilde{\Phi}$ is uncertainty related to the buyer's utility which is increasing in ω.

4. The marginal willingness to pay for the reserved quantity Q in state H is at least as large as the execution fee, i.e., $U^H(Q) > e$. Furthermore assume that the spot price in the low state and the one in the high state differ to such an extent that $P^{s,L} < e < P^{s,H}$.

The buyer's indirect utility is represented in the following quasi-linear form:

$$\tilde{V}(\tilde{q}^e, \tilde{q}^s, \tilde{P}^s, Q) = \tilde{U}(\tilde{q}^e + \tilde{q}^s) - rQ - e\tilde{q}^e - \tilde{P}^s \tilde{q}^s, \tag{1}$$

where $\tilde{q}^e$ is the number of options executed in the spot market, $\tilde{q}^s$ the capacity purchased in the spot market. The following program yields the optimal state-contingent consumption portfolio $\{\tilde{q}^e, \tilde{q}^s\}$:

$$\max \ \tilde{V}(\tilde{q}^e, \tilde{q}^s, \tilde{P}^s, Q) \quad \text{s.t.} \quad \tilde{q}^s \geq 0 \text{ and } Q \geq \tilde{q}^e \geq 0. \tag{2}$$

To solve this program, we need to distinguish between the two states L and H, which results in the following lemma.

Lemma 1 *In the spot market, the buyer consumes from the contract and the spot market as given in table 1.*

Contract Consumption	Spot Consumption	State
0	$(a\alpha\Phi^L/p\Psi^L)^{1/(1-\alpha)}$	L
Q	0	H

Table 1: Contract and Spot Consumption in the Spot Market.

Proof: Apply the theorem of Kuhn and Tucker to the program given through equ. (2).

Therefore the buyer executes either all options or none; he buys from the spot market in state L only. We are now able to compute the buyer's expected utility, which results in:

$$E[\tilde{V}(Q;r,e)] = -rQ + \pi^H U^H(Q) - \pi^H e Q + const., \tag{3}$$

where the *const.* term does not depend on Q.

From (3), we can derive a first order condition to determine the optimal reservation quantity $Q^*(e,r)$, quantified in the following theorem.

Theorem 1 *The optimal number of options Q^* the buyer obtains in period 0 is given by: $Q^*(e,r) = (a \alpha \pi^H \Phi^H / (r + \pi^H e))^{1/(1-\alpha)}$, if $r + \pi^H e \leq \pi^H p \Psi^H$. Otherwise $Q^*(e,r) = 0$.*

Proof: Differentiate equ. (3) with respect to Q and set to zero. Note that we need to require $U^{H'}(Q^*) > e$ and $U^{H'}(Q^*) < p\ \Psi^H$, conditions derived in computing the consumption portfolio provided in lemma 1, which yields the two regimes for Q^*.

We can interpret theorem 1 in the following way: The buyer is increasingly willing to pay higher reservation fee r in the contract market, the more likely state H occurs and the larger the difference between the spot price in that state and the execution fee. State H is the favorable state for the buyer, since in that case the execution fee is lower than the spot price and he therefore benefits from contracting capacity in period 0. The term $r + \pi^H e$ is the expected price the buyer is going to pay for options since he executes his options in state H only. Note that the buyer requires this price to be strictly smaller than the expected spot price, since, from theorem 1, $r + \pi^H e \leq \pi^H p\ \Psi^H < E[p\ \tilde{\Psi}]$. Traditional reasoning would suggest equality with the expected spot price.

For the seller, however, state H is less favorable, since in that case he would be able to sell his capacity in the spot market at a higher price. As a consequence, he insures himself against this case by demanding a larger reservation fee.

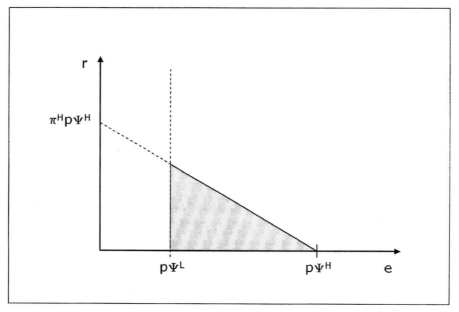

Figure 1: The Range or (r,e)-Values for Which Q > 0 is Indicated by the Triangle.

Figure 1 shows the triangular region of *(r,e)*-values for which the buyer is willing to reserve capacity in the contract market. Note that the lower limit on *e* is imposed by our assumptions. Thus if e is set equal to the spot price in the high state, then the acceptable reservation fee r shrinks to zero. The reservation fee is maximal for the lowest allowable execution fee.

Corollary 1 The optimal number of options $Q^*(e,r)$ the buyer obtains in the contract market decreases strictly in the reservation r and the execution fee e.

Proof: Follows immediately from theorem 1.

The corollary states the expected result that the demand for options decreases with price. We now know how the buyer reacts to any tariff (e,r) announced by the seller, who will choose the tariff relying on this information, such that his profit is maximized. This task is undertaken in the next section.

3.2 The Seller's Optimal Tariff

As we did in the buyer's case, we state a few assumptions concerning the seller's profit.

1. Total capacity K is exogenously fixed.

2. The per unit cost $\tilde{\beta}$ of holding capacity K is state-contingent.

3. The marginal cost $\tilde{b}$ of production is constant with respect to output quantity and is state-contingent.

4. Most importantly, and this is key to our options analysis in the context of cost management, we postulate a difference between the cost $\tilde{b}^c$ associated with providing capacity reserved through a long-term contract as opposed to the cost $\tilde{b}^s$, which is incurred if capacity is demanded on a short-term basis, i.e., in the spot market: $\Delta \tilde{b} \equiv \tilde{b}^c - \tilde{b}^s > 0$. We shall discuss in a later section in what industries this difference is particularly pronounced.

5. It is reasonable to assume that the marginal cost increases as the state of the economy improves, thus $b^{(c,s)L} < b^{(c,s)H}$. Furthermore let $b^{c,H} < p\,\Psi^H$, since otherwise the seller would not be able to operate profitably in state H.

The expected seller's profit then is

$$E[\Pi(r,e,\tilde{b}^c,\tilde{b}^s,Q)] = E[rQ + \tilde{q}^e\,(e - \tilde{b}^c) + m\,(K - \tilde{q}^e)(\tilde{P}^s - \tilde{b}^s)^+ - \tilde{\beta} K], \quad (4)$$

where the first two terms account for the profit generated through the long-term contract market, the third term represents the profit from selling into the spot-market. It may well be that there is a risk for the seller of not finding a buyer on short notice, which is true in particular for goods or services that are customer specific. We therefore introduced the risk factor m, with $0 < m \leq 1$. Hence, as m decreases, the risk of not finding a last-minute buyer increases. The factor m may vary substantially from industry to industry and it may also be a function of the spot price, where a higher spot price results in pronounced risk. For our purposes, however, it is sufficient to model m as a constant. Furthermore, as far as spot-market sales are concerned, we assume that no sales into the spot-market occur when price is below cost, as is evident by the $(...)^+$ operator. The last term, finally, represents the cost of holding capacity K.

The seller maximizes his profit according to the following program:

$$\max E[\Pi(r,e,\tilde{b}^c,\tilde{b}^s,Q)] \quad \text{s.t.} \quad K \geq Q. \tag{5}$$

The following theorem results.

Theorem 2 *The optimal reservation and execution fee (r^*,e^*) is given by:*

$$r^* + \pi^H e^* = \pi^H \min[(1/\alpha)(b^{c,H} + m(p\Psi^H - b^{s,H})^+), p\Psi^H], \quad Q^* < K,$$

$$r^* + \pi^H e^* = (\pi^H a \alpha \Phi^H / K)^{1/(1-\alpha)}, \quad Q^* \geq K.$$

Proof: Differentiate equ. (4) with respect to $r^* + \pi^H e^*$ to get the first order condition. Take into account theorem 1 for the case $Q^* \geq K$.

Note that in the present two-state case the reservation fee and the execution fee cannot be determined separately, contrary to the more general case of a continuous state-space which is analyzed in Spinler, Huchzermeier and Kleindorfer[12]. If we set the execution fee e^* equal to marginal cost, i.e., $e^* = b^{c,H}$ (which is possible if $b^{c,H}$ is larger than $p\Psi^H$, see our assumptions for the buyer's problem and figure 1), then we can interpret r as being the margin the seller is able to extract from the buyer. The reservation fee r contains the term $\pi^H m (p\Psi^H - b^{s,H})^+$, which represents the opportunity cost of reserving capacity in the contract market. This reserved capacity is going to be executed by the buyer in state H at a fixed price e, which is lower than the spot price. Thus the need for the seller to account for this case in the reservation fee.

Having computed the optimal execution and reservation fee, we can determine the equilibrium quantity.

Corollary 2 *The strategies given in theorem 1 and 2 for the buyer and the seller, respectively, lead to the following equilibrium quantity Q^*:*

$$Q^* = (a \alpha \Phi^H / \min[(1/\alpha)(b^{c,H} + m(p\Psi^H - b^{s,H})^+), p\Psi^H])^{1/(1-\alpha)}.$$

Proof: Combine theorems (1) and (2).

---

[12] See Spinler, Huchzermeier, Kleindorfer (2001b).

4 Welfare Properties

For the additional contract market to make economic sense, it should yield higher welfare than a pure spot market scenario. In this section, we shall compare the welfare generated in the two different scenarios. We define the welfare as $W \equiv E[\tilde{V}] + E[\tilde{I}]$. Let W^o be the one associated with the options case, W^s the one related to the pure spot market, and let $\Delta W \equiv W^o - W^s$. We assume that transaction costs occurring in the contract market are zero, which is justified by the fact that search and information gathering costs decrease dramatically for electronic markets.

The following theorem states the superiority of the combined spot and contract market in terms of economic efficiency.

Theorem 3 *The gain in efficiency ΔW provided by the addition of the contract market to the spot market is strictly positive, i.e., $\Delta W > 0$. The welfare difference can be represented as $\Delta W = \pi^H [(1-m)(p \Psi^H - b^{s,H})^+ + \Delta b^H]$.*

Proof: Calculate ΔW with Q^* given by corollary 2 and the consumption for pure spot market being in state L $X^L = (a\alpha\Phi^L/p\Psi^L)^{1/(1-\alpha)}$ and in state H $X^H = (a\alpha\Phi^H/p\Psi^H)^{1/(1-\alpha)}$.

With regard to implementing the novel market scheme, it is of interest what parameters impact the efficiency gain.

Corollary 3 *The efficiency gain ΔW increases with increasing cost difference Δb^H and with increasing risk of not finding a last-minute buyer, i.e., with decreasing m.*

Proof: Follows directly from theorem 3.

So we have obtained the key result that the efficiency gain increases (in this case linearly) with the cost differential between short- and long-term allocation. As a matter of fact, the gain is still positive even in the case of a completely riskless spot market, i.e., for $m = 1$. Thus the message is clear: Those industries where this cost difference is high are particularly suited to adoption of the spot and contract market. The implications of this important finding will be discussed in the next section.

5 Cost Management to Enhance Efficiency Gains

What factors impact the difference of marginal costs based on short-term vs. long-term allocation (to simplify notation in the following, let us denote the former, a little loosely, by "short-term costs" and the latter by "long-term costs")? This certainly depends on the industry supplying the good or service and on the time gap between the contract and the spot market.

The latter point involves a trade-off: on the one hand, the longer the period between the contract and the spot market, the more the seller is capable of making arrangements for reducing long-term costs by, e.g., optimizing his fleet and route allocation in the air cargo business or by dedicating lowest cost generators to the demand indicated early via options in the electric power business.

On the other hand, the further away the actual day of use when the contracting takes place, the less precise the initial forecast of demand on the buyer side. This may lead to reduced willingness to trade in the contract market, in particular, if, as was assumed for our modeling purposes, there were no secondary market enabling options trade among the buyers at an intermediary point of time. In practice, however, such a secondary market would be essential for a well functioning market set-up. By the time the secondary market takes place, the buyer will have updated his prior conditional demand probability distribution.[13] As a consequence, the buyer may find it in his interest to purchase additional options, if available, or sell them into this market. Thus the secondary market partially mitigates the downside of opening the contract market early with respect to the day of use.

Let us take a look at an example in the air cargo industry to see how the procedure of capacity allocation currently applied there works and how it could be modified upon implementing contingency contracts to aid cost management in the sense discussed above.

Lufthansa Cargo AG (LH Cargo) belongs to the Deutsche Lufthansa AG Group and is considered market leader in the global air cargo sector with a global market share of 7%[14]. Hellermann[15] points out that LH Cargo currently finalizes its long-term capacity planning process about 15 months prior to actual use. Thus if one wanted to keep the planning cycle, it would be reasonable to have the contract market take place that long before the spot market. LH Cargo, at this point in time, bids reservation fees for each route, which may differ depending on potentially more profitable opportunities of selling into the spot market (see Theorem 2), and the corresponding execution fees. The buyers, having learned the tariff, would then purchase options according to their likely demand. It is important to recognize that the level of options purchase provides LH Cargo with more accurate information on future demand levels than the current practice of relying on historical demand data. This early demand indication now allows LH Cargo to optimize their network supporting the various destinations and their fleet on a given route and thereby reduce the long-term marginal cost.

---

[13] Models analyzing this updating process are generally referred to as Bayesian Models in the literature, see Sengupta (1985).

[14] See Lufthansa AG (2001).

[15] Hellermann (2001).

Then, six months before use[16], the secondary market for options trading among the buyers would take place, where corrections could be made with regard to the now fixed schedule or with regard to the quantity needed. Finally, a few days prior to the transportation date, spot market interactions would occur: The buyer decides whether or not to execute the option or to satisfy his demand from a back-stop technology in the spot-market. LH Cargo in turn allocates pre-contracted capacity now called and attempts to sell remaining capacity into the spot market. Note that the remaining capacity will entail higher marginal costs than the pre-contracted capacity, as discussed earlier.

This new type of contract would replace or complement the currently used Guaranteed Capacity Agreement (GCA), which entitles the buyer to a specified quantity of capacity for the next six months and the right to return excess capacity at certain points in time. From the seller's point of view, enhanced cost savings potential could be exploited because demand data utilized for long-term capacity planning would no longer be based on historical demand but on actually materializing options sales. From the buyer's point of view, he would gain flexibility in terms of usage of capacity, thus being able to tailor capacity to his needs in the secondary and spot market. The opportunity for LH Cargo to reduce marginal costs thanks to the long-term contract market yields a benefit accruing to *both* parties. This stems from the larger welfare generated through the combination of an options and a spot market when compared with a pure spot market or a fixed contract, as has been discussed in section 4.

6 Conclusion

We have provided a game theoretic market model to value contingency contracts under demand, cost *and* price uncertainty, which demonstrates that economic efficiency can be enhanced in a market set-up consisting of a contract and a spot market versus a pure spot market. The efficiency gain is positively correlated with the marginal cost difference between capacity allocated on short notice, i.e., through the spot market, and that allocated on a long-term basis. Thus the novel market scheme we propose makes it possible to exploit this cost difference and thereby link cost management on the seller side provided by long-term planning to efficiency gains in the supply chain. We have sketched an example in the air cargo industry of how the type of contingency contract analyzed here could be implemented.

Our research lays the foundation for future work in this area: The trade-off alluded to in section 5 between marginal cost difference and the timing of the contract and the spot market is worth being incorporated explicitly into the model. Empirical

---

[16] Which is the lifetime of a current schedule, see Hellermann (2001).

research will shed light on further industries where the type of cost management discussed here could be put into practice via contingency contracts.

7 References

Black, F., Scholes, M. (1973): The Pricing of Options and Corporate Liabilities, in: Journal of Political Economy, Vol. 81 (1973), p. 637-654.

Dixit, A., Pindyck, R. (1994): Investment under Uncertainty, Princeton University Press, Princeton, New Jersey.

Gale, I., Holmes, T. (1992): The Efficiency of Advance-Purchase Discounts in the Presence of Aggregate Demand Uncertainty, in: International Journal of Industrial Organization, Vol. 10 (1992), p. 413-437.

Harris, M., Raviv, A. (1981): A Theory of Monopoly Pricing Schemes with Demand Uncertainty, in: The American Economic Review, Vol. 71 (1981), p. 347-365.

Hellermann, R. (2001): Market Requirements for Trading Options on Transportation Capacity, Diploma Thesis, WHU Vallendar, Germany.

Huchzermeier, A., Cohen, M. (1996): Valuing Operational Flexibility under Exchange Rate Risk, in: Operations Research, Vol. 44 (1996), p. 100-114.

Lufthansa AG (2001): Logistics.
URL: http://www.Lufthansa.com/dlh/en/htm/ profil/felder/logistik.html. 25.09.2001.

Newbery, D. (1998): Competition, Contracts, and Entry in the Electricity Spot Market, in: RAND Journal of Economics, Vol. 29 (1998), p. 726-750.

Oren, S., Smith, S., Wilson, R. (1985): Capacity Pricing, in: Econometrica, Vol. 53 (1985), p. 545-567.

Sengupta, J. K. (1985): Optimal Decisions under Uncertainty, Springer, New York.

Spinler, S., Huchzermeier, A., Kleindorfer P. R. (2001a): Optionen auf Kapazität: Anwendungen für E-Transportplattformen (Options on Capacity: Applications to e-Transport Platforms), in: Sebastian, H.-J., Grünert, T. (eds.): Logistik Management (Logistics Management), Teubner, Stuttgart, p. 305-315.

Spinler, S., Huchzermeier, A., Kleindorfer P. R. (2001b): Capacity Options: Theory and Applications, Working Paper, WHU Vallendar, Germany.

Tsay, A., Nahmias, S., Agrawal, N. (1999): Modeling Supply Chain Contracts: A Review. In: Tayur, S., Ganeshan, R., Magazine, M. (eds.): Quantitative Models for Supply Chain Management, Kluwer, Boston, p. 299 – 336.

Wu, D., Kleindorfer, P. R., Zhang, J. (2001): Optimal Bidding and Contracting Strategies for Capital Intensive Goods, Working Paper, Drexel University, Philadelphia.

Part 4
Extending the Scope Beyond Cost

Using Internet-based Purchasing Tools in Supply Chains – Insights from a Retail Industry Analysis

Mirko Warschun, Uwe Schneidewind

1	Introduction	364
2	Purchasing Objectives As a Starting Point for a Purchasing Concept	365
3	The Purchasing Process	367
4	Internet Applications Which Support the Purchasing Process	368
5	Evaluation of Internet-based Purchasing Applications	376
6	Conclusion	377
7	References	378

Summary:
As a central part of the operations of retail companies, purchasing makes an important contribution to strengthening the competitive position. To support the activities which take place within the commercial purchasing process, new applications are being developed based on the internet. These will change the whole face of purchasing in the future. In order to fully utilize the added value offered by the use of the internet, consistent orientation to the objectives defined by purchasing policy is necessary.

Key words:
Purchasing, Supply Chain Management, Internet, Electronic Commerce, Retail Industry

1 Introduction

In a large number of retail companies in the consumer goods industry the average purchasing volume amounts to between 70% and 80% of the net turnover. Seen from a cost perspective, the importance of purchasing implies that the operating result is highly sensitive to relative changes in the costs of goods purchased.[1] In addition to this, purchasing processes incur additional costs for retailers. Some examples of this are administrative costs for purchasing, storage costs, in-plant transport costs and capital tie-up costs. Along with these cost implications, purchasing also influences sales revenue. The non-availability or obsolescence of goods in demand can lead to lost sales revenue. In addition to the supply function which makes goods available for the sales process, the range of products specific to the retail format greatly influences profits through the effects on sales revenue. Purchasing is thus a central part of the operations of retail companies and makes a major contribution to strengthening their competitive position.

Today, trade with consumer goods is characterized by complex flows of information, goods and finance in the purchasing process. By the time retail companies have the desired purchase objects available for sale, numerous parties have been involved in the sourcing process along the supply chain in addition to the manufacturers and their suppliers (for example: purchasing associations, wholesalers, providers of logistics services, financing and import firms). Today these flows are not only complex; they are also time-consuming and involve the loss of a great deal of information at the interfaces.

Within the scope of this article, the hypothesis will be proposed that internet-based information and communication technologies will change the face of purchasing in the future, as new applications are developed. This development markedly increases the transparency of offers, prices, costs, capacities and capabilities within the value creation system.[2] Increased digitalization and networking can reduce the information loss between the parties involved at the interfaces. Conditions are created for better cooperation with a high specialization of labor and for easier exchange of information between organizations.[3] Specialists can develop along the value chain. They concentrate on certain parts of the supply chain and offer specific purchasing services in a new intermediary function.

---

[1] Using the example of Metro AG a 1% reduction in the costs of goods purchased, which amounted to 78.3% of the net turnover in the financial year 2000, would lead to a 36% increase in the operating result. See Metro (2001), p. 82.

[2] See Porter (1999), p. 63-96.

[3] See Choi, Stahl, Whinston (1997), p. 539-578; Picot, Reichwald, Wigand (2001) p. 145-189; Wirtz (2000).

2 Purchasing Objectives As a Starting Point for a Purchasing Concept

A differentiated understanding of fundamental purchasing objectives is a prerequisite for the analysis and development of purchasing in a commercial situation. Different academic and practical concepts for identifying purchasing objectives have already been developed. The three approaches selected here – the transaction cost approach, the total cost of ownership concept, and the efficient consumer response concept – have been developed in different fields of theory and application and thus offer different approaches to purchasing.

2.1 Transaction Costs

The transaction cost approach is part of the new institutional economics.[4] This approach centers on all information and coordination costs which are incurred in the preparation, agreement, implementation, supervision and adjustment of reciprocal commercial relations.[5] However, seen from a cost perspective, transaction costs are just one factor in purchasing. For a comprehensive overall cost perspective the actual production costs or costs of goods purchased, as well as physical transfer costs incurred, particularly need to be included as further parameters for evaluating purchasing.

2.2 Total Cost of Ownership

The total cost of ownership concept, which comes from the field of purchasing management, is based on an overall cost concept.[6] It expands the theoretical concept of the transaction cost approach and includes a large number of cost elements along the phases of a procurement process: "TCO considers total cost of acquisition, use/administration, maintenance and disposal of a given item/service."[7] However, it remains to be ascertained that elements beyond the dominating cost focus, for example cross-supplier assortment planning and aspects of cooperative product development, are not examined.[8]

---

[4] See Coase (1937); Williamson (1990).
[5] See Picot (1982), p. 270.
[6] See Ellram (1993).
[7] Ellram (1999), p. 597.
[8] See Seuring (2001), p. 106-113.

2.3 Efficient Consumer Response

The concept of efficient consumer response reaches far beyond the dominating cost focus of the first two approaches.[9] This concept, developed by manufacturers and retailers in the consumer goods sector, strives for the cooperative optimization of the whole value creation system from the manufacturer, to retailers and the final consumer. ECR comprises two basic thrusts: orientation to the needs of the final consumer (category management) and the optimization of goods flows (supply chain management). Instead of pure cost orientation, examples of further purchasing objectives considered are lowering cycle times, improving the product assortment, and (possibly) product development.

2.4 Development of a Comprehensive Purchasing Objective System

The different focuses of the three purchasing approaches selected – the transaction cost approach (TC), the total cost of ownership concept (TCO) and the efficient consumer response concept (ECR) – allow a look at and understanding of purchasing in different ways. They form the basis for developing a comprehensive purchasing objective system. The criteria for a purchasing decision discussed in the concepts described can be structured along four target dimensions which form a conceptual grid for further examination (see Figure 1).

The key initial activity for *opening up new sources of supply* is the search effort involved in identifying new suppliers. *Reducing the costs of goods purchased* for purchase objects which have already been defined is the most important purchasing objective from a cost angle. In addition to purchase prices, the manufacturer's contribution to advertising expenses, listing money, and rebates and discounts must be considered. In *developing the retailer's internal potential* the focus is particularly on order execution processes and internal handling and transport processes. In addition, the reduction of mark-down costs is a central purchasing objective for trade. These activities, which are primarily isolated, are extended by *the manufacturer and the retailer cooperating to tap joint potential.* For example, inter-organizational cooperation enables cross-company optimization of logistics processes and replenishment. Within the framework of intensifying a manufacturer-retailer relationship, cooperation in the fields of product assortment shaping, planning of sales promotion activities and cooperative product development can take place.

---

[9] See Homburg, Grandinger, Krohmer (1996); Kurt Salmon (1993).

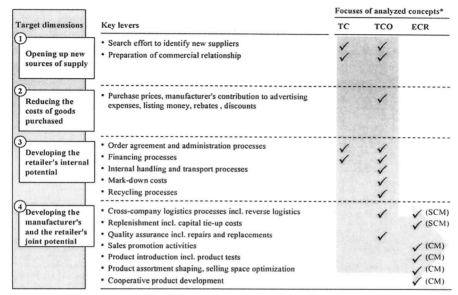

Figure 1: Analysis Framework for a Purchasing Objective System

Different purchasing applications along the four target dimensions introduced will be analyzed and evaluated in the further course of this article.

3 The Purchasing Process

Retail companies realize the purchasing function within a purchasing process. The individual sub-processes and activities can be structured based on the practically-oriented generic terms "assortment" and "supplier management" (see Figure 2).[10]

The elements of *assortment management* include both assortment planning and – in the case of private labels – product design. The *supplier management* sub-

---

[10] The order of events for individual sub-processes and activities within the purchasing process is not necessarily purely sequential. Communication and feedback loops enable comprehensive information and coordination. The processing and sequence of the purchasing activities are especially determined by specific assortment requirements.

processes can be divided into the phases preparing the ground for purchasing, purchase agreement and implementation of purchasing.[11] The preparation phase consists of identifying and assessing potential products and suppliers. In the agreement phase negotiations are conducted with suppliers and, depending on their outcome, a contract is concluded and an order placed. The implementation phase comprises order management, incoming goods, financial transactions and, if necessary, handling of returns. The results of the activities of every sub-process enter into the respective end products.

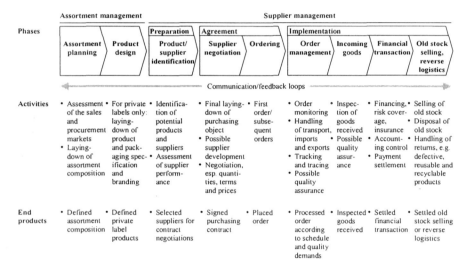

Figure 2: Purchasing Process

4 Internet Applications Which Support the Purchasing Process

New internet-based applications are being developed to support the activities which take place within the commercial purchasing process: "The technology now allows you to do extremely content-rich communication and develop tools that

---

[11] For the basic process structure see Schmid, Lindemann (1998), p. 193-194.

enable you to manage many more inter-business processes."[12] A selection of possible internet applications which contribute to efficient organization of the purchasing process is summarized in Figure 3.[13]

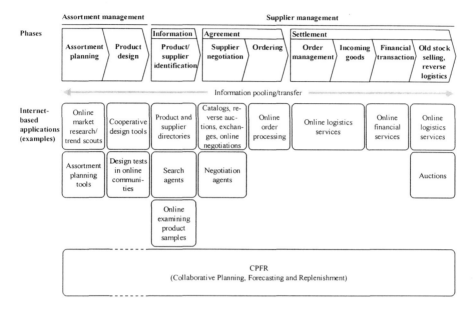

Figure 3: Internet Applications Supporting the Purchasing Process

Among other things these internet-based applications aim to improve the quality of assortment planning and product design, identify new suppliers, reduce the costs of goods purchased and automate order management. Subsequently, selected applications for supporting assortment management and supplier management as well as general applications will be described and assessed.

4.1 Internet Applications for Assortment Management

Within the framework of assortment management a retail company decides on the assortment planning and possibly on the product design.

---

[12] Spencer Marlow, Marketing Manager GE Global eXchange Services. Interview September 12th, 2000.
[13] Internet applications are assigned to the individual sub-processes based on the respective focus of activity within commercial purchasing; it is thus not an exclusive field of application.

In addition to an assessment of the sales and procurement markets, assortment planning also lays down demand-oriented assortments. Internet applications allow the inclusion of a comprehensive and up-to-date information base. Special analysis tools make it easier to evaluate complex, assortment-specific correlations. As a relatively new internet-based service *online market research companies/trend scouts* offer information on the latest developments on the sales markets. Since 1998 Worth Global Style Network (WGSN) has provided users with multimedia information on the latest developments in the fields of zeitgeist, consumer types, fashion trends and packaging design.[14] *Assortment planning tools* can simulate sales scenarios and lay down the future assortment structure. Until now this task has been supported by retailers' internal merchandise information systems. However, a retail company is now able to use the internet to evaluate historical sales developments and market analyses interactively with selected manufacturers. Seen from a commercial point of view this allows direct access to the manufacturer's product-related knowledge, and enables the quality of assortment planning to be improved.

The product design phase comprises laying down the product and packaging specifications and branding. The internet offers an opportunity to support cooperative development activities between retailers and manufacturers. *Cooperative design tools* allow direct interaction between players.[15] So-called *design tests in online communities* present new product ideas to potential customers online and facilitates their discussion.

As well as improving the opportunities for integration and cooperation via the internet, the market feedback process is accelerated. "Collaborative product design and development via the Internet speeds innovation and time to market."[16]

4.2 Internet Applications In Supplier Management

Supplier management follows assortment management. The sub-processes of supplier management can be divided into the phases preparing the ground for purchasing, agreeing on the purchase and implementation of purchasing. Next, internet-based applications taking place within these phases will be examined.

4.2.1 Applications Which Prepare the Ground for Purchasing

In the preparation phase the focus is on the identification and assessment of potential products and suppliers. So-called internet-based agents, product and

---

[14] Information on WGSN under http://www.wgsn.com. Enquiry dated 12.07.2001.
[15] See Upton, McAfee (1996), p. 127-133; Weiber (1997), p. 78-79.
[16] Gerry Palmer, Executive Vice President and CTO GlobalNetXchange. Interview February 5th, 2001.

supplier directories, and online examinations are developing in the consumer goods industry to support these activities.

Internet agents are software programs which independently execute tasks on the internet on behalf of a user.[17] In order to improve the quality of the results during their employment, agents can have a certain ability to learn. This (artificial) intelligence allows problem solution which is oriented towards the particular purchasing situation. Within the preparation of the ground for purchasing, agents can especially be employed to carry out search and filter functions. In addition to this, the use of agents is conceivable in the agreement phase. The retailer's agents can independently conduct negotiations about price and terms with the manufacturer's agents in a fully automated market process. As well as comprehensive procurement and preparation of information, the employment of agents aims to accelerate and reduce the costs of the search and negotiation process. In practice, only limited use is made of agents at present, despite this increasing opportunity for effectiveness and efficiency.[18] So far, the main reason for this is the lack of clear parameters and data on complex product and supplier specifications.

To optimize the preparation for purchasing, structured *product and supplier directories*, which assist a worldwide, systematic search for suppliers and products, are becoming increasingly available on the internet. Up-to-date company profiles and multimedia product catalogs are offered as a new internet-based service.[19] For example, the company Apparelcommerce has made information available on the internet about manufacturing plants in the textile and clothing industry in Eastern Europe and North Africa since 1999.[20] In addition to a company profile, this includes up-to-date information on short-term and long-term availability of capacity, and a standardized assessment of operative capabilities. This markedly increases the transparency of offers, costs, capacities and capabilities.

Examining product samples describes goods presentations which give the retailer's buyers an overview of the range of goods available on the procurement markets.[21] At present these activities are largely carried out physically at the manufacturer's company and at central fairs. This entails a lot of traveling. The employment of internet-based applications enables some of these activities to be

---

[17] See Moukas, Zacharia, Guttman, Maes (2000); Tolle, Chen (2000).
[18] See Clement, Runte (1999), p. 189.
[19] Examples of companies offering product and supplier directories via the internet include Asian Sources (http://www.asiansources.com), Europages (http://www.europages.com), The Green Book (http://www.thegreenbook.com), Thomas Register (http://www.thomasregister.com) and WLW (http://www.wlw-online.de).
[20] Information on Apparelcommerce under http://www.apparelcommerce.com. Enquiry dated 17.07.2001.
[21] See Tietz (1993), p. 161 and p. 520-521.

moved to a virtual level. Multimedia product representations allow at least a first assessment of the product range. As well as accelerating the process and reducing costs, a further advantage of online applications is the availability of product information around the clock. An obstacle to widespread implementation is especially found in the limited acceptance of many buyers who believe physical contact with the product is necessary in order to assess it.[22] The opportunities for using internet-based applications for product selection are therefore determined by the degree of characteristic features which can be communicated by the purchase object.

4.2.2 Applications for Agreeing Purchasing

The purchase agreement phase comprises the negotiations with suppliers and the ordering process. Among the negotiations conducted between the retailer and a potential supplier, the parameters of the supply contract are fixed, especially quantities, terms, prices, and delivery schedules. A large number of internet-based *trading mechanisms* are being developed to support these coordination activities between manufacturers and retailers. In the following, a distinction is made between mechanisms for preparing for trade and mechanisms for direct contract coordination (see Figure 4).

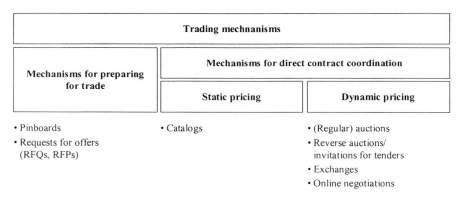

Figure 4: Classification of Internet Trading Mechanisms

So-called *pinboards* are one mechanism for preparing for trade. Specified intentions to buy and sell are published to initiate a transaction relationship. The aim of publishing the intention to purchase is to openly approach as many interested suppliers as possible beyond the familiar business partners.

---

[22] See Weber (2001), p. 30.

Compared with this, *requests for offers* are characterized by directly approaching potential buyers or sellers.[23] For example, manufacturers selected via the internet in a request for offers covering product and supply specifications are asked to submit a first offer. Based on this, a retail company narrows down the choice of participants for the negotiation process. The actual contract negotiation takes place at a later time. Internet-based requests for quotes thus allow the inclusion of a wide manufacturer base and also clearly accelerate the negotiation process.

In addition to the mechanisms which prepare for trading, other mechanisms used for direct coordination of purchasing contracts via the internet include catalogs, (regular) auctions, reverse auctions, exchanges and online negotiations (Figure 5).

	Catalogs	(Regular) auctions	Reverse auctions/ invitations for tenders	Exchanges	Online negotiations
Price fixing	Static	Dynamic	Dynamic	Dynamic	Dynamic
Price influence	Supplier	Buyers (supplier sets minimum price)	Suppliers (buyer sets maximum price)	Suppliers and buyers	Suppliers and buyers
Suppliers	One or many	One	Many	Many	One
Buyers	One or many	Many	One	Many	One
Price transparency (fixed price, bids)	Open	Open or closed	Open or closed	Open or closed	Open
Key targets for retailers	• Reduction of search and negotiation time/costs • Simplification of order processing • Poss. reduction of costs of goods purchased (by means of price comparison, standardization of purchasing objects, supplier consolidation)	selling of old stock • Increase in turnover • Opening up new and inclusion of a large number of potential buyers • Reduction of sales and negotiation time/costs	• Reduction of costs of goods purchased • Opening up new and inclusion of a large number of sources of supply • Reduction of search, demand announcement and negotiation time/ costs	• Inclusion of a large number of suppliers and buyers • Reduction of search and negotiation time/costs	• Reduction of costs of goods purchased • Poss. developing the supplier's and the retailer's joint potential, definition of product specifications and/or supplier development

Figure 5: Characteristics of Mechanisms for Direct Contract Coordination

Internet-based *catalogs* provide an electronic overview of products, possibly supplemented with multimedia illustrations.[24] The potential buyer is able to select the purchase objects needed from a pre-defined assortment which is structured according to product groups. In total the supplier stipulates the prices as fixed. If

---

[23] Depending on the characteristics, a distinction can be made between Requests for Quotes (RFQs) and Requests for Proposals (RFPs). See Monczka, Trent, Handfield (1998), p. 36

[24] See Baron, Shaw, Bailey (2000); Eyholzer (1999), p. 9-11.

several interested companies have access to a catalog, it is possible to specify different terms and conditions for specific buyers.

While catalogs are characterized by static price fixing, a dynamic pricing process is a central characteristic of *auctions*.[25] At auctions, several takers compete for the products or services of a supplier. With regard to price transparency and bidding procedure, a distinction can be made between four basic auction forms: English auctions, Dutch auctions, first price sealed bid auctions and second price sealed bid auctions.

The (regular) auctions organized by suppliers focus on securing a high price.[26] In contrast, auctions organized by takers aim to secure a price which is as low as possible. The distinguishing feature of these *reverse auctions* or *invitations for tenders* is a mirror-image bidding procedure. A taker invites tenders for examination of the special product or service required, and several suppliers then compete to supply it. Reverse auctions are thus the main type of auction used within the framework of commercial purchasing. The focus is on reducing the prices for the purchase objects. Using the internet enables the inclusion of a large number of manufacturers worldwide. This can increase the number of potential tenderers, and is conducive to an intensification of competition between the individual tenderers.[27] In addition to price reductions, auctions noticeably accelerate the tendering and negotiation processes.

Compared with auctions, which are initiated by a supplier or a taker, at *exchanges* – also called double auctions – several players, both suppliers and takers, are involved at the same time.[28] Suppliers place offers to sell and takers place offers to buy. An independent intermediary compares the offers and determines the price which achieves maximum transaction volume. Exchanges tend to be used more for homogeneous goods. They have not so far been used by retail companies to purchase consumer goods to be offered for sale because of the low level of standardization of the goods and procurement situations.

The trade mechanisms of auctions and exchanges are usually characterized by an exclusive focus on the contract parameter price.[29] In contrast, *online negotiations* enable matters beyond agreements about prices and terms to be negotiated – for example product and packaging specifications, or supplier development measures. Here, individual retailers enter into a direct negotiation process with individual manufacturers via the internet.[30]

---

[25] See Beam, Segev (1998); McAfee, McMillan (1987); Vickrey (1961).
[26] (Regular) auctions are above all used in trade to sell remaining stock, for example fashion articles at the end of the season.
[27] See McAfee, McMillan (1987), p. 729.
[28] See McAfee, McMillan (1987), p. 702 and p. 725-726.
[29] See Ströbel (2000).
[30] See Runge (1998).

Following the conclusion of a contract, the retailer places a first order. Unlike classic systems, *online order processing* via the internet also enables electronic data interchange with smaller suppliers and suppliers who are only temporarily active. This supports improved integration and automation of cross-company and internal activities.

4.2.3 Applications for Purchasing Implementation

The outcomes of purchasing agreements are signed purchasing contracts and the placement of orders. The purchasing implementation phase follows and comprises order management, incoming goods, financial transactions and, if necessary, handling of returns.

The main elements of order management and incoming goods are order monitoring, handling of transport, imports and exports, consignment tracking, inspection of goods received and quality assurance. The use of the internet within the framework of these supply chain activities provides a comprehensive and up-to-date information basis for all those involved. A so-called logistics database forms the basis for new *online logistics services*. As a communication platform independent of time and place, the internet offers those involved direct access to data which meets their specific requirements.[31] The increased transparency – for example consignment tracking systems – enables optimization of the information flows which accompany and are ahead of goods flows. Closer coupling and coordination of the players involved in the value creation system are conducive to shorter order throughput times, more exact delivery date predictions, and better planning of capacities and stock along all stages of the value chain. In addition to this, additional internet-based services are developing, for example transport catalogs, auctions and exchanges, which serve as electronic mediation systems between shippers, carriers and hauling contractors.[32]

As a further element of purchasing implementation, financial transactions mainly cover the financing activities themselves, risk coverage, insurance, accounting control and payment settlement. In this connection *online financial services* enable processes to be completed more quickly, and allow advisory services which are independent of time and place. Via the internet the retailer's internal systems can be directly connected to the systems of banks, insurance companies, import companies and customs authorities. In the event of faulty articles which can be reused, retail companies handle so-called returns. In addition to *online logistics services* for information support to goods flows, the sale of remaining stock provides an opportunity for the use of *internet-based trading mechanisms*. For example, retailers can make use of (regular) internet auctions to sell fashion articles at the end of the season and thus reach potential takers worldwide.

---

[31] See Pfohl, Koldau (1999), p. 39.
[32] See Alt, Schmid (2000), p. 86-87.

4.3 General Applications

In addition to internet applications, which support the individual phases of assortment and supplier management, general applications are also used that cover multiple phases.

The application *CPFR (Collaborative Planning, Forecasting and Replenishment)*[33] is of particular importance for purchasing. This supports cooperative planning, forecasting and inventory management between retailers and manufacturers of consumer goods. CPFR focuses on boosting sales through improving the availability of goods at the point of sale. Simunltaneously it aims at reduced costs by optimizing stock and production capacity with higher forecasting accuracy. In an interactive coordination process a retailer and the respective supplier analyze and discuss business plans, demand and order forecasting, deviations, order fulfillment and sales developments, with the aim of developing mutual understanding as a prerequisite for joint management of the relevant planning, forecasting and replenishment processes. The willingness of the retailer and the manufacturer to make the necessary data available in a database with a sufficient level of detail and topicality is essential for the success of CPFR. In practice, this has so far only been realized to an insufficient degree.

5 Evaluation of Internet-based Purchasing Applications

The analysis shows that a large number of new internet-based applications are developing along the purchasing process. A classification of the different procurement applications on the basis of the purchasing objective system developed in chapter 2 illustrates the different points of emphasis of the individual applications for the retailer (see Figure 6).

In summary, the task of purchasing is to realize the given purchasing objectives within the framework of the purchasing policy in long-term action plans which are adapted to the sales positioning of the retailer. The selection and development of purchasing applications must be oriented towards this.

---

[33] See VICS (1998).

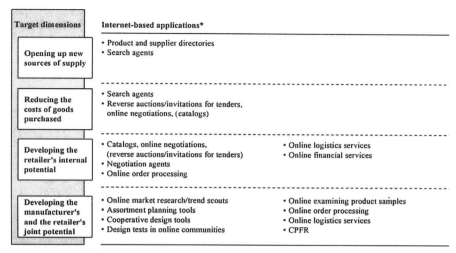

Figure 6: Classification of Internet Applications On the Basis of Procurement Objectives

6 Conclusion

The success of the development and the practical implementation of new manufacturer-retailer business models greatly depends on the extent to which added value can be secured for and by the companies involved.[34] This added value largely results from the implementation of innovative internet applications and services. In order to ensure the generation of added value, the specific procurement situation of the particular company must be taken into consideration. In the planning stage of new internet applications, attention should be paid to the special features which are related to purchasing. Against this background, it is possible to generate added value in all phases of the purchasing process.

However, in company practice internet applications have only been realized in limited areas. The focus has so far been on applications for contract negotiation and ordering. Applications such as CPFR and design tools which assist cooperation between retailers and manufacturers are frequently still in the development and piloting phase. MARLOW, Marketing Manager GE GXS, explains this: "Most existing internet-based purchasing solutions such as auctions

---

[34] For new internet-based manufacturer-retailer business models being developed see Behrenbeck, Menges, Roth, Warschun (2001).

do not add value to the industry but move profits between players in a zero-sum game. The high improvement potential is in integrated tools that support collaboration between manufacturers and retailers."[35] The integration of all applications which frequently just support isolated individual sub-processes is therefore necessary in order to fully tap the added value offered by the use of the internet. In this way the creation of new interfaces and media breaks can be avoided. The internet offers opportunities for generating added value – on condition that it is possible to integrate and ensure the interaction of all parties involved along the supply chain.

7 References

Alt, R., Schmid, B. (2000): Logistik und Electronic Commerce. Perspektiven durch zwei sich wechselseitig ergänzende Konzepte (Logistics and Electronic Commerce), in: Zeitschrift für Betriebswirtschaft (ZfB), Vol. 70, No. 1 (2000), p. 75-99.

Baron, J. P., Shaw, M. J., Bailey, A. D. Jr. (2000): Electronic Catalogs In the Web-based Business-to-Business Procurement Process, in: Shaw, M., Blanning, R., Strader, T., Whinston, A. (eds.): Handbook On Electronic Commerce, Springer Verlag, Berlin et al., p. 385-410.

Beam, C., Segev, A. (1998): Auctions On the Internet. A Field Study, Working Paper 98-WP-1032, Fisher Center for Information Technology & Marketplace Transformation, Haas School of Business, University of California, Berkeley/CA.

Behrenbeck, K., Menges, S., Roth, S., Warschun, M. (2001): Choosing the Right Option In the B2B Marketplace, in: European Business Forum (EBF), Issue 5, Spring (2001), p. 64-67.

Clement, M., Runte, M. (1999): Internet-Agenten (Internet Agents), in: Albers, S., Clement, M., Peters, K. (eds.): Marketing mit interaktiven Medien. Strategien zum Markterfolg, 2nd Edition, FAZ-Institut,, Frankfurt am Main, p. 179-192.

Coase, R. H. (1937): The Nature of the Firm, in: Economica, Vol. 4, November (1937), p. 386-405.

Choi, S.-Y., Stahl, D. O., Whinston, A. B. (1997): The Economics of Electronic Commerce, MacMillan Publishing, Indianapolis.

Ellram, L. M. (1993): Total Cost of Ownership. Elements and Implementation, in: The International Journal of Purchasing and Materials Management, Vol. 29, No. 4 (1993), p. 3-11.

Ellram, L. M. (1999): Total Cost of Ownership, in: Hahn, D. (ed.): Handbuch industrielles Beschaffungsmanagement. Internationale Konzepte – innovative Instrumente – aktuelle

---

[35] Spencer Marlow, Marketing Manager GE Global eXchange Services. Interview September 12th, 2000.

Praxisbeispiele (Handbook of Industrial Sourcing), Gabler Verlag, Wiesbaden, p. 595-607.

Eyholzer, K. (1999): Electronic Purchasing, Working Paper No. 116, Institute for Business Computing Science, Department for Information Management, University of Bern, Bern.

Homburg, C., Grandinger, A., Krohmer, H. (1996): Efficient Consumer Response (ECR). Erfolg durch Kooperation mit dem Handel, Wissenschaftliche Hochschule für Unternehmensführung, Vallendar.

Kurt Salmon (Kurt Salmon Associates Inc.) (ed.) (1993): Efficient Consumer Response. Enhancing Consumer Value In the Grocery Industry, in: Food Marketing Institute (ed.), Washington/DC.

McAfee, R. P., McMillan, J. (1987): Auctions and Bidding, in: Journal of Economic Literature, Vol. 25, June (1987), p. 699-738.

Metro (Metro AG) (2001): Geschäftsbericht 2000. Konzernabschluss der Metro AG (Annual Report 2000), Düsseldorf.

Monczka, R., Trent, R., Handfield, R. (1998): Purchasing and Supply Chain Management, South-Western College Publishing, Cincinnati/OH.

Moukas, A., Zacharia, G., Guttman, R., Maes, P. (2000): Agent-Mediated Electronic Commerce: An MIT Media Laboratory Perspective, in: International Journal of Electronic Commerce, Vol. 4, No. 3 (2000), p. 5-21.

Pfohl, H.-C., Koldau, A. (1999): Auswirkungen des Electronic Commerce auf die Logistik (Implications of Electronic Commerce on Logistics), in: Industrie Management, Vol. 15, No. 5 (1999), p. 36-41.

Picot, A. (1982): Transaktionskostentheorie in der Organisationstheorie: Stand der Diskussion und Aussagewert (The Concept of Transaction Costs in Organizational Theory), in: Die Betriebswirtschaft, Vol. 42 (1982), p. 267-284.

Picot, A., Reichwald, R., Wigand, R. T.. (2001): Die grenzenlose Unternehmung: Information, Organisation und Management (The Borderless Company: Information, Organization and Management), 4th Edition, Gabler Verlag, Wiesbaden.

Porter, M. A. (1999): Wettbewerbsvorteile: Spitzenleistungen erreichen und behaupten (Competitive Advantage), 5th Edition, Frankfurt/Main.

Runge, A. (1998): The Need for Supporting Electronic Commerce Transactions with Electronic Contracting Systems, in: Electronic Markets, Vol. 8, No. 1 (1998), p. 16-19.

Schmid, B. F., Lindemann, M. A. (1998): Elements of a Reference Model for Electronic Markets, in: Proceedings of the 31st Annual Hawaii International Conference on Systems Science HICCS'98, Vol. IV, Hawai January 6-9, 1998, p. 193-201.

Seuring, S. (2001): Supply Chain Costing – Kostenmanagement in der Wertschöpfungskette mit Target Costing und Prozesskostenrechnung (Supply Chain Costing With Target Costing and Activity Based Costing), Verlag Franz Vahlen, München.

Ströbel, M. (2000): On Auctions as the Negotiation Paradigm of Electronic Markets, in: Electronic Markets, Vol. 10, No. 1 (2000), p. 39-44.

Tietz, B. (1993): Der Handelsbetrieb. Grundlagen der Unternehmenspolitik (The Retail Company), 2nd Edition, Verlag Franz Vahlen, München.

Upton, D. M., McAfee, A. (1996): The Real Virtual Factory, in: Harvard Business Review, Vol. 74, No. 4 (1996), p. 123-133.

Vickrey, W. (1961): Counterspecutation, Auctions, and Competitive Sealed Tenders, in: The Journal of Finance, Vol. 16, No. 1 (1961), p. 8-37.

VICS (Voluntary Interindustry Standards Association) (1998): Collaborative Planning, Forecasting and Replenishment Voluntary Guidelines, Lawrenceville/NJ 1998, http://www.cpfr.org/Guidelines.html, Abfrage July 28, 2001.

Weber, B. (2001): Musterungen am Monitor (Online Examinations of Product Samples), in: Lebensmittel-Zeitung, Vol. 53, No. 14 (2001), p. 1 and p. 30.

Weiber, R. (1997): Der Cyberspace als Quelle neuer Marktchancen. Wettbewerbsvorteile durch Informationstechnik (The Cyberspace As Source for New Market Opportunities), in: Absatzwirtschaft, Vol. 40, No. 8 (1997), p. 78-83.

Williamson, O. E. (1990): Die ökonomischen Institutionen des Kapitalismus: Unternehmen, Märkte, Kooperationen (The Economic Institutions of Capitalism: Firms, Markets, Relational Contracting), Verlag Mohr, Tübingen.

Wirtz, B. W. (2000): Electronic Business, Gabler Verlag, Wiesbaden.

Complexity Management in the Supply Chain: Theoretical Model and Empirical Investigation in the Italian Household Appliance Industry

Giovanni Miragliotta, Marco Perona,
Alberto Portioli-Staudacher

1	Introduction	382
2	Background	383
3	A Conceptual Framework to Complexity	384
4	The Empirical Study	392
5	First Results	395
6	Concluding Remarks	396
7	References	397

Summary:
This paper describes a research program investigating the impact of complexity on manufacturing industries: the innovative perspective of this study is represented by the focus on every function of the company and on different stages in the supply chain. A methodology results which helps assess the optimum trade-off between improving effectiveness performances (e.g. variety) and reducing efficiency performances. A classification of complexity dimensions and of potential sources is provided, together with a selection of physical drivers which work as intermediate variables and as output variables. After that, a scheme for treating and interrelating these variables is discussed, thus defining a conceptual model for the complexity issue. Finally, the paper presents some early results acquired from the application of this methodology to the Italian Household Appliances industry.

Keywords:
Supply Chain Management, Complexity Reduction, Complexity Management, Household Appliance Industry.

1 Introduction[1]

Technology innovation, globalization of markets and more and more demanding customers are trends companies cannot escape. Beating the competition is based on mastering this evolution, and particularly mass customization: customers have all their basic needs satisfied and want their specific needs fulfilled as well. Companies have to supply an ever-growing number of products at the same, at even lower prices, tailored to customers' individual needs, causing a ballooning of variety and a fall in lot sizes. As an example, in the mid 1960s the Chevrolet Impala was the best selling car in the USA. The platform on which it was based was selling 1.5 million units a year. In 1991 the best selling car was the Honda Accord, and the platform on which it was based was selling 400,000 units a year. Despite the increase in the market size the number of units per model decreased by a factor of four[2].

After exploiting all internal resources in seeking efficiency improvements, companies have started to focus more closely on their supply chain, seeking an overall cost reduction and increase in efficiency. Therefore, besides the increase in the number of products and components, competition now involves suppliers and distributors, thus making the overall system more complex. As a matter of fact, many managers are realizing that the management of this overall complexity is a strategic issue for the company and the whole supply chain.

Unfortunately, most cost management systems are focused on direct costs only (in particular manpower costs) and indicate no understanding of the impact of this increase in complexity, although nowadays in most companies direct manpower costs are no longer 60 to 70% of total cost, but 10 to 15%. This highlights the necessity to tackle complexity indirect costs.

One of the main reasons why complexity costs are not explicitly addressed is that there is no clear and straightforward relation with quantifiable elements. Therefore a two-year research program was started in strict conjunction with companies belonging to manufacturing businesses, aiming at:

1. Identifying the main elements related to complexity, in terms of dimensions of complexity and drivers of complexity

---

[1] This paper is the result of research collaboration among authors. Nevertheless, sections 1 and 2 were written by A. Portioli Staudacher, sections 3, 4 and 5 were written by G. Miragliotta, and section 6 was written by Marco Perona.

[2] Clark and Wheelwright (1992).

2. Investigating the relationships between the complexity drivers and the correlation with a company's performance
3. Identifying which levers can be used by firms in order to modify the drivers' values (in other words, which action can be performed to reduce and manage complexity)

This paper will concentrate on the first two issues, providing a complete overview of the theoretical approach developed and some early findings derived from its application to a relevant case, namely the Italian Household Appliance industry. To this extent, the paper will be arranged as follows. Chapter 2 will discuss an introductory background of the complexity research issue, while Chapter 3 will highlight the main features of the new developed approach. Chapter 4 will present the operationalization of the model, while Chapter 5 will discuss some early results which give hints how the developed methodology can be applied. Finally, Chapter 6 provides some concluding remarks.

2 Background

Complexity comes from the Latin word *cum plexus*, which means "entwined, twisted together". Therefore, in order to have something complex you need two or more components which are strictly joined in such a way that it is difficult to separate them. Many parts and intimate, sometimes counterintuitive links between them: that's complexity, and that's why a system is more complex than each of its parts.

From a firm's point of view, the complexity issue is closely connected to the variety which exists within its boundaries; variety, in all its meanings (variety of products, of distribution channels, of suppliers, of components, etc.), is a well-known managerial subject: remarkable works have been devoted to discuss how enhancing the competitive strength by increasing variance is not always a safe strategy, since the competitive gains due to variety increase are counterbalanced by complex, interrelated, unpredictable effects which can reduce or even cancel those benefits. For instance, Quelch and Kenny (1994) state that unchecked product line extension can weaken a brand's image, disturb trade relations and cause cost increase; in fact, even if marketing managers see an overall sales increase, manufacturing and logistics managers may be overwhelmed by the additional complexity: as a global effect, excessive line extension will lead to lower brand loyalty, stagnant category demand, poorer trade relations due to the increase in space requirement, etc. Since differentiation has an enormous importance in today's business background in setting a competitive advantage, complexity management reveals a cornerstone of modern managerial science.

Nevertheless, it is clear that variety has advantages and disadvantages. No clear management principle can be found in the literature to support the trade-off decision between improving effectiveness performances (by increasing variety) and reducing efficiency performances (as an effect of the increased complexity). Moreover, managerial literature is unable to provide clarification about measurement approaches: for instance, while Stalk (1988) says that a 50% decrease in end items variety increases productivity by 30% and decreases costs by 17%, Hardle and Lodish (1994) present examples where product line extensions raised entire company performances.

In this background, one point which remains certain is the following one: even if increasing variety increases complexity, it is incorrect to believe that variety itself is the only driver of complexity. Complexity can be reduced, as well as managed. For instance, Suzue and Kohdate (1990) propose five techniques to decrease the number of parts in a product and diminish the number of processes to produce it, without changing the variety of finished items: this allows a decrease in internal complexity without affecting the market, and underlines the fact that smart intervention of management practices can shift the trade-off equilibrium by improving both efficiency and effectiveness.

So what is actually lacking is a model that is able to explain the relationships among all relevant variables, and able to address a company's efforts in reducing (if needed) or in managing complexity. Moreover, unlike the bulk of works presented in literature which address the complexity issue with a partial view (end items line extension, product components, production processes, etc.), a comprehensive view of the whole company is missing. Even more interestingly, a comprehensive view of the whole supply chain is missing.

The present research work aims to close this gap by addressing the complexity issue in all functions of the company and for different companies at different levels in the supply chain, thus investigating supply chain behavior and the improvement space which opens when significant complexity reduction/management efforts are completed.

3 A Conceptual Framework to Complexity

3.1 Dimensions of Supply Chain Complexity

As stated before, the main purpose of this research work was to develop a comprehensive model helping managers of manufacturing companies assess the optimum trade-off between improving effectiveness performances (by increasing complexity sources, e.g. variety) and reducing efficiency performances (as an effect of the increased effort to manage complexity). To reach this point, the objective methodology should be complete (i.e. able to catch every relevant factor), precise (i.e. able to catch correctly the impact of each factor on company complexity) and based on reliable and quantitative data.

Therefore, the first objective to be pursued is providing a framework of the multidimensionality of complexity management. To this extent, we classified all competitive variables within a manufacturing company in "dimensions"; variables belonging to a given dimension have to satisfy the following two conditions:

1. Variables must be "linked" with each other (for instance, the number of distribution stages and the stock management policy
2. Relationships with variables belonging to other dimensions have to be set by means of a strategic interface, and therefore by a company steering committee

The second condition helps to understand that, even if there is a significant degree of interdependency between different dimensions, the extent of this interdependency is a result of company strategy. The final number of complexity dimensions is thus an outcome of this process.

Starting from these considerations, we classified all competitive variables and were able to isolate five dimensions of complexity, as illustrated in Figure 1; those dimensions were purposely defined for manufacturing companies (on which this research project was focused), but we can be confident that, *mutatis mutandis*, they remain valid also for different ones (for instance service companies).

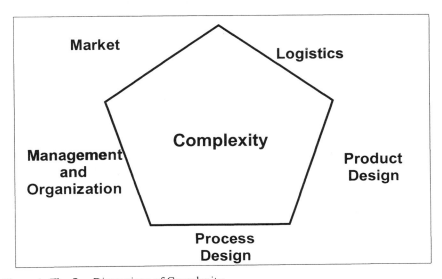

Figure 1: The five Dimensions of Complexity

The five dimensions can be described as follows:

1. *Market* includes those competitive variables characterizing the company and its relationship with its market in terms of product line breadth, services offered, number and location of customers, etc.;
2. *Logistics* includes variables such as the structure of the distribution system, the number of packaging systems, and the degree of co-operation with logistic service providers;
3. *Product design* dimension includes those variables related to the inherent product structure, such as the number of levels in the Bill of Material, the modularization degree, the exploitation of commonalities, the resort to partnerships with strategic suppliers, etc.;
4. *Process design* includes variables such as process flow type, production technologies, lay-out architecture, workforce organization, service plants and maintenance;
5. *Management and organization* includes those competitive variables related to human resource skills, organizational leanness, depth of the control chain, procedural coherence, support tools' availability, and so on.

These five dimensions do not pretend to be exhaustive, but we believ they represent a valid basis to start the analysis. In fact, each side of the pentagon is related by means of company strategy. For instance, market positioning and distribution channels have to be "tuned", and this is done by defining the whole company strategy. For instance: a first mover or a fast follower; on the whole, this results in a simple but not simplistic model.

Once the complexity dimensions are defined, the second step of the analysis is represented by the selection of physical, easily measurable drivers to assess the level of complexity within each dimension. These drivers should have two main properties:

1. They should be effectively mixable together to create a set of complexity indexes. To this extent, we were conscious that the actual number of drivers that could be related to the five dimensions is quite large, so we had to point out an optimal "depth of analysis" in order to collect the right amount of information to develop a tool which could be at the same time real-life fitting and operatively applicable.
2. They should catch the implications of complexity along the supply chain. To this extent, they have to include drivers which get both the upstream and downstream perspective of the same phenomenon, for instance, of supply orders. To fully exploit this potential, a coherent design of the research target has to be performed in the data acquisition phase (cf. Section 4).

As a result of these guidelines, an appreciable number of drivers described were selected. In the following paragraphs we will provide only a brief description and reminder of the reasons for considering them, being impossible to provide the complete list of selected drives. Moreover, in the following pages we will not discuss in detail the way each single driver has been transposed into a numerical index for two reasons: first, this would require much time and space and, second, this matter actually does not represent the innovative strength of this research project, but rather a first attempt to put into practice the developed model and to close the feedback loop.

With regard to the *market* dimension, four research areas were selected, namely product, service, time and customers. For each of them, some drivers were pointed out: not all of them are strictly quantitative items (e.g. the *commercial channel* driver is actually a list of activated commercial channels, from sales agents to internet), nor do all of them have the same extent (e.g. variety has been split into high and low level variety, with consequent sub-drivers, while service has been divided only into financial and non-financial services, grouping into the second category every service which has an operational and logistic impact). Finally, not all drivers can work only as measures of complexity sources, and some of them may represent output variables describing the system performances (e.g. the number of product families accounting for 80% of turnover); this list, anyway, is useful to understand the breadth and the depth of the analysis, providing also a quick recognition on the possible measures which can be obtained mixing and merging these basic data.

In the *logistics* dimension, three research areas have been pointed out, i.e. the inbound, the outbound and the internal logistics areas. Regarding the selected drivers, quantitative measures prevail, including flows and stock data, as well as information regarding available equipment and level of automation, up to the number of cycles (loading, handling and packaging) performed per year. Some qualitative data has been collected too, especially with regard to the distribution system architecture.

With regard to the *product design* dimension, 4 areas were selected, one focusing on the product inherent structure, one on the degree of vertical integration in product design, one on the co-design efforts and a final one focusing on the availability of design support software tools. Special attention has been paid to this dimension since traditionally the complexity matter has been studied starting from the product design perspective, and many methodologies exist to control and reduce product variety, standardize the components' panel, and reduce the impact of product design on other operative activities (e.g. Design For X methodologies). Many quantitative items have been included, but an extensive inquiry has been initiated regarding important inter-company qualitative items such as co-operation level and codesign practices.

The fourth dimension, i.e. the *process design*, has been studied focusing on four areas, namely production resources, production processes, quality control and process engineering. Of these, the first two have been deeply investigated collecting quantitative data related to the vertical integration degree and number of components/sub-assemblies to be produced, as well as unstructured information such as plant lay-out. With regard to the quality area, as confirmed by many managers, we treated quality drivers such as output variables rather than input variables because product quality is actually an outcome of the product design and of the process engineering phases, while quality control is supposed to contribute to complexity management only in a minor way (e.g., by eliminating defective products and thus avoiding returns, customer quarrels and so on). The same considerations stay true for incoming materials.

Finally, the *management and organization* dimension has been divided into three areas: informative systems, human resources and management processes. This dimension has revealed itself asone of the most difficult to study since various non-quantitative aspects had to be addressed, and many of them, such as the complexity acknowledgement degree and the managers' skills, are quite relevant to the studied subject. As before, some of the collected drivers were also targeted in order to be used as a company's performance measure (e.g. workforce amount for each activity), so as to empower the descriptive capabilities of the new methodology.

The list of drivers presented, together with the definition of the five-dimension model, represent a rigorous approach to the study of complexity in manufacturing companies. In our opinion, it can be considered as the state-of-the-art attempt to identify the main elements related to complexity, and an effective compromise between completeness and manageability, fulfilling the first objective declared in Section 1.

3.2 The Conceptual Model

The conceptual model development has indeed kept pace with the work described in the previous paragraph, since the deeper the insight on the complexity dimensions and drivers, the more complete the perception of the relationships among them became. Here, for the sake of convenience, this subject has been discussed after having provided a first holistic discernment on this matter, even if these phases overlapped.

During the conceptual model development phase some guidelines were followed in order to assure the success of the modeling effort.

The first guideline was represented by the purpose of investigating precise relationships between complexity sources (i.e. drivers) and output variables. This led to a slight difficulty, since it is very hard to isolate output variables which are universally related to complexity drivers. For instance, product variety can be feasibly considered one of the main effectiveness boosting levers; to measure the benefits of increasing complexity (by increasing product variety) one could consider measuring the turnover increase. Actually, we know that too many different factors contribute to the turnover final result, such as general market trends, raw material cost modifications, and new competitor entrance, so that this measure is not *precise*, i.e. is not able to catch the exact impact of the input variables on the output variables. To solve this point, we decided to focus only on those local measures easily linkable with complexity sources. For instance, one of the most important is the direct/indirect employees ratio, since complexity usually impacts the workforce effort needed to keep the system under control. This guideline reduced the set of correlations to be investigated, but increased the precision of the supposed relationship.

A second important guideline was inspired by the objective of developing a methodology able to help managers understand the proper amount of complexity. In fact, as we know, a certain level of complexity is necessary to compete in today's markets, but increasing complexity over value doesn't improve the effectiveness performances while reducing global efficiency. To acquire this point, the conceptual model should have to deal with this *basic complexity* assessment to understand which complexity reduction space is actually available.

This remark points out a third important guideline which is represented by the managerial levers in the analysis. Broadly speaking, managerial levers are classified into two main groups: complexity reduction levers (e.g. sub-suppliers resort, components standardization) and complexity management levers (e.g. investments in informative systems); for each of them the impact on physical drivers and thus on output variables should be analyzed.

Finally, during the conception of the model, we had to remember that the implications of complexity cannot all be studied with the same methodological approach. For issues such as automation impact, a widespread survey-based study can assess feasible conclusions while for others such as codesign strategy, case studies could represent the appropriate research approach. This fourth guideline molded the model conception and model validation phase, since the conceptual model should take care of the data which would have been collectable given the selected research methodology (cf. Section 4.1).

Starting from these introductory considerations, we distinguished three different levels at which complexity can be measured:

1. *Basic Complexity*: this represents the minimum amount of complexity which is needed in a given business to effectively compete with other actors

2. *Actual Complexity*: this represents the level of *physical* complexity which can be measured inside a company. This value is related only to physical drivers, for instance the average number of suppliers for each component

3. *Net Complexity*: this represents the level of complexity which remains to be faced after some has been filtered by complexity management tools (e.g. informative system, production resource automation).

According to Figure 2, given its knowledge about the environment, its strategic objectives and the available financial, technological and human resources, the company defines its operative strategy which, if perfectly followed, will lead to a certain level of complexity.

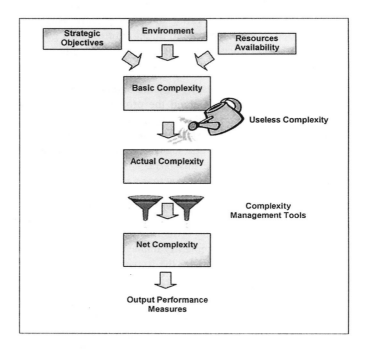

Figure 2: The Conceptual Model

We will refer to this as *Basic Complexity*. As a matter of fact no company is able to positively put into practice its operative strategy; historical heritage, imperfect information, lack of co-ordination and so on will lead to a situation in which physically observed complexity[3] is greater than what is strictly needed in order to get the same market results. We will refer to this as *Actual Complexity*. As we mentioned before, given the objective effectiveness performances, this results in an increased complexity level and therefore in a reduction in efficiency performances. In other words, some interventions are available to reduce costs without de-

---

[3] i.e. The actual values of the physical drivers used to measure complexity.

creasing customer satisfaction, while others keep the same costs and increase customer satisfaction.

As a third step, a company is endowed with many complexity management tools which, given a physical level of complexity, reduce the perceived impact of the complexity itself. We will refer to this perceived impact as *Net Complexity*. For instance, let's consider two companies, both of which have 30,000 end items, the first one being endowed with a complete Enterprise Resource Planning (ERP) system, while the second one manages all the information on local workstations: the *Physical Complexity* is the same for both companies, but the *Net Complexity* is very different. Even if some other complexity management tools exists, e.g. organizational roles, investments in informative systems represent the most common way to control and manage existing complexity. Starting from the *Net Complexity*, company processes are run and local and global performances are derived, both in terms of efficiency and effectiveness measures.

Notice in Figure 2 the role played by the *Useless Complexity* item. While it is easy to understand that physical drivers, tools and outcomes are observable variables, one may think that *Useless Complexity* in not supposed to be an observable variable, thus leaving undefined the *Basic Complexity*. Actually, we believe that given the environmental variables, the strategic objectives and resource availability, each complexity driver can be questioned to determine whether its value is optimal or not[4]. This process cannot be automated and must be performed in conjunction with a company's people to exploit their knowledge, but it allows an estimation of what could be the *Basic Complexity* and, from there, the corresponding amount of complexity to be eliminated and the impact on complexity drivers and output variables.

Provided that this scheme seems to carefully describe the operative stages through which the internal complexity is defined, created and managed, the modeling approach will be based on the following three steps.

1. *Assessment of company operating conditions.* This phase will point out a description of company operating conditions which can be linked to the company complexity level. For instance, we may consider a commitment to reducing the number of suppliers rather than the width of the product families range.

2. *Measurement of complexity drivers.* This step is devoted to establishing a theoretical link between the operating condition and a certain complexity dimension and then a link to a specific driver belonging to that dimension. The underlying hypothesis is that the higher the value of the driver, the higher the complexity degree. With reference to the above mentioned examples, measurement drivers could be, respectively, the number of suppliers for each

---

[4] Higher optimal values are more frequent than lower ones.

bought component and the number of components to be designed and updated by R&D personnel.

3. *Measurement of output variables*. Finally, this step is devoted to establishing a theoretical link between the complexity drivers and an output variable. With reference to the above mentioned examples, output variables could be the service level assured by active suppliers and the R&D personnel productivity.

By means of this three-step analysis, a theoretical assessment of complexity impact on company performances can be hypothesized, and an empirical validation pursued. One important point to be discussed is the connection between complexity drivers and costs. Due to research time constraints and confidentiality needs, no direct analysis on the cost impact of each driver was performed.[5] Our hypothesis is that, if the model is able to show the existence of a relationship between, for instance, investments in automated handling tools and correspondent reduction in man-hours effort, the companies will be able to estimate the amount of potential savings. To this extent, we had to remember that drivers were selected as much as possible according to the principles of the Activity Based methodology[6] in order to ease this estimation which has been kept outside the boundaries of this study.

This conceptual model, according to us, represents an effective approach, both rigorous and suitable to the theory-building target of this research program, thus fulfilling the second objective declared in Section 1.

4 The Empirical Study

4.1 Data Collection Methodology

The defined research objectives and the depth of the matter made the selection of the appropriate data collection methodology easier, since a survey approach would not have been able to assure the needed depth, breadth and quality of the gathered information. Furthermore, research time constraints and the purpose of assessing some generalizable conclusion made it unfeasible to take an action research approach. We decided to address traditional case studies as they are also particularly suitable for theory building studies like present one. Moreover, case studies are appropriate support for collecting data regarding management levers to reduce and manage complexity, thus accomplishing the third research objective (which is not discussed in this paper, cf. Section 1).

---

[5] Actually, some data on percentage cost split have been gathered from cost accountants in order to validate the precision of the model in assessing the company current state.

[6] See Kaplan, Johnson (1987).

If this appeared to be a natural choice, the extreme heterogeneity of the subject required collecting a vast amount of data to assure a certain level of rigor in the analysis, and therefore raised the need for a rather large number of cases to be conducted. This, in addition to the depth of information collected for each company, held a potential risk of research resources depletion; in order to manage it, we decided to plan the data collection phase according to the following framework:

1. *Interview structure*: the interviews were structured in accordance with a standard form which helped the interviewers concentrate on those aspects in Section 3. The form was beta-tested on a few companies in the early steps of the research project and then, after some modifications, frozen.

2. *Multiple respondents for each interviewed company*: to increase the availability and the quality of the gathered information, the whole form was divided into modules (eight modules, about ten pages each), and submitted to different managers at the company. Selected respondents were CEOs, sales officers, logistics and production planning managers, R&D managers, process engineering officers, quality managers, plant managers and cost accountants. Each respondent was responsible for the fulfillment of his own module.

3. *Performing the interviews*: modules were sent to each respondent two weeks before the planned interview. In the interview (about two hours for each respondent) the research team examined collected data to discuss and validate it. A short de-briefing at the end of the meeting was planned to help the research team and managers clarify on missing or incoherent answers. If needed, a follow up was planned in the following weeks.

Thanks to this operating procedure, it was possible to collect a significant amount of information with limited costs and in a relatively short time.

Before closing, we would like to assure that, given the above mentioned objectives and the methodology chosen to fulfill them (i.e. case studies), no statistical analysis or correlation measure will be provided, but rather a set of evidences which support the existence of a relationship between management choices, complexity drivers and output variables. In our opinion, this does not portray a limitation in this first stage of the research project in which the theory-building purpose represents the main concern. Likely, as a next step, a restriction on the established relationships will allow more focused feed-back and data integration, sample redesign and quantitative inference about the hypothesized implications.

4.2 Sample Selection

The selection of the business on which to test the developed model represented a critical aspect for two reasons. First, according to research objectives, a supply chain oriented approach should be adopted. Therefore, the studied industry should allow easy access to many companies at different levels in the supply chain. This was not so easy since, for instance, companies belonging to the textile-apparel supply chain (quite important in the Italian economic scenario) have very different levels of concern about complexity topics, and while producers are very interested in complexity management, fabric suppliers are more focused on cost reduction and product quality increase.

As a second reason, even if the interviews were an excellent source of information, a significant *a priori* level of knowledge about the studied business was necessary in order to support the modeling and data validation phases, as well as attract commitment from companies.

These two conditions led the research team to the Italian Household Appliance industry (dishwashers, washing machines, refrigerators and cookers). Besides being a very relevant business[7], both producers and component suppliers are traditional manufacturing companies interested in complexity-related issues. Moreover, the research team was rather familiar with the business because of previous research experiences (cf. Perona et al., 1998).

Given this point, a call for interest was addressed to Italian companies belonging to the Household Appliance industry. Thirteen companies, including some of the most relevant players in the business agreed to participate. As expected, none of them belong to the distribution stage, which in Italy is currently undergoing a deep change due to the entrance of big foreign players which force incumbent distributors to stay focused on this process.

Key Item	Passive components suppliers	Active components suppliers	Manufacturers
Number of firms	2	6	5
Average turnover (Eu·10^6, 2000)	59	177	246
Average employees (2000)	240	610	650
Average Value added (% on turnover, 2000)	51%	48%	31%
Average turnover trend (3 years)	+6.5%	+3.5%	+12.4%

Table 1: Sample Description

As illustrated in Table 1, to address a consistent set of topics, participating companies were divided into two groups, namely components suppliers and manufac-

---

[7] White Goods Italian plants volumes account for almost 50% of total European production.

turers. A further distinction was made among suppliers (passive and active ones) to take into consideration that a passive component (e.g. plastic shell, gasket, cable) requires a much simpler production and logistic system than an active one (e.g. engine, compressor).

5   First Results

In the following section we present two different evidences drawn following the methodological approach described in Section 4. The purpose of this section is to point out what kind of understanding should be expected as output of the research project.

The first evidence is related to the Market presence dimension, and tries to show that the more the company concentrate on less customers, the better performances are assured to them. This operating condition was identified by measuring the number of customers which accounts for 80% of total turnover; the selected complexity driver is the percentage of Sales & Marketing total workforce effort devoted to activities directly related to customer care (e.g. advising *ex ante* and *ex post*, audits to customer) Finally the output variable is a normalized index ranging from 0 to 100, the higher the better, which summarizes measured delivery performances, namely average delivery lead time, % of late orders and average delay. The relevant values are shown in Table 2.

Key Item	Passive components suppliers	Active components suppliers	Manufacturers
% of customers which account for 80% turnover	19.4%	15.3%	14.8%
Customer care effort / total effort (Sales & Marketing Workforce)	6.8%	9.6%	10.6%
Performance index (0÷100)	60	78	77

Table 2: Customer Focusing Impact on Complexity

If we compare passive component suppliers with Active component suppliers we notice that a reduction of about 25% in the percentage of customer which accounts for 20% of total turnover (from 19.4% to 15.3%) implies an increase in customer care focused activities of about 35% (from 6.8% to 9.6%), with a global improvement in delivery performances of about 30%. The situation doesn't change if the comparison is made with manufacturers. Apart from the numerical value of the performance index, which may be affected by the adopted law, this evidence indicates that a complexity reduction effort made to select and focus on fewer customers may represent a competitive advantage through the concentration of effort toward customer care activities. These indications may represent interesting empirical evidence if delivery performances represent the critical factor of success in that business.

A second example is related to the logistics dimension, and shows that the more careful the plant layout design, the higher the handlers' productivity. This operating condition was identified by measuring the average distance of internal handling operations. The selected complexity driver is the % of handling cycles which is performed with non-automated equipment. Finally, the output variable is the handling personnel's productivity (handling cycles/year). The measured values are shown in Table 3.

Key Item	Passive components suppliers	Active components suppliers	Manufacturers
Average distance for internal handling operations (mt)	25	65	145
% of manual cycles on total handling cycles (Internal Logistics Workforce)	10%	30%	36%
Handler productivity (cycle/year)	29.100	20.600	13.200

Table 3: Lay-out Design Impact on Complexity

The depicted trend may seem obvious, but it underlines the space which is available for complexity management investment if a critical analysis of the productive system is performed. These values are actually very helpful to managers in evaluating which improvement space is too often neglected on the basis of a consolidated way of doing things.

6 Concluding Remarks

This paper presented a two-year research project aimed at developing an innovative methodology to evaluate quantitatively the complexity level within a supply chain, and assessing whether the current complexity level represents the optimum equilibrium between the target effectiveness and efficiency performances. After describing the whole methodology, both in terms of basic assumptions and in terms of modeling approach, the paper has presented some early findings drawn by the application of the methodology to the Italian Household Appliance industry. The specific perspective adopted is that one of supply chain management achieved by interviewing a set of suppliers and finished goods producers.

The methodology has shown to be a powerful interpretive tool, and a valid support in analyzing the impact of complexity on specific aspects of the operative and organizational structure. Moreover, thanks to the selected validation approach, it also suggested several correlations between strategic choices and operating conditions, complexity drivers and performance variables. Naturally, the highlighted correlations must be tested by means of different empirical methodologies (e.g. surveys) which represent a natural research stream to be pursued from now on. An additional point of strength is represented by the possibility of tailoring the core model to various businesses, thus opening other interesting theory proposal and validation opportunities. A limitation of the designed model may be found in the subjectivity with which the complexity matter can be treated; actually this may become a drawback, but may also represent a good opportunity for "putting numbers on soft things", which is often the real concern for many managers around the world.

7 References

Clark, K. B., Wheelwright, S. C. (1992): Managing the New Product and Process Development, The Free Press, New York, NY.

Hardle, B. G. S., Lodish, L. M. (1994): The Logic of Product Line Extensions, in: Harvard Business Review, Vol. 72, November-December (1994), 53-62.

Perona, M., Cigolini, R., Chessa, M., Angellara, S., Adani, M., et al (1998): The Integrated Management of Logistic Chains: A Field Research in Italy, Proceedings of 10th international Working Seminar On Production Economics, IGLS, 16-20 Feb. 1998.

Quelch, J. A., Kenny, D. (1994): Extend Profits, Not Product Lines, in: Harvard Business Review, Vol. 72, September-October (1994), p. 153-160.

Stalk Jr., G. (1988): Time-The Next Source of Competitive Advantage, in: Harvard Business Review, Vol. 66, July-August (1988), p. 95-103.

Suzue, T., Kohdate, A. (1990): Variety Reduction Program, Productivity Press, Cambridge, Massachusetts.

Using the Balanced Scorecard for Interorganizational Performance Management of Supply Chains – A Case Study

Klaus Zimmermann

1 Introduction 400
2 Description of the Chemicals Supply Chain 400
3 Research Methodology 401
4 Supply Chain Balanced Scorecard Chemicals 402
5 Conclusion 413
6 References 414

Summary:
This study discusses an action research project carried out at two companies in the chemical industry, which had established a non-equity strategic partnership. This partnership was between an international producer of chemicals and one of its key distributors, both based in Europe. One of the results of the joint project was the development of an inter-enterprise Supply Chain Balanced Scorecard in order to implement a joint supply chain strategy and to support supply chain improvement efforts. The following case study illustrates the extension of the Balanced Scorecard concept as related to the management of supply chains. It describes the development steps of the joint scorecard and analyses its features. The study closes with a critical assessment of its benefits, provides recommendations for further implementations and highlights implications for further research.

Keywords: Supply Chain Management, Performance Measurement, Balanced Scorecard

1 Introduction

Although a number of studies point out the advantages of an inter-enterprise approach to supply chain management, true inter-organizational projects are still relatively scarce. It has been argued that one of the reasons for this is the lack of appropriate performance measurement systems, which make the performance of the whole chain comprehensible and demonstrate the benefits of partnership to the participating companies.[1] Additionally, it has been stated that traditional performance measurement systems are designed for single entities and do not readily support supply chain perspectives.[2] In this context, it is not surprising that supply chain performance evaluation has attracted the attention of many researchers and companies worldwide. However, the development of inter-organizational performance measurement systems is still in an initial stage and such systems lack empirical evidence.[3]

In the last few years, the Balanced Scorecard has gained increasing acceptance in industry as an instrument for the implementation of corporate or business unit strategies. While currently representing the most widely recognized performance measurement framework[4], the Balanced Scorecard is neither specifically designed for inter-enterprise measurement nor for the evaluation of supply chain performance measurement.

2 Description of the Chemicals Supply Chain

The following case study is based on the results of a joint project between a large, international producer of chemicals, referred to herein as 'International Chemicals', and a medium-sized distributor called 'ChemTrade'. International Chemicals produces final chemical products from raw materials. ChemTrade represents a major distribution channel for International Chemicals and acts as the

---

[1] See Cooper, Lambert, Pagh (1997), p. 10; Lummus, Vokurka (1999), p. 15; Ballou, Gilbert, Mukherjee (2000), p. 7; Gunasekaran, Patel, Tirtiroglu (2001), p. 72.
[2] See Van Hoek (1998) p. 187; Cullen et al. (1999), p. 30; Gericke et al. (1999), p. 16; Schweier, Jehle (1999), p. 83.
[3] See Berry et al. (1997), p. 74; Cullen et al. (1999), p. 30; Kaluza, Blecker (1999), p. 19-20; Seal et al. (1999), p. 303; Kummer (2001), p. 81. For an example of an inter-organisational implementation of the Balanced Scorecard in an Efficient Consumer Response Project see Zimmermann, Kohl (2001), p. 36-40.
[4] See Klingebiel (1998), p. 8; Neely et al. (2000), p. 1122.

sole national distributor for certain product groups. In most cases, ChemTrade sells the chemicals directly to the final consumers, sometimes via another distributor (see Figure 1).

Figure 1: Chemicals Supply Chain.

The non-equity strategic partnership between International Chemicals and ChemTrade had been based on a long-term contract, which granted mutual exclusivity in certain regions. In January 2000, a joint project was started with the objective to improve all processes from International Chemicals to the final consumer. The joint project team consisted of the top management of ChemTrade and divisional marketing and logistics management of International Chemicals. One of the results of the project was the development of a joint supply chain Balanced Scorecard between International Chemicals and ChemTrade.

3 Research Methodology

The author and a fellow colleague supported the companies in the development and implementation of the joint scorecard. The researchers initially were brought in to offer solutions and were mainly perceived as impartial facilitators of the process. Participating as neutral intermediaries provided them with the opportunity to analyze the scorecard process in this dyadic supply chain partnership. The research and resulting case study is based on the scorecard-related workshops, meetings and interviews conducted on numerous occasions over a period of ten months from December 2000 to September 2001.

In methodological terms, this research may be classified as a case of "action research" whereas the research output results 'from an involvement with members of an organization over a matter, which is of genuine concern to them'[5]. As discussed by Kaplan, the objective of action research is 'to modify and extend the emerging theory in light of knowledge gained through experience'[6]. In terms of the typology of Scapens the following case study may be most appropriately

---

[5] Eden, Huxham (1996), p. 75.
[6] Kaplan (1998), p. 91.

classified as an illustrative case study because it 'attempts to illustrate new and possibly innovative practices developed by particular companies'[7].

4 Supply Chain Balanced Scorecard Chemicals

4.1 Objectives

The development of the scorecard began approximately one year after the project kicked off, after various improvement initiatives had already been started. Therefore, one of the main objectives of the scorecard was to measure the success of the project to date. Other objectives included:

- Demonstrate the success of the co-operation.
- Clarify the strategic objectives of the supply chain partners.
- Provide a focus on critical performance measures.
- Identify further potentials for improvement.

4.2 Development Steps

The Supply Chain Balanced Scorecard Chemicals was developed during a series of four workshops over a period of six months. Participants of these workshops were managers and employees of both companies. When this case study was written the scorecard design was completed (see Figure 2).

Since a shared vision and joint strategic objectives between the two companies had not yet been formulated, the first step in the scorecard development process was to define these objectives. In contrast to the 'classic' approach the shared vision process was postponed and the strategic objectives were defined first (see Figure 2). The rationale for this was that the workshop participants considered the definition of strategic objectives as more relevant and specific than the shared vision process and thus representing a more logical start for the joint process. The following strategic objectives were defined:

- Profitable growth,
- Increased customer satisfaction,
- Reduction of inventory costs,

---

[7] Scapens (1990), p. 265.

- Enhancement of delivery service,
- Improved administrative processes (order processing, pricing process, data interchange, complaint handling),
- Use of e-commerce,
- Increased satisfaction of employees involved in co-operation,
- Joint marketing strategies and actions.

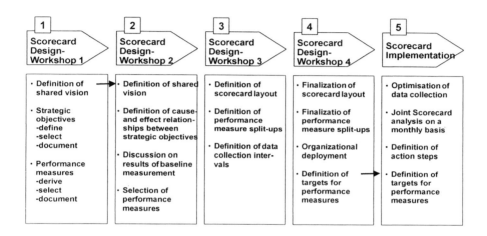

Figure 2: Development Steps of the Supply Chain Balanced Scorecard Chemicals.

Performance measures were identified based on these objectives. In the first workshop, performance measures which would best measure the achievement of the defined strategic objectives were defined. After this workshop, a first data collection ('baseline measurement') of these performance measures was performed in order to verify the availability of the required data. As a result, some performance measures were abandoned in the second workshop due to the related data collection effort. Moreover, cause and effect relationships between the strategic targets were discussed and the following shared vision was defined: 'Together better, faster and stronger at the market'. Between the second and third workshops data was collected and actions were taken to improve data quality. In the third workshop the layout of the scorecard was defined. The group decided to show all performance measures on one page in order to provide an overview as well as to compile the scorecard on a monthly basis. Additionally, certain performance measures were assigned to product groups ('split-ups') for detailed analyses, and it was decided that such analyses would be based on company and inter-company data. In the fourth workshop, further refinements on the display of the performance measures and the split-ups were defined. In addition, roles and responsibilities for the scorecard at each company were defined and assigned. Furthermore, it was also agreed upon to postpone the definition of targets for the performance measures and to combine this task with the budgeting process. During the implementation phase, the group plans to continuously optimize data collection and perform joint scorecard analyses on a monthly basis, including the determination and assignment of action steps.

4.3 Features

The author will analyze the Supply Chain Balanced Scorecard Chemicals as to whether its features correspond to those of the traditional Balanced Scorecard which typically comprises:

- Balanced set of measures,
- Performance measures derived from strategy,
- Multiple performance dimensions,
- Cause and effect relationships,
- Focus on few performance measures,
- Hierarchy of performance measures.

As mentioned in Section 1, the evaluation of the performance of the whole supply chain is critical for the management of the supply chain. Therefore, in addition to the aforementioned features the Supply Chain Balanced Scorecard Chemicals will also be analyzed as to whether it contains inter-enterprise performance measures.

4.3.1 Balanced Set of Measures

As discussed by Kaplan and Norton the Balanced Scorecard consists of a balanced set of financial and non-financial performance measures, lagging and leading indicators as well as internal and external performance measures.[8] Table 1 shows an allocation of the performance measures of the Supply Chain Balanced Scorecard Chemicals as related to these categories.

---

[8] Financial performance measures are expressed in monetary terms. Lagging indicators such as market share or profitablity reflect the results of actions. Leading indicators such as error rates or cycle times provide early feedback on the success of strategy implementation and are considered as drivers of performance. External performancee measures are oriented toward the shareholders of the company whereas internal performance measures are directed to the business processes and the innovation and growth potential of the company. See Kaplan, Norton (1997a), p. VII, 30, 71, 144-145; Kaplan, Norton (1997b), p. 5-6.

All performance measures of the Supply Chain Balanced Scorecard Chemicals correspond to the mentioned categories, albeit with a different weighing (see Table 1). The scorecard is dominated by non-financial measures. Only one of the nine performance measures represents a financial performance measure ('turnover'). Similarly, leading indicators are represented to a much larger extent than lagging indicators (seven of nine performance measures). The reason for the emphasis on non-financial and leading indicators lies in the objective of the joint project itself, which is to identify and realize improvement potential. With respect to internal and external performance measures, there is a balanced presentation. One performance measure ('sales volume') represents an external measure as well as an internal measure (see Table 1).

Performance Measure	Definition	Financial	Non-Financial	Lagging Indicator	Leading Indicator	External	Internal
Turnover	Turnover of International Chemicals and ChemTrade	x		x		x	
Market share	Market Share according to sales people of ChemTrade (on an annual basis)		x	x		x	
Customer satisfaction index	Index of customer satisfaction according to questionnaire (on an annual basis)		x		x	x	
Complaint number	Number of complaints received by International Chemicals and ChemTrade		x		x	x	
Complaint quota	Number of complaints divided by number of ChemTrade orders		x		x	x	
Delivery reliability	Confirmed customer delivery date divided by actual delivery date or availability (if pick-up)		x		x		x
Inventory	Average inventory of International Chemicals and ChemTrade		x		x		x
Sales days' coverage	Average inventory divided by monthly sales (International Chemicals and ChemTrade)		x		x		x
Sales volume	Sales of International Chemicals and ChemTrade in tons		x		x	x	x

Table 1: Performance Measures Supply Chain Balanced Scorecard Chemicals.

From the partnership point of view, this performance measure represents an external one because it comprises the sales from ChemTrade to its customers. From that perspective 'sales volume' may also be considered a supply chain internal performance measure as it also includes the sales from International Chemicals to ChemTrade.

4.3.2 Performance Measures Derived from Strategy

A main characteristic of the Balanced Scorecard and other performance measurement systems is to define performance measures based on strategy.[9] In the case of the Supply Chain Balanced Scorecard Chemicals, the selection of performance measures is based on jointly defined strategic objectives. However, performance measures are not defined for all objectives. This is due to the fact that either adequate performance measures which effectively measured the respective objective, could not be identified or the collection of the data had resulted in an economically unjustifiable effort.

4.3.3 Multiple Performance Dimensions

Another typical feature of the traditional Balanced Scorecard is the allocation of strategic objectives and performance measures according to the four dimensions: Financial ('how do we look to our shareholders?'), Customer ('how do customers see us?'), Processes ('what must we excel at?') and Development ('how can we continue to improve and create value?').[10] The Supply Chain Balanced Scorecard Chemicals follows this generic framework. Strategic objectives for all four dimensions are defined.

Dimension	Strategic Objective	Performance Measure
Financial	Profitable growth	Turnover
		Market share
Customer	Higher customer satisfaction	Customer satisfaction index
		Complaint number
		Complaint quota
Processes	Enhancement of delivery service	Delivery reliability
	Reduction of inventory costs	Inventory
		Sales days' coverage
	Improved administrative processes	Sales volume
Development	Use of e-commerce possibilities	Not yet defined
	Increased satisfaction of employees involved in co-operation	Not yet defined
	Joint marketing strategies and actions	Not yet defined

Table 2: Allocation of Strategic Objectives and Performance Measures.

---

[9] See for example Kaplan, Norton (1992), p. 77-78; Kaplan, Norton (1996), p. 68.
[10] See Kaplan, Norton (1992), p. 72.

However, performance measures are not derived for all strategic objectives. As a result, the development dimension is not represented by performance measures (see Table 2).

Nearly half of the performance measures (four out of nine) are allocated to the process dimension, followed by the customer and financial perspective (see Table 2). As is demonstrated by the table above, the main focus of the Supply Chain Balanced Scorecard Chemicals is on customer satisfaction and logistics processes.

4.3.4 Cause and Effect Relationships

As discussed by Kaplan and Norton, the strategy of an organization is a system of hypotheses about cause and effect.[11] Therefore, the strategic objectives are to be linked by cause and effect relationships.[12] Additionally, the performance measures shall be linked with each other by these relationships and thus connect the performance dimensions with each other.[13] The main purpose of this is to make these relationships explicit in order to be able to manage and validate them.[14] This allows analyzing the causes of outcomes of passed actions while simultaneously providing an early warning system.[15] In the case of the Chemicals Supply Chain cause and effect relationships were merely discussed for the strategic objectives and not for the performance measures (see Figure 3).

The direction of the arrows points out a reinforcing effect. An example for a cause and effect relationship from the Supply Chain Balanced Scorecard Chemicals would be: Increased employee satisfaction will lead to better handling of orders which in turn improves delivery service. If customers receive a better delivery service (in terms of delivery reliability, time, quality or flexibility) they are likely to be more satisfied and may purchase further products, which fosters revenue and growth of the supply chain. As illustrated by Figure 3, a mutual reinforcing effect between some strategic objectives is perceived by International Chemical and ChemTrade. For example, the improvement of administrative processes, such as handling of complaints, is considered to increase employee satisfaction. Conversely, it is assumed that higher employee morale will lead in turn to better performance of the complaint process. The link between 'better delivery service' and 'less inventory costs' indicates that these are the two main objectives in the processes dimension being of equal importance and interdependent.

---

[11] See Kaplan, Norton (1997b), p. 5.
[12] See Kaplan, Norton (1997a), p. 144.
[13] See Kaplan, Norton (1996), p. 65; Kaplan, Norton (1997a), p. 28-30; Kaplan, Norton (1997b), p. 5.
[14] See Kaplan, Norton (1996), p. 65.
[15] See Kaplan, Norton (1997a), p. 28; Kaplan, Norton (1997b), p. 5.

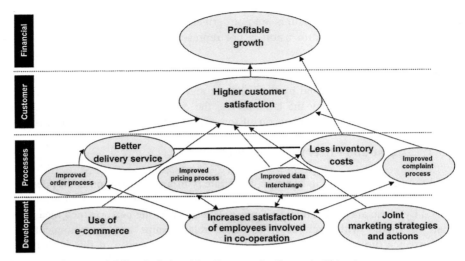

Figure 3: Cause and Effect Relationships Between the Strategic Objectives.

4.3.5 Hierarchy of Performance Measures

A function of the Balanced Scorecard is to cascade the top-level Balanced Scorecard down to lower hierarchical levels.[16] Having Balanced Scorecards in place at all hierarchical levels supports the strategy implementation throughout a company.[17] Neither at International Chemicals nor at ChemTrade was a Balanced Scorecard implemented prior to the joint project. Therefore, no connection of the Supply Chain Balanced Scorecard Chemicals with scorecards of the companies could be established. However, a decomposition of the strategic company objectives took place as the divisional objectives from marketing and logistics of International Chemicals and the company objectives from ChemTrade formed the basis for the definition of the joint supply chain objectives.

4.3.6 Focus on few Performance Measures

Kaplan and Norton argue that numbers should not overload the Balanced Scorecard and they suggest 15 to 20 performance measures as a general guideline.[18] The Supply Chain Balanced Scorecard Chemicals consists of nine

---

[16] See Kaplan, Norton (1997b), p. 9.
[17] See Kaplan, Norton (1997a), p. 34-35.
[18] See Kaplan, Norton (1993) p. 135. However, the limitation on few strategically relevant performance measures does not represent an innovation of the Balanced Scorecard concept. The focus on few performance measures was much earlier discussed by Reichmann and Lachnit. See Reichmann, Lachnit (1976), p. 707-708.

Supply Chain Balanced Scorecard 409

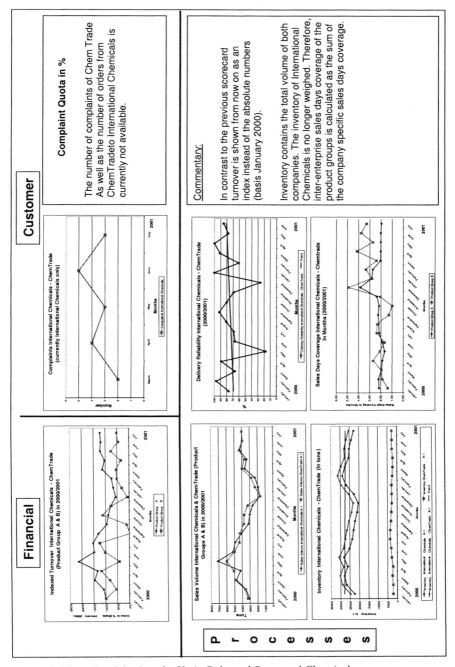

Figure 4: Example of the Supply Chain Balanced Scorecard Chemicals.

performance measures of which seven are collected monthly and two on an annual basis ('market share' and 'customer satisfaction index', see Table 1). Therefore, the number of performance measures is below the recommended amount. Figure 4 provides an example of the Supply Chain Balanced Scorecard Chemicals.

However, Kaplan and Norton point out that the number of performance measures is rather insignificant as long as the performance measures are aligned to a single strategy.[19]

4.3.7 Inter-Enterprise Performance Measures

The traditional Balanced Scorecard concept is focused on individual companies and therefore does not include inter-enterprise performance measures. If the Balanced Scorecard is applied to the management of supply chains it needs to incorporate inter-enterprise performance measures as well as individual enterprise performance measures. While inter-enterprise performance measures show all members how the supply chain is performing, enterprise performance measures can serve as a diagnostic on where problems are occurring within members of a partnership.[20] The Supply Chain Balanced Scorecard Chemicals consists of four inter-enterprise performance measures: 'complaint number', 'complaint quota', 'inventory' and 'sales days' coverage'. For these performance measures data of International Chemicals and ChemTrade were combined. 'Complaint number' and 'complaint quota' comprise the number of complaints, which are received by each of the companies. 'Inventory' encompasses the total of inventory of both companies. For 'sales days' coverage' the companies' sales day's coverage figures are added up. For 'inventory' and 'sales days coverage' the enterprises' data are displayed in addition to the inter-enterprise data for further analysis. During the project certain actions were initiated to reduce inventory of certain product groups. Therefore, the Supply Chain Balanced Scorecard Chemicals contains an appendix of analysis sheets by product group for the performance measures 'sales volume', 'inventory' and 'sales days' coverage'. However, due to the dyadic nature of the partnership the inter-enterprise data is limited to two companies

4.3.8 Features Supply Chain Balanced Scorecard Chemicals versus Traditional Balanced Scorecard

The traditional Balanced Scorecard concept and the Supply Chain Balanced Scorecard Chemicals have a number of common features. As Table 3 illustrates the main differences lie in a stronger emphasis on non-financial performance measures and leading indicators, the use of the supply chain strategy instead of a company strategy as a basis for performance measures, and the use of inter-

---

[19] See Kaplan, Norton (1996), p. 68.
[20] See Brewer, Speh (2000), p. 84.

enterprise performance measures. Other differences seem mainly to be the result of the specifics of this particular case study, such as no cause and effect relationships between performance measures or no links between the supply chain scorecard and the company Balanced Scorecard simply because the latter was not existent.

Features	Traditional Balanced Scorecard	Supply Chain Balanced Scorecard Chemicals
Balanced set of performance measures	• Balance of financial and non-financial performance measures, leading and lagging indicators, external and internal performance measures	• Focus on non-financial performance measures (8 out of 9) and leading indicators (7 out of 9) • Balance of internal and external performance measures
Performance measures derived from strategy	• Basis: In the majority of empirical cases business unit or company strategy	• Basis: Joint supply chain strategy
Multiple performance dimensions	• Dimensions according to strategy • Dimensions reflecting specifics of the company • Generic framework: , 4-Dimensions-Balanced Scorecard'	• Dimensions according to strategy • Dimensions reflecting specifics of the supply chain • 4-Dimensions-Balanced Scorecard' framework applied
Cause and effect relationships	• Between strategic objectives • Between performance measures	• Only between strategic objectives
Hierarchy of performance measures	• Top-down decomposition of the Balanced Scorecard from company level to individual level within company	• No top-down decomposition possible. Supply Chain Balanced Scorecard was the first scorecard of the two companies
Focus on few performance measures	• Recommendation 15 - 20 performance measures	• 9 performance measures of which 7 are collected monthly and 2 yearly
Inter-enterprise performance measures	• N/A	• 4 inter-enterprise performance measures

Table 3: Features of the Traditional Balanced Scorecard Concept versus the Supply Chain Balanced Scorecard Chemicals.

4.4 Benefits

When this case study was written, the design of the Supply Chain Balanced Scorecard Chemicals had just been completed (see Chapter 4.2). Therefore, the following list of benefits is preliminary and should be evaluated as such:

- Trust amongst the supply chain partners was increased through information exchange.
- The success of the supply chain co-operation could be continuously monitored.
- The result of actions initiated by the partnership could be evaluated.
- The scorecard provided a focus on critical performance measures.
- By using inter-enterprise performance measures potentials for improvement in the supply chain could be identified and implemented.
- Planning security could be enhanced through better information exchange.
- The Balanced Scorecard provided an effective framework to discuss joint improvement efforts in a structured way.

4.5 Recommendations

In respect to benefits of the Balanced Scorecard, the following recommendations have been developed. The reader should keep in mind the relatively early compilation of this study with regard to the Supply Chain Balanced Scorecard Chemicals process. It is also worth noting that some of these recommendations may also apply to the development of a company Balanced Scorecard:

1. Top management commitment from the participating companies for the joint scorecard is required; trust seems to be another indispensable prerequisite. Without trust the supply chain partners would not be willing to pass on their data fearing that another company in the supply chain would take advantage of this information.

2. Select performance measures which may be collected with an economically justifiable effort. Therefore, it is important to perform a first data collection as a test ('baseline measurement') prior to the final selection of performance measures to clarify the data collection effort.

3. If performance measures show inter-enterprise data, for example the total of inventory in the supply chain, the additional display of the performance of the supply chain partners can be useful in order to show the contribution of each company and to identify potential for improvement.

4. Keep the complexity of the Balanced Scorecard itself to a minimum. Selecting few performance measures maintains focus on the relevant data and reduces the data collection effort.
5. It is decisive to define clear responsibilities for the implementation of the scorecard. This comprises the assignment of responsibilities at each company for data collection and the selection of a responsible person for the regular compilation of the scorecard.
6. For the development of the scorecard an external facilitator is considered helpful.
7. It is important to continuously check whether the scorecard provides the relevant data, to constantly improve data quality and to reduce the data collection effort. The participants in the supply chain must perceive that the benefits of the scorecard outweigh the efforts associated with compiling it.

5 Conclusion

This case study discusses how the Balanced Scorecard may represent an effective instrument to support the management of inter-enterprise supply chains. However, since the development of a Supply Chain Balanced Scorecard involves revealing company objectives and data, its implementation is not feasible if trust does not exist between the partnering companies. Taking this into account, a Balanced Scorecard shared by all companies in the supply chain would require extensive trust throughout. At the same time, jointly developing a Balanced Scorecard and sharing data may re-enforce trust and strengthen the partnership. However, a supply chain-wide implementation of the Balanced Scorecard, although theoretically desirable, seems rather unlikely in practice. Further empirical evidence of shared Balanced Scorecards are therefore most likely identified in dyadic relationships. It would be worthwhile analyzing the findings of other dyadic Balanced Scorecard implementations and comparing them with those identified in this case study.

6 References

Ballou, R. H., Gilbert, S. M., Mukherjee, A. (2000): New Managerial Challenges from Supply Chain Opportunities, in: Industrial Marketing Management, Vol. 29, No. 1 (2000), p. 7-18.

Berry, T., Ahmed, A./Cullen, J., Dunlop, A., Seal, W., Johnston, S., Holmes, M. (1997): The Consequences of Inter-Firm Supply Chains for Management Accounting, in: Management Accounting (British), No. 11 (1997), p. 74-75.

Brewer, P.C., Speh, T.W. (2000): Using the Balanced Scorecard to Measure Supply Chain Performance, in: Journal of Business Logistics. Vol. 21, No. 1 (2000), pp. 75-93.

Cooper, M. C., Lambert, D. M., Pagh, J. D. (1997): Supply Chain Management: more than a new Name for Logistics, in: The International Journal of Logistics Management, Vol. 8, No. 1 (1997), p. 1-14.

Cullen, J., Berry, A. J., Seal, W., Dunlop, A., Ahmed, M., Marson, J. (1999): Interfirm Supply Chains: the Contribution of Management Accounting, in: Management Accounting (British), No. 6 (1999), p. 30-32.

Eden, C., Huxham, C. (1996): Action Research for Management Research. In: British Journal of Management, Vol. 7, p. 75-86.

Gericke, J., Kaczmarek, M., Schweier, H., Sonnek, A., Stüllenberg, F., Wiesehahn, A. (1999): Anforderungen an das Controlling von Supply Chains (Requirements for the Controlling of Supply Chains), in: Logistik Spektrum, Vol. 11, No. 2 (1999), p. 13-16.

Gunasekaran, A., Patel, C., Tirtiroglu, E. (2001): Performance Measures and Metrics in a Supply Chain Environment, in: International Journal of Operations and Production Management. Vol. 21, No. 1/2 (2001), p. 71-87.

Kaluza, B., Blecker, Th. (1999): Integration von Unternehmung ohne Grenzen und Supply Chain Management (Integration of the Enterprise without Limits and Supply Chain Management), Discussion Paper of the College of Business Administration Universitiy of Klagenfurt, Austria.

Kaplan, R. S. (1998): Innovation Action Research: Creating new Management Theory and Practice, in: Journal of Management Accounting, Vol. 10, p. 89-118.

Kaplan, R. S., Norton, D. P. (1992): The Balanced Scorecard - Measures that Drive Performance, in: Harvard Business Review, Vol. 70, No. 1 (1992), p. 72-79.

Kaplan, R. S., Norton, D. P. (1993): Putting the Balanced Scorecard to Work, in: Harvard Business Review, Vol. 71, No. 5 (1993), p. 134-142.

Kaplan, R. S., Norton, D. P. (1996): Linking the Balanced Scorecard to Strategy, in: California Management Review, Vol. 39, No. 1 (1996), p. 53-79.

Kaplan, R. S., Norton, D. P. (1997a): The Balanced Scorecard: Translating Strategy into Action, Schaeffer-Poeschel, Stuttgart.

Kaplan, R. S., Norton, D. P. (1997b): Why does Business Need a Balanced Scorecard?, in: Journal of Cost Management, Vol. 11, No. 3 (1997), p. 5-10.

Klingebiel, N. (1998): Performance Management – Performance Measurement, in: Zeitschrift für Planung, Vol. 9, No. 1 (1998), p. 1-15.

Kummer, S. (2001): Supply Chain Controlling, in: Kostenrechnungspraxis, Vol. 45, No. 2 (2001), p. 81-87.

Lummus, R. R., Vokurka, R. J. (1999): Defining Supply Chain Management: A Historical Perspective and Practical Guidelines, in: Industrial Management & Data Systems, Vol. 99, No. 1 (1999), p. 11-17.

Neely, A./Mills, J./Platts, K./ Richards, H./ Gregory, M./Bourne, M./Kennerley, M. (2000): Performance Measurement System Design: Developing and Testing a Process-Based Approach, in: International Journal of Operations and Production Management, Vol. 20, No. 10 (2000), p. 1119-1145.

Reichmann, T., Lachnit, L. (1976): Planning, Management and Control with Performance Measures, in: Zeitschrift für betriebswirtschaftliche Forschung, Vol. 28 (1976), p. 705-723.

Scapens, R. W. (1990): Researching Management Accounting Practice: the Role of Case Methods, in: British Accounting Review, Vol. 22 (1990), p. 259-281.

Schweier, H., Jehle, E. (1999): Controlling of Logistic Networks: Conceptual Requirements and an Approach for Instrumental Design, in: Industrie Management, Vol. 15, No. 5 (1999), p. 83-87.

Seal, W., Cullen, J., Dunlop, A., Berry, T., Ahmed, M. (1999): Enacting a European Supply Chain: a Case Study on the Role of Management Accounting, in: Management Accounting Research, Vol. 10, No. 3 (1999), p. 303-322.

Van Hoek, R. I. (1998): „Measuring the Unmeasurable" – Measuring and Improving Performance in the Supply Chain, in: Supply Chain Management, Vol. 3, No. 4 (1998), p. 187-192.

Zimmermann, K., Kohl, M. (2001): Projekt-Scorecard - Wie Continental eine ECR-Initiative steuert (Project-Scorecard: How Continental Manages an ECR-Initiative), in: Absatzwirtschaft, Vol. 44, No. 6 (2001), p. 36-40.

Editors

Dr. Stefan Seuring Dipl.-Betriebswirt, M. Sc. Chem., M. Sc. Env. M.

Born 1967, 1987-90 studies in Business Administration at the University of Cooperative Education Stuttgart (D), 1990-95 studies in Chemistry at the Universities of Bayreuth (D) and Bristol (UK), 1995-98 research assistant at Faculty of Environmental Technology, University of Paderborn (D), 1997-98 distance studies in Environmental Management at the University of Kent at Canterbury (UK). In 2001 completion of PhD at the University of Oldenburg (D). 1998-2001 lecturer, since April 2001 senior lecturer at the Department of Production and the Environment, Faculty of Business, Economics and Law, University of Oldenburg (D). Research carried out in close co-operation with major companies from various sectors, specially chemistry and textiles.
Research interest: supply chains, cost management, environmental management.

Supply Chain Management Center, Institute for Business Administration,
Carl von Ossietzky University Oldenburg, 26111 Oldenburg, Germany
Tel. +49 441 798 4188   Fax: +49 441 798 5852
Email: stefan.seuring@uni-oldenburg.de, http://www.uni-oldenburg.de/scmc

Maria Goldbach Dipl.-Oec., Diplômée de l'INSEEC Bordeaux

Born 1973, 1993-1999 studies in Business Administration and Economics at the University of Kassel, Germany. In this context, 1997-1998, studies in Business Administration at the INSEEC (Institut des Hautes Etudes Economiques et Commerciales) in Bordeaux, France. In 1999 research assistant in the Research Group for Environmental Policy at the University of Kassel. Since January 2000 research assistant and lecturer at the Department of Production and the Environment, Faculty of Business, Economics and Law, University of Oldenburg, Germany. Co-ordination of a joint research project with five research partners as well as two major companies in the textile sector.
Research interest: Organisational Theory, Environmental Management, Supply Chain Management, Cost Management.

Chair for Produktion and the Environment, Institute for Business Administration,
Carl von Ossietzky University Oldenburg, 26111 Oldenburg, Germany
Tel. +49 441 798 4142   Fax: +49 441 798 5852
Email: maria.goldbach@uni-oldenburg.de, http://www.uni-oldenburg.de/ecomtex

Authors

Prof. Dr. Layek Abdel Malek

Born in June 1947 in Cairo, Egypt, holds a Bachelor of Science and a Master degree in Mechanical Engineering both from Cairo University, Computer Sciemce Diploma from National Planning Institute in Cairo, and a Ph.D in Operations Reseach from Polytechnic University in New York, USA. Dr. Malek has numerous publications and book chapters in the areas of robotic assembly, flexible manufacturing and inventory control. He is the recipient of many awards from National Science Foundation, AT&T, New Jersey State and CNR of Italy. Dr. Malek serves on the Editorial Boards of the Journal of Manufacturing Systems, International Journal of Industrial Engineering, and the Engineering Economist. Currently he is the Associate Dean of Engineering and professor of Industrial & Manufacturing Engineering.

New Jersey Institute of Technology,
University Heights, Newark, NJ 07102-9895, USA
Tel. +973 596-3648   Fax +973 596-3652
Email: malek@adm.njit.edu

Kourosh Bahrami Diplom-Kaufmann, CEMS Master

Born 1971 in Tehran, Iran, 1991-1998 studies in Economics and Business Administration at the Universities of Bonn and Cologne, Germany, 1994-1998 program of the Community of European Management Schools (CEMS) in International Business at the University of Cologne, Germany, and 1995 at the École des Hautes Études Commerciales (HEC) in Paris, France. Since 2000 PhD student at the Wirtschaftsuniversität Wien, Austria.

Since 1998 inhouse consultant for Supply Chain Management with Henkel KGaA, specialization: distribution concepts within Europe.

Research interest: strategic management, supply chain management, logistics cooperation

Henkel KGaA / Euro-Logistics
Henkelstr. 67, 40191 Düsseldorf (Germany)
Tel. +49 211 797-2781   Fax: +49 211 798-10736
Email: kourosh.bahrami@henkel.de

Monica Bartolini

Born 1974 in Ravenna, Italy – 1993/98 studies in Business Administration at the University of Bologna (I), Forlì Campus - Since 1998 PhD student in Business Administration at the University of Pisa (I) - Since 1998 researcher at the

CRESEM (research centre, University of Bologna, Forlì Campus) – Since October 2000 visiting at the Lean Enterprise Research Centre at the Cardiff Business School (UK) - Lecturer in Accounting, Cost Management Accounting, and Business Administration (University of Bologna, Forlì Campus).
Research interests: cost management, strategic cost management, management control.
University of Bologna, Forlì Campus, P. le Vittoria, 15, 47100, Forlì (FC), Italy
Tel. +39 0543 450 267   Fax: +39 0543 450 269
Email: monicabartolini@hotmail.com

Prof. Dr. Khurrum S. Bhutta

Born 1969 in Lahore, Pakistan, 1988-93 Mechanical engineering at University of Engineering & Technology Lahore, 1994-96 Master of Business Administration at Lahore University of Management Sciences, 1997-98 Research Assistant at Lahore University of Management Sciences, 1998-01 PhD Operations Management And Research Assistant at University of Texas At Arlington TX, U.S., Since January 2001 Assistant Professor Department of Information Systems at Nicholls State University Thibodaux LA, U.S. Research carried out in areas of Multinational Corporations and Supplier Selection for Textile Industry.
Research interest: Supply Chains, Cost Management, and International Trade

Department of Information Systems,
Nicholls State University, Box 2042, Thibodaux, La. 70310, USA
Email: is-mkb@nicholls.edu

Marco Fischer Dipl.-Kaufmann

Born 1975 in Karl-Marx-Stadt (today Chemnitz), Germany, 1996-2001 studies in Business Administration and Economics, emphasis Production and Industrial Management, Controlling and Computer Science in Economics at Chemnitz University of Technology, Germany, since 2001 research assistant at the Faculty of Economics and Business Administration (chair Production and Industrial Management) at Chemnitz University of Technology.
Research interest: ERP-systems, cost management, production nets, swarm intelligence, especially ant-colony-optimization.

Chair for Production and Industrial Management, Faculty of Economics and Business Administration, Chemnitz University of Technology,
09107 Chemnitz, Germany
Tel. +49 371 531 4205   Fax: +49 371 531 3958
Email: marco.fischer@wirtschaft.tu-chemnitz.de,
http://www.tu-chemnitz.de/wirtschaft/bwl7

Prof. Dr. Peter Hines

Born 1962 in Banbury, England, Professor of Supply Chain Management and Director of the Lean Enterprise Research Centre at Cardiff Business School. He holds a BA (MA) in geography from Cambridge University and an MBA and PhD from the University of Cardiff. Peter followed a successful career in distribution and manufacturing industry before joining Cardiff Business School in 1992. Since that time he initially led the Materials Management Unit and now leads the 24 strong Lean Enterprise Research Centre together with Professor Dan Jones.
He has undertaken extensive research into the Supply Chain in both the automotive and other industries.

Professor of Supply Chain Management, Cardiff Business School, Aberconway Building, Colum Drive, CF10 3EU, Cardiff, UK
Email: peterhines@hotmail.com

Prof. Dr. Arnd Huchzermeier

Born 1961 in Heidelberg, Germany, he is the Chair in Production Management of the Otto-Beisheim Graduate School of Management of the WHU in Vallendar. In 1991, he received a Ph.D. degree from the Wharton School of the University of Pennsylvania, Philadelphia, Pennsylvania, USA. Among others, he is Member of the ECR Academic Partnership and the Editorial Board of the ECR Journal; Academic Director of the German industry competition 'Industrial Excellence Award' of INSEAD; and Associate of the Real Options Group.
Research interests: real options in R&D, supply chain management respectively; product bundling and pricing, management models for Industrial Excellence as well as promotion planning and store performance optimization.

Department for Production Management, WHU Otto-Beisheim Graduate School of Management, Burgplatz 2, 56179 Vallendar, Germany
Email: ah@whu.edu

Prof. Dr. Faizul Huq

Born 1958 in Dhaka, Bangladesh, is an Associate Professor in the Department of Information Systems and Management Sciences of the College of Business Administration at the University of Texas at Arlington. He received his DBA from the University of Kentucky in 1990. His research interests are in the areas of Logistics and Supply Chain Management, Job Shop Scheduling, Group Technology and Cellular Manufacturing. His articles have appeared in numerous journals. He is a member of INFORMS, DSI, SME, and POMS.
Research intersts: Production Management, Logistics/Distribution Management, Manufacturing Engineering

Associate Professor, Department for Information Systems and Management Science, University of Texas at Arlington, P.O. Box 19437, Arlington, TX 76019, USA,
Tel. +1 817 272-3528
Email: huq@uta.edu

Michael Kaczmarek Diplom-Kaufmann

Born 1973 in Radevormwald, Germany, 1993-1998 studies in Business Administration at the University of Dortmund, since 1998 Research Assistant and Lecturer at the University of Dortmund, Faculty for Economic and Social Sciences, Chair for Operations Management and Logistics, since 1998 member of the Collaborative Research Center 559 „Modelling of Large Logistics Networks", Subproject A3 „Management of integrated Supply Chains".
Research interest: supply chain management, modelling, simulation

Chair for Operations Management and Logistics, Faculty for Economic and Social Sciences, University of Dortmund, D-44221 Dortmund, Germany
Tel. +49 231 755 3225   Fax +49 231 755 3189
Email M.Kaczmarek@wiso.uni-dortmund.de,
http://www.wiso.uni-dortmund.de/lsfg/ibl

Dr. Peter Kajüter MBA

Born 1966 in Hamburg, Germany, 1986-1988 Deutsche Bank AG, 1989-1993 studies in Business Administration at the University of Münster (D) and Edinburgh University Management School (UK), 1993-1999 Programme Director and Head of Tailored Executive Programmes at USW Schloss Gracht, Erftstadt (D), since 1999 senior lecturer at the Department of Auditing and Control, Faculty of Business and Economics, University of Düsseldorf (D).
Research interest: cost management, management accounting and control, risk management, international financial accounting, auditing.

Department of Auditing and Control
University of Düsseldorf, Universitätsstr. 1, D-40225 Düsseldorf, Germany
Tel. +49 211 81-11882   Fax +49-211-81-11883
Email: kajueter@uni-duesseldorf.de, http://www.wiwi.uni-duesseldorf.de/upb/

Prof. Dr. Joachim Käschel

Born 1951 in Olbernhau, Germany, 1969-1973 studies in mathamatics at Technische Hochschule Karl-Marx-Stadt, Germany, 1973-1989 research assistant at the Faculty of Mathematics, PhD-thesis in 1977, 1981-1985 research at the USSR Academy of Science computer center, 1989-1993 assistant professor at the Faculty of Economics and Business Administration at Chemnitz University of Technology, habilitation in 1991, since 1993 professor in Economics and Business Administration, especially Production and Industrial Management at Chemnitz University of Technology, 1996-2000 dean at Faculty of Economics and Business Administration at Chemnitz University of Technology.
Research interest: production planning, supply chains, supply nets.

Chair for Production and Industrial Management, Faculty of Economics and Business Administration, Chemnitz University of Technology, 09107 Chemnitz, Germany
Tel. +49 371 531 4244   Fax: +49 371 531 3958
Email: j.kaeschel@wirtschaft.tu-chemnitz.de,
http://www.tu-chemnitz.de/wirtschaft/bwl7

Prof. Dr. Paul R. Kleindorfer

Born 1940 in Illinois, USA, he is Universal Furniture professor of Decision Sciences and Economics, Professor of Operations and Information Management, and Professor of Public Policy and Management at the Wharton School of the University of Pennsylvania. Dr. Kleindorfer is Co-Director of the Wharton Risk Management and Decision Processes Center.
His research interests include operations management, regulatory and environmental economics, risk management and energy policy. He is coauthor of Decision Sciences: An Integrative Perspective (Cambridge University Press, 1993) as well as over 100 research papers and 15 books in decision sciences and economics.

The Wharton School
University of Pennsylvania, Philadelphia, PA 19104-6366, USA,
Email: Kleindorfer@wharton.upenn.edu

Prof. Dr. Herbert Kotzab

Born 1965 in Vienna, Austria. 1984-91 studies in Business Administration at the Vienna University of Economics and Business Administration (WU-Wien), 1991 to 1992 assistant to the CEO of Velux-Austria, 1992 - 1996 lecturer and Ph.D. student at the Department for Retail Marketing at the Vienna University of Economics and Business Administration, 1996 to 1999 senior lecturer at this department, 1999 to 2001 assistant professor for International Supply Chain Management at the Department of Operations Management at the Copenhagen Business School (CBS), from 2001 associate professor at the Department of Operations Management at the CBS. In 1998 visiting scholar at the Center for Transportation Studies at MIT.

Associate Professor, Dept. of Operations Management, SCM-Group
Copenhagen Business School, Solbjerg Plads 3, DK-2000 Frederiksberg
Tel.: +45 3815 2450   Fax.: +45 3815 2973
Email: hk.om@cbs.dk

Rolf Krüger Dipl.-Kaufmann

Born 1973 in Essen, Germany, 1993-98 Studies in Business Administration at Universität-GH Essen, since 1998 Research Assistant and Lecturer at Ruhr-Universität Bochum, Faculty of Economics and Business Administration, Department of Production Management. Practical work experience: Participation in production and logistics projects for companies in Germany, Canada and Brazil. Research interests: Logistics, International Supply Chain Management, Controlling

Lehrstuhl für Angewandte BWL I/Produktionswirtschaft
Ruhr-Universität Bochum, Universitätsstr. 150, 44801 Bochum, Germany
Email: Rolf.Krueger@ruhr-uni-bochum.de

Prof. Dr. Francine Maubourguet

Born 1955 in Miossens, France, attended and received her Graduate Degree in Engineering and Computer Science from University of Bordeaux, France, in 1978. From 1978 to 1992 she served as Project Manager for several French IS services companies leading projects in the areas of Accounting and Financial Systems Development,Sales Force Administration and Automation, and Production & HR Systems. In 1992 she joined the faculty at Groupe ESC Pau (French Grande Ecole) as Professor of MIS. Since 1998 she has served as the Deputy Director of ESC Pau.

Her Research interests are in Information Strategies for New Organizations, and Supply Chains and Information Technologies.

Deputy Director, Groupe ESC Pau, 3 rue Saint John Perse, 64000 Pau, France
Tel: +33 5 59 92 64 64
Email: fm@esc-pau.fr

Dr. Messaoud Mehafdi BSc, MSc

Born 1959 in Algiers, Algeria where he studied for a BSc (Honrs) in Accounting and Finance and graduated in 1981. Joined the University of Wales in 1982 where he completed an MSc in Management in 1983, including a dissertation on divisional performance measurement. Between 1985 and 1990 he worked part-time as a tutor at Greenwich University and read for a Ph.D. on the behavioural aspects of transfer pricing in large UK companies. He then joined Lancaster University as a Lecturer in Management Accounting. In 1995 he moved to the University of Huddersfield where he has been since as a senior lecturer. He taught management accounting and strategic management accounting on various post-experience and international MBA programmes in the UK, France and Oman. Research interests: transfer pricing, cost management and management control.

Department of Accountancy
The University of Huddersfield, Queensgate, Huddersfield HD1 3DH, UK
Email: m.mehafdi@hud.ac.uk

Giovanni Miragliotta

Born 1973, in San Benedetto del Tronto, Italy, 1992-1998 studies in Management Engineering at Politecnico di Milano (I); 1998 - 1999, research assistant and lecturer of Industrial Plants and Industrial Tecnhologies at Politecnico di Milano (I) and at Università di Brescia (I). Since 1999 doctoral student at Politecnico di Milano. Researches carried out in close co-operation with other research institutions and companies, especially production control software companies.
Research interest: supply chains, cost management, multisite industrial production management.

Dipartimento di Economia e Produzione
Politecnico di Milano, P.za L. da Vinci 32, I-20133 Milano, Italy
Email: giovanni.miragliotta@polimi.it

Prof. Dr. Marco Perona

Born 1963 in Padova, Italy. 1982-87 degree in Mecanical Engineering at the Born 1963 in Padova, Italy. 1982-87 degree in Mecanical Engineering at the Politecnico di Milano (I). 1988-1989 Research fellow at Mecanical Engineering Department of the Politecnico di Milano. 1990-1992 Research fellow at the Economics and Production Department of the Politecnico di Milano. 1993-1997 Research Professor at the Economics and Production Department of the Politecnico di Milano. 1997-2001 Associate Professor of Industrial Technologies at the University of Brescia (I). 2001-to date Full professor of Industrial Technologies at the University of Brescia. Board member at MIP, Business School of the

Politecnico di Milano. Director of the Master of Supply Chain Management at the University of Brescia.

Dipartimento di Meccanica, Università degli Studi di Brescia,
Via Branze 38, I-25123 Brescia, Italy
Email: perona@bsing.ing.unibs.it

Prof. Dr. Alberto Portioli Staudacher

Born 1964 in Milan, Italy, is Associate Professor of Operations Management at Politecnico di Milano, where he started working in 1990. Professor Portioli Staudacher teaches graduate and post graduate courses in the areas of Operations strategy, Production planning and control, Supply Chain Management, and New product development, adopting an integrated approach considering Technological, Managerial and Organisational aspects simultaneously. In these areas he has published 2 books and over 45 articles, and is a member of the editorial board of the *International Journal of Robotics and Computer Integrated Manufacturing*. Professor Portioli is the Director of the Laboratory on Operations Management, and leads a number of service and consulting activities Politecnico di Milano offers to Italian and European companies.

Dipartimento di Ingegneria Gestionale, Politecnico di Milano,
P.za L. da Vinci 32, I-20133 Milano, Italy
Email: alberto.portioli@polimi.it

Andrea Raschi

Born 1975 in Forlì, Italy, 1994-1999 studies in Business Administration at the University of Bologna (I), Forlì Campus. Since January 2000 collaboration at CRESEM, Bologna University Research Centre, Forlì Campus (I). January-May 2001 visiting at LERC, Lean Enterprise Research Centre, Cardiff Business School (UK).
Research interests: lean thinking, supply chain management, cost management.

Research Fellow, University of Bologna, Forlì Campus,
P.le Vittoria, 15, 47100, Forlì (FC), Italy
Tel. +39 0543 450 267   Fax: +39 0543 450 269
Email: raschi2000@libero.it

Gerald Rebitzer Dipl.-Ing.

Born 1967 in El Paso, USA; 1989-95 studies in Environmental Engineering at TU Berlin, Germany; 1995-96 freelance consultant in waste management, Berlin; 1996-2001 research engineer in Design for Environment (DfE) and 1997-2001 project manager in method and software development for DfE at the TU Berlin; since 2001 researcher (Ph.D. studies) at the Swiss Federal Institute of Technology, Lausanne, Switzerland. Research carried out in various sectors, including automotive, electronics, aerospace, and water treatment. Editor for Life Cycle Costing in the Scientific Journal Gate to Environmental and Health Science.
Research interests: DfE, Life Cycle Management, Life Cycle Costing, Life Cycle Assessment (more than 47 publications in these areas to date)

Swiss Federal Institute of Technology,
EPFL-Ecublens, CH-1015 Lausanne, Switzerland
Tel. +41-21-693-5526   Fax: +41-21-693-5529
Email: Gerald.Rebitzer@epfl.ch, http://dgrwww.epfl.ch/GECOS/DD/

Dr. Gabriele Schneidereit

Born 1969 in Magdeburg, Germany, 1987-1992 studies in Mathematics at the (Technical) University "Otto von Guericke" Magdeburg, 1992-1995 post-graduate study in Mathematics at the same university, 1995 gaining a doctorate in Mathematics, since 1995 scientific assistant at the University of Technology "Carolo Wilhelmina" Braunschweig, Department of Business Administration, Information Systems and Information Management.
Research interests: supply contracts, information systems, logistics.

Abteilung Allgemeine Betriebswirtschaftslehre, Wirtschaftsinformatik und Informationsmanagement, Institut für Wirtschaftswissenschaften,
Technische Universität Braunschweig, Abt-Jerusalem-Str. 7,
D-38106 Braunschweig, Germany
Tel. +49 531 391 3215   Fax: +49 531 391 8144
Email: g.schneidereit@tu-bs.de, http://www.winforms.phil.tu-bs.de/

Prof. Dr. Uwe Schneidewind

Born 1966 in Cologne, Germany, 1986-91 studies in Business Administration at the University Cologne (D) and HEC, Paris. 1991-92: Strategic Consultant in Environmental Management at Roland Berger & Partner, Düsseldorf, 1993-1997: research assistant at the Institute for Economy and the Environment (IWO-HSG) at University of St. Gall (PhD- and Habilitation thesis on strategic environmental management issues), since 1998 full professor for Production Management and

the Environment at the University of Oldenburg.
Research interest: E-Organization in Business and Society

Chair for Production and the Environment, Institute for Business Administration,
Carl von Ossietzky University Oldenburg, 26111 Oldenburg, Germany
Tel. +49 441 798 4181   Fax: +49 441 798 4193
Email: uwe.schneidewind@uni-oldenburg.de,
http://www.uni-oldenburg.de/produktion

Prof. Dr. Riccardo Silvi

Born 1963 in Chiaravalle, Ancona, Italy, Associated Professor at the University of Bologna – Forlì Campus. Lecturer of Accounting and Cost Management Accounting. Co-ordinator of the Lean Management Accounting international research programme together with the Cardiff Business School (UK). He has been visiting professor at the Babson College in Wellesley (USA), where he carried out some research programmes at the Center for Innovation in Management Accounting and he was lecturer at the MBA programme. Lecturer at the Auditing and Control Master at the University of Pisa and at the Finance and Control Master of Profingest (Bologna).
Research interests: management control, performance measurement systems, strategic cost management.

Business Administration, University of Bologna, Forlì Campus,
P.le Vittoria, 15, 47100, Forlì (FC), Italy
Tel. +39 0543 450 268   Fax: +39 0543 450 269
Email: rsilvi@spfo.unibo.it

Prof. Dr. Regine Slagmulder

Born 1966 in Aalst, Belgium, she is currently an Associate Professor of Accounting and Control at INSEAD. Prior to joining INSEAD, she was a Professor of Management Accounting at Tilburg University (The Netherlands) and visiting professor at the University of Ghent (Belgium). Her current activities focus on the link between management accounting and control systems and firm strategy. More specifically, she is interested in strategic cost management (incl. activity-based costing and supply chain cost management) and performance measurement. She is the co-author of several books and has articles published in both academic and practitioner journals, including *Sloan Management Review*, *Management Accounting Research*, *International Journal of Production Economics*, and *Strategic Finance*.

INSEAD, Boulevard de Constance, F-77305 Fontainebleau Cedex, France
Email: regine.slagmulder@insead.edu

Prof. Dr. Riurik V. Skomorokhov

Born 1954 in Lipetsk, USSR, 1982-1986 Moscow Institute of Radioengineering, Electronics and Automation, Assistant Professor, Department. of Enterprise Economics, 1986-1998, The Plekhanov Russian Economic Academy, Associate Professor, Department. of Enterprise Economics and Organization, 1996-1997 Machine-building @ Hydrolic (joint-stock company), Director of Economy and Operations, since 1998 Professor at Moscow Institute of International Economics & Business and the Bauman Moscow State Technical University, independent consulting and researching. Research carried in close co-operation with leading companies from various sectors, specially machine-building industry.

Research interest: production and operations management, supply chain management, system optimization of manufacturing, scheduling

Bauman Moscow State Technical University, 2-ya Baumanskaya, 5 Moscow, Russia,
Email skomorokhov@mtu-net.ru

Stefan Spinler Dipl.-Ing.

Born 1970 in Coburg, Germany, 1991-97 studies in Electrical Engineering at Erlangen University and University College London (UK), 1996- 1997 research stay at Bell Labs, Murray Hill, NJ (USA), 1997-1999 Responsible for Process Integration in DRAM Manufacturing at Infineon Technologies Dresden (D), since October 1999 Research Associate and Lecturer in Production Management WHU Vallendar (D), in 2000 Visiting Scholar at Kellogg Graduate School of Management, IL (USA), Member of the Jury "Industrial Excellence Award" 2000 and 2001.

Research interests: Real options, Supply Chain Management, Risk Management and Industrial Excellence.

Department for Production Management, WHU Otto-Beisheim Graduate School of Management, Burgplatz 2, D-56179 Vallendar, Germany
Email: Sspinler@whu.edu

Dr. Lars Stemmler MSc. Logistics, Dipl.-Kfm.

Born 1972 in Hamburg, Germany, Lars is a project manager with BLG Consult GmbH, a member of the BLG Logistics Group AG & Co., KG. Prior to joining BLG Consult GmbH he worked in various functions for Deutsche Schiffsbank AG, a leading ship finance institution, and for the Oldenburg Chamber of Industry and Commerce. He is also a guest lecturer in logistics at Oldenburg University.

He completed a PhD on infrastructure policy of the European Community. He received a MSc. in logistics from Cranfield University in 1998. He also holds a masters degree in business studies. He pursues an interdisciplinary approach to logistics.

Im Hollergrund 50, D-28357 Bremen, Germany
Email: l.stemmler@gmx.de

Frank Stüllenberg Diplom-Kaufmann

Born 1971 in Bochum, Germany, 1993-1998 studies in Business Administration at the University of Dortmund, since 1998 Research Assistant and Lecturer at the University of Dortmund, Faculty for Economic and Social Sciences, Chair for Operations Management and Logistics, since 1998 member of the Collaborative Research Center 559 „Modelling of Large Logistics Networks", Subproject M3 „Network Controlling".
Research interest: logistics, supply chain management, controlling, interorganizational cooperations

Chair for Operations Management and Logistics, Faculty for Economic and Social Sciences, University of Dortmund, D-44221 Dortmund, Germany
Tel. +49 231 755 3226   Fax +49 231 755 3189
Email Frank.Stuellenberg@wiso.uni-dortmund.de,
http://www.wiso.uni-dortmund.de/lsfg/ibl

Dr. Tobias Teich

Born 1966 in Zwickau, Germany, 1987-1992 studies in Computer Science at Chemnitz University of Technology, Germany, 1992-1993 research assistant at the Faculty of Computer Science at Chemnitz University of Technology, 1992-1995 studies in Business Economics at Chemnitz University of Technology, since 1994-1998 research assistant at Faculty of Economics and Business Administration (chair Production and Industrial Management) at Chemnitz University of Technology, PhD-thesis in 1998, since 1998 assistant professor at Faculty of Economics and Business Administration (chair Production and Industrial Management) at Chemnitz University of Technology.
Research interest: ERP-systems, SCM-systems, production nets, production control.

Chair for Production and Industrial Management, Faculty of Economics and Business Administration, Chemnitz University of Technology, 09107 Chemnitz, Germany
Tel. +49 371 531 4193   Fax: +49 371 531 3958
Email: tobias.teich@wirtschaft.tu-chemnitz.de,
http://www.tu-chemnitz.de/wirtschaft/bwl7

Dr. Christoph Teller Mag.

Born 1972 in Wolfsberg, Austria, 1992-1998 studies in Business Administration at the Vienna University of Economics and Business Administration, from 1998 PhD-Student, form 1999 research assistant and lecturer at the Department of Retailing and Marketing (Vienna University of Economics and Business Administration), completion of PhD in 2001.
Research interest: retail logistics, euro-changeover

Department of Retailing and Marketing, Vienna University of Economics and Business Administration, Augasse 2-6, A-1090 Wien, Austria
Tel.: (01) 313 36/46 19   Fax.: (01) 313 36/717
Email: christoph.teller@wu-wien.ac.at

Giovanni Valentini Laurea Ind. Eng.

Born 1973 in Brescia, Italy. 1992-1997 studies in Industrial Engineering and Management at the University of Brescia (I) and Coimbra (P), 1998-2000 temporary lecturer at the Department of Mecahnical Engineering of the University of Brescia (I) and at the Polytechnic of Milan (I), since October 2000 Ph.D. student in Management at IESE Business School, Barcelona (E). Involved in research projects concerning product innovation and operations management.
Present research interests: competitive strategy and innovation strategy.

IESE Business School – Doctoral Program
Avda. Pearson 21, 08034 Barcelona, Spain
Tel. +34 620180855   Fax: +34 932534343
Email: GValentini@iese.edu, http://www.iese.edu

Prof. Dr. Stefan Voß

Born 1961 in Hamburg, Germany, is a full professor and head of the department for Business Administration, Information Systems and Information Management at the University of Technology Braunschweig (Germany) since 1995. He holds degrees in Mathematics (diploma) and Economics from the University of Hamburg and a Ph.D. and the habilitation from the University of Technology Darmstadt. His current research interests are in quantitative/information systems approaches to operations management and logistics including public mass transit and telecommunications. Stefan Voß serves on the editorial board of some journals including being Associate Editor of INFORMS Journal on Computing and Area Editor of Journal of Heuristics.

Technische Universität Braunschweig, Abt-Jerusalem-Str. 7, D-38106 Braunschweig, Germany
Email: stefan.voss@tu-bs.de

Dr. Mirko Warschun Dipl.-Kaufmann, CEMS Master

Born 1969 in Düsseldorf, Germany. 1992-97 studies in Economics and Business Administration at the University of Cologne, Germany, 1993-97 program of the Community of European Management Schools (CEMS) in International Business at the University of Cologne, Germany, and 1994-95 at the Stockholm School of Economics, Sweden. 2000-01 PhD student at the Faculty of Business, Economics and Law at the University of Oldenburg, Germany. Since 1998 consultant with McKinsey & Company. Research interest: strategic management, electronic commerce, purchasing, supply chain management.

McKinsey & Company, Inc., Prinzregentenstr. 22, D-80538 München, Germany
Tel. +49 89 5594 8526   Fax +49 89 5594 8527
Email: Mirko_Warschun@mckinsey.com

Prof. Dr. Lucio Zavanella

Born 1958 in Collio Val Trompia (Italy), 1977-1982 studied at the Polytechnic of Milan, where he graduated in Industrial Engineering (1982). Currently, he is associate professor at the University of Brescia (Italy) – Faculty of Engineering, where he teaches Production Planning and Plant Services. His publications have been published in International Journals in the area of Production Research, Production Economics and Manufacturing. He has also held many presentations at International Conferences and Workshops. Themes discussed vary from maintenance, to management of resources in manufacturing. Present research interests are supply chains, environmental management, application of heuristic techniques.

Department of Mechanical Engineering, Faculty of Engineering
University of Brescia, Via Branze 38, I-25123 BRESCIA (Italy)
Tel.: +39 030 37151   Fax: +39.030.3702.488
Email: zavanell@ing.unibs.it, http://www.unibs.it

Klaus Zimmermann Dipl.Betriebswirt

Born 1966 in Mannheim (D), 1989-1993 studies in European Business Administration at Middlesex University, London (GB) and Fachhochschule Reutlingen (D), 1993-1999 project manager at Arthur Andersen Business Consulting, Hamburg (D), since 1999 project manager of two supply chain projects and responsible for supply chain management research at the European Business School, Institute for Environmental Management and Business Administration, Oestrich-Winkel (D). Research interests: Supply Chain Management, Performance Management, Balanced Scorecard.

ESPRiT Consulting AG, Am Sandtorkai 74, D-20457 Hamburg
Email: klausgzimmermann@web.de

Index

Activity-Based Costing ....
...................23, 35, 77, 92, 113, 201

Airbus... 140

Aircraft Industry............................... 140

Apparel Industry............... 111, 118, 299

Balanced Scorecard.................. 159, 402

Buyer-Supplier Interface 80

Car Industry.......................... 42, 65, 137

Case Study...
..........42, 65, 118, 140, 207, 223, 399

Category Management 199, 366

Chemical Industry 400

Competence Cells............................. 179

Complexity................................ 149, 383

Computer Industry............................ 207

Consignment Stock 326

Consumer Goods...................... 214, 364

Continuous Replenishment............... 199

Contribution Margin......... 184, 242, 291

Cooperation...17, 85, 101, 178, 269, 310
   Horizontal 218

Cost Accounting....................................
............21, 34, 54, 113, 235, 242, 292

Cost Aggregation.............................. 190

Cost Driver ....
.... 33, 71, 92, 113, 167, 187, 238, 310

Cost Management 3, 91
   Concepts.................................... 5, 36
   Customer 77
   Institutional.................................... 91
   Operationalization 40
   Proactive........................... 31, 39, 159
   Supplier 77
   System......................................40, 43
   Three Cost Levels............. 22, 94, 117

Cost Reduction 26, 43,
   84, 101, 117, 166, 228, 262, 311, 382

Cost Simulation 279

Costing System 35, 76, 186, 236

Data-Processing Model..................... 180

Design for Environment.................... 136

Direct Cost................................. 23, 113

Distribution Network 214, 221

Economic Order Quantity................. 327

Economies of Scale........................... 312

Efficient Consumer Response.................
.... 196, 214, 365, 366

Electronic Data Interchange....................
.... 20, 80, 198, 259, 328, 375

Environmental Performance 139

Index

Finance 166
Ford 137
Functionality-Price-Quality Trade-offs
.... 38, 82
Game Theory 266, 351
Global Logistics Network 319
Globalization 178, 310
Henkel 223
Household Appliance industry 383
Information Flow 2, 17, 198
Information Sharing 168
Internet 368
Interorganizational Cost Management ....
.... 5, 22, 24, 37, 75, 79, 80, 116
Intra-Firm Partnerships 153
Inventory 172, 290, 326
Joint Cost Reduction 122
Lean Accounting 53
Lean Management 56
Life-Cycle Assessment 129
Life-Cycle Costing 132
Life-Cycle Management 128
Logistic 234, 258, 263, 274
Logistical Cost Management 236
Logistics Costs 278, 316
Logistics Network 319

Logistics Reach 316
Lost Sales 290
Management Accounting 35, 57, 76, 148
Marketing 56, 153, 291
Mass Customization 54, 382
Material Flow 2, 17, 131, 172
New Institutional Economics 22, 90, 365
Optimization Methods 338
Order Fulfillment 177
Order-Neutral Costs 186
Order-Related Costs 187
Organizational Theory 34, 90, 152
Outsourcing 149
Payment Terms 169
Performance Measurement ....
.... 149, 216, 246, 283, 404
Policy Deployment 56
Polyester Linings 119
Process Activity Map 63
Process Chain Map 277
Process Optimization 20, 36, 226
Product Design 19, 81, 386
Production Network 19, 177
   Non-Hierarchial 178
Product-Relationship-Matrix 17
   Three Cost Levels 27

Index   435

Profit Distribution 191
Purchasing 294, 365
Purchasing Process 367
Reference Model 20, 264
Retailering 364
Retailing 296
Return on Investment 167
Safety Stock 291
Scheduling 342
Schwarzkopf 223
SCOR-Model 21, 275
Service Level 205
Shareholder Value 148
Simulation 264, 278
Small and Medium Sized Enterprises
.... 178, 234
Strategic Cost Management .. 37, 56, 237
Strategic Management 33, 57
Structure Optimization 228
Supply Chain
  Coordination 259
  Modeling 275
  Performance 285, 338
  Planning 264, 274
  Relationships 17, 85, 150

Supply Chain Costing . 3, 15, 38, 94, 112
Supply Chain Finance 170
Supply Chain Management 2, 36
  Product Dimension 17
  Relationship Dimension 17
Supply Chain Target Costing 96, 111
Supply Contracts 255, 351
Survey 239, 299
Sustainable Development 128
Systems Thinking 129
Target costing 35
Target Costing 82, 93, 114
  Chained 116
  Market-Driven Costing 115
  Product-Level Target Costing 115
  Target Achievement Plan 44
Total Cost 44, 112, 236, 314
Total Cost of Ownership ....
.... 22, 24, 155, 158, 365
Transaction Costs ....
.... 23, 34, 94, 113, 157, 254, 260, 365
Transfer Pricing 148
Transportation Costs . 222, 260, 314, 359
Value Stream Mapping 55
Vendor Managed Inventory 263, 281
Virtual Enterprise 54, 178